Lucille Ball FAQ

Movie star Lucille Ball in the 1940s.

Lucille Ball FAQ

Everything Left to Know About America's Favorite Redhead

James Sheridan and Barry Monush

An Imprint of Hal Leonard Corporation

Published in 2011 by Applause Theatre & Cinema Books
An Imprint of Hal Leonard Corporation
7777 West Bluemound Road
Milwaukee, WI 53213

Trade Book Division Editorial Offices
33 Plymouth St., Montclair, NJ 07042

All images are from the personal collections of the authors.

The FAQ Series was conceived by Robert Rodriguez and developed with Stuart Shea.

Printed in the United States of America

Book design by Tony Meisel

Library of Congress Cataloging-in-Publication Data

Sheridan, James, 1988-
  Lucille Ball FAQ : everything left to know about America's favorite redhead /
James Sheridan and Barry Monush.
      p. cm.
  Includes bibliographical references and index.
  ISBN 978-1-61774-082-4 (pbk.)
  1. Ball, Lucille, 1911-1989. 2. Entertainers–United States–Biography. 3.
Comedians–United States–Biography. I. Monush, Barry. II. Title. III. Title: Lucile
Ball frequently asked questions.
  PN2287.B16S54 2011
  792.702'8092–dc22
  [B]
                              2011016466

www.applausepub.com

Contents

His, Mine, and Ours

When my publisher approached me about suggestions for expanding Hal Leonard's *FAQ* series of books outside the realm of music, I thought it was a great idea but did not immediately picture myself as the person to do the job. I figured whoever the celebrity in question might be as the first non–music industry *FAQ* subject, the person writing the book couldn't just be a casual fan, but would have to know the performer inside and out to provide the reader with something new and revealing. And my love of the entertainment world is so vast that it gets rather unfocused. There's so much to know about so *many* people and things that my tiny brain hardly has room to hold it all, let alone concentrate almost exclusively on one area. Sure, there are plenty of performers whom I adore and whose work I follow as fervidly as possible, stars whose movies I see repeatedly or collect, but I never thought of myself as the sort who could pop facts off the top of my head about *any* of my favorites to the degree that others could. As much as I love Fred Astaire, for example, I've met *plenty* of people out there (some perfectly sane) who are much more adept at remembering facts, dates, and trivia on Fred than I am.

If not me, then I certainly had the exact person in mind that *could* do a detailed book on a star, provided that star was going to be Lucille Ball. He could do this well, do it affectionately, do it knowledgably, and have fun doing it. That person was and is James Sheridan. Please indulge me while I embarrass my collaborator with praise.

When I met James he was all of nineteen years old and yet possessed a degree of knowledge about Lucille Ball that one might imagine only someone who had lived as long as Lucy herself did could cram into his head. There didn't seem to be anything about her that he didn't know, and, refreshingly, it went beyond her iconic television series, *I Love Lucy*, encompassing her motion picture career, her television specials, her personal life, her relatives, where she lived, who she dated, those many show business names with whom she came into contact, and even those she *almost* encountered. Nothing mentioned about the lady was *too* trivial for James; you had only to name it and he not only knew about it, but told you the *true* facts if perhaps *your* facts were off the mark. And thankfully he did not do this in a manner that could in any way be construed as obnoxious or arrogant.

On the contrary, his manner of informing you was and is always helpful, friendly, enthusiastic, and respectful. By now he's squirming with discomfort reading this, so enough of that.

Anyway, I agreed to come along for the ride and help out, this being James's first effort at book writing. And I'm glad I did. It was if nothing else educational. Although I had spent my youth growing up with Lucy, as did pretty much all of my peers—enjoying her at one point three times a day, when she could be seen in the New York market in the morning on *The Lucy Show* reruns (provided you were not at school), after dinner in the syndicated run of *I Love Lucy*, and then (provided it was Monday) on the primetime schedule in *Here's Lucy* —I never pretended to be an expert on her. However, I clearly liked her more than the average *I Love Lucy* aficionado because I also enjoyed exploring her career beyond what she accomplished on the small screen, watching as many Lucille Ball *movies* as I came across. To me, Lucille Ball was a terrific screen presence who made an indelible impression and could be looked upon as most definitely having "made it" in the industry, even *before* television came along and turned her into not just a superstar but a seminal entertainment icon of the twentieth century, one of the handful of people who can truly be called a show business legend.

So, although I could come up with some perfectly nice things to tell you about Lucille Ball, I couldn't surprise you much with little bits of trivia that were guaranteed to make you say "Hey, I didn't know *that*!" That was James's department, and he certainly delivered. In fact, he delivered beyond what I assumed he could deliver, as just when you feel you've heard all the facts about a certain Lucy credit or show, he'll bowl you over with five or ten more. Thanks to him, I promise you you'll find out things in *Lucille Ball FAQ* that you never knew before.

Barry Monush

ACKNOWLEDGMENTS

A huge thank-you to my co-author Barry Monush for proposing this book in the first place and for all the hard work he put into it.

I would like to thank my parents, Jim and Lorraine Sheridan, for all of their support through the years, as well as my sister, Maggie, and brother, Patrick. I would like to thank the rest of my family, especially my aunt, MaryLou Meehan, who took me to the Museum of Television & Radio for the first time when I was ten years old.

My thanks go out to Lucy superfans Brock Weir, Laura Johansen Garrett, Neil Wilburn, and Claude Courval for their friendship and generosity through the years, as well as to all others who love Lucy. Thanks also to Anndrew Vacca, David Lempka, and Ron Simon.

My sincere thanks to all the employees of the Paley Center for Media.

Lastly, I would like to thank my late grandmother, Helen Muniz, who introduced me to Lucy and watched all 507 *Lucy* episodes with me over and over again.

James Sheridan

Thanks first and foremost to James Sheridan, my amazing collaborator. I couldn't have done it without him.

Thanks for absolutely everything to Tom Lynch; to John Cerullo for giving us the go-ahead on the project; to Marybeth Keating for putting it together; to Rebecca Paller for her support and interest.

A special mention to my sister Michelle, my brother Bryan, and my mom, with whom I spent many a formative year watching all kinds of Lucy programs (my dad could take or leave them).

And to those who added a bit of expertise to the mix, including Jim Pierson, Paul Roy Goodhead of the Anthony Newley Appreciation Society, and Olivia from Mel Tillis Enterprises.

Barry Monush

THE KEY TO LUCY

For those who know, live, and breathe Lucille Ball, it is pretty easy to skim through this book and catch references and meanings instantly. However, for the casual fan or those with a mere cursory knowledge of Lucy and her career, it would be helpful to read the timeline up front as well as the background on the important people in her life, personally and professionally. This done, you will then realize why throughout the text certain people are referred to in passing by their first names only.

For example, her first husband and most famous co-star, Desi Arnaz, is simply "Desi," of course. Her children, Lucie Arnaz and Desi Arnaz Jr., are "Lucie" and "Desi Jr.," respectively. Second husband Gary Morton is "Gary," her mother "DeDe," her brother "Fred" (not to be confused with grandpa Fred Hunt or the character of Fred Mertz played by William Frawley on *I Love Lucy*), her cousin and "sister" figure Cleo Mandicos/Smith "Cleo." Frequent co-star and pal Vivian Vance is referred to as "Vivian" or "Viv."

Similarly, in certain sections, rather than listing the titles of her television series over and over again, we use their initials. Hence, *ILL* for *I Love Lucy* (an abbreviation that Lucy herself, by the way, detested); *LD* for *The Lucy-Desi Comedy Hour*; *TLS* for *The Lucy Show*; *HL* for *Here's Lucy*; and *LWL* for *Life with Lucy*.

Introduction

I do not remember Lucille Ball not being in my life. I have always been a Lucy fan. Lucille Ball passed away when I was only seven months old, so I never saw any of her shows during their original run, but I started watching reruns of *I Love Lucy* with my grandmother before I can even remember. In 1995, before I was seven years old, I went to the "Lucy: A Tribute" exhibition in Universal Studios Florida. Although I was already a big Lucy fan, I only knew her as Lucy Ricardo (and, to a lesser extent, Lucy Carmichael). Because of this exhibit, which included clips from her various acting roles, I was amazed at the scope of her career and all that she had accomplished beyond the series I knew her from. After seeing this, I began recording all of Lucy's shows and movies that were aired on television and reading everything about her that I could get my hands on. My interest in Lucy also introduced me to many other talented performers from the "Golden Age of Hollywood" who I became fans of as well.

I find Lucy's talent astonishing. In her six decade-long career, Lucille Ball achieved more success than nearly anyone else in the entertainment industry, in television, films, stage, and radio. Although known for her comedic genius, she was equally adept at drama. Although neither a trained singer nor dancer, she was often seen doing both with an infectious enthusiasm in her films and on television, not to mention in her one Broadway credit. Her first series, *I Love Lucy*, revolutionized the way television shows were made. In 1952, it became the first show to be watched by over 10 million people. A year later, it was being viewed by over 40 million. In the nineteen-sixties, Ball became the first woman to head a major production company on her own and was responsible for green-lighting some of the most popular and profitable television series of all time (*Star Trek, Mission: Impossible*, et al.).

Lucille Ball made $50 a week when she started at RKO in 1935 and within a few years became known as "Queen of the Bs," referring to the lower-budgeted films to which she was assigned. Two decades later, she owned the whole studio. She starred in three highly successful sitcoms in three successive decades, picking up four Emmys and numerous other awards along the way. *TV Guide* has written, "the face of Lucille Ball has been seen by more people more often than the face of anyone else who ever lived."

Despite all the years that have passed since Lucy's death, her popularity remains extraordinarily high and shows no sign of slowing down. I hope with this book that readers learn a few things about Lucille Ball they did not know before, as well as information about people, places, and things associated with her. Who knows, you may end up an even bigger fan of Lucy's than you already are.

James Sheridan

Lucille Ball FAQ

"I Thought You Wanted to Know Something about HER"

Lucille Ball: A Timeline

August 6, 1911: Lucille Desirée Ball is born on Sunday, August 6, 1911 to Henry Durrell and Desirée Eveline Hunt Ball. She is born at 5:00 in the afternoon at the home of her maternal grandparents at 123 Stewart Avenue, Jamestown, New York.

February 28, 1915: Lucy's father, Henry Durrell Ball, dies of typhoid fever at their home in Wyandotte, Michigan.

July 17, 1915: Lucy's brother, Frederick Henry Ball, is born in Jamestown.

September 17, 1918: Lucy's mother, DeDe, marries Edward Peterson, a metal polisher. On the day of the wedding, Lucy asks Ed if he was now her "new daddy." He simply shook her hand and told her to call him Ed. DeDe and Ed go to Detroit to work, and Lucy is left in the care of Ed's stern parents. DeDe and Ed will later divorce.

July 3, 1927: Eleven-year-old neighbor Warner Erickson is accidently shot in Lucille's family's backyard. Lucy's grandfather, Fred Hunt, had given Lucy's brother, Fred, a .22 caliber rifle as an early birthday present. Warner was accidently shot by a visiting friend, Joanna Ottinger, and was paralyzed for the rest of his short life. The Erickson family sued Fred Hunt, which resulted in the family losing their house. The family always referred to this incident as "the breakup," and it led Lucy to care for her family for the rest of her life.

June 24, 1930: Lucy opens in the Jamestown Players Club production of *Within the Law* at Jamestown's Nordic Temple. Lucy played con artist Aggie Lynch in the play and was the first thing mentioned in the local newspaper review, which described her as "a potential Jeanne Eagels."

July 11, 1933: Lucy signs a contract with Samuel Goldwyn Productions that will bring her out to Los Angeles. One sweltering Wednesday, Lucy was walking down Broadway in front of the Palace Theatre when she was stopped by an acquaintance, agent Sylvia Hahlo. Hahlo told Lucy that Samuel Goldwyn needed a showgirl immediately for the Eddie Cantor vehicle *Roman Scandals*. Twelve girls were required, and one of the ones selected had to drop out because her mother would not let her go to California. Hahlo sent Lucille upstairs to Goldwyn's New York representative Jim Mulvey, whose office was in the Palace building. All of the girls were required to be poster girls, which Lucy indeed was. Lucy was the "Chesterfield Girl," since a portrait of her painted by artist Walter Ratterman was used on billboards for Chesterfield Cigarettes. Lucy was hired as a Goldwyn Girl at a salary of $125 a week for what was originally supposed to be a six-week assignment. Lucy and the eleven other girls left New York for California that Saturday.

October 7, 1933: Movie patrons get their first opportunity to see Lucille Ball on a movie screen when *The Bowery* is released. Although Lucy first began work on *Roman Scandals, The Bowery* is the first film in which she appears to open in theaters. Two more Lucy credits, *Broadway Thru a Keyhole* and *Blood Money,* will both be in theaters before the December 29, 1933 opening of *Roman Scandals.*

September 23, 1934: Lucille signs a contract with Columbia Pictures and joins their stock company, which is dissolved shortly thereafter.

March 25, 1935: Lucille Ball is signed by RKO. She will spend seven years under contract there and one day own the studio.

March 19, 1936: In a move that will come back to haunt her years later, Lucy registers with the Communist Party to please socialist Grandpa Hunt, who had had a stroke. DeDe and Fred Ball sign shortly thereafter. Lucy had no intention of voting for anyone in the Communist Party and never did. Lucy's registration expires after two years.

January 21, 1937: Lucy opens in the Broadway-bound play *Hey Diddle Diddle* at Princeton, New Jersey's McCarter Theatre. Lucy plays the role of aspiring actress Julie Tucker. Conway Tearle was the play's star, and the cast also featured Keenan Wynn, who would later appear with Lucille in several of her MGM films. Following the New Jersey engagement, the play moved to Philadelphia and then Washington DC.

February 13, 1937: *Hey Diddle Diddle* closes in Washington DC after leading man Conway Tearle becomes seriously ill. Lucy will not appear onstage for another decade.

October 14, 1938: *The Wonder Show,* starring Jack Haley, premieres on CBS Radio. Lucy co-stars on the series along with Virginia Verrill, Artie Auerbach (who married Lucy's cousin, Cleo), bandleader Ted Fio Rito, and announcer Gale Gordon. The series ran until April 7, 1939.

Lucille as dancer Bubbles, who will soon become burlesque queen Tiger Lily White, in *Dance, Girl, Dance* (1940).

November 30, 1940: Lucille Ball marries Desi Arnaz. For much of the previous week, Lucy was on a public appearance trip in Milwaukee. She was supposed to spend only one day in the city, but it ended up being five. After a grueling day on November 28, Lucy arrived back at her hotel, and, while still in the lobby, accepted a phone call from Desi. He accused her of staying in Milwaukee because actor Joseph Cotten was also in the city, and he believed she was with him. Lucy told him she did not know Cotten and she was going to be in New York by morning. Just as Lucy was denying she was meeting Cotten, he walked into the hotel lobby. She asked the actor to drive her to the airport. The following afternoon, Desi arrived at Lucy's hotel room at the Hampshire House between his shows at the Roxy Theatre. Lucy was in the middle of giving an interview for a magazine about how she and Desi would never marry. After the reporter left, Desi asked Lucy to marry him. He had been waiting for her to come back to New York to ask. Lucy was a bit apprehensive and suggested that they just live together, but Desi wanted to marry. Lucy accepted his proposal. Desi had arranged for them to travel to Greenwich, Connecticut the following morning with Desi's business manager, Deke Magaziner, and his theatrical agent, Doc Bender. In his haste, Desi forgot to get a ring for Lucy, so Magaziner and Bender bought a brass ring at Woolworth's, which was the only store open in the area. Lucy and Desi were married by Justice of the Peace John P. O'Brien, who suggested that he perform the ceremony at a nearby country club, the Byram River Beagle Club, rather than his chambers. After the ceremony, the new Mr. and Mrs. Arnaz drove back to New York where Desi had to perform at the Roxy. He had already missed his first show of the day, and the curtain was being held for the second. Desi introduced his bride on-stage, and the entire audience pelted the couple with rice, supplied by the management of the Roxy. That night, Desi threw a party at El Morocco to celebrate the marriage. Guests included many who were involved with *Too Many Girls*: Richard Rodgers and Lorenz Hart, George Abbott, book writer George Marion Jr., RKO president George Schaeffer, and the leading man in the musical's Broadway incarnation, Richard Kollmar, and his new wife, Dorothy Kilgallen. Lucy and Desi spent their wedding night at the Pierre Hotel and then stayed at The Cabin in Onaway, Michigan before arriving in Los Angeles on December 22, 1940.

August 6, 1942: On her thirty-first birthday, Lucille Ball signs a contract with Metro-Goldwyn-Mayer.

September 7, 1944: Lucy files for divorce from Desi. Saying they separated the day before, she claimed that Desi caused her "grievous mental suffering with provocation."

October 16, 1944: Lucy testifies in court and gets her divorce from Desi. The night before, Desi met with her and the two patched up their differences. Lucy left Desi in the morning to go to court, saying that everyone would expect her to be there to divorce him. Lucy went to court and claimed that Desi was overly extravagant and that ultimately led to their separation. Lucy received her divorce, but it was immediately nullified when she went back to Desi after leaving the courtroom.

June 23, 1947: Lucy opens in *Dream Girl* at the McCarter Theatre in Princeton, New Jersey (the site of her previous stage appearance, *Hey Diddle Diddle*, ten years earlier). Lucy played the role of daydreaming bookshop proprietor Georgina Allerton in summer stock into the winter of 1948. Lucy played stock engagements in such places as Detroit, Toronto, San Francisco, and even took the show to New York, albeit Brooklyn and the Bronx. Lucy finally got the opportunity to play the role in Los Angeles in January 1948, but became ill with a virus shortly after opening. The show closed soon thereafter.

July 5, 1948: *My Favorite Husband* airs on CBS radio as a one-time program with Lucille Ball and Lee Bowman as Liz and George Cugat. The series begins airing weekly starting July 23 with Richard Denning in the role of George. With the January 7, 1949 episode, the Cugats become Liz and George Cooper. It is on this program that Lucille will work with Jess Oppenheimer, Madelyn Pugh, and Bob Carroll Jr. for the first time. These three will have a major impact on Ball's future career.

June 19, 1949: Lucy and Desi remarry in the Catholic Church. Desi's mother Lolita believed that the couple could not have children because they were not married in the eyes of God. Lucy took instructions in the Catholic faith and, although she seriously considered converting to Catholicism (she was born Protestant), never officially did. Lucy and Desi agreed to raise their children Catholic, though. They remarried at Our Lady of the Valley Church in Canoga Park and then had a lavish reception at their Chatsworth home. Lolita served as Lucy's matron of honor, and Kenny Morgan, husband to Lucy's cousin Cleo, was best man.

March 2, 1951: On Desi's thirty-fourth birthday, a very pregnant Lucy shoots the pilot for *I Love Lucy*.

March 31, 1951: The final episode of *My Favorite Husband*, "The April Fool Joke," airs.

July 17, 1951: Lucy gives birth to her first child, Lucie Desirée Arnaz, via an emergency caesarean section at 8:15 a.m. at Cedars of Lebanon Hospital. That night, Desi and friend Eddie Maxwell write the song "There's a Brand New Baby (At Our House)."

September 3, 1951: Rehearsals begin for the first episode of *I Love Lucy*, "Lucy Thinks Ricky Is Trying to Murder Her." Lucille Ball and Vivian Vance meet for the first time. The episode is filmed on September 8.

October 15, 1951: *I Love Lucy* premieres with the episode "The Girls Want to Go to a Nightclub," the second episode filmed. Following the rehearsal for that week's episode, "The Séance," the cast and crew (sans William Frawley, who went home to watch a boxing match on television) go to the home of director Marc Daniels and his wife, series camera coordinator Emily Daniels to watch the premiere.

January 19, 1953: Desiderio Alberto Arnaz IV is born at Cedars of Lebanon Hospital at 8:20 am. That night, Lucy Ricardo gives birth on *I Love Lucy*. Forty-four million people, the largest television audience ever up to that time, watch the episode "Lucy Goes to the Hospital." The birth of Lucy's baby becomes the biggest news story in the country, and makes the front pages of the newspapers on January 20 instead of the inauguration of Dwight Eisenhower that would occur that day.

September 4, 1953: Lucy, DeDe, and Fred Ball have a private meeting with House Un-American Activities Committee investigator William A. Wheeler. The family individually explained they each registered with the Communist Party to please an ill Fred Hunt. The Balls were all cleared and were told the meeting would remain confidential.

September 11, 1953: News breaks that Lucille Ball once registered with the Communist Party. Walter Winchell had announced on his radio program on September 6 that America's top redhead comedienne had Communist connections. Lucy heard the report at home and thought Winchell was talking about Imogene Coca. It becomes front page news on September 11. Lucy and Desi awaken with reporters outside their home asking for a statement. That night, the first *I Love Lucy* episode after the summer hiatus, "The Girls Go into Business," was scheduled to be filmed. The cast and crew rehearsed the show as usual, but were not sure what would happen. A doctor stood by in case Lucy collapsed. CBS and Philip Morris soon told the Arnazes they would stick by them. That day, Representative Donald L. Jackson announced that there was no evidence that Lucy was ever a member of the Communist Party. Before the night's filming, Desi gave a speech telling them not to believe what they had read in the newspapers and announced that Lucy was cleared of any wrongdoing. Desi introduced Lucy by calling her "my favorite redhead" and followed by saying, "That's the only thing red about Lucy is her hair, and even that is not legitimate." The audience gave Lucy a huge ovation that left her in tears. She ended the filming by telling the audience, "God bless you for being so kind." Lucy was on the front pages again the next day stating that she had been cleared. Lucy and Desi host a press conference in their backyard the following day. It was clear that the public still loved Lucy.

May 6, 1957: The series finale of *I Love Lucy*, "The Ricardos Dedicate a Statue," airs.

November 17, 1957: *The Lucille Ball-Desi Arnaz Show* premieres with a seventy-five minute episode, "Lucy Takes a Cruise to Havana" with guest stars Hedda Hopper, Ann Sothern, Cesar Romero, and Rudy Vallee.

December 11, 1957: Plans are finalized for Desilu to purchase RKO Studios. Desi had agreed to buy the studio during a break in rehearsals for the second *Lucille Ball-Desi Arnaz Show*, "The Celebrity Next Door." Lucy now owns the studio she once started at for fifty dollars a week.

March 2, 1960: Nine years to the day after playing the character for the first time, Lucy plays Lucy Ricardo for the final time when the last installment of *The Lucille Ball-Desi Arnaz Show*, "Lucy Meets the Mustache," is filmed.

March 3, 1960: Lucy files for divorce from Desi on the grounds of mental cruelty. She testifies in court on May 4, and the divorce is granted that same day.

December 16, 1960: Lucy makes her Broadway debut when *Wildcat* opens on Broadway at the Alvin Theatre. The show was scheduled to open on December 15, but the producers were forced to push it back a day after three trucks carrying sets, costumes, and props from Philadelphia, where the show played its out-of-town tryouts, to New York were stuck on the New Jersey Turnpike during a snowstorm.

December 20, 1960: Lucy meets Gary Morton.

May 24, 1961: Lucy collapses onstage during the matinee performance of *Wildcat*. This was the second time she collapsed onstage, the first being April 22. She never returned to the show. Performances ceased June 3, and the announced August 15 reopening never occurred.

November 19, 1961: Lucille Ball and Gary Morton are married by Dr. Norman Vincent Peale at the Marble Collegiate Church, 1 West 29th Street, in New York. Jack Carter and Paula Stewart, who introduced the couple, served as best man and matron of honor, respectively. Among the

Lucy strikes a pose in 1965.

forty people in attendance were Lucie; Desi Jr.; DeDe; Gary's mother, Rose Goldaper; and friends Hedda Hopper, Jean Kean, and Russell Markert. Outside the church, 1,500 fans waited to wish Lucy and Gary good luck.

October 1, 1962: The premiere episode of *The Lucy Show*, "Lucy Waits Up for Chris," airs. It is the highest-rated episode of the series.

November 8, 1962: Lucille buys out ex-husband Desi's share of Desilu. She purchased Desi's 300,350 shares of Desilu stocks for just over $3 million. As a result, she owns 52 percent of the company. Lucy becomes the first female studio owner in Hollywood.

September 7, 1964: *Let's Talk to Lucy*, a daily ten-minute radio show, premieres on CBS Radio. Lucy interviews some of the biggest stars in show business and some of her close friends. This is her first project to be produced by her husband Gary and cousin Cleo, who will later produce *Here's Lucy*. The radio show lasts for one season.

February 14, 1967: Gulf and Western Industries acquired Desilu Studios for an excess of $17 million. The previous year Gulf and Western had purchased Paramount Pictures, located next door to Desilu Studios. Gulf and Western had the fence separating the two studios torn down, and the two were merged.

March 11, 1968: *The Lucy Show* airs its final episode, "Lucy and the 'Boss of the Year' Award." With the sale of Desilu, Lucy no longer owns *The Lucy Show* and with enough episodes for syndication, she decides to create a new series featuring her own children.

September 23, 1968: The first episode of *Here's Lucy*, "Mod, Mod Lucy," airs. The episode will be the second highest-rated show of the week (following the series premiere of *Mayberry R.F.D.*, which immediately followed *Here's Lucy* on the CBS schedule).

January 6, 1972: Lucy breaks her leg while skiing at her Snowmass, Colorado condo. Lucy was spending the holiday season at Snowmass with Gary, DeDe, Lucie and her husband Phil Vandervort, and Desi Jr. and his girlfriend Liza Minnelli. Lucy had just gotten off a ski lift when another skier crashed into her, breaking Lucy's right leg. Lucy is forced to film the first several episodes of the fifth season of *Here's Lucy* in a cast. The break also postpones the filming of Lucy's film *Mame* until the following January.

March 7, 1974: Lucy's final film, *Mame*, opens at New York's Radio City Music Hall.

March 18, 1974: *Here's Lucy* ends its 144-episode run with "Lucy Fights the System."

July 20, 1977: Lucy's mother, DeDe Ball, dies of a stroke at her home in Brentwood, California.

September 20, 1986: *Life with Lucy* premieres on ABC. It comes in at number 23 for the week in the Nielsen ratings.

November 6, 1986: *Life with Lucy* is cancelled by ABC. The series was ranked sixty-sixth in the ratings out of sixty-seven shows (*The Ellen Burstyn Show*, which followed on the ABC schedule, was the only show lower). The thirteenth and final episode of the series, "World's Greatest Grandma," is filmed the same day as the cancellation. Aaron Spelling is the first one notified by ABC of the series' fate. He has his assistant tell Gary Morton, who does not mention the news until after that night's episode is filmed. In their car on the way home, Gary tells Lucy the bad news. The final episode, "Mother of the Bride," airs on November 15. Five episodes were left unaired.

December 2, 1986: Desi Arnaz dies in his daughter's arms soon after midnight. Lucy spends the day taping *Super Password* with *Life with Lucy* co-star Ann Dusenberry and Betty White and Estelle Getty.

May 11, 1988: Lucy suffers a minor stroke at her home.

March 29, 1989: Lucille Ball makes her final public appearance at the 61st Academy Awards. After being greeted with a thunderous standing ovation, Lucy and friend Bob Hope introduce a musical number featuring "The Oscar Winners of Tomorrow." Following the ceremony, Lucy and Gary attend agent Irving "Swifty" Lazar's famous post-Oscar party at Spago's. While leaving, Lucy delights the crowd outside by kicking up her legs.

April 18, 1989: Lucy complains of chest pains and shortness of breath, but refuses to go to the hospital until Gary and Lucie beg her. Lucy arrived at Cedars-Sinai Medical Center by ambulance at around noon, and doctors discovered that she has a tear in her aorta. An hour later, surgeons began operating. Lucy has a seven-hour surgery in which part of her aorta and aortic valve are replaced. Doctors are optimistic about her recovery. In the

Lucille Ball, star of *Life with Lucy* (1986).

following days, the hospital, known for its celebrity patients, receives a record number of cards, flowers, and faxes for Lucy. Across the street, the Hard Rock Café erects a banner that reads "Hard Rock Loves Lucy." Two days after surgery, she is able to get out of bed. Lucy is aware of the public outpouring of love and support and is deeply touched.

April 26, 1989: Lucy awakes with sharp pains in her back and loses consciousness. She has developed a tear in her aorta, but not in the area that was operated on. She goes into cardiac arrest, and doctors unsuccessfully attempt to revive her. Lucille Ball is pronounced dead at 5:47 in the morning with the cause of death being a ruptured aorta. The news sweeps the nation. Flags in Los Angeles are lowed to half-mast. The Hollywood Chamber of Commerce sets out a roll of paper down Hollywood Boulevard for people to write a message dedicated to Lucy. The following weekend, Gary, Lucie, and Desi Jr. privately inter Lucy's ashes at Forest Lawn Cemetery in the Hollywood Hills alongside DeDe. (In 2002, their ashes are moved to Lake View Cemetery in Jamestown to be with Henry Ball and the Hunt family.) Lucy never wanted a funeral, but three memorial masses are held for her on May 8 in New York, California, and Chicago. On May 14, Mother's Day, fifty of Lucy's family members and closest friends hold a picnic in Lucy's memory on property once owned by Robert Taylor in Mandeville Canyon. Lucy receives numerous posthumous accolades throughout the year including the Emmy's Governors Award and the Presidential Medal of Freedom.

"I'm from Jamestown!"

Lucy's Family

The world loved Lucy, of course, but no star can exist exclusively on the devotion of the public. Throughout her life and her career there were certain people who were key figures in her story, who were instrumental in providing Lucille Ball with love and support, certainly within her close-knit family, and also among some of her acting colleagues whom she could depend on to deliver the goods on her series.

Here are the family members and associates who were most important in the life of Lucy. Certainly no book about Lucille Ball could be written without their mention.

Fred and Flora Belle Hunt

Lucy's maternal grandparents played an important part in her early life. Frederick Charles Hunt was born on July 24, 1865 in Jamestown, New York to Reuben and Eveline Bailey Hunt. Flora Belle Emeline Orcutt was born on June 19, 1867 in Shumla, New York to William and Helen Sprague Orcutt. Although Lucille would later say that Flora Belle was one of five sets of twins, this does not appear to be true. Census records indicate that Flora indeed was a twin (she had a twin brother, Frederick), but her other siblings (eight children total as of 1880) were all of various ages and not twins (unless there were twins that died in infancy). Flora Belle's parents died before she was even seventeen, leaving her and her siblings orphans. Fortunately, Flora managed to keep them all out of orphanages and raised them herself.

Flora Belle found a job as a chambermaid at a hotel owned by Reuben Hunt. Another employee at the hotel was Reuben's son, Fred. The two married on April 10, 1889 in Sinclairville, New York, and soon had three children, Harold Reuben (born September 24, 1890), Desire Eveline, and Lola Marion (born September 10, 1897). Fred had a variety of jobs through the years including grocer, postman, optical instruments maker, chiropractor, and, finally, wood turner. He made marvelous wooden objects like doll-houses and doll furniture and sleds for his granddaughter. When Lucy was in her sixties, she said that the most treasured gift she owned was the hand-carved doll furniture her grandfather gave her for Christmas when she was five. Flora worked as a nurse and midwife, which included delivering her three grandchildren. The Hunts' eldest child and only son, Harold, died of tuberculosis on July 8, 1909 at the age of eighteen. Fred Ball, a father whose son had died, was thrilled when his namesake grandson, a son whose father had died, was born. Young Lucille and her brother Freddy called their grandfather "Daddy." Grandpa Hunt loved the vaudeville shows in Jamestown and took his granddaughter there frequently. As a result, Lucille wanted to be a vaudeville performer. Flora Belle developed uterine cancer and died on July 1, 1922. She was just twelve days past her fifty-fifth birthday.

After the July 1927 shooting accident that left a neighbor's child paralyzed (see "59 Eighth Street, Celeron" entry in "Where Lucy Lived" for further details), Fred was sued for everything he had. Lucille later said, "He just became an old man overnight," referring to the remorse her grandfather felt over the incident. The family was horrified when someone testified that Hunt had deliberately made a target out of the injured boy, Warner Erickson. Hunt was sent to jail but released almost immediately. However, the judge declared that he would have to stay within the city limits of Mayville, the county seat, for a year. During this time, Hunt took up residence with some relatives on their farm in Mayville. Lucy became incensed when she learned that her grandfather was given nothing but strawberries to eat and vowed that she would someday give him a happy life.

Fred Hunt had very progressive political views, and because he was a factory worker in the days prior to unions, he became a champion of the working man. He began to follow the ideals of Socialist Eugene V. Debs, beliefs that were further heightened by the Great Depression. Jamestown was extremely affected by the economic turmoil as several of its once-thriving factories went under. Many residents lost everything, just as Fred had following the tragic incident involving the Erickson family. Hunt witnessed even more economic hardships when he and the family moved to Manhattan.

Fred Hunt became a much happier man when the family took up residence in Southern California. He and other like-minded working men would meet in the garage of Lucy's rented house on Ogden Drive to discuss political and social issues. Although it was not necessary for her father to have any cash, DeDe would give him five dollars a week. Hunt, always eager to help the working class, would walk over to a nearby corner of Sunset Boulevard, go up to one of the streetwalkers who gathered there, give her the five dollar bill, and tell her to take the night off. Uncomfortable with this routine, the family had to stop giving him money. Lucy used to laugh over the fact that when her dates would wait for her at her house, Grandpa Hunt would read them excerpts from *The Daily Worker.* Fred was also able to persuade his daughter, eldest granddaughter, and grandson to register for the Communist Party. Although they had no interest, they did so anyway just to please their ailing loved one, a decision that would come back to haunt Lucy in later years.

Hunt eventually suffered several strokes, dying of one on January 4, 1944. He was buried next to his wife at the Lake View Cemetery in Jamestown.

Henry Ball

Lucille's father, Henry Durrell Ball, was born on September 25, 1887 in Busti, New York to Jasper and Nellie Durrell Ball. The sixth of seven children, he was preceded by George, Frank, Clinton, Maude, and Mabel and followed by Blanche. After Jasper and Nellie divorced, Jasper had several more children with different wives, well into his seventies. The Balls were of Scottish descent.

Henry Ball, nicknamed "Had," reportedly had a great sense of humor. Along with his older brother, Frank, their father, Jasper; and others, Henry helped set up the Independent Telephone Company in Butte, Montana. According to Lucille, her father also spent some time working for the Anaconda Copper Company in Anaconda, Montana.

While visiting the rest of his family in Jamestown, Henry met Desirée Ball. The two married on September 1, 1910 in Jamestown and then went back to live in Montana. They returned to Jamestown for their daughter Lucille's birth there, on August 6, 1911, and then moved back to Montana. Henry loved to play with his daughter and would throw her up in the air, catching her just before she hit the ground, something that Lucille adored.

Ball eventually took a job in Wyandotte, Michigan as a telephone lineman foreman. During the winter of 1915 "Had" contracted typhoid, thought to be the result of eating ice cream at a local shop.

Henry died on Sunday, February 28, 1915 at the family home at 126 Bidle Avenue South in Wyandotte. He was twenty-eight years old. His funeral was held on March 4 back in Jamestown. During the service, Lucille let out a bloodcurdling scream as the casket holding her father's body was lowered into the ground. Following her father's death, Lucille had practically no contact with the Ball family.

Lucy and her mom, DeDe, clown for some enlisted men during World War II.

DeDe Ball

Lucille Ball's beloved mother, Desire Eveline Hunt, was born on September 21, 1892 in Jamestown, New York. Despite the name on her birth certificate, she preferred to be called Desirée. When her niece Cleo began calling her DeDe, she decided this suited her best of all and kept that name. Desirée was of French, English, and Irish descent. She attended Jamestown High School.

Before she was eighteen years old, she became a bride, marrying Henry Ball at her parents' house on August 31, 1910. She then moved to Montana, where her husband worked, but returned to Jamestown for the birth of her first child, so it could be delivered by DeDe's midwife mother. After giving birth to daughter Lucille Desirée she was back in Montana, until the Balls later moved to Michigan. When DeDe was five months pregnant with her second child her husband died of typhoid fever. Her son, whom she named Frederick Henry Ball, was born on July 17, 1915. DeDe had married at seventeen, become a mother at eighteen, and was widowed at twenty-two. So depressed was she at this dreadful turn of events that her family sent her to California in hopes that the change of locale would alleviate her grief. While she was west, Lucy was sent to live with DeDe's sister Lola and her husband George, while Lucy's baby brother Fred stayed with DeDe's parents.

After DeDe returned, she met metal polisher Edward Peterson, and the two married on September 18, 1918. Shortly thereafter, Peterson went to Detroit in search of work, leaving Lucy in the care of his parents, while Freddy remained with the Hunts. Ed Peterson had no interest in kids, but a very definite interest in drinking. Although he never did anything to hurt his stepchildren, they were never close to him. To help make ends meet, DeDe worked as a hat salesperson at Jamestown's chic Marcus Department Store. The stress, however, gave her terrible migraine headaches, requiring her to spend a great deal of time lying down.

DeDe became very involved in her daughter's schooling and directed many of the school plays that Lucy appeared in. The two of them would take all the furniture from their house and cart it over to the school to use as set pieces. Although her children had chores and responsibilities, DeDe was not terribly strict. As a woman with very definite ideas, supporting her daughter's theatrical ambitions in a more narrow-minded time, Desirée Ball created a small local scandal when she allowed Lucille to go to drama school in New York when she was only fifteen. There was much whispering behind her back about the woman who encouraged her daughter to become an actress. Needless to say, DeDe would have the last laugh.

After DeDe and Ed Peterson separated, DeDe and Grandpa Hunt moved to New York City where Lucille and Fred lived, the four of them renting an apartment together. Divorced from Peterson, DeDe took a job working at Stern's Department Store on 42nd Street. Ed would die on April 8, 1943 at the age of fifty-nine. His mother survived him.

DeDe and her father joined Lucille and Fred in California in 1934, all of them settling into Lucy's rented house on Ogden Drive. Getting pretty steady jobs in movies, Lucy refused to let her mother work, and as a result DeDe's migraines ceased. In the nineteen-forties, Lucille bought a house for DeDe in Canoga Park, near Chatsworth, that was actually built by her brother Fred. Lucy said that not having DeDe around that much when she was growing up made her appreciate her mother all the more. She spoke to DeDe on the telephone every day; and every year, on Lucy's own birthday, August 6, she would send her mother flowers as a thank-you.

After the birth of Lucie and Desi Jr., DeDe went over to the house on Roxbury Drive every day to watch her grandchildren. Never wanting to live with her own children for fear of feeling like a burden to them, DeDe kept a separate residence while her daughter's career continued to climb, eventually moving into a house in Brentwood. When Lucy went to New York to do *Wildcat,* DeDe came along with her for the duration of the show, sharing Lucy's apartment with the children. Although she never officially converted to Catholicism, DeDe took Lucie and Desi Jr. to church every Sunday. The children were extremely close to their grandmother.

When Lucy began work on *My Favorite Husband* on the radio in 1948, DeDe became a fixture in the audience. Lucy called her mother her "biggest fan," as DeDe was present for nearly every audience filming of each one of her daughter's shows, taking a spot in the last row along with a group of friends. Lucy loved the fact that she could hear her mother's laughter on her reruns long after she had passed away. When Lucy ended *Here's Lucy,* a furious DeDe supposedly asked her, "Now what am I going to do Thursdays?"

In addition to being an audible part of Lucy's television legacy, DeDe made one on-camera appearance, in the *Here's Lucy* episode "Lucy and Johnny Carson," playing an audience member at *The Tonight Show Starring Johnny Carson.* When Lucy keeps on singing her "Stump the Band" selection, "Snoops the Lawyer," a wearied Johnny sits down on the arm of DeDe's chair. Although she spoke no dialogue, she did receive billing in the episode's closing credits.

In 1972, DeDe was a guest on a talk show for the first time when she was interviewed on *The Merv Griffin Show,* sharing the stage with other mothers of show business figures, including Jack Carter's and Lenny Bruce's. In 1975, she was a guest on *Dinah!* with daughter Lucy and granddaughter Lucie, marking the first time that the three generations were all interviewed together. Active in the Motion Picture Mothers Club, she was interviewed alongside other members of the group comprised of celebrities' mothers on *The Peter Marshall Variety Show,* in 1976.

DeDe loved the condo Lucy purchased in Snowmass, Colorado and was frequently spotted sledding down hills at forty miles an hour when she was over the age of eighty.

Lucille was devastated when DeDe died at her home in Brentwood on July 20, 1977 at the age of eighty-four.

Fred Ball

Lucille's Ball only sibling, younger brother Frederick Henry Ball, was born on July 17, 1915 in Jamestown, New York. His first name came from his maternal grandfather, while his middle name was in tribute to his late father, who had passed away several months before the boy was born. After his sister went to New York City, Fred eventually moved in with her and finished his schooling there. Following Lucille's relocation to Los Angeles

and Fred's high school graduation, her brother joined her out west, finding a job as a page at the recently opened Club Trocadero. When he turned
21 and was eligible to vote, Fred's grandfather persuaded him to register
with the Communist Party, just as he had coaxed Lucy and her mother into
doing. It was because of his political affiliation that Fred was fired from his
job at the Vega Aircraft Corporation. Despite this blot on his record, he was
able to secure jobs with several other aircraft companies over the next several years in both California and Kansas before entering the army.

Fred married a redheaded actress also named Lucille, who by marriage
became a second Lucille Ball. She reportedly said to her famous sister-in-
law, "I guess one of us will have to change her name!" The couple had a
daughter, Pamela, before divorcing. When his brother-in-law formed the
Desi Arnaz Orchestra in the mid forties, Fred became the band manager.
Fred would go on to serve as an executive at Desilu.

Fred's second wife was Phyllis Brier of Jamestown. In 1956, he married
his third wife, Nanzoma (Zo) Roznos, who was a secretary at Desilu. Zo,
like Fred (and niece Lucie), was born on July 17, but four years after Fred.
Following the wedding, Zo was forced to leave her job with the company
because Desilu, owned by a married couple, prohibited a husband and
wife both working for them. Desi reportedly fired his former brother-in-law
from Desilu when Fred attempted to speak to him about how Desi's escalat-
ing drinking was affecting the company. Once Lucy became president of
the company, she installed her brother as Desilu's director in charge of real
estate investments. Fred was the general manager of the Indian Wells Hotel
that Desi opened, but Lucy later controlled, until it was sold in 1970. Fred
and Zo went on to operate a motel in Cottonwood, Arizona.

In addition to daughter Pam from his first marriage, Fred had three
more children, Melissa, April, and Geoffrey. Fred Ball passed away on
February 5, 2007.

Cleo Smith

Lucy's cousin Cleo was born on May 12, 1919 to George (who was born
in Greece) and Lola Marion Hunt Mandicos. Her parents married on
October 22, 1917, and Lucille lived with them for a time while her mother
was in California. Cleo spent her early life in Detroit, Michigan. When the
Mandicos eventually returned to New York, they moved into Lola's parents'
home in Celeron, which also housed DeDe, Ed Peterson, Fred Ball, and
Lucille. Since they were raised in the same house, Lucy and Cleo always
regarded each other as sisters rather than cousins.

Lola operated her own beauty shop, which Lucy loved. This led to a lifelong love of hairstyling for Lucy, who later said that if she had not gone into show business she would have liked to have been a beautician. Lola and George eventually divorced, and Lola went into nursing, leaving Cleo in the care of DeDe and Fred Hunt while she went away to nursing school. George Mandicos moved to Buffalo. On August 15, 1930, Lola died of peritonitis while working at a Long Island mental hospital. The absent George Mandicos returned and wanted Cleo to live with him in Buffalo. A custody battle developed between DeDe and George, with the court ultimately siding with the girl's father. Cleo moved with her father to a Greek community in Buffalo.

When Cleo turned sixteen, she could legally decide where she could live and chose to join Lucille, Fred, DeDe, and Grandpa Hunt in California. Cleo travelled 3,000 miles by Greyhound Bus to Los Angeles, where Lucy met her at the terminal direct from the set of *I Dream Too Much,* still in full makeup. Cleo settled into the family's home on Ogden Drive.

Lucy got Cleo work as an extra, including a bit as one of the campers in *Having Wonderful Time.* Cleo began to go by the professional name of "Cleo Manning." In 1938, she married Artie Auerbach. Lucy and Artie were both regulars on Phil Baker's radio program and on Jack Haley's *The Wonder Show,* where Auerbach played a variety of wacky characters. The couple eventually divorced. Cleo lucked out when she was given a kissing scene with Clark Gable in his 1941 movie *Honky Tonk,* only to have the moment cut from the release print.

In 1941, Cleo married publicist Kenneth Morgan. During the war, the couple lived in an army camp in North Carolina and had a son, Scott. After the war, Ken took a job in Johannesburg, South Africa, and the couple moved there for a year. When they returned, he became the head of public relations for the newly formed Desilu Productions. He also appeared as Ricky's press agent in the first season *I Love Lucy* episode "Men Are Messy." Cleo and Ken appeared together in the party scene in "Lucy's Last Birthday." The Morgans are named among the guests Ricky invited for Lucy's surprise party. During this time, Cleo took college classes and eventually became involved in social work.

The Morgans went along on the Arnazes' ill-fated final trip to Europe in 1959, and like Lucy and Desi, Cleo and Ken were soon divorced. Cleo took a job as a receptionist for *Look* magazine, eventually working in the promotion department. Among her coworkers at the magazine was Wanda Clark. When Lucy asked Cleo if she knew of someone who could be her secretary, Cleo recommended Wanda, who would stay in Lucy's employ for the rest of Lucy's life.

While in Las Vegas, Lucy introduced Cleo to Cecil Smith, the television critic of the *Los Angeles Times*. The two would marry and eventually add two more children to their family, a son, Marcus, and a daughter, Tina.

When Lucy began her radio show, *Let's Talk to Lucy,* in 1964, Cleo applied for and got the job of the series' producer. As a result, she left her job with *Look* and decided to concentrate on this area. She served as the Executive in Charge of Production for *Lucy in London* and, in 1969, became one of the few women producers on television when she took over these responsibilities on *Here's Lucy;* a position she held until the series ended in 1974. Keeping with the family feeling of the series, Cecil Smith appeared as himself in "Lucy Meets the Burtons." Cleo and Cecil's son Marcus appeared as the ring bearer at Lucy's aborted wedding ceremony in the episode "Lucy and Her Prince Charming," a role he actually held at Lucie Arnaz and Phil Vandervort's wedding the previous year.

The Smiths eventually retired to San Luis Obispo, California. Cecil Smith passed away on July 11, 2009 at the age of ninety-two.

"Mr. and Mrs."

The Men Lucy Married

Desi Arnaz

L ucy's first husband, her most famous co-star and the person to whom her name would be forever and most inextricably linked, Desiderio Alberto Arnaz y de Acha III, was born on March 2, 1917 in Santiago de Cuba to Desiderio Alberto Arnaz II and Dolores Acha Arnaz. Desiderio II was a distinguished doctor, while Dolores, known to all as "Lolita," was considered one of the most beautiful women in the country.

The happy couple, Lucy and Desi Arnaz, out for a night on the town.

Desi's paternal grandfather, the first Desiderio, was a doctor who charged up San Juan Hill with Theodore Roosevelt and the Rough Riders during the Spanish-American War. Desi's maternal grandfather was one of the founders of the Bacardi Rum Company.

In 1923, Desi's father became the youngest mayor of Santiago at the age of twenty-three. His brother became the chief of police. Two Arnazes holding these positions gave the family an incredible degree of wealth and power. The Arnazes had many homes, while young Desi had horses and boats. His father's status rose even higher in 1932 when he was elected to Congress. All of this came crashing down the following year when the Machado regime in Cuba was overthrown. The Arnazes were targets of the new regime, and Desi and his mother barely escaped with their lives. The revolutionaries burned down their home, destroyed all their possessions, and slaughtered all their animals, forcing them to hide with relatives of Desi's mother for several months. Desiderio Arnaz, who was off in Havana at the time of the uprising, was jailed for several months along with other government officials. After he was released, he went to Miami and soon sent for his son. The Arnazes now had nothing. Desi's plan of going to Notre Dame to study medicine no longer had much hope of being fulfilled. When Desi first arrived in the United States, he and his father lived in a small rooming house. But their fortunes sank even lower when the once-privileged Arnaz men found themselves having to move into a rat infested, unheated warehouse. To make ends meet, they went into business selling bananas and later broken tiles. Desi completed his high school education at Miami Beach's Saint Patrick's High School, where his best friend was Al Capone Jr. To earn extra money, Desi took a job cleaning canary cages. Desi's mother was eventually sent for to reunite with her family.

In 1936, Desi entered show business when he joined the Siboney Septet, a band at Miami Beach's Roney Plaza (coincidentally, Vivian Vance had an engagement there several months earlier). This led to a job with the Xavier Cugat Orchestra that took him to New York. Cugat didn't pay much, so Desi decided to strike out on his own. Also leaving behind his job with Cugat was his secretary, Louis A. Nicoletti, who became Desi's band manager and continued to work for him for years. At the time of his death in 1969, he was the assistant director on *Here's Lucy*.

Cugat allowed Desi to use his name ("Desi Arnaz and His Xavier Cugat Orchestra") and told him he would send him some musicians. Those he sent were Italian, Spanish, and Jewish musicians who knew nothing about Latin music. The group was so awful that their jobs were in jeopardy. They were actually told they were going to be fired at the end of the night. Rescue came by way of the conga, which Desi remembered from Cuba. He figured *anybody* could play that, so they worked it into their act. This not only meant that Desi could officially take credit for introducing the conga to Miami, but helped turned the conga line dance into such a sensation in the city that the club where they performed soon changed its name to La Conga. Offered a job at a new Manhattan nightclub that also went under the name La Conga, Desi returned to New York. Not unlike the Miami Conga, this too became one of the biggest hotspots in the city.

Lyricist Lorenz Hart saw Desi perform at Miami's La Conga and thought he would be perfect for the new college musical he and Richard

Rodgers were writing. Desi, who had never even seen a Broadway show before, auditioned for the role of Manuelito, a Latin American football star, in *Too Many Girls* and won the part. Diosa Costello, who was also appearing at La Conga, was cast in the musical as well. The show opened at the Imperial Theatre on October 18, 1939 with Richard Kollmar, Marcy Wescott, Eddie Bracken, and Hal LeRoy filling the other principal roles and, in the chorus, Van Johnson. Johnson served as understudy to Kollmar, Bracken, and, of all people, Desi. However, the freckle-faced redhead never had to go on in Desi's place and pass himself off as a Latin.

Desi and Diosa Costello were doing double duty. After playing in *Too Many Girls* in the evening, they would perform at La Conga until the early hours of the morning. It is possible that during this time Desi made his television debut performing alongside Costello at the World's Fair. This would predate Lucy's first television appearance by about eight years.

Desi became engaged to dancer Renée DeMarco, but they could not marry right away because her divorce from former dance partner Tony DeMarco (they were the famous Dancing DeMarcos) was not yet finalized. Renée (who Desi referred to as "Freckles" in his 1976 autobiography), did not seem to mind her fiancé's roving eye. His other dates at the time included Betty Grable who was then co-starring on Broadway in *Du Barry Was a Lady*, which was playing at the 46th Street Theatre next door to *Too Many Girls*. Also in 1939, Desi's parents divorced. Lolita moved in with her son in his subleased duplex apartment on Central Park West. Desi's father would eventually remarry to a woman named Ann and adopt her young daughter, Connie.

RKO bought the film rights to *Too Many Girls* and originally had Ginger Rogers in mind for the female lead. However, Lucille Ball ended up being cast in the role instead. In December 1939, before it was definite that Lucy would be starring in the film version, she was sent to New York by RKO for personal appearances. She was told to go see *Too Many Girls* while she was in town and ended up being mesmerized by Desi Arnaz. Although she did not go backstage after the performance, Lucy and her friend Russell Markert went to the La Conga, only to learn that Desi had the night off, so she did not get to meet him. *Too Many Girls* closed in May 1940 when many of the cast members went out west to do the film.

When Desi first saw Lucille Ball at the RKO studios in Hollywood, she had just finished filming her fight scene with Maureen O'Hara in *Dance, Girl, Dance*. Her hair was in disarray, her clothes were torn, and she was wearing a fake black eye. Desi was shocked to find out that this person was the one who would be starring in his movie debut. When a more glamorous Lucille Ball walked into the room a few hours later, Desi exclaimed,

"Whatta *honk* of a woman!" He had no idea who she was. He had to be told that was Lucille Ball, whom he had met earlier that day. Desi asked her if she wanted him to teach her the rumba, so they went to El Zarape, a Mexican restaurant over a market on Sunset Boulevard, with the gang from *Too Many Girls*. While others involved in the film, including Ann Miller and George Abbott, did the Conga, Lucy and Desi quietly talked. Lucy said she fell in love with Desi in five minutes.

A few days later, they met up at a cast party at Eddie Bracken's house. Lucy and Desi got to talking and by the following day, Desi had ended his engagement with Renée DeMarco and Lucy broke off her relationship with Al Hall. The two dated for months despite the long periods of separation due to their respective careers. The stage cast of *Too Many Girls* played the show in Chicago (with Van Johnson replacing Richard Kollmar), while Lucy went on a personal appearance tour to promote *Dance, Girl, Dance*. They met up in New York on November 29, 1940 where Desi was performing at the Roxy Theatre. Desi told Lucille that he wanted to marry her the following morning, and she happily accepted. The two were wed on November 30, 1940 in Greenwich, Connecticut.

Desi was supposed to star in another Broadway musical written by *Too Many Girls* scriptwriter George Marion Jr., *Yours for a Year*, but that project never materialized. RKO, wanting to capitalize on the couple's much-publicized romance, announced in November 1940 that, after Desi's Broadway commitment, he and Lucy would film a movie called *Havana*. This would be the first of many projects that would have teamed the two that never happened. In 1941, it was announced that Desi would likely play Lucille's love interest in *Look Who's Laughing*, but when the picture was filmed, Lee Bonnell had the part. Lucy and Desi wanted to co-star in a movie, but got the impression that the studio did not think people would accept them as a couple. They decided to do a vaudeville act together and played New York and Chicago, among other places. Desi sang many of his popular numbers, and Lucy joined him for the song "You and I." The couple got an offer to do the act at the London Palladium, but turned it down when Lucy discovered she was pregnant. Unfortunately, Lucy had a miscarriage, the first of several in their marriage.

Four Jacks and a Jill (which had its basis in the 1937 film *That Girl from Paris* starring Lucille Ball), *Father Takes a Wife*, and *The Navy Comes Through* were Desi's three other pictures under his RKO contract. A stint in the revue *The Ken Murray Blackouts* led to a contract with Metro-Goldwyn-Mayer, the same studio where his wife was employed at the time. Taking a role in the war picture *Bataan*, Desi was praised for his final scene in which he dies from malaria. He received a Photoplay Award for Performance of the

Month, but despite this and his favorable reviews, this was the only film he made under his MGM contract.

Desi wanted to join the service immediately after World War II was declared, but he was not yet an American citizen. Although he was not made a citizen until October 1943, Desi was drafted that May. He wanted to go into the Air Force, but the day before he was to report to basic training, he injured his knee playing softball, tearing a cartilage, which required surgery. Desi was eventually stationed at Birmington Hospital, close to the Arnazes' ranch in Chatsworth. Despite the closeness to the house, he was rarely at home. Lucy suspected he was philandering and filed for divorce. The divorce was voided when the two cohabitated together before the decree was issued.

With no prospects for his movie career, Desi decided to form a new Desi Arnaz Orchestra. They opened at Ciro's in Hollywood, where Desi added a number into his act that would forever be identified with him, "Babalu." This was followed by his first top-billed role in a motion picture, in the hour-long Universal musical *Cuban Pete*.

After he and his band were the featured orchestra for one season on Bob Hope's *The Pepsodent Show*, they went on tour. While driving through Indiana on the way to Akron, Ohio, the band's bus driver fell asleep and crashed into a truck. Customarily, Desi and brother-in-law Fred Ball always travelled with the band, but this particular time they decided to go to Detroit to see Lucy onstage in *Dream Girl*. The front of the bus where the two traditionally sat received the bulk of the damage, and the band member who sat in their seat, Charlie Harris, was hurt the most badly; he ended up losing an eye. This close call made the Arnazes evaluate their relationship and vow to spend more time together.

Wanting some control over their future joint ventures, Lucy and Desi formed Desilu Productions in 1950. Hoping that their next project together could be on television, the two did a vaudeville act to show CBS that the American people would buy them as a couple. While on the road, Lucy felt ill and went to the doctor, who gave her a pregnancy test. She would not hear the results until Monday, a few days later. On Sunday night before their performance, Lucy and Desi were both in their respective dressing rooms listening to Walter Winchell's radio show when Winchell announced that the Arnazes were *infant*-icipating. The couple soon cancelled all their future commitments, but Lucy again had a miscarriage. She did, however, get pregnant again, and they were overjoyed when their daughter Lucie Desirée Arnaz was born on July 17, 1951, finally fulfilling their long cherished dream of having a child together. A son, named for his father, came along eighteen months later.

Desi was given his own CBS Radio show, a musical game show, *Your Tropical Trip*, that premiered on January 21, 1951, but this credit would soon slip off the radar as the Arnazes' careers were about to turn around in a major way. On Desi's thirty-fourth birthday, March 2, 1951, they shot the pilot for *I Love Lucy*. Once the show took off, Desi extended his involvement to becoming its executive producer. Soon Desilu grew from a production company into an empire with shows like *December Bride* and *The Untouchables* produced by the studio at which Desi served as president. Desi was praised by those who knew him for his brilliant business acumen.

At the height of their phenomenal success, Desi gave Lucy two options. They could either quit right then and not have to worry about anything for the rest of their lives, or they would have to expand. Not wanting to quit, Lucy took the second option. Desilu became an even bigger force within the industry to the degree that the Arnazes were able to purchase RKO, where they had met seventeen years before. In 1958, Desi became the host of the anthology series *The Westinghouse Desilu Playhouse*, which ran for two seasons.

While all this success might have led the public to believe that life couldn't possibly be better for the Arnazes, Desi became overworked and his drinking escalated. In the spring of 1959, the couple, their children, and Cleo and Kenny Morgan went on a trip to Europe. Lucy had hoped this would save her crumbling marriage, but it only did more damage. The two returned home not speaking to each other. Desi's infidelity was not a secret, and in September 1959 he was arrested for public drunkenness in front of a house of ill repute on Hollywood Boulevard. Lucy couldn't bear the fact that her private humiliations were being made public. It was clear to them both that their union would have to come to an end. In November 1959, Desi told his wife he wanted a divorce. Lucy filed for divorce on March 3, 1960, the day after the final *Lucille Ball-Desi Arnaz*

Lucy and Desi film their wedding scene in their final movie together, *Forever, Darling* (1956).

Show was filmed. Despite the split, Desi continued to send red and white carnations to Lucy on their anniversary every year for the rest of his life.

After the divorce, Desi purchased a house in Del Mar, California, where the Arnazes had vacationed for several summers. He also owned homes, at various times, in Palm Springs and Las Cruces, Mexico. In 1957, he had opened the 42-room Desi Arnaz' Western Hills Hotel (later the Indian Wells Hotel), which adjoined the Indian Wells Country Club in Palm Springs.

Desi took an active role in his former wife's first (and only) venture into Broadway, *Wildcat*, which was bankrolled by Desilu. They were spotted out together in New York, leading to public speculation over whether the two were reconciling. No reconciliation took place, and by the end of 1960, Lucy was romantically involved with Gary Morton. Desi and Lucy were, however, able to maintain their working relationship, for a while. In January 1962, Lucy requested that Desi direct the sketch she would appear in for the Desilu pilot *The Victor Borge Comedy Theater.* When Lucy returned for *The Lucy Show*, Desi served as the executive producer, but only for the first fifteen shows. Studio execs were worried that Desi's drinking was getting out of hand and talked Lucy into exercising her option of being able to buy her ex-husband out of Desilu, which she did for an excess of $3 million.

Desi began dating Edith Mack Hirsch, whom he had met years earlier at the Santa Anita Racetrack, where she worked as a cigarette girl. In the interim, she had married dog food magnate and racehorse owner Clement Hirsch, and was still legally bound to him when she began her relationship with Desi. Hirsch had two private investigators follow Desi and Edie, while Desi, in turn, hired two detectives of his own to follow Hirsch's men. A few days after Edie was granted a divorce from Hirsch in Juarez, New Mexico, she and Desi married on his forty-sixth birthday at the Sands Hotel in Las Vegas. Present at the wedding were Jimmy and Marge Durante, Van Johnson, and Marc and Marcella Rabwin. Lucy sent the couple a horseshoe-shaped wreath of flowers with the message, "Congratulations. You both picked a winner." Edie was only a few weeks younger than Desi, having been born on April 15, 1917. She was also the mother of a son, Greg.

Not content in retirement, Desi decided to return to the television industry, forming Desi Arnaz Productions and setting up shop at Desilu. He was now a tenant at the studio he created. Desi engaged Bob and Madelyn to write several pilot scripts. The results were *Gussy, My Girl* with Ken Murray; *Brother Bertram* (a sitcom about monks in a monastery, an idea that was resurrected by Lucille Ball Productions in 1981 as *Bungle Abbey*); *The Carol Channing Show*, and *The Mothers-in-Law*. Another pilot produced by Desi Arnaz Productions was *Land's End* with Rory Calhoun. *The Mothers-in-Law* was the only show to get on their air.

Bob and Madelyn created *The Mothers-in-Law*, a sitcom about two couples who have lived next door to each other for years and then become even closer when their children marry and move into a garage apartment between the houses. Eve Arden and Ann Sothern were considered for the titular mothers, but this idea was dropped when it was decided that the two ladies seemed too similar. Kaye Ballard, seventeen years younger than Eve Arden, was selected to be her co-star. In addition to producing the series and directing many of the episodes, Desi appeared in four episodes as matador Señor Raphael del Gado. He was joined by his son in two of these and even sang a song he himself wrote, "I Love You," on the show. *The Mothers-in-Law* ran for two seasons from 1967 to 1969.

After he directed the first eight *Mothers-in-Law* installments, Desi, Edie, Lucie, and Desi Jr. went on a yachting trip in July 1967 and stopped in San Juanico, Mexico. The family was sitting on a veranda when a heavyset man sat on the railing causing it to collapse, sending everyone plummeting four feet. Desi landed on a metal stake in the ground, which punctured his side. Because the town did not have a hospital, Desi had to be flown to Scripps Memorial Hospital in La Jolla, California, where several blood clots had to be removed. In the next few years, he would undergo four surgeries for diverticulitis.

In October 1970, Desi co-hosted a week of *The Mike Douglas Show*. Guests on the show included Vivian Vance, his son, and his daughter. Desi was reduced to tears when Lucie performed a musical tribute to him. Keeping busy in a variety of ways, Desi taught a class on television production for a semester at San Diego State University in 1972. Two years later, Desi played amateur sleuth Dr. Juan Domingo in an episode of *Ironside*. A spinoff was proposed featuring Desi's character, but did not happen.

Desi's memoirs, which he titled, simply, *A Book*, were published to great success in 1976. To promote the book, Desi hosted an episode of the new series *NBC's Saturday Night* (before it changed its name to *Saturday Night Live*), which featured takeoffs on *I Love Lucy* and *The Untouchables*. Desi Jr. also appeared on the show as his father's guest. Desi performed "Cuban Pete" and "Babalu" and became the series' first host to also be credited as the musical guest. Desi made his final sitcom appearance in an episode entitled "The Cuban Connection" (2/26/78) on *Alice*, which was produced by his old friends Bob Carroll Jr. and Madelyn Davis and directed by *I Love Lucy*'s William Asher. He also planned a second memoir, entitled, of course, *Another Book*, but this was never written.

In 1980, Desi made his final acting appearance with the movie *The Escape Artist*, billing himself as "Desiderio Arnaz" because he wanted his son to drop the "Jr." from his name and become simply Desi Arnaz. The movie, in which Desi played a crooked mayor, did not receive a theatrical release until 1982. That same year, in March, he was named King of the Miami Carnival and was joined by his two children for a show at the Orange Bowl in front of 30,000 fans. Lucie played "Sally Sweet" to her father's "Cuban Pete" and wore the same costume her mother had worn over thirty years earlier. On May 23, 1983, Desi performed for the last time on television on *Late Night with David Letterman*, where he was interviewed and sang.

Desi's wife, Edie, succumbed to cancer on March 23, 1985. Finally admitting that he had a drinking problem, Desi sought help. The year following his wife's death, he was diagnosed with lung cancer. As his conditioned worsened, Lucie Arnaz moved in with him. On November 30, 1986, Lucy and Desi spoke to each other on the telephone for the last time. Lucy repeated over and over again how much she loved him. Desi told her he loved her too. It would have been their thirty-sixth wedding anniversary.

Desi Arnaz passed away in his daughter's arms five minutes after midnight on December 2, 1986. He was survived by his mother, Lolita, who had Alzheimer's at the time and never knew of her son's death. Dolores de Acha Arnaz died on October 24, 1988 at the age of ninety-two.

Gary Morton

Lucy's second husband, Gary Morton, was born Morton Goldaper on December 18, 1924 in The Bronx, New York. He had a sister, Helen. During World War II, Gary was stationed in Fort Riley, Kansas, where he entertained his fellow soldiers with impressions. Feeling fulfilled by the experience, Gary decided to pursue a career in comedy. When he told his family of his show business aspirations, he promised them he would quit if he did not make it to the stage of the Paramount Theatre in five years' time. Three years later, he was there. In 1953, Gary married Jacqueline Imoor, who acted under the name Susan Morrow. Her sister, Judith Campbell Exner, would later gain notoriety when she claimed to be John F. Kennedy's mistress. Following the demise of his marriage (it was annulled), Gary was linked in the gossip columns with actress Cleo Moore (who, coincidently, would get married on Gary and Lucy's wedding day).

Although he never reached the upper echelons of stardom during his stand-up days, Gary Morton was known in the business as a talented comedian who also played the trumpet and threw some celebrity impressions into his act, a favorite being Bette Davis. Gary opened for such singers as Johnnie Ray, Paul Anka, and Vic Damone, and then dabbled in legit theatre when he appeared as a replacement in a bit part in the Broadway musical *Mr. Wonderful* starring Sammy Davis Jr., sharing the stage with his friend Jack

Lucy and Gary Morton pose with the statuette awarded to Lucy for her induction in the Television Academy Hall of Fame in 1984.

Carter. He made several appearances on television during this time, including *The Bob Crosby Show.*

Lucille Ball and Gary Morton would refer to December 20, 1960 as the beginning of their relationship. Although Lucy usually credited her *Wildcat* co-star Paula Stewart with introducing them, her first actual encounter with her future husband took place prior to their official "first date," which involved Stewart. While out with Danny Welkes, an agent, at Danny's Hideaway, a restaurant on East 45th Street, Lucy was introduced to Gary. When he went to shake her hand, his tie fell into her cup of coffee. She ended up sending him three new ties to replace the one he ruined. When later asked on *The Merv Griffin Show* how she and Gary first met, Lucy said, "I happened to see him one night and I didn't forget him. And then, eventually, I met him." Following their initial meeting, Paula Stewart, who was engaged to Jack Carter at the time, invited Lucy out on a double date. Her date turned out to be Gary. The group went to the Silver Moon Pizza Place on Second Avenue. Gary admitted to his famous date that he had never actually seen an episode of *I Love Lucy.* Lucy became extremely interested in this man, thirteen years her junior. Beginning in February 1961, the gossip columns began reporting the two as an item. When Lucy went to Miami to get some rest from *Wildcat,* Gary met her there. Not surprisingly, Gary began to get even more bookings as a result of his much-publicized romance with the First Lady of Television. Club owners thought audiences would want to see the man they read so much about in the gossip columns and would flock to their establishments to see if Lucy would show up.

On another pizza double date with Jack and Paula Carter, Lucy discovered a ring on an anchovy in her pizza. Gary proposed. This was fairly early in their courtship, very likely April 12, 1961, as Lucy's driver, Frank Gorey, recalled that the date they decided to wed was the same day Yuri Gagarin became the first man to go into outer space. When *Wildcat* closed and Lucy returned to California, Gary followed along, taking up residence in her guesthouse on Roxbury Drive.

When Lucy and Gary flew back to New York in November 1961 for Lucy to begin work on the TV special *The Good Years,* they finally set a date to marry. When the two applied for a marriage license on November 13, the groom gave his age as forty-four (Lucy would later claim he was forty-six when they married, when in reality he was not even thirty-eight), which made it seem like less of an age difference. Without Lucy's knowledge, Gary signed a prenuptial agreement waiving any rights to her money. Lucille Ball and Morton Goldaper (he did not legally change his name to Gary Morton until 1965) were married by Doctor Norman Vincent Peale at the Marble Collegiate Church on November 19, 1961. The extent of his new wife's fame hit Gary when they exited the church to over a thousand well-wishers crowded outside. Just weeks after his marriage, Gary made his debut as a comic on *The Ed Sullivan Show* on December 10, 1961. He appeared again on the show the following January 7.

With his marriage, Gary inherited two stepchildren, whom he always praised and who always praised him in return. His favorite pastime was golf, and he very quickly fell in love with the California weather, which allowed him to indulge in the game all year round. He was also an avid car collector and loved clothes.

Mr. and Mrs. Morton made their first joint television appearance as contestants on *Password* on September 26, 1963. The couple would return to the game show many times over the next several years, including appearances with Lucie and Desi Jr., as well as such friends as Vivian Vance, Peter Lawford, Gale Gordon, Mary Wickes, Carole Cook, and Richard Crenna. In 1966, Gary served as a guest panelist on *I've Got a Secret* with Lucy as the celebrity contestant.

During the run of *The Lucy Show,* Gary took on the job of warming up the audience prior to the filming, a position Desi had held during the *I Love Lucy* years. He made his first appearance on *The Lucy Show* during its second season in the episode "Lucy Takes Up Golf," playing, most appropriately, Lucy Carmichael's golf-loving boyfriend, Gary Stewart. The following season he had a small role as a casino pit boss in "Lucy Goes to Vegas" (where he received billing as "Morton Goldaper.") He played record producer Mr. Morton in "Lucy Discovers Wayne Newton," and was featured in the series finale "Lucy and the 'Boss of the Year' Award," as an emcee.

By the mid sixties, Gary had pretty much ended his stand-up career, choosing instead to become more involved in his wife's projects. When Lucy began work on her daily, ten-minute radio show, *Let's Talk to Lucy,* Gary served as both associate producer and announcer. With the formation of Lucille Ball Productions in 1968, Gary was made vice president. That same year he became executive producer of his wife's newest series, *Here's Lucy.* During its six-season run, he played an emcee in "Lucy and the Andrews Sisters," an actor in "Lucy and Sammy Davis Jr.," a carnival barker in "Lucy Makes a Few Extra Dollars," and, finally, himself, in "Lucy Carter Meets Lucille Ball," in which he gave Lucy Carter a passionate kiss, mistakenly thinking she was his wife.

Lucy loved making her workplace a family affair and hired many of her relatives through the years, including members of Gary's family. Among the actors most frequently seen on *The Lucy Show* and *Here's Lucy,* was Gary's cousin, Sid Gould, a standup comic, twelve years older than Gary, who had achieved success in the comedy field before him. Sid made his first appearance in a Lucille Ball project shortly after the Mortons married when he played a cab driver in her film *Critic's Choice,* although he did not share any scenes with Lucy. His first role on *The Lucy Show* was in the first-season episode "Lucy Is a Kangaroo for a Day."

Sid's wife, actress Vanda Barra, began appearing on *The Lucy Show* starting with the sixth season, when she played a wisecracking waitress in the episode "Lucy and Robert Goulet." She could also be seen that same season in a recurring role of a bank employee named Vanda Wilson. On the same network, she was a regular on *The Jonathan Winters Show* during its two season run (1967–69). Once *Here's Lucy* began, Barra became a more frequent guest. In the opening scene of the third-season premiere, "Lucy Meets the Burtons," she appeared as a friend of Lucy's, appropriately named Vanda. The creators took this one step further by actually casting Vanda Barra as a recurring character named Vanda Barra, another secretary who worked in the same office building as Lucy Carter. Vanda Barra would show up to play Vanda Barra quite often starting with season four.

Although Sid Gould would continue to play other bit characters throughout the remainder of the series, he also had the recurring role of Sam, the waiter in the coffee shop located downstairs in the office building where Lucy, Harry, Mary Jane, and Vanda worked. The characters of Vanda and Sam were established as a couple. All of the episodes featuring the two were written by Madelyn Davis and Bob Carroll Jr. with the exception of the fifth-season episode "A Home Is Not an Office" (which was penned by Fred S. Fox and Seaman Jacobs). Although Vanda and Sid did appear in the series finale, "Lucy Fights the System," they did not play the characters fans of the series had come to know them by. The two were also featured in the later Lucille Ball specials and a 1978 Bob Hope special with Lucy, while Vanda worked with Lucy on *The Mary Tyler Moore Hour*.

In 1974, Gary Morton made his feature film debut in the biopic *Lenny*, starring Dustin Hoffman as controversial comedian Lenny Bruce. Gary received excellent reviews for his portrayal of comic Sherman Hart, modeled after his friend Milton Berle (who had turned down the role). Although Lucy spoke out about the explicit language and sexual content in films during this period, she apparently had no objections to her husband appearing in a film that featured plenty of both.

After the demise of *Here's Lucy*, Gary remained in charge of the day-to-day business of Lucille Ball Productions and filled a small role as a casino boss in Lucy's 1975 *Lucy Gets Lucky* special. He spent months looking at film clips of his wife's shows (which meant that he finally got around to catching up on those *I Love Lucy* episodes he had missed) to put together *CBS Salutes Lucy: The First 25 Years*, which premiered in November 1976, with Gary credited as executive producer. With Lucille Ball Productions, Gary produced the 1983 Tom Cruise film *All the Right Moves* and the made-for-television movie *Sentimental Journey* that same year. For its brief run, Gary served as executive producer with Aaron Spelling and Douglas S. Cramer on his wife's final show, *Life with Lucy*. Through the years Lucy and Gary appeared together frequently on talk shows like *The Merv Griffin Show, Dinah!*, and *The Mike Douglas Show*.

Gary accepted several honors on behalf of his late wife in 1989 including her Emmy's Governors Award and the Presidential Medal of Freedom. In 1990, Gary made his second, and final, feature film appearance, in *Postcards from the Edge*, as Meryl Streep's sleazy business manager.

In 1994, Gary married golf pro Susie McAllister, who was nearly twenty-three years his junior. Lucie and Desi Jr. both attended the wedding. Gary continued to live in the Rancho Mirage home he once shared with Lucy until his death on March 31, 1999 of lung cancer.

4

"Lucille Ball Is Old Enough to Be Your Mother"

Lucy's Children

Lucie Arnaz

Lucie Desirée Arnaz was born on July 17, 1951 at 8:15 a.m. in Los Angeles at Cedars of Lebanon Hospital, six weeks before her parents started work on *I Love Lucy*. The couple, who was thrilled to finally have a baby after nearly eleven years of marriage, had planned to name their child Susan if it was a girl. However, after Lucy had fallen asleep following the birth, which had turned out to be an unplanned caesarean, Desi put the name "Lucie" on the birth certificate. He spelt it with an "ie" so that no one would get confused. Instead, it led to confusion for the rest of their daughter's life.

Lucie's first official television appearance came when she and her baby brother Desi Jr. were briefly

Desi Arnaz Jr., age three-and-a half, and Lucie Arnaz, age five, with their mother on the set of the *I Love Lucy* episode "The Ricardos Visit Cuba."

seen as extras in the *The Lucille Ball-Desi Arnaz Show* episode "Lucy Goes to Sun Valley" in 1958. (They would show up alongside their parents in a Ford Motor commercial that aired during the same episode, as well.) She made her speaking television debut when she and Desi Jr. joined their mother as guests on *The Tonight Show with Jack Paar* on December 29, 1960. Following their parents' divorce, Lucie and Desi Jr. moved to New York with their mother while she did *Wildcat* on Broadway. After the musical's closing, the family moved back to California in 1961.

When her mother returned to do *The Lucy Show*, Lucie was seen in the third episode of the series to air, "Lucy the Referee," as one of the extras watching the football game. Later that season, Lucy asked her real-life daughter if she was interested in playing Cynthia, the best friend of her TV daughter Chris (Candy Moore) in the episode "Lucy the Soda Jerk." Eleven-year-old Lucie agreed to do it, but although "Cynthia" was mentioned many times over the next few seasons, the character was seen in only one other episode, "Lucy Is a Chaperone," which aired only a few weeks after her first appearance. She could also be seen with Vivian Vance and Moore in the Jell-O commercial that accompanied the episode.

Although she no longer played Cynthia, Lucie returned several times to *The Lucy Show*: in "Lucy at Marineland," as a nameless spectator sitting next to brother Desi in the bleachers, asking an overly excited Lucy Carmichael to sit down; in "Lucy and the Ring a Ding Ding," as a shoeless hippie who encounters Mr. Mooney and an incapacitated Lucy, who has taken too many relaxation pills; and in "Lucy Gets Her Diploma," as Patty Martin, one of the students Lucy befriends when she has to go back to high school. (Another student was played by young actor Philip Vandervort, who began dating Lucie at this time.) More curiously, at age sixteen, Lucie showed up as "Dorothy," an adult friend of her mother's character in "Lucy and Robert Goulet." Later, she drifted back to bit player, as a dancing teenager in the episode "Lucy Gets Involved," which featured Phil Vandervort in a larger role.

Throughout the mid sixties, Lucie and Desi Jr. appeared with their mother and stepfather on the game show *Password*. Although her brother appeared several times on the show their father produced and directed, *The Mothers-in-Law*, Lucie's sole appearance there was as an extra whizzing by on a golf cart in the show's second episode, "Everybody Goes on a Honeymoon."

Although initially shy as a child, especially in comparison to her extroverted younger brother, Lucie became more outgoing the older she got. Her interest in musical theater led to her creating her own theatrical group in the family garage at Roxbury Drive. Lucy was so supportive of this endeavor that she had a stage built there, complete with a spotlight for her daughter. Because of its theater program, Lucie decided to go to Immaculate High School, which could boast of having its productions reviewed in *Variety*. While there, Lucie ended up in such shows as *Oklahoma!* and *The Boy Friend*. What inspired her to go into show business for real was (ironically) seeing Angela Lansbury star in the Broadway production of *Mame*.

When Lucy invited her children to play her character's offspring on her new series, *Here's Lucy*, Lucie worried that if she was poorly reviewed, it would hurt whatever show business career she was hoping to have in the future. She told her mother that if the critics were against her joining the show, she wanted to be written out. Her mother agreed to this condition. Lucie had considered going to Northwestern to study theater when she graduated high school, but because she was now committed to the series, abandoned those plans. Although she spent part of her junior and senior year receiving on-set tutoring, Lucie followed the lesson plans provided by her school, Immaculate Heart, and was able to graduate with her friends.

At first, the *Here's Lucy* writers weren't quite sure what Lucie Arnaz (in the role of Kim Carter) could do, but soon began writing to her strengths as a fine singer, dancer, and mimic. The show gave Lucie the opportunity to sing and dance with such people as Ginger Rogers, Carol Burnett, Wayne Newton, and Donny Osmond.

Soon after she turned eighteen, Lucie moved into her own apartment in nearby Century City. She dated documentary filmmaker and occasional actor Phil Vandervort, whose real name was actually Philip Vandervort Mernegeaux. The two were married on Lucie's twentieth birthday in the backyard of the Roxbury Drive house she had grown up in. Among the 200 guests were Gale Gordon, Carol Burnett, Jeff and Beau Bridges, Ruta Lee, Jack Carter, and Ken Berry. Best man was actor Dick Gautier, and Lucie's maid of honor was her mother's beloved secretary Wanda Clark. Desi, who gave the bride away, sang to his daughter the title song from the last picture he and Lucy had made together, *Forever, Darling*, which brought Lucy to tears. Lucie and Phil separated after only a year together, although it would be several more years before they would finally be divorced.

In 1972, Lucie made her dramatic television debut, scoring her first acting role outside of one of her mother's series, when she guest starred on the paranormal show *The Sixth Sense*.

Encouraged by Vivian Vance to pursue stage work in order not to get typecast in a sitcom, as Vance had, Lucie auditioned for and won the role of Sally Bowles in the San Bernardino Civic Light Opera production of *Cabaret*. This did not keep her from continuing on *Here's Lucy*. In fact, her involvement with the show was more needed than ever after her mother broke her leg prior to the production of the fifth season.

Lucille Ball Productions planned a Kim Carter spin-off series of *Here's Lucy*, with the final episode of the fourth season, "Kim Finally Cuts You-Know-Who's Apron Strings," serving as the pilot. CBS did not purchase the show, however. Lucie would only appear in twelve of the twenty-four episodes of the sixth season of *Here's Lucy*. During this period, she devoted her time to another production of *Cabaret* and to playing Princess Winifred in *Once Upon a Mattress* with the Kenley Players in Ohio.

When Lucie won the lead role of Gittel Mosca in the national tour of the musical *Seesaw*, she announced that she would not be returning to *Here's Lucy* if it was renewed for a seventh season. The show ended after six seasons, with Lucie taking center stage in the final episode, "Lucy Fights the System." She had appeared in 113 of the 144 episodes.

Seesaw was restructured from Broadway in order to put even more emphasis on Lucie's character, including the show-stopping first act finale, "The Party's On Me." Lucie received raves from the critics and garnered comparisons, not to her famous parents, but to musical powerhouses like Barbra Streisand and Ethel Merman. The first time Lucy saw the show, she broke down and cried, marveling at her daughter's performance.

On the small screen, Lucie fulfilled a long-held dream of guest starring on *Marcus Welby, MD* and had the title role in *Who Is the Black Dahlia?*, playing real-life homicide victim Elizabeth Short, whose brutal 1947 murder remains unsolved. Unexpectedly, she wound up competing in the ratings with her mom as this NBC telefilm aired on March 1, 1975 directly opposite CBS's *A Lucille Ball Special: Lucy Gets Lucky*. That same month television audiences got a taste of Lucie's musical abilities when she hosted the *Wonderful World of Disney* special "Welcome to the World," which found her performing again with one of her *Seesaw* co-stars, Tommy Tune.

In 1976, she found success in a straight play when she starred with Stockard Channing and Sandy Duncan in the first West Coast production of *Vanities*. That same year, she had landed her first role in a theatrical feature, in Tom Laughlin's *Billy Jack Goes to Washington*, playing a variation of the same character Jean Arthur had done in *Mr. Smith Goes to Washington*, only to have the picture get shelved indefinitely because of legal hassles involving the original movie. A chance to rectify this by taking on the part of Rizzo in the movie of *Grease* never came to be, because Lucie could not wait forever for the producers to make a signed commitment and was obliged to fulfill her contract to play Rosie in Wisconsin's Melody Top Theatre production of *Bye Bye Birdie*. Her *Vanities* co-star, Stockard Channing, ended up being cast in the *Grease* film. Movie audiences finally got to see Lucie Arnaz up on the big screen when she was promoted to the female lead (after Deborah Raffin vacated the part) in Neil Diamond's 1980 remake of *The Jazz Singer*, garnering among the few good reviews given the picture and getting the chance to share the screen with Laurence Olivier. She received a Golden Globe nomination for her performance.

While playing Annie Oakley in *Annie Get Your Gun* at Long Island's Jones Beach Theatre, Lucie was invited to audition for a new musical slated for Broadway, *They're Playing Our Song*. She won the role of kooky lyricist Sonia Walsk in what was essentially a two-character piece; Neil Simon's script was loosely based on the relationship between the show's composer, Marvin Hamlisch, and lyricist Carole Bayer Sager. Robert Klein was cast in the "Hamlisch" part, neurotic composer Vernon Gersch. On February 11, 1979, Lucie made her Broadway debut at the Imperial Theatre, the same place her father had made *his* Broadway bow, in *Too Many Girls* forty years prior. She even had the same dressing room he did. Lucie won the prestigious Theatre World Award for her outstanding Broadway debut, as well as the Outer Critics Circle Award for Best Actress in a Musical and, for her performance during the pre-Broadway tryouts in California, the Los Angeles Critics Circle Award. She was also nominated for a Drama Desk Award. Although *They're Playing Our Song* received five Tony nominations, Lucie Arnaz, most surprisingly, was not in the running for Best Actress in a Musical. Nominated or not, she performed a rousing version of her musical's title tune at the award ceremony that year. Tony Roberts would eventually replace Robert Klein opposite Lucie. None other than Stockard Channing would be Lucie's replacement once she left.

During the run of *They're Playing Our Song*, Lucie met Laurence Luckinbill, who was concurrently starring in another Neil Simon show on Broadway, *Chapter Two*. Nearly seventeen years older than Lucie, Luckinbill (born November 21, 1934 in Fort Smith, Arkansas), had just ended his marriage to actress Robin Strasser, with whom he had two sons, Nicholas (born in 1969) and Benjamin (born in 1975). Luckinbill had achieved great success in the stage and film versions of *The Boys in the Band* and received a Tony nomination for *The Shadow Box* in 1977.

On September 10, 1979, Lucie and Larry were introduced at the after-theater hangout Joe Allen and eventually began dating. Just as Gary Morton, upon meeting Lucy, admitted to having never seen an episode of *I Love Lucy*, Luckinbill could make the same claim. During their engagement, the couple starred in the made-for-television movie *The Mating Season*.

On June 22, 1980, Lucie Arnaz and Laurence Luckinbill married in a small wedding at an apple orchard in Kingston, New York. The guests included Lucy and Gary; Desi and Edie; Desi Jr. and his wife, Linda Purl; and

Larry's two sons. As he had done at his daughter's first nuptials, Desi sang "Forever, Darling," and Lucy once again erupted in tears. The newlyweds quickly went to work together again, starring in the national tour of the drama *Whose Life Is It Anyway?*, alternating the roles of the paralyzed sculptor and the doctor, the former part having been given a sex change during the play's original Broadway run.

Arnaz and Luckinbill also did a sitcom pilot for CBS entitled *One More Try* that bore several similarities to their real lives. They played a couple, each with a divorce behind them, who marry. Like Larry, the husband has two children from his first marriage. Lucie's character's name was DeDe in tribute to her beloved grandmother.

Lucie would give birth to her first child, Simon Joseph Luckinbill, on December 9, 1980. He was named for the playwright whose shows she and Larry were starring in when they met. Their second son, Joseph Henry Luckinbill (born December 31, 1982), received his middle name in honor of the late Henry Fonda, who had sent Lucie notes and flowers from his own hospital room while Lucie was recovering from the birth of her first child. A moved Lucy mistakenly believed that "Henry" had been selected in tribute to her own father, and Lucie never told her otherwise. The Luckinbills' third child, Katharine Desiree, was born on January 11, 1985, named for her mother's favorite actress, Katharine Hepburn.

At the time she learned she was pregnant with Katharine, Lucie had started work on her own weekly television series, *The Lucie Arnaz Show*, based on a British sitcom called *Agony*. Lucie played an unmarried psychologist, Jane Lucas, trying to balance a radio show, a magazine column, a private practice, and a personal life. Her *second* leading man from *They're Playing Our Song*, Tony Roberts, played Jane's boss at the radio station. Filmed in New York, the show received a six-episode commitment from CBS, premiering on April 2, 1985. Three other episodes aired that month and the remaining two in June. CBS did not place the series on their fall 1985 schedule.

In 1988, the Luckinbills moved to Brentwood, California near Lucie's mother. That same year Lucie did the telefilm *Who Gets the Friends?* and began work on a new project. Asked to put together a nightclub act in celebration of Irving Berlin's 100th birthday to play in Italy, Lucie accepted the assignment and found that she loved cabaret work, continuing to do a club act for years to come.

Lucie returned again to weekly television in 1991 with CBS's hour-long family comedy-drama, *Sons and Daughters*, playing Tess Hammersmith, the single mother of a ten-year-old adopted daughter. The series lasted for thirteen episodes. Following its cancellation, Lucie and her family relocated back to New York. Although she decided to cut back on performing in order to raise her three children, she did not stop working completely. She returned to the New York stage in Neil Simon's Pulitzer Prize-winning *Lost in Yonkers*, garnering superb reviews.

During her *Yonkers* run, Lucie was simultaneously working on a documentary about her parents, inspired by the home movies she discovered of Lucy and Desi early in their marriage. Lucie wove these silent images in with new interviews featuring such people as Fred Ball, Cleo Smith, Carole Cook, Marcella Rabwin, Marco Rizo, Bob Hope, Ann Miller, and 105-year-old George Abbott. The Luckinbills produced the documentary through their company Just ArLuck Productions (a combination of both their surnames). Premiering on NBC on February 14, 1993, *Lucy and Desi: A Home Movie* received widespread acclaim and won the couple an Emmy Award. Lucie would later call this project her "proudest professional accomplishment." That same year, Lucie released her first solo album, *Just in Time*, and would go on to release a pair of CD-ROMS in 1997. One, *Lucy & Desi: Made for Each Other*, was dedicated to her parents, while the other was devoted to helping people save their own family history.

In 2001, Lucie earned another Emmy nomination, as one of the executive producers of *The "I Love Lucy" 50th Anniversary Special*.

Onstage, in the 1980s, the Luckinbills did the first American production of *Educating Rita*; Lucie reunited with Tommy Tunc for a national tour of *My One and Only*, which brought her a Sarah Siddons Award; appeared opposite one of her mother's favorite actors, John Ritter, in *A Place to Stay*; and joined her husband for a national tour of *Social Security* (at one point she hoped to turn it into a movie for her mother, in order to help her recover following the painful cancellation of *Life with Lucy*, but this never came to be). Off-Broadway she was seen opposite Estelle Parsons in *Grace and Glorie* (1996); made her London debut in the 2000 musical version of *The Witches of Eastwick* (in the role Cher had done in the film); and in 2006 was back on Broadway (returning to the Imperial Theatre) when she joined the company of *Dirty Rotten Scoundrels*. Also in the cast at the beginning of Lucie's run was Rachel York, who had played her mother in the 2003 CBS TV movie *Lucy*.

Lucie starred in several plays produced at the Coconut Grove Playhouse in Miami, Florida in the 2000s: *Once Removed, A Picasso, Ann & Debbie*, and *Sonia Flew*, in which she co-starred with her daughter Kate in the theater's final production before it was shuttered for good.

Lucie has also continued her critically acclaimed cabaret act and, in 2010, released another album, *Latin Roots*.

Lucy with her two children in 1965.

Desi Arnaz Jr.

On January 19, 1953, Desiderio Alberto Arnaz IV was born at Cedars of Lebanon Hospital in Los Angeles at 8:05 a.m. and caused a worldwide media sensation. His mother's pregnancy had been incorporated into the storyline of *I Love Lucy*, which meant the public was eagerly anticipating the birth of both Lucille Ball's fictional and real-life baby. Because Desi's birth had to be a scheduled caesarean and Lucy's obstetrician always performed caesareans on a Monday, the same day *I Love Lucy* aired on television; it was decided to have the two births coincide on the same day.

Desi Arnaz desperately wanted a son. None of his father's brothers had a son, so if Desi did not produce a male offspring, the Arnaz name would die with him. One of the reasons the *I Love Lucy* writers gave the character of Ricky Ricardo a boy was because they were well aware of how much having a male offspring meant to Desi and figured if he ended up with another daughter in real life, he could at least have a son on television.

The Arnazes were thrilled when Lucy did indeed give birth to a boy. So newsworthy was this event that five minutes later it was being reported as far off as Japan. The *I Love Lucy* episode aired that night, "Lucy Goes to the Hospital," was the highest-rated television program ever up to that point, with 44 million people watching. The next day, Desi Jr.'s birth was the chief headline of newspapers across the country, rating more attention than the fact that Dwight Eisenhower was being inaugurated that day. In April 1953, Desi Jr. dominated the cover of the first national issue of *TV Guide*, while his mother was seen in a smaller insert picture. The banner headline read "Lucy's $50,000,000 Baby."

Although he never appeared on *I Love Lucy* as Little Ricky, Desi Jr. did show up as an extra in the final scene of the last episode, "The Ricardos Dedicate a Statue" (his sister Lucie did not, however, despite some sources indicating that she did). Both Arnaz children did appear as extras a year later in "Lucy Goes to Sun Valley" on *The Lucille Ball-Desi Arnaz Show*. In 1957, minus any family members, Desi was a guest on *Art Linkletter's House Party* and appeared with the *real* Little Ricky, Keith Thibodeaux, on *The Dinah Shore Chevy Show* in 1960. Later that year, after he and his sister moved to New York with their mother while she appeared on Broadway in *Wildcat*, the three were guests on *The Tonight Show* (with guest host Hugh Downs).

Since *The Lucy Show* featured two young boys around his age, Desi popped up several times on the show, whenever they needed to fill the scene with additional friends, teammates, and whatnot. Desi Jr. made his first appearance in "Lucy Is a Referee," as a football player. On three occasions he played Billy Simmons, whose mother, Audrey (Mary Jane Croft), was a friend of Lucy and Viv's. The character of Billy appeared in "Lucy Visits the White House" (as a cub scout), "Lucy and the Little League" (a little league player), and "Lucy and the Scout Trip" (once again, a scout). He was also an extra in his sister's big debut episode, "Lucy Is a Soda Jerk," and made his last appearance on *The Lucy Show* in the fourth-season premiere, "Lucy at Marineland," sitting behind Lucy during the aquatic show.

Desi was inspired to take up the drums by watching Keith Thibodeaux play them on *I Love Lucy*. The two would become best friends. While at

Beverly Hills Catholic School, Desi befriended Dino Martin (son of Dean Martin) and Billy Hinsche, both of whom were slightly older than him. (Dino was in his sister Lucie's class.) Both guitarists, Dino and Billy joined forces with drummer Desi, first by playing in Lucy's garage and eventually rehearsing in the Martins' living room. Their big break came when Frank Sinatra was invited to the Martins' house to hear the boys play and liked them so much he signed them to his Reprise Records label. Calling themselves simply Dino, Desi & Billy, the group scored two top twenty-five hits in 1965, "I'm A Fool" (also the title of their debut LP) and "Not the Lovin' Kind." As a youthful pop band sensation, the trio went on tour with the Beach Boys and opened for other groups like Paul Revere & the Raiders. During their brief moment in the spotlight, Desi and his group showed up to sing on the first color episode of *The Ed Sullivan Show,* as well as on *The Hollywood Palace* and the teen-oriented *Hullabaloo.* They also were seen in the 1966 Dean Martin/Matt Helm adventure *Murderers' Row,* making this Desi Jr.'s big screen debut. Later, Lucy said agreeing to let her son be in a rock band and go on tour at the age of twelve was "the worst mistake we ever made." She was deeply concerned about the instant success her son achieved at such a young age, believing he was growing up too quickly. Furthermore, she worried that the heavy focus on music and traveling meant Desi was not concentrating enough on school. Ironically, Lucy was unable to get the trio on her own show because their price was too high.

When Desi's father returned to television producing *The Mothers-in-Law,* Desi Jr. made several appearances on the series. He and his sister zoomed by on a golf cart in the opening moments of the second episode, "Everybody Wants to Go on a Honeymoon"; and in "Career Girls," he was unbilled as a drummer in a scene also featuring a pre-fame Rob Reiner. More notable was the episode "The Hombre Who Came to Dinner, Part Two," in which Desi Jr. joined his famous father, who was guest starring as Señor Raphael del Gado. The younger Desi played Tommy the grocery delivery boy, who auditioned for the show Señor del Gado was putting on by singing "Babalu." In character, Desi asked what the name of the song was and when given the answer, replied, "Never heard of it!" Desi Jr. got to accompany his father on the drums while the elder Desi sang "The Straw Hat Song." The "Two Desi Arnazs" (as they were humorously credited) made their last *Mothers-in-Law* appearance in "The Matador Makes a Movie," in which Desi Jr. played a production assistant on a movie set. In the scene, Desi Sr. remarked that he looked "very familiar."

In 1968, Desi joined his sister and mother on *Here's Lucy,* portraying Lucy Carter's son, Craig. Two years into the run of the show, seventeen-year-old Desi became a ubiquitous face on the cover of the gossip magazines when he began dating recently divorced, twenty-three-year-old Oscar winner Patty Duke. Desi accompanied Patty to the Emmy Awards in 1970, where she won for her performance in the TV movie *My Sweet Charlie* and then gave an incomprehensible acceptance speech (which she later blamed on her undiagnosed bipolar disorder), which brought her a good deal of negative press. When Duke discovered she was pregnant, she married rock promoter Michael Tell, whom she barely knew, on June 26, 1970, a union that was annulled after thirteen days. Patty got back together with Desi, and the tabloids had a field day claiming that Desi was the father of Patty's baby. Lucy was portrayed as a villain, someone who would not let her seventeen-year-old son marry his pregnant girlfriend. After Patty gave birth to a son, Sean Duke, on February 25, 1971, Desi said that the baby was his. Although Desi Sr. and Lucie both visited Patty in the hospital, gossipers were quick to note that Lucy was not present. Lucy, who believed the entire time that the baby was not her son's, did, however, visit Patty at home and invited her to visit Lucy's home with the baby. Although Desi and Patty quickly broke up, Desi remained a part of Sean's life. In 1972, Duke married John Astin, who adopted Patty's son, who would later become well known as the actor Sean Astin. When Sean was in his twenties, paternity tests concluded for certain that his biological father was Michael Tell. In 1990, Duke produced and starred in a TV movie based on her autobiography *Call Me Anna*. In it, Desi Jr. was played by a pre-*Friends* Matthew Perry.

Initially, the kids only had three-year contracts with *Here's Lucy*, and for Desi that was sufficient. During the third season, he was offered one of the leads in the film *Red Sky at Morning*. Wanting to pursue a movie career, he accepted the role, which necessitated him being written out of several *Here's Lucy* episodes. Desi certainly received encouragement for his decision to pursue work outside his mother's series when he was given the Golden Globe for Best Promising Newcomer for his performance in *Red Sky*. After making his first dramatic television appearance as a dying escaped convict in a segment of *Night Gallery*, he starred in a string of made-for-TV movies like *Mr. and Mrs. Bo Jo Jones*, *Voyage of the Yes*, and *She Lives!* During *Here's Lucy*'s fifth season, Desi made one final appearance as Craig Carter, in the episode "Lucy and Joe Namath."

In 1971, the son of Desi Arnaz and Lucille Ball began dating the daughter of Vincente Minnelli and the late Judy Garland, Liza Minnelli. Lucy loved Liza, whom she had known since Liza was a little girl, saying "I feel like she's one of my children." When Desi returned to California between movie gigs, he and Liza stayed in Lucy's guesthouse. There was talk of an episode of the fifth season of *Here's Lucy* teaming Desi with Liza, but this never materialized. In May 1972, it was announced that Desi Arnaz Jr. and

Liza Minnelli were engaged. The following March, Desi escorted Liza to the Academy Awards, where she won the statuette for Best Actress for *Cabaret*. Almost one year to the day after it was made public, it was announced that the Arnaz-Minnelli engagement was off. Liza soon proclaimed her love for Peter Sellers, who was twenty-seven years older than Desi. In record time, that relationship ended as well.

Desi had briefly attended the California Institute of the Arts to study music, only to drop out in order to star as young Marco Polo in the movie musical *Marco*, which was filmed in Japan. Desi's next project took him to Israel where he played the title role in the western *Billy Two Hats*, opposite Gregory Peck. These back-to-back assignments meant that Desi was away on location for close to two years. During that time Lucy purchased a house in Beverly Hills and rented it to her son so he would have a place to call home.

In 1974, Desi made his professional stage debut in the Kenley Players production of *Sunday in New York* and, in 1976, joined his father when he hosted *NBC's Saturday Night* (prior to its name change to *Saturday Night Live*), portraying Ricky Ricardo in a sketch. He joined a cast of other young actors who were also the children of performers—Robert Carradine (son of John Carradine), Melanie Griffith (daughter of Tippi Hedren), and Anne Lockhart (daughter of June Lockhart)—for the movie *Joyride* and then played the groom in Robert Altman's *A Wedding*, one of a huge ensemble cast that included Carol Burnett, Mia Farrow, Dennis Christopher, Vittorio Gassman, Amy Stryker (as the bride), and Lillian Gish.

After Desi and Linda Purl portrayed a couple in the telefilms *Having Babies* (1976) and *Black Market Baby* (1977), they began dating and married on January 13, 1980. Lucie flew in from New York, where she was starring in *They're Playing Our Song*, to serve as a bridesmaid. Desi's former band-mate, Dino Martin, and Tony Martin Jr. (son of Tony Martin and Cyd Charisse) served as ushers. Lucy and Gary Morton and Desi and Edie Arnaz were all present. The couple spent their honeymoon at Desi Sr.'s house in Las Cruces, Mexico. Unfortunately, Desi Jr. had no better luck with his first marriage than his sister had with hers, and the couple separated by December and divorced the following year. In 1981, Desi Jr. joined his mother for a special week of *Password Plus*.

In 1982, after years of drug and alcohol abuse, Desi finally decided to stop and pull his life together. Lucy, Gary, and Lucie attended meetings with him as a family, which was therapeutic for all. Because of his own experiences in fighting addiction, Desi Jr. was later able to persuade his father to seek treatment for his alcoholism. Several years earlier, Desi had read the book *The Mystic Path to Cosmic Power*, by self-help expert Vernon Howard. As a result, he became deeply involved with Vernon's New Life Foundation in Boulder City, Nevada, and would eventually settle there.

Both of Desi's parents were in attendance when he starred in a summer stock production of *Promises, Promises* in Milwaukee, Wisconsin, in 1983. That same year, he returned to series television in the science fiction show *Automan*, playing Walter Nebicher, a police officer and computer expert, who has created a holographic crime fighter. The series premiered on ABC in December and ended the following April.

On October 8, 1987, Desi married Amy Bargiel, a ballerina. Amy was a divorcée with a ten-year-old daughter, Haley, whom Desi adopted. The couple had met when Desi was the spokesperson for the New Life Foundation and Amy was a student of the organization. Lucy and Gary Morton and Lucie and Larry Luckinbill attended the wedding in Boulder City, Nevada.

While watching a ballet competition on television one day, Amy noticed a fellow dancer she had been roommates with for a summer in New York in the early seventies. The name on the screen was Kathy Thibodeaux. When Desi informed her that his friend Keith Thibodeaux had also married a ballet dancer they soon came to a realization: Lucy and Desi's real-life son and their TV son both married ballerinas who had been roommates! Both Amy Arnaz and Kathy Thibodeaux also ended up running ballet companies with their husbands' assistance.

It was predestined that Desi Jr. return to feature films when Oscar Hijuelos's Pulitzer Prize-winning novel *The Mambo Kings Play Songs of Love* was adapted for the big screen, because the script required someone to play Desi Sr. He initially turned down the role, thinking that it was too soon after his parents' deaths, but after over 100 actors were auditioned without success, he was approached again. Desi was told that other actors could play Ricky Ricardo, but did not have a sense of who the real Desi Arnaz was. Convinced, Desi Jr. accepted the role and spent time at his father's former home in Las Cruces, Mexico that the family still owned, where he practiced speaking in the older Desi's unmistakable accent. In the film (whose title was shortened to *The Mambo Kings*), Desi helps out two Cuban singers (Armand Assante and Antonio Banderas) by casting them in the *I Love Lucy* episode "Cuban Pals." Footage of Desi's mother as Lucy Ricardo taken from the episode was spliced into the film so it looked like Desi Jr.'s Ricky was interacting on camera in the scene with Lucy. Desi was praised for his uncanny performance.

In 1997, Desi and Amy formed the Boulder City Ballet Company for children, and the following year, bought and restored the Boulder Theater in their town. Around this time, Desi reteamed with Billy Hinsche to form

Ricci, Desi & Billy. Ricci was the brother of the late Dino Martin, who was killed in a plane crash in 1987. The three performed together in various venues including the Arnazes' theater.

In 2010, Desi joined his sister Lucie in celebrating the music of the Desi Arnaz Orchestra. Desi played percussion in the show that Lucie hosted, wrote, and staged originally at New York's 92nd St. Y. They later performed the show, entitled *Babalu*, in Miami, joined in both places by performers Raul Esparza and Valarie Pettiford. Desi continued his work with Boulder City Ballet Company as well.

5

"Friendship. Just the Perfect Blendship."

Lucy's Friends and Co-stars

Gale Gordon

T he man Lucille Ball spent more time acting with than any other, Gale Gordon, was born Charles Thomas Aldrich Jr. on February 20, 1906 in New York City to Charles and Gloria St. Leger Aldrich. His parents were both vaudevillians, his father being a quick-change artist and pantomimist, his mother a singer and actress. Two years after the birth of Charles Jr., his sister Jewell St. Leger (his mother's stage name for a time) Aldrich was born (she later went by the name Judy). Charles Aldrich Sr.

Lucy and Harry (Gale Gordon) perform "By the Light of the Silvery Moon," with piano accompaniment by Liberace, in the *Here's Lucy* episode "Lucy and Liberace."

taught his son and his daughter at a young age to do a cartwheel, which Gale would frequently execute on the *Lucy* shows and could still do into his eighties. When he was a year old, the Aldrich family moved to London, England. Having been born with a cleft palate Gale was unable to speak a single word until he was three years old. He underwent an operation in England during his childhood to correct the condition. The Aldriches returned to New York after eight years in London, settling in Queens, New York. The family returned again to England when Gale was seventeen, and he finished school there.

On his return trip to America, Gale met Baron Rothschild on the ship. Rothschild gave Gale a letter of introduction to the Shubert family of theatrical impresarios. At the age of seventeen, Gale made his Broadway debut in a nonspeaking role in the Shuberts' *The Dancers,* starring Richard Bennett. He was paid fifteen dollars a week for his stage work and an extra ten dollars for serving as Bennett's dresser. Another member of the cast was Gale's mother. Not wanting to be the second Charles T. Aldrich, the younger Charles decided to adopt the stage name Gale Gordon, although he never legally changed it. Richard Bennett was aware of Gale's speech affliction and helped him with voice training. Gale would later be known for his perfect diction.

In 1925, Gale Gordon went to Hollywood for the first time and made his first appearance on radio the following year. On the Los Angeles station KFWB, he played ukulele and sang "It Ain't Gonna Rain No Mo'." In 1929, he played Judas in the film version of *The Pilgrimage Play.* That same year, Gordon became a member of the California-based Henry Duffy Players. Another member of the theater troupe was Eunice Quedens, who would soon after change her name to Eve Arden. Gale was making $2.50 a radio show ($2.25 net profit because the radio station acted as their own agency and took out 10 percent) and ended up on so many other programs that he was, at one time, the highest-paid actor in the medium, earning fifteen dollars a show.

In the mid-thirties, Gale co-starred on *Mary Pickford and Company.* When the show relocated to New York, Gale went along and also landed a role in the Broadway play *Daughter of Atreus,* which had a short run in 1936. Prior to this, he had originated the role of Flash Gordon on radio's *The Amazing Interplanetary Adventures of Flash Gordon* in 1935. While performing on the series *Death Valley Days* in New York, Gale met fellow performer Virginia Curley. The two married on December 27, 1937. In 1938, Gale became the announcer of *The Wonder Show,* starring Jack Haley, which also featured Lucille Ball in the cast. The two did the show together for a season. Strangely enough, neither of them ever later publicly mentioned this collaboration after they started working together on television in the nineteen-sixties.

Gale's radio work had been almost exclusively dramatic until he landed a guest spot on the popular *Fibber McGee and Molly* in 1941. This led to a regular role on the series as blustery Mayor LaTrivia. Playing an entirely different role, Gordon appeared with Fibber and Molly in the film *Here We Go Again*, which was a sequel to the previous year's *Look Who's Laughing*, which had co-starred Lucy. Gale joined the Coast Guard in 1942 and stayed in the service until 1945. He returned to his role on *Fibber McGee and Molly* and his other shows.

In 1948, Gale Gordon was approached to play Osgood Conklin, the principal of Madison High School, on the new radio comedy *Our Miss Brooks*. Gale requested that his salary be $150 per show since that was what he was making at the time on *Fibber McGee and Molly*. CBS turned him down. Joe Forte played the role in the pilot, but the producers were so displeased with his performance that they hired Gordon at his asking price. Gale was therefore reunited with his Henry Duffy Players co-star, Eve Arden. Playing Gale's wife on the series was his real-life wife, Virginia.

Our Miss Brooks began as a summer replacement radio series on July 19, 1948. A few weeks earlier, Lucille Ball had debuted in her own radio series, *My Favorite Husband*. Gale was reunited with his old *Wonder Show* co-star when he played a judge in the *My Favorite Husband* episode "Valentine's Day" on February 12, 1949. He returned several weeks later in the episode "Mother-in-Law" (March 4, 1949) playing the boyfriend of George Cooper's mother (Bea Benaderet). The following week, Gale assumed the role of Rudolph Atterbury, George's boss, and became a series regular. Bea Benaderet soon joined as his wife, Iris. During the summer of 1950, Gordon and Benaderet starred on a summer replacement series, *Granby's Green Acres*, which was the forerunner of the sixties sitcom *Green Acres*. In 1950, movie audiences could see Lucille Ball and Gale Gordon in the film *A Woman of Distinction*, although they did not appear on camera together.

When Lucy decided to venture into television with husband Desi, she wanted Gale and Bea Benaderet to join her. Bea, however, was already co-starring on *The George Burns and Gracie Allen Show*. Gale knew that he could command a large salary on radio, while he would only be paid scale on Lucy's show. In 1951 alone, he was a regular on seven radio series: *My Favorite Husband*, *Our Miss Brooks*, *Fibber McGee and Molly*, *The Phil Harris-Alice Faye Show*, *Halls of Ivy*, *The Great Gildersleeve*, and *The Dennis Day Show*. All of these assignments took only an average of twenty hours a week, which meant he made a lot of money for little work. He was therefore unable to accept Desilu's offer. Gale did, however, appear in two episodes of *I Love Lucy* during the first season, as Ricky's boss, Alvin Littlefield, in "Lucy's Schedule" and "Ricky Asks for a Raise."

Gale Gordon was soon working on the Desilu lot permanently when *Our Miss Brooks* transferred to television in 1952. During its first season, it was filmed on the stage adjacent to *I Love Lucy*, with a door adjoining the two sets. In September 1953, Gale and Virginia Gordon were in a car accident that resulted in a bad whiplash for Mrs. Gordon. As a result, she left her *Miss Brooks* role as Mrs. Conklin and was replaced by Paula Winslowe. Gale received an Emmy nomination for the series in 1955. The TV version of *Our Miss Brooks* ran until May 1956, while the radio version, which had continued despite the move to television, ended a month later. A movie version of *Our Miss Brooks* was released by Warner Bros. that same year, featuring Gordon and other recurring characters, although the film's plot did not follow the continuity of the television and radio series. Gale became very close to the actress who played his daughter on *Our Miss Brooks*, Gloria McMillan, and even gave her away when she married. During this time, Gale's mother, Gloria, was acting on another CBS television and radio sitcom, *My Friend Irma*, playing landlady Mrs. O'Reilly.

When *Our Miss Brooks* ended, Gale became the star of his own television series for the only time in his career, the CBS sitcom *The Brothers*. Bob Sweeney, who had been a regular on *Our Miss Brooks* during its final season, was the other sibling in question. *The Brothers* lasted a single season, as did Gale's next venture into weekly television, *Sally*, supporting Joan Caulfield, who had starred in the television version of *My Favorite Husband*. Gale also appeared frequently as landlord Mr. Heckendorn on *The Danny Thomas Show* and made multiple appearances on the Jess Oppenheimer-created *Angel*. In 1958, Gale appeared in *The Lucille Ball-Desi Arnaz Show* episode "Lucy Makes Room for Danny," as a judge. The following year, he co-starred in a Desilu sitcom pilot, *Where There's Smokey*, playing Soupy Sales's fire marshal brother-in-law. The show did not sell.

The Gordons bought a 150-acre ranch in Borrego Springs, California that they named "Tub Canyon." Surrounding themselves with their many dogs, Gale and Virginia made this their home, Gale running the ranch by himself without any hired hands. When he became Borrego Springs' honorary mayor, he joked, "They wanted a celebrity-type. One day, I was out working around my septic tank when someone called to ask if I'd be honorary mayor. I said I would because it was better than what I was doing at the moment." Gordon served in that capacity for years.

In January 1962, Gale appeared alongside Lucy in a sketch in the Desilu pilot for *The Victor Borge Comedy Theatre*. Lucy was considering a return to television in the fall in a new series and wanted Gale to be a part of it. Gale would soon have prior commitments that would make this impossible. On February 17, 1962, Joseph Kearns, who had been co-starring as Mr. Wilson on *Dennis the Menace*, then in its third season, suddenly died. It was immediately announced that Gale Gordon would be replacing Kearns as his character's brother. (Gordon, in fact, more closely resembled the character of Mr. Wilson that Hank Ketcham had created for the daily comic strips than Kearns did.) He stayed with the series until it ended in the spring of 1963. That fall, Gale joined the cast of *The Lucy Show* as banker Theodore J. Mooney. Gale would earn two Emmy nominations for the series (1967, 1968). During this time, he also appeared in stage productions of *The Merry Widow* and *Damn Yankees,* as well as such movies as *Sergeant Deadhead* (also featuring Eve Arden) and *Speedway* with Elvis Presley.

Harry tries to help Lucy with her problem involving Kim's new boyfriend in the *Here's Lucy* episode "Lucy and the Professor."

Gale received his fourth and final Emmy nomination for the third season of *Here's Lucy.* That season had kicked off with the famed "Lucy Meets the Burtons" episode. During rehearsals for the show, Richard Burton was wowed by Gale Gordon and asked Gary Morton to tell him more about him. When Gale walked by, Burton said to him, "You must be English. You act so well; you couldn't be American." Gale stayed with the show until *Here's Lucy* ended in 1974. It was Gale in fact, not Lucy, who had the series' final line. After being hit in the face with a pie, he sighed, in recognition of the character's years of physical abuse at the hands of Lucy Carter, "I knew it would end like this.

A few months later, Gale stepped into the role of millionaire Osgood (another Osgood!) Fielding in the California production of the musical *Sugar*, based on the film *Some Like It Hot*, after Cyril Ritchard, who had played the role on Broadway, suffered a heart attack onstage during previews. The following year, Gale made his first dinner theater appearance when he starred in *The Sunshine Boys* teamed with frequent *Lucy* character actor Irwin Charone. Gale would continue to do dinner theater for the rest of his career, primarily in Canada.

Lucy and Gale reunited for two of her specials, *Lucy Calls the President*, with Gale cast as her father-in-law, and *Lucy Moves to NBC*, as himself. During the seventies and eighties, Gale appeared on several talk shows with Lucy, often popping up unannounced to surprise her, including *Dinah!*, *The Mike Douglas Show*, *The Merv Griffin Show*, and *The John Davidson Show*.

In 1981, Gale starred as the head of a San Francisco monastery in the sitcom pilot *Bungle Abbey*, produced by Lucille Ball Productions. It was significant for being Lucy's only solo directorial credit on television. Five years later, Gale and Lucy teamed up one last time for her short-lived series *Life with Lucy*. When Gale made his final movie appearance, in 1989's *The 'Burbs*, pictures of himself and Lucy were visible in his character's house in the film, which was released only two months before Lucy's death. In 1991, he played his final acting roles, on the premiere installment of the sitcom *Hi Honey, I'm Home!* reprising the character of Theodore J. Mooney, and in an episode of *The New Lassie*.

Gale and Virginia moved into an assisted living facility in Escondido, California. Virginia died in 1995 and Gale passed away several weeks later, on June 30, 1995, of lung cancer.

Gale Gordon appeared in 267 episodes of Lucille Ball's television series total; two *I Love Lucy* episodes, one *Lucille Ball-Desi Arnaz Show*, 111 episodes of *The Lucy Show*, 140 episodes of *Here's Lucy*, and 13 *Life with Lucy*s.

Vivian Vance

The woman who partnered Lucille Ball on television more frequently than any other female, Vivian Roberta Jones was born on July 26, 1909 in Cherryvale, Kansas to Robert and Euphermia (Mae) Ragan Jones. Vivian was the second child born to the couple; her sister Venus was born in 1905.

The Joneses would go on to have four more children, Dorothy, Maxine ("Mickey"), Robert, and Lou Ann, with a twenty-one-year age gap between the eldest, Venus (nicknamed "Mimi"), and the youngest, Lou Ann. At one point, one of the Jones' neighbors was future silent screen star Louise Brooks, who was nearly three years older than Vivian.

The family eventually settled in Independence, Kansas. Around the age of eighteen, Vivian made her theatrical debut, in a touring company of the New York stage success *Broadway*. For her acting career, Vivian adopted the last name Vance after the folklorist Vance Rudolph. On October 6,

Vivian tries to help when Lucy sues Mr. Mooney after his barking dog creates a neighborhood disturbance in *The Lucy Show* episode "Lucy is Her Own Lawyer."

1928, nineteen-year-old Vivian Jones married twenty-three-year-old Joseph Danneck, eventually moving to Albuquerque, New Mexico, where Vivian's parents had recently settled. The Dannecks' marriage, however, was short-lived.

Continuing her show business career, Vivian was featured in the vaudeville show *Cushman's Revue* and then joined the newly formed Albuquerque Little Theater group, appearing in their first presentation, *This Thing Called Love*. Another of the roles that Vivian played with the company was Aggie Lynch in *Within the Law* in March 1932. Less than two years earlier, Lucille Ball played that same part in a local Jamestown production. Both actresses received rave reviews from the local critics. In August 1932, the Albuquerque Little Theater put on *The Trial of Mary Dugan* with Vivian in the title role. The money the company earned for this production was used to send Vivian to New York. She had planned to study under renowned teacher Eva LaGallienne, but was not accepted into her program. Instead, she landed a part in the chorus of the Jerome Kern-Oscar Hammerstein II musical *Music in the Air*. Like Lucille Ball would twenty-eight years later,

Vivian Vance made her Broadway debut at the Alvin Theatre. On January 6, 1933, Vivian married violinist George Koch.

In the summer of 1933, while Lucille Ball was making her screen debut in California, Vivian Vance was doing the same thing 3,000 miles away. Sans credit, she played a dance hall girl in the Universal film *Take a Chance*, filmed at Astoria Studios in New York. Vivian was given a verse of the song "Eadie Was a Lady" to sing in the film's finale, backing up the picture's star, Lillian Roth (taking over the part Ethel Merman had done on Broadway). In the meantime, her future television co-star beat her to the big screen, as Lucy's movie *The Bowery* was released a couple of short weeks before *Take a Chance*. A year later, Vivian was working on Broadway with Ethel Merman in *Anything Goes*. Although Vivian was only in the ensemble (playing a character named "Babe"), she also served as Merman's understudy and stepped in for the star for two performances. As a reward for her good work, Vivian was given the lead role of Reno Sweeney in a second national tour of the show opposite the leading men from Broadway, Victor Moore and William Gaxton. Between legit stage gigs, Vance also performed in nightclubs. In 1936, *Anything Goes* songwriter Cole Porter, book writers Howard Lindsay and Russel Crouse, producer Vinton Freedley, and leading lady Ethel Merman teamed up again for *Red, Hot, and Blue*. Jimmy Durante and Bob Hope co-starred. A character was written with Vivian in mind (she was even named Vivian), but by the time the show opened, she only had one line.

Vivian took yet another chorus job in the musical *Hooray for What!* with a book by her friends Lindsay and Crouse, music and lyrics by Harold Arlen and E. Y. Harburg and direction by Vincente Minnelli. Ed Wynn was the star. Vivian would also be serving as the understudy to Kay Thompson, who would be making her Broadway debut in the role of spy Stephanie Stephanovich. The musical was a mess in its out-of-town tryouts in Boston, with the first performance reportedly running six hours long. Choreographer Agnes de Mille was fired and several cast members left the production, including Roy Roberts, who would later play Mr. Cheever in the post-Viv years on *The Lucy Show*. Kay Thompson was abruptly fired as well, and, after much speculation over who would replace her, it was eventually decided to give understudy Vivian the role permanently. Vivian now had three songs (all of which were arranged by Thompson herself) to sing including the act one finale and the musical's most enduring tune, "Down with Love." The show was a hit, running 200 performances.

Vivian followed this by appearing in a tour of a straight comedy play, *Kiss the Boys Goodbye*, directed by Antoinette Perry (for whom the Tony Awards are named). Also in the cast was Philip Ober. Viv and Phil fell in love despite the fact that they were married to others. Vivian soon returned to Broadway and received favorable reviews for her performance in the play *Skylark* starring Gertrude Lawrence. *Skylark* played at the Morosco Theatre on West 45th Street, just down the street from the Imperial Theatre, which, at the time, housed *Too Many Girls* with Desi Arnaz featured in the cast. The two shows, in fact, opened within the same week.

Vivian left *Skylark* to do another play, *Out from Under,* also directed by Antoinette Perry and again featuring Philip Ober in the cast. Vivian divorced George Koch in July 1940, while Ober's marriage ended early the following year. On August 12, 1941, she wed Philip Ober. That same year, she had her biggest musical hit on Broadway when she co-starred in another Cole Porter show, *Let's Face It!,* alongside Danny Kaye, Eve Arden, and Edith Meiser (the latter would appear as Mrs. Littlefield in two episodes during the first season of *I Love Lucy*). Making their Broadway debuts in the musical were Nanette Fabray and Carol Channing (who understudied Eve Arden).

In 1944, Mr. and Mrs. Ober would go on one of the first USO tours in North Africa and Italy in the play *Over 21.* What Vivian experienced there would have a profound impact on her psychologically. The following year, she joined the Chicago company of *The Voice of the Turtle,* starring husband and wife Hugh Marlowe and K. T. Stevens (who would later appear as neighbor Mrs. O'Brien in the *I Love Lucy* episode "New Neighbors"). Vivian played the caustic "other woman," Olive Lashbrooke. During one performance, she found herself unable to move an ashtray as per the script. Viv knew something was wrong with her but did not bother to tell her husband, who was performing in San Francisco at the time. On New Year's Eve 1945, Vivian had a complete nervous breakdown, and her husband was sent for. Phil took her to San Francisco with him, and she was replaced by her understudy, future Oscar winner Patricia Neal. Come spring 1946, Vivian was able to rejoin the cast of *Voice of the Turtle* in the San Francisco leg of the tour. Because of her breakdown, she became deeply involved in psychoanalysis and a tireless advocate for mental health for the rest of her life.

In 1950, the Obers travelled to the West Coast, where they appeared in the film *The Secret Fury,* directed by their friend Mel Ferrer. Vivian made another screen appearance shortly thereafter in *The Blue Veil* in the minor role of Charles Laughton's secretary-turned-wife. By the time the film was released on October 25, 1951, Vivian had a steady job on the small screen.

Mel Ferrer asked Vivian to appear with him in a production of *The Voice of the Turtle* that he was putting on at the La Jolla Playhouse, a little over 100 miles from Los Angeles. She immediately wanted to turn down the show because of the bad memories attached to it, but her husband talked her into doing it. She would once again be playing Olive Lashbrooke, this time with Mel Ferrer and Diana Lynn. Concurrently, those involved in developing *I Love Lucy* were trying to find someone to play the role of landlady Ethel Mertz. Director Marc Daniels, who had previously directed Vivian in a production of *Counselor-at-Law*, thought she might be ideal for the part. On July 28, 1951, Desi Arnaz, producer/head writer Jess Oppenheimer, and Daniels made the trek down to La Jolla to see Vivian in the play. Lucille Ball did not accompany them because she had just given birth to daughter Lucie Arnaz eleven days earlier. During the intermission, Desi exclaimed, "I think we found our Ethel Mertz!" The three gentlemen went backstage after the show to speak to Vivian. When she was offered the part, she initially refused. She had a movie about to be released and thought there could be more in the future. However, she figured if a big star like Lucille Ball was willing to take the gamble, she should too. Vivian assumed the whole thing would be over in thirteen weeks. On September 3, 1951, the day of the first rehearsal for *I Love Lucy*, Lucille Ball and Vivian Vance were introduced for the first time. As far as Lucy was concerned, Vivian did not fit her image of the character at all, but Vance's down to earth demeanor soon impressed the star. It very quickly became evident that Vivian had been the ideal choice, playing Ethel Mertz so well that it was unthinkable that anyone else could have been considered for the role. In 1954, Vivian Vance became the first winner of a Best Supporting Actress Emmy Award.

Vivian's husband showed up in the series' fifth episode, "The Quiz Show," portraying an actor pretending to be Lucy's long-lost first husband for a stunt on the game show *Females Are Fabulous* and then pretended to be MGM head Dore Schary in the episode "*Don Juan* Is Shelved," when the real Schary backed out. (Schary bore no resemblance to Ober, but few audiences knew what the movie exec looked like, so it hardly mattered.) During his wife's time on *I Love Lucy*, Ober made many appearances in films and television, most notably playing Deborah Kerr's cuckolded husband in the Oscar-winning smash *From Here to Eternity*. However, most of his roles were small character parts. It was clear who the real star in the family was, and Ober became increasingly jealous of his famous wife. The Obers' marriage eventually became unbearable, and the couple separated in 1958. Allegedly, Ober was abusive toward Vivian, although it was he who filed for divorce, on the charges of "mental cruelty."

In 1957, Vivian's name was bandied about for the role of Vera Charles in the movie version of the Broadway hit *Auntie Mame*. Although she did not end up doing the film, she soon was acting in another property based on the writings of Patrick Dennis. In 1959, Vivian made a sitcom pilot for Desilu entitled *Guestward Ho!*, which was written by Bob Schiller and Bob Weiskopf. The show derived from a book by Patrick Dennis and Barbara

Hooton that was based on Hooton and her husband's experience of moving from New York City to a ranch in New Mexico. In the pilot, Vivian played Babs Hooten and Leif Erickson was her husband, Bill. Reportedly, Vivian became overwhelmed at the realization that she would be center stage for once, which made for a difficult shoot. The pilot did not sell with Vivian and, a year later, Desilu filmed a new version with Joanne Dru and Mark Miller as the Hootens. The new pilot was picked up by ABC, but only ran for a single season. By this point, Vivian had completed her duties as Ethel Mertz.

In 1960, Barbara and Bill Hooton invited Viv to the Santa Fe Opera Ball and arranged a blind date for her. The man was San Francisco-based publisher John Dodds, On January 16, 1961, Vivian Vance and John Dodds married at the Hootons' Santa Fe ranch. Vivian's good friend, actor John Emery, gave the bride away. The couple soon moved to Stamford, Connecticut, and Dodds took a job with G. P. Putnam & Company. Vivian was a frequent guest on the New York-based *The Tonight Show with Jack Paar*, on one occasion joined by Lucy. She spent much of her time, however, aiding in mental health causes.

In 1962, Lucy went to Connecticut to try to persuade Vivian to join her on her new series. Vance initially rejected the proposition, but relented with some conditions attached. She insisted that her new character be more feminine and allowed to wear nicer clothes than Ethel Mertz had been given and that her name be Vivian. Lucy said, "Her loyalty to me—and a hefty paycheck—won her back to be my sidekick."

In order to do the show, Vivian commuted 3,000 miles. On Sunday night or Monday morning, John Dodds would drive his wife from their Stamford house to Kennedy Airport in New York. With the time difference, she was at Los Angeles International Airport in three hours and forty minutes. Renita Reachi, her on-set stand-in, would meet her at the airport and take her to the Beverly Hills Hotel. After the filming of that week's episode at Desilu on Thursday night, Renita would drive her back to the airport where she would take a flight back east at eleven o'clock that evening. John would greet her at the airport and take her home. A few days later, the process would start all over again. Despite the commuting, Vivian enjoyed playing the role of Vivian Bagley much more than she did Ethel Mertz. She also loved the fact that she played a mother on the show, and she adored her on-screen son, Ralph Hart.

Lucy announced her intention to cease production on *The Lucy Show* at the end of its second season, which greatly pleased Vivian, who was tired of commuting and eager to stay on the East Coast with her husband. Thinking her television series was over, Vivian accepted an offer to star in the Broadway play *Beekman Place,* written by her friend Samuel Taylor. That all changed when Lucy decided to keep the series going. When *Beekman Place* opened (and closed) in October 1964, Arlene Francis had the lead. Also in the cast was a young actor named Laurence Luckinbill, who sixteen years later would marry Lucie Arnaz.

Vivian agreed to return for the third season of *The Lucy Show* if she was not obliged to appear in every episode. As a result, she was seen in only twenty of the twenty-six episodes produced for the 1964–65 season. Vivian also announced prior to the third season that she would definitely not be returning for the fourth. Between the second and third seasons of *The Lucy Show,* she had filmed the period comedy *The Great Race,* playing Hester Goodbody, the feminist wife of a newspaper editor. Viv hoped that this film would launch her into a new career in the movies. Unfortunately, what was already a small part got even smaller overseas when most of the scenes set in the newspaper office were cut from the epic-length movie's foreign prints since they were not exactly essential to the plot. In 1966, Vivian accepted the lead role in the Woody Allen comedy *Don't Drink the Water* during its pre-Broadway tryout, only to leave the show, reportedly because of problems with co-star Lou Jacobi.

While doing much stock work throughout the nineteen-sixties and seventies, Vivian Vance was still visible in the medium that had made her a star. In 1968 alone, she appeared several times with Lucy. She returned for two episodes of *The Lucy Show.* The first, which aired on New Year's Day 1968, was a clip show featuring some of the best moments with Lucy and Viv from the early years of the series. The second, "Lucy and the Lost Star," featured an infamous guest appearance by Joan Crawford. The latter would mark Vivian's final appearance on *The Lucy Show,* which ended its run only two weeks later. Vivian surprised Lucy as a guest on a *Mike Douglas Show* that aired in April 1968. In December of that year, Vivian made her first appearance on *Here's Lucy,* playing Lucy Carter's childhood best friend, Vivian Jones (an early draft of the script named the character Vivian Dodds). Vivian ultimately appeared in six episodes of *Here's Lucy* in its first four seasons.

Claudette Colbert taught Vivian to "get before the public every year—let 'em see you every year—then they don't realize you're getting any older because they're getting old right along with you." In 1970, in addition to *Here's Lucy,* Vivian also appeared in *The Kraft Music Hall Presents Desi Arnaz* and a television adaptation of *The Front Page.*

The Dodds moved from Connecticut to New Mexico to New York before finally settling in the San Francisco Bay area. In 1973, Vivian was diagnosed with breast cancer and underwent a mastectomy.

Vivian was one of the stars who appeared on Lucy's *Dean Martin Celebrity Roast*, which aired in February 1975. Later that year, Viv surprised Lucy on *Dinah!* in an episode also featuring Lucie Arnaz, DeDe Ball, and Zsa Zsa Gabor. On the show, Vivian read aloud a contract once given to her by Lucy as a gag gift. Among the provisions listed were that she had to remain twenty pounds heavier than the star of the show. This piece of fiction would later erroneously be reported as fact. At this time, Viv also played Maxine the coffee lady in a popular series of Maxwell House coffee commercials. In 1975, she was back on a hit sitcom on CBS's Monday night schedule when she played a next-door neighbor in a much-publicized guest appearance on *Rhoda*.

Vivian reunited with Lucy for *A Lucille Ball Special: Lucy Calls the President*, playing Lucy's longtime neighbor and best friend, Vivian. Vivian's health was faltering, however, as she learned during rehearsals that her cancer had returned. She also developed Bell's palsy during the taping. Despite her illness, Vivian continued to appear on television. She was among the more than 100 stars gathered by CBS to celebrate their fiftieth anniversary in *CBS: On the Air*, in March 1978. Lucy also appeared, although the two co-stars and friends were not placed near each other in the star-studded opening or the grand finale lineup (which was in alphabetical order, shot on the walkway in front of CBS Television City). This would be the last time Lucille Ball and Vivian Vance would be seen in the same television program. Vivian made her final television appearance in the short-lived Mark Harmon series *Sam*, which aired on March 14, 1978.

Knowing how bad Vivian's illness was, Lucy and Mary Wickes visited their good friend at her home. The three had a wonderful visit, after which Lucy and Mary cried all the way back in the car, knowing that they would never see Vivian again. Vivian Vance died at her home in Belvedere, California on August 17, 1979. This, coming after the end of her weekly television series in 1974 and the death of her mother DeDe in 1977, was a terribly difficult time for Lucy. For the rest of her life, she would usually tear up at the mention of Vivian's name while being interviewed.

Vivian appeared in 175 episodes of *I Love Lucy*, 13 *Lucille Ball-Desi Arnaz Shows*, 81 episodes of *The Lucy Show*, and 6 episodes of *Here's Lucy*. Ultimately, Vivian appeared in 275 episodes of Lucille Ball's series.

Ricky and Fred (William Frawley) hang around as the gang tries to upstage Ethel in her one woman show in the *I Love Lucy* episode "Ethel's Hometown."

William Frawley

Lucy's indispensable *I Love Lucy* co-star, William Clement Frawley, was born on February 26, 1887 in Burlington, Iowa to Michael and Mary Brady Frawley, the second of four children. John ("Jay") was the eldest, then William, followed by Paul, then Mary. After high school, Bill Frawley worked at the Burlington Railroad as a traffic instructor and then took on a variety of jobs, including working as a court reporter in Chicago and then back to the railroad business with a clerk job for Union Pacific in Omaha, Nebraska.

At the age of twenty, Frawley launched his show business career when he accepted a job in the chorus of a show in Chicago, *The Flirting Princess*. Frawley's mother was so dead set against her child going into show business that William soon returned to his railroad job. The performing bug, however, bit not only William but younger brother Paul, and the two would team up in a show written by Bill entitled *Fun in a Vaudeville Agency* that they played in their native Burlington. The Frawley Brothers toured vaudeville, but Paul eventually heeded their mother's wishes and went to college. The younger Frawley would eventually return to the business, however, with quite a bit of success in his day.

In 1914, William Frawley married Edna Louise Broedt, with whom he created another vaudeville act, Frawley and Louise, which toured the country. The duo became most admired for a one-act playlet they performed, entitled "Seven A.M." In 1916, Bill Frawley made his film debut in the silent *Lord Loveland Discovers America*, followed that same year by a short, *Persistent Percival*, with his wife. The Frawleys divorced in 1927, and he never remarried.

During this period, Bill Frawley claimed to have introduced the standards "Carolina in the Morning" and "My Melancholy Baby," both of which he later performed as Fred Mertz. (Frawley's claim on "Carolina" is especially unlikely, as the song debuted in the Broadway revue *The Passing Show of 1922*, of which he was *not* a member of the cast.)

Frawley made his Broadway debut as a replacement in the musical *The Gingham Girl* in 1923. The show starred Edward Buzzell, who, once he went to Hollywood and switched to directing, would become one of Lucy's mentors. He kept very busy on Broadway over the next decade, with *Merry, Merry; Bye, Bye Bonnie; Talk About Girls* (featuring a pre-fame Ruby Keeler); *Here's Howie;* and his longest-running show, the straight play *Sons O' Guns,* which opened in 1929. According to Frawley, he was fired from the cast of *She's My Baby* starring Beatrice Lillie, Clifton Webb, and Irene Dunne for punching Webb in the nose. William was not the only Frawley on Broadway at the time. His brother Paul was enjoying great success, appearing in more than a dozen shows over a fourteen-year period, including *Sunny* (1925–26) opposite Marilyn Miller and *Top Speed* (1929–30), which featured Ginger Rogers in her Broadway debut. Like Vivian Vance, Paul co-starred with both Ed Wynn (*Manhattan Mary;* 1927–28) and Gertrude Lawrence (*Treasure Girl;* 1928–29) on Broadway.

During the 1932–33 Broadway season, William Frawley would star in his most enduring play, the Hecht & MacArthur comedy *Twentieth Century*. Also in the cast was Roy Roberts, who would play bank president Mr. Cheever on *The Lucy Show*. When Columbia released a film version the following year, Frawley was nowhere to be seen. Nearly twenty years earlier, Harry Cohn had been a song plugger trying to interest all the big vaudevillians in the tunes he was peddling. He knocked on Frawley's dressing room door, and Frawley politely told him to wait outside with the other song pluggers and he would talk to him. Cohn was furious at this dismissal. By 1933, Cohn was the head of Columbia Pictures. When he attended a performance of *Twentieth Century*, he again knocked on Frawley's dressing room door. This time, however, he vindictively announced, "I've just bought this show for Columbia, and I just came backstage to tell you're *not* going to be in the picture!" Roscoe Karns (who would play newspaper editor Mr. Foley in "Lucy Is a Reporter" on *The Lucy Show*) played the part on film.

Frawley made his last Broadway appearance in *The Ghost Writer*, after which he signed a contract with Paramount Pictures and moved to Hollywood in 1933. Between this time and *I Love Lucy*, Frawley appeared in approximately 100 movies. These included *Bolero* (1934, with Lucy's friends George Raft and Carole Lombard); *The Adventures of Huckleberry Finn* (1939), as the phony "Duke"; the Oscar-winning *Going My Way* (1944), purchasing the song "Swinging on a Star" from Bing Crosby and thereby providing Bing's parish with some needed money; both the 1934 and 1951 versions of *The Lemon Drop Kid*; and, perhaps most memorably, *Miracle on 34th Street* (1947), as the crafty political adviser who makes sure Judge Harper (Gene Lockhart) doesn't ruin his career by declaring Kris Kringle (Edmund Gwenn) a fraud. Frawley also appeared as landlord to Fanny Brice and Hume Cronyn in "The Sweepstakes Ticket," a sketch in *Ziegfeld Follies*, a film that featured Lucille Ball with big billing and a small part. Despite his long list of movie credits, this was the closest William and Lucy ever got to being seen in the same picture.

In 1951, William Frawley called up Lucille Ball, whom he barely knew, and asked if there might be a part for him in her upcoming television series. His film career had slowed and he was looking for work on the small screen, having already been seen on such shows as *The Alan Young Show* and *The Silver Theatre*. Earlier that year, he came close to accepting a radio job announcing for the New York Yankees alongside Mel Allen. Although he would no doubt have loved this gig, since he enjoyed spending his time with sportsmen more than anyone else, he decided he would rather stay in Hollywood than relocate to New York. The *I Love Lucy* team was looking for someone to play the role of Fred Mertz. Both Gale Gordon and

James Gleason had both been approached, but neither could commit. CBS had been advised against hiring Frawley as it was known in the industry that he had a drinking problem. Desi, however, was interested and met with the actor, over drinks. Convinced that Frawley was perfect for the part, Desi told the network he wanted him for the job and assured them that if Frawley's drinking ever interfered with the show, he would immediately be fired. Frawley agreed with this and kept to his word, never once causing any problems during production because of alcohol.

Vivian Vance, however, was not pleased that she was playing the wife of Bill Frawley, who was twenty-two years her senior. Early on, she made the comment that she thought the sixty-four-year-old actor should really be playing her *father*. Frawley was incensed when he overhead this remark, and whatever relationship they had before that only got worse. Although never less than professional in reporting for work and doing his job, the only parts of the script Frawley ever read were his own. Because of this, he admitted that he often wasn't sure what the episode they were filming was even about.

Frawley was nominated for five Emmys for his performance as Fred Mertz, but never won the coveted award. Never missing a chance to spew some venom at his former TV wife, Frawley was quoted as saying in a 1963 interview, "It doesn't surprise me. I knew they didn't know what they were doing when Vivian Vance got one."

During the run of *I Love Lucy* Frawley resided at the Knickerbocker Hotel, north of Hollywood Boulevard. He lived there with his sister until her death in 1957. By this time, his two brothers were in a local hospital due to alcoholism, their care paid for by Bill. At the end of his life, Frawley lived by himself in an apartment on North Rossmore Avenue in Los Angeles. In 1958, he released an album, *Bill Frawley Sings the Old Ones . . .*, which featured "Carolina in the Morning" and "Melancholy Baby." The following year, he starred in an installment of *The Westinghouse Desilu Playhouse*, "Comeback" (3/1/59).

A few days before the last *Lucille Ball-Desi Arnaz Show* aired, it was announced that William Frawley would be back on television in the fall of 1960, co-starring with Fred MacMurray on a new ABC sitcom, *My Three Sons*. Desi was furious that Frawley would accept a job with another production company while still under contract to Desilu. Although he threatened to sue his former co-star, he never did. Ironically, *My Three Sons* was filmed at Desilu Studios, although it was not owned by the company. Actually the first actor to be cast, Bill played Michael Francis O'Casey, affectionately known to all as "Bub," who lived with his widowed son-in-law Steve Douglas (MacMurray) to help raise his three grandchildren. Enlisted to do most of the housekeeping chores, Bub basically served as the mother figure in the house. Frawley and MacMurray had previously worked together in the films *Car 99* (1935) and *The Princess Comes Across* (1939) and, more recently on *The Lucille Ball-Desi Arnaz Show* episode "Lucy Hunts Uranium." Bill Frawley became extremely close with the three young actors who played his grandsons, Tim Considine, Don Grady, and Stanley Livingston, who loved his stories, his drinking, and his colorful language. He often enlisted young Livingston in helping him perpetrate pranks against Vivian Vance, who was filming *The Lucy Show* next door on the Desilu lot.

In January 1961, Bill Frawley had an edition of Ralph Edwards's testimonial series *This is Your Life* dedicated to him. Because she was in New York doing *Wildcat* at the time, Lucy was not able to attend but did a taped tribute to her former co-star. One of the surprise guests who *did* show up was Bill's ex-wife Edna Louise. To say he was greatly displeased to see her would be an understatement.

Frawley's final film, *Safe at Home!*, was released in 1962. Frawley received third billing in the baseball-themed movie after real-life Yankees Mickey Mantle and Roger Maris. Among those others co-starring in the picture was Patricia Barry, who had also appeared in the pilot for *My Three Sons*. The wife of Philip Barry Jr. (son of the noted playwright), she was forty-one years younger than Bill. Despite this, she and Bill became extremely close, although the exact nature of their relationship was unclear to many people. She received the bulk of Frawley's estate when he died.

Before the fifth season of *My Three Sons* began, Frawley was unable to pass his physical, which meant the producers could no longer insure him. They decided not to tell him right away that he would have to be dropped from the show, instead filming thirteen episodes for the season with Bill, giving them time to find a replacement. Bill's health began to fail even further, causing him great difficulty remembering his lines and to nod off in the middle of a scene, sometimes even while standing up. Frawley was heartbroken when he was told that he could no longer continue on the series, a feeling shared by everyone else connected with the show. Bill's last appearance on the series had Bub going off to Ireland. William Demarest, an actor whom Frawley never cared for, was brought in to play Bub's brother, Charley. Still smarting from his dismissal, Frawley visited the set often and would comment on Demarest's performance. The producers had no choice but to inform Frawley that his presence was no longer welcome. *My Three Sons* continued for an astounding seven additional seasons.

William Frawley and Lucille Ball worked together one last time in the episode "Lucy and the Countess Have a Horse Guest," from the fourth season of *The Lucy Show*. Frawley played a horse trainer whom Lucy and the

Countess (Ann Sothern) encounter at a stable. He had two lines. After he exited, Lucy Carmichael remarked, "You know, he reminds me of someone I used to know." The end credits read "Our Bill Frawley as The Trainer."

With his failing health, Frawley hired a male nurse to help him. On March 3, 1966, Frawley and his nurse went to the movies to see *Inside Daisy Clover* starring Natalie Wood, who, as a child, had appeared with Bill in *Miracle on 34th Street* and *Chicken Every Sunday*. While walking down Hollywood Boulevard, Bill collapsed. The nurse dragged him inside the lobby of the Knickerbocker Hotel where Bill had lived for so many years. William Frawley died of a heart attack.

William Frawley appeared in 174 episodes of *I Love Lucy*, 13 episodes of *The Lucille Ball-Desi Arnaz Show*, and 1 episode of *The Lucy Show;* 188 episodes total.

Mary Jane Croft

While never an official Lucy series regular, the pert Mary Jane Croft was an actress Lucille Ball could always depend on and did, frequently. Born on February 15, 1916 in Muncie, Indiana, Mary Jane attended Muncie's Ball State University. On February 6, 1934, just before her eighteenth birthday, she began her acting career playing the featured role of Dolly Cadwalader in the comedic play *Expressing Willie* in the Muncie Civic Theater. She would star in two more plays with the theater troupe that year, *There's Always Juliet* and *The Dover Road*.

She was invited to join the company of Cincinnati's Guild Theatre, which led to a job as a staff performer at WLW, Cincinnati's top radio station. Croft worked there from 1935 to 1939, when she moved to California. While at WLW, she met another radio performer, Jack Zoller, and the two married. Zoller would go on to produce such radio shows as *Cavalcade of America*, which Mary Jane appeared on. On August 4, 1944, son Eric Zoller was born.

Lucy and Mary Jane (Mary Jane Croft) react to Lucy's new housemate Carol in *The Lucy Show* episode "Lucy Gets a Roommate."

Mary Jane's innumerable radio credits included *The Beulah Show* (in which she played Alice Henderson, the title character's employer), *The Mel Blanc Show*, and the lead in the soap opera *The Story of Sandra Martin*, playing a crusading reporter. One of Croft's most famous radio jobs was on *Our Miss Brooks*, playing Daisy Enright, fellow English teacher at Madison High School and Miss Brooks's chief rival for the affections of biology teacher Mr. Boynton. Her stint on this series allowed her to share airtime with Gale Gordon. Mary Jane continued her characterization of Miss Enright in the television version of *Our Miss Brooks*, but was used far less often.

For three seasons, Mary Jane became a television favorite without ever being seen on camera. Unbilled, she provided the voice of Cleo the basset hound on Jackie Cooper's sitcom *The People's Choice* (1955–58). Making droll observations about the events on hand, Cleo's voice could be heard by the television audience but not the characters on the show. During the series' run, Mary Jane also joined the cast of *The Adventures of Ozzie and Harriet*, which was then in its fifth season. Playing next-door neighbor Clara Randolph (married to Joe Randolph, played by Lyle Talbot), Mary Jane would continue on the show for nine seasons, until it ended in 1966. At times, she worked on *Ozzie and Harriet* concurrently with *The Lucy Show*.

March 26, 1950 marked the first time Mary Jane worked with Lucille Ball, when she was a guest on *My Favorite Husband*, playing Dr. Margaret Baldwin, PhD, a former college girlfriend of Liz's husband, George, in "Liz's Radio Script." Mary Jane made her first appearance on *I Love Lucy* in the March 29, 1954 installment "Lucy Is Envious," as Lucy's wealthy former schoolmate Cynthia Harcourt, who gets Lucy and Ethel to inadvertently donate $500 each to her charity. When Mary Jane returned in the fifth season finale, "Return Home from Europe," she was now playing Evelyn Bigsby, who sat next to Lucy Ricardo on the airplane trip from France to New York in which Lucy tried to disguise a twenty-five-pound cheese as a baby. When the Ricardos moved to Westport, Connecticut, Mary Jane once again changed characters, portraying next-door neighbor Betty Ramsey, which she would do for five episodes.

Television pretty much claimed Mary Jane Croft as its own, although she did manage to make a single big-screen appearance, playing Patty McCormick's guardian Aunt Harriet in the 1958 Christmas-themed film *Kathy O'*.

In 1960, Mary Jane married Elliott Lewis, who had been involved in some capacity with nearly every show during the Golden Age of Radio, earning him the moniker "Mr. Radio." One of his jobs as an actor found him playing the title character in *The Definitive Casebooks of Gregory Hood* for three years, a role originated by Gale Gordon. He also took over the

Franchot Tone role in the radio adaptation of the movie *Her Husband's Affairs*, opposite Lucy.

When Lucille Ball returned to television with *The Lucy Show*, Elliott Lewis joined the series as producer. It was only natural that his wife would appear on the new *Lucy* series as well. In the eighth episode, Mary Jane made her first appearance as Lucy and Viv's friend Audrey Simmons, returning to the part eight times during the first two years. Elliott Lewis left *The Lucy Show* at the end of the second season. The writing staff of the series underwent a change following this season, which probably accounted for why none of Lucy and Vivian's other friends appeared during season three, although the character of Audrey was mentioned frequently.

When *The Lucy Show* returned for its fourth season, it underwent a massive change. Vivian Vance had left the show, and Lucy Carmichael had moved to Los Angeles. In the second episode of the new format, "Lucy and the Golden Greek," Mary Jane was introduced as Lucy's neighbor, Mary Jane Lewis (her married name). Mary Jane Lewis was unlike any of the previous characters the actress had played on Lucy's series. She was rather ditzy and had a speaking voice that drew comparisons to that of a chipmunk. While she was appearing on *The Lucy Show*, Mary Jane's only child, Eric, was killed in action while serving in Vietnam on January 22, 1967.

When Lucy returned in *Here's Lucy*, Mary Jane was back as Lucy's best pal, once again named Mary Jane Lewis, although this time she worked in the same office building as Lucy and was secretary to a lawyer. Mary Jane did not actually appear on the show until near the end of the first season in the episode "A Date for Lucy," which aired on February 10, 1969. At that time, Mary Jane also appeared in the final episode of Desi's production *The Mothers-in-Law*, "The Not-So-Grand Opera," playing Carol Yates, the head of Eve and Kaye's opera club. It was directed by her husband Elliott. The following season, she only appeared in three episodes of *Here's Lucy*. After this, the number of episodes featuring Mary Jane increased and during seasons five and six, she appeared in a total of nineteen episodes.

Mary Jane made her final *Here's Lucy* appearance in "Mary Jane's Boy Friend," the only time her name was featured in the title of an episode. She also appeared with Lucy in a commercial for the game Body Language during the run of the series. In fact, during her time on *Here's Lucy*, Mary Jane did little else on television, although she did play a judge in a 1972 episode of *The Don Rickles Show*.

In 1977, Mary Jane was reunited with the Lucy gang one last time for *A Lucille Ball Special: Lucy Calls the President*, playing Midge Bowser, the wife of Mayor Wally Bowser (James E. Brodhead). In the late seventies, there was a bit of a renaissance in radio dramas, and Elliott Lewis produced and directed the CBS Radio series *Sears Radio Theater* (later *Mutual Radio Theater*) from 1979 to 1980, which frequently featured Mary Jane. Mary Jane and Elliott would eventually settle in Oregon, where he died on May 23, 1990 at the age of seventy-two.

Mary Jane was honored with the first "Lifetime of Excellence" Award by the We Love Lucy Fan Club at the Third Annual Loving Lucy Convention in 1998. She passed away of natural causes at her home in Century City, California on August 24, 1999.

Mary Jane Croft appeared in 7 episodes of *I Love Lucy*, 39 episodes of *The Lucy Show*, and 33 episodes of *Here's Lucy;* 79 episodes total.

6

"Is She Still Entertaining in Her Beverly Hills Mansion?"

Where Lucy Lived

The world of show business has always been known as a nomadic one, often forcing its participants to relocate at the drop of a hat, to go months without an actual stomping ground, or to establish residence somewhere just to be close to a studio or theater of employment. Lucille Ball actually moved around quite a bit even *before* she made the decision to become a performer, living in three different states before she had even reached the age of five. As with most actors, once she was in pursuit of work, there were digs both in New York City and the Los Angeles area, the latter including her most famous and longest-lasting residence, on star-studded Roxbury Drive in Beverly Hills.

123 Stewart Avenue. Jamestown, New York

Lucille Desirée Ball was born on Sunday, August 6, 1911 at 5:00 p.m. at 123 Stewart Avenue, Jamestown, New York, to Henry Durrell and Desirée (called DeDe) Eveline Hunt Ball, in a house belonging to her maternal grandparents, Frederick Charles and Flora Belle Orcutt Hunt. At the time, Lucille's parents were residents of Anaconda, Montana, but Desirée wanted to return to her hometown of Jamestown so that her midwife mother could deliver the child. Shortly after Lucille's birth, the Balls returned to their home in Montana.

Anaconda, Montana

Henry and Desirée Ball were living in Anaconda, Montana when daughter Lucille was conceived. Henry was working at the Independent Telephone Company, which was established by Henry, his father, his brother, and some others. The Ball family originally lived at 120 West Park Avenue before moving to Commercial Avenue (on the southwest corner of Oak Street, where Henry's brother Frank lived). The Balls, however, could not deal with the Montana weather and the differences from the Western New York area where they were raised and eventually moved to Michigan. When Lucy went to New York in the nineteen-twenties, she began telling people she was from Montana, which she thought sounded more exciting and glamorous than Jamestown. Interested in her family history, and in order to appear more convincing as a native Montanan, she wrote to the Chamber of Commerce in Anaconda and Butte for informational pamphlets and soon knew more about the towns than probably many people who actually lived there. Lucille continued to publicly state she was from Montana for many years after.

126 Biddle Avenue South. Wyandotte, Michigan

In 1914, the Ball family moved to Wyandotte, Michigan, where Henry worked at the Michigan Bell Company. Lucille's earliest memories came from this house, including having hot tea accidently spilt on her. Years later, when an adult Lucy and DeDe visited the place, Lucy was able to recall everything about the house.

Only a year after the move to Michigan, Lucy's father became ill with typhoid fever. The house was placed under quarantine. With her husband ill, a pregnant DeDe would tie Lucille to a clothesline so she couldn't run away. Whenever someone passed by, Lucille, anxious to escape her awkward confinement, would pretend that she had gotten caught in the clothesline accidently and ask them to help her get loose. This only added to DeDe's stress, as she was then forced to search the neighborhood for her daughter.

During this same period, three-year-old Lucille Ball got her first opportunity to perform for a crowd when DeDe asked Mr. Flower, the neighborhood grocer, to keep an eye on her daughter. Lucy acted out little routines she had learned from her parents and would frequently be rewarded with pennies or candy from those shopping in the grocery store.

Lucille vividly remembered the events that happened at Biddle Avenue on Sunday, February 28, 1915; her father died there at the age of twenty-eight. In later years, Lucy would recall her mother telling her that her father had died; simultaneously, a picture fell off the wall. That same day, a bird flew into the house through the window; according to superstition a sign of bad luck. This memory left Lucille with a lifelong phobia of pictures of birds. By Thursday, March 4, Lucille and DeDe were back in Jamestown. For the next several years, Lucille lived alternately with her maternal grandparents and DeDe's sister and brother-in-law, Lola and George Mandicos.

20 Twelfth Street. Jamestown, New York

Following DeDe's marriage to Ed Peterson on September 17, 1918, the newlyweds moved to Detroit, figuring they stood a better chance of finding work there than in Jamestown. Thinking that DeDe's parents could not handle two children by themselves, the Petersons decided that younger brother Fred (who had been born in Jamestown on July 17, 1915) should stay with them while Lucille would be entrusted in the care of Ed's parents, Charles and Sophia Peterson. Lucy estimated that she lived with the Petersons for two-and-a-half years, but said it felt like six or eight. Grandma Peterson was a devout Christian who tried to rid the house of any sense of enjoyment. As a result, Lucille's life with the Petersons mainly consisted of chores and punishments. "It was a little confining; it was a little embarrassing, it was a little hard for a child to understand," Lucy later said about living with the Petersons, "but a lot of good things came out of it." Namely, her strong work ethic, which Lucy always credited to Grandma Peterson. She also attributed her love of gardening and her pastime of crocheting to her. After moving to Hollywood, Lucy visited Grandma Peterson every time she was in the Jamestown area.

On her first return visit to her hometown in 1934, Lucy stayed with Ed, who was now divorced from DeDe and living with his mother. She visited them again in early 1936 when she was on the East Coast following the closing of her play, *Hey Diddle Diddle*. On April 3, 1943, Ed Peterson died at the age of fifty-five. When Lucy returned to Jamestown the following January for the burial for Grandpa Hunt, she visited Sophia Peterson and tried to persuade her to move out to California with her rather than live alone, but was unsuccessful.

59 Eighth Street. Celeron, New York

On February 1, 1920, Lucy's grandparents, the Hunts, purchased a house at 59 Eighth Street in the village of Celeron from Fred and Lucy Hall for $2,000. The Hunts, DeDe and Ed Peterson, and the Ball children all moved into the three-bedroom house. They were soon joined by Lola and George Mandicos and their newborn daughter Cleo. Grandma Flora Belle gave up her nursing career to stay home and take care of Cleo and the other children. However, on July 1, 1922, Flora Belle died after a long bout with uterine cancer. (Her funeral was held in the house.) With her passing, this meant that all the adults were out of the house earning a living during the day, so Lucille was entrusted with taking care of the two younger children. Lola eventually divorced George and left her career as a beautician for nursing. Although she herself moved from Eighth Street, Lola left Cleo in the care of her family. Next door was the Lopus family, who had a daughter, Flo Pauline, Lucille's age who became her best friend.

Lucille loved her bedroom that overlooked the backyard surrounded by lilac bushes. The children would put on shows in the house, using the red and green velvet portieres that divided the hallway and the parlor as "stage" curtains. Lucy, Fred, and Cleo would spend the day playacting until they saw DeDe get off the streetcar from Jamestown at the end of the street. The kids would then try to get the chores they neglected all afternoon done before DeDe walked in the door. Among Lucille's fondest memories of this time were the attractions at nearby Celeron Park and being taken to the vaudeville shows on weekends by Grandpa Hunt. When Lucy began appearing in her school plays, such as *Charley's Aunt* (in which she played Charley), she would take the furniture from her own house to use as set pieces, which didn't exactly thrill Ed Peterson as it left him no place to sit down. DeDe typically directed the school plays.

Lucy's first thought of being a performer was the result of Ed Peterson taking her to see monologist Julius Tannen perform, fascinated by his ability to make an audience both laugh and cry. (Tannen would later have a small role in Lucy's film *The Big Street* two decades later, but is probably most recognized for doing the talking picture demonstration in *Singin' in the Rain.*)

Not all memories of Celeron were pleasant ones. On July 2, 1927, Fred Ball received an early birthday present from his grandfather—a .22 caliber rifle. The next day in the backyard, Fred Hunt explained all about the gun to his three grandchildren and Joanna Ottinger, a girl about Fred Ball's age, who was visiting family in town. Eight-year-old Warner Erickson who lived down the street and was a friend of Cleo's, had showed up uninvited and, when his presence was noticed, was told to stay out of the way. The younger Fred practiced on a target of tin cans his grandfather set up and Joanna followed. At the same time, Warner's mother, Francis, screamed for him to return home. Warner jumped up just as Joanna fired the gun. The bullet severed Warner's spinal cord, and he was permanently paralyzed from the waist down. The Ericksons filed a lawsuit against Fred Hunt. Fearing a dire financial outcome, Fred's lawyers advised him to deed his house to DeDe and Lola for one dollar. Although Lucille, DeDe, Fred Ball, and Cleo all testified on Fred Hunt's behalf, he lost the case and was told by the court that he owed the Ericksons $4,000. He paid them every cent he had and declared bankruptcy. All the family had left was the house on

Eighth Street because it was under DeDe and Lola's names. Warner's family sued a second time, claiming that the Hunts were trying to defraud them by transferring Fred's house to his daughters. The Ericksons won again, and the house was foreclosed on and eventually bought at auction by Zuhr and Bernice Faulkner. The Faulkner family owned the house into the next century. Lucy and Desi toured the house on Lucy's final trip to Jamestown in February 1956.

Eighth Street was renamed Lucy Lane in 1989.

Dyckman Street. New York City

Lucille Ball, age fifteen, travelled to New York City to attend the John Murray Anderson–Robert Milton School of the Theatre and Dance, located at 128-130 East 58th Street. Lucy lived quite a distance away on Dyckman Street in the uptown neighborhood of Inwood (north of the Cloisters), where she stayed with some friends of the family. Lucy's classes at the school included eccentric dancing and elocution. Despite her best efforts, Lucy was quickly told that she had no talent, and DeDe received a letter from the school saying that she was wasting her money. Lucy left the school.

Not wanting to go back to Jamestown a failure, Lucille stayed in New York and searched for jobs in the chorus of various stage productions. She eventually moved into a rooming house near Columbus Circle. Lucy was hired for five different shows, but fired from all of them after weeks of un-paid rehearsal time. In need of a job, she decided to seek employment as a model and landed her first such stint, modeling coats at a Seventh Avenue wholesale house. At her next modeling job, Lucy went by the name Diane Belmont, which she thought sounded much more glamorous than her given name. She always liked the name Diane, and the surname Belmont came to her while driving past the famous Long Island racetrack where she frequently appeared in fashion shows.

Homesickness later made Lucy return to Jamestown, but she was not through with New York. Reverting back to her real name, she found work with the famous designer Hattie Carnegie in Manhattan. Among Hattie's distinguished clientele were Constance Bennett, Joan Bennett, Joan Crawford, and Gloria Swanson. Lucille specialized in modeling for the Bennett sisters and decided to bleach her hair blonde and style it the same way Joan did. Lucy would later serve as Constance Bennett's stand-in during her early days in Hollywood. During this period nearly all of Lucy's free time was spent posing for artists and photographers for extra money.

20 East Fifth Street. Jamestown, New York

In 1928, the family lost their Eighth Street house, and Grandpa Hunt was arrested. Although he spent only a brief time in jail, he was not allowed to leave the city limits of Mayville, the county seat, for a year. The rest of the family moved into a room in the Wilcox Apartments on East Fifth Street in Jamestown. As a result, Lucy was forced to transfer to Jamestown High School. Her aunt, Lola Mandicos, was working as a nurse at a Long Island hospital when she died of peritonitis in 1930. Her ex-husband George Mandicos was insistent that his daughter Cleo no longer be kept in DeDe's care and come live with him in Buffalo. A custody battle between George and DeDe resulted with Cleo's father winning.

When Lucy lived in Jamestown, she had a variety of jobs including soda jerk at Walgreens (she loved to later claim that she was fired from a soda jerk job for forgetting to put the banana in the banana splits), an elevator operator, and a salesgirl at a dress shop. Lucy returned home to Jamestown after collapsing with excruciating pains in her legs while working at Hattie Carnegie's. Lucy said she was diagnosed with rheumatoid arthritis and spent several years bedridden in Jamestown before she was sufficiently recovered.

201 West 74th Street. New York City

When Lucy returned to New York in the spring of 1931, she took up residence at the Hotel Kimberly on West 74th Street and Broadway. This time she did not go alone, bringing along her best friend from Jamestown, Marion Strong. The two ladies had made their way to New York by coaxing a ride out of a Cleveland newspaperman named Eddie Murphy, who was on his way there. Lucy and Marion settled in room number 712 at the ladies' hotel, sleeping in twin beds and sharing a bureau for eighteen dollars a week. Marion worked at an antiques shop on East 51st Street for twenty dollars a week, while Lucy made twice as much as a freelance model. After several months, Marion decided the hustle and bustle of New York City life was not for her and returned to Jamestown. Lucy, not wanting to be left alone, chose to depart with Marion.

Undaunted, Lucy eventually returned to New York and the Hotel Kimberly, this time inviting her friend Gertrude Foote, who was then working as a hairdresser in Jamestown, to join her. However, Gertrude, whom Lucy nicknamed "Footie," felt the same way Marion did and was back in Jamestown after only three months. Lucille later claimed that while she was living at the Hotel Kimberly, a gang war broke out in the neighborhood and, while she was taking a bath, a bullet hit the tub and drained all the water.

58 East 53rd Street. New York City

Lucille eventually moved into an apartment over an Italian restaurant on East 53rd Street. The rent was more expensive than she was used to paying and the eatery below smelled of garlic, but Lucy liked that it was not a massive walk-up apartment. At this time, Lucille worked at a clothing store owned by E. A. Jackson and his wife located at 530 Seventh Ave (off 39th Street). The designer there was Rose Roth, who had once been Hattie Carnegie's business partner. Lucy loved working at the new establishment because it was frequented by average women rather than the society types Hattie Carnegie's catered to. Lucy ended each fashion show in a bridal gown.

Lucy convinced DeDe to send her brother Fred to live with her and attend high school there in New York. With her two children gone, her sister having died, and Cleo being taken away to Buffalo, it was only a matter of time before DeDe (along with Grandpa Hunt) decided to move to the City as well, with the family renting an apartment together.

North Formosa Street. Hollywood

Lucy's first home in California was a single room complete with Murphy bed on North Formosa Street in Hollywood. Three blocks away was the United Artists Studios where Samuel Goldwyn's production headquarters were located and *Roman Scandals* was filmed. Lucy eventually bought a secondhand bicycle for ten dollars to ride to the studio. On occasion, she would be so tired after a long day of working that she would take a cab home, convincing the driver to let her take the wheel while he sat in the back, holding the bicycle out the window.

1344 North Ogden Drive. Hollywood

Lucy's goal was to reunite her family in California.

Fred Ball was the first to come out to Hollywood, joining his sister in a three-bedroom house at 1344 North Ogden Drive she had rented for eighty-five dollars a month. Although the house was furnished, Lucy was given permission to do some redecorating, so she asked fellow Columbia contract player Ann Sothern (who earlier in the year was one of the headliners of *Kid Millions*, while Lucy was just an unbilled Goldwyn Girl), if she could give her some decorating advice. Sothern gladly came over and helped. Lucy later described the home as "a blue and white dollhouse." Shortly after Lucy informed DeDe and Grandpa Hunt that she was ready for them to join her in California, she and the rest of the Columbia stock company were released from their contracts. Lucy would later recall telling DeDe, "Don't take the train, save money and take the bus." Movie star George Raft, a friend of Lucy's who was the employer of her boyfriend Mack Gray and the boyfriend of her friend Virginia Peine, loaned her $65 and his limousine so that Lucille could meet her family at the station in style. When Lucy brought her mother and grandfather to the house, DeDe cried when she first saw it, so happy was she at her daughter's accomplishment.

Grandpa Hunt, who was never truly happy living in New York City, greatly improved his spirits as a result of the move. Lucy would write in her autobiography, "Keeping that household afloat was the greatest thing that ever happened to me." Soon after Cleo turned sixteen on May 12, 1935, she left her father's custody in Buffalo and was finally reunited with her family in the house on Ogden Drive in Hollywood. Lucy purchased a secondhand 1933 Studebaker Phaeton and met her shocked cousin at the Greyhound bus terminal during a break from filming *I Dream Too Much,* still in full makeup for her role.

One job Grandpa Hunt had at the new house was to repeatedly fix the back of the garage because Lucy would frequently forget to stop in time when pulling in her Studebaker and knock out the back wall. Grandpa also took to holding political meetings in the garage, until he was incapacitated by a stroke and thereafter spent much of his time sitting on the porch. Annoyed by a tree in front of the house that he claimed blocked his view, he wanted to cut it down, but Lucy and the family repeatedly informed him that the tree was not theirs, it was city property. Grandpa warned them that the offending tree would fall down during a storm if it was not removed. During a storm, the tree did come down right on top of Lucy's car. It was apparent that the tree's roots had been carefully sawed to make this happen. Lucy and her family realized that Grandpa Hunt had gradually cut them, so when there finally was a storm, it would fall over.

1403 North Laurel Avenue. Hollywood

With DeDe, Grandpa Hunt, Fred, and Cleo all living at the Ogden Drive house, Lucy decided to get her own apartment nearby, moving only a couple of blocks away to 1403 North Laurel Avenue. Lucy hosted an all-girl housewarming party at the apartment on November 17, 1937, and guests included DeDe, Cleo, and RKO friends Ginger Rogers, Eve Arden, Phyllis Frasier (Ginger's cousin), and Florence Lake. One of the other tenants in this building was F. Scott Fitzgerald, who died in December 1940. Lucy and Desi lived here until March 1941.

19700 Devonshire Drive. Chatsworth, California

The newly married Arnazes wanted their own home.

Lucy's frequent co-star Jack Oakie had recently moved into a house previously owned by Barbara Stanwyck in Northridge in the San Fernando Valley. While the Arnazes were visiting his home, Oakie put the couple in contact with a real estate developer in the area named Bill Seson. Seson showed the Arnazes a five-acre ranch on Devonshire Drive in Chatsworth, the same street Oakie lived on. The place, which contained a swimming pool and 200 orange trees, was exactly what Lucy and Desi had in mind. However, they could not afford the price Seson asked (Desi recalled the figure to be $14,500, while Lucy later claimed they paid $16,900). The developer, wanting some high-profile clients, said they could put a down payment on the property. Desi told him they could give him $1,500 up front, and Seson agreed that they could pay the rest over a ten-year period. The Arnazes had their dream home. Inspired by Mary Pickford and Douglas Fairbanks calling their home Pickfair by combining the first syllables of their surnames, the Arnazes christened the place Desilu.

The ranch was soon filled with animals including 300 chickens, three roosters, a pig, and a cow. The cow, named the Duchess of Devonshire, grew to be over 1,000 pounds and fell in love with Desi, at one point crashing through their bedroom wall to be near him. All of their animals died of natural causes since Lucy refused to kill any of them for food. Desi, with Grandpa Hunt's help, built a small house on their property as a place for him to retreat to when he and Lucy had a fight or as a place for the couple to throw a party. The finished house contained a main room, kitchen, and bathroom. The Arnazes loved to host parties at the Desilu ranch starting with a surprise thirtieth birthday party Desi threw for Lucy a few months after they moved in. Among the other celebrations held there was the wedding reception for Lucy's brother Fred and his wife Phyllis Brier. Lucy and Desi held their own reception at their home when they married for the second time at the nearby Our Lady of the Valley Church on June 19, 1949. When Lucy discovered she was pregnant the following year, Desi added a two-room nursery wing, which, at $23,000, cost more than the house. Although, sadly, Lucy miscarried that baby, the Arnazes were finally able to use the nursery when Lucie Desirée was born on July 17, 1951.

By 1954, the lengthy commute from Desilu the ranch to Desilu the studio and back had become too much for the Arnazes. This, combined with the scare of kidnapping threats against the children, convinced Lucy and Desi to find a place closer to work. Lucy and Desi sold their Chatsworth home to former child star Jane Withers. For a short time before they vacated the premises, the Arnazes kept the trailer used in their film *The Long, Long Trailer* parked at the back of the property. This was used as a guesthouse and was frequently occupied by the Arnazes' friend June Havoc.

Lucy and Desi show off their Rancho Mirage home.

40-241 Club View Drive. Rancho Mirage, California

Lucy and Desi created a weekend retreat in 1954. In a poker game, Desi won a vacant lot in Rancho Mirage, near Palm Springs, on which Paul Williams was hired to design a home for the property. The eventual ranch house had six bedrooms and the same number of bathrooms, faced the San Jacinto Mountains, and was located on the seventeenth hole of the Thunderbird Golf Course. Although his own home was on the course, Desi was prohibited from golfing there because he was Cuban.

Lucy received this house as part of her divorce settlement with Desi. The Rancho Mirage home became a favorite of golf lover Gary Morton. However, he too was not permitted to golf at Thunderbird because he was Jewish. Gary instead became a member of the nearby Tamarisk Golf Course. Lucy and Gary would typically drive out to their Rancho Mirage home after that week's Lucy episode filming. As one of the city's most prominent residents, Lucy was named the first Honorary Mayor of Rancho Mirage. Lucy's close friend Ginger Rogers lived down the street at 40-230. Gary Morton lived at this house until his death in 1999.

1000 North Roxbury Drive. Beverly Hills

When her realtor took her to 1001 North Roxbury Drive, Lucy was none too thrilled with the place the broker showed her. However, on her way out, the house across the street, at 1000 North Roxbury Drive, at the corner of Lexington Road, caught her eye. Curious as to *its* availability, Lucy rang the doorbell, and the owner of the house, a Mrs. Bang, answered. Lucy asked her if she would be willing to sell her house. As chance would have it, Mrs. Bang's son had recently been killed, and because the place held too many memories, she and her husband were thinking of moving. Lucy called Desi with the news, and he instructed her to buy the house if she wanted. Mr. and Mrs. Bang agreed to sell the place, which had been built in 1936, for $85,000. During the six months the Arnazes spent remodeling the house, the family stayed at the nearby Beverly Hills Hotel on Sunset Boulevard.

Because of the many stars that lived in the neighborhood, tour buses constantly cruised through the streets. This became the basis of the *I Love Lucy* episode, "The Tour," in which the exterior of Lucy and Desi's newly purchased house was used to represent Richard Widmark's Beverly Hills home; a scene filmed *before* the Arnazes actually moved in. By the time the episode aired on May 30, 1955, the family was living there and found themselves having to put up with occasional fans who would climb the brick wall that surrounded the property, thinking that it was all right to do so because Lucy Ricardo did it.

The Arnaz family officially moved into the house on May 5, 1955. As Desi carried his wife over the threshold, he discovered that the pipes had burst, leaving the place in a complete state of disarray. Enraged, he started tearing the damaged walls down with his bare hands. Horrified at this unbridled display of temper, DeDe escorted the children out of the house, telling them that their father was rehearsing. Lucy later stated that this was her first indication that the Desilu empire was becoming too much for her husband and cited this particular outburst in her divorce testimony.

Lucy's favorite room of the house was what she called the "lanai" (Hawaiian for "porch"). It contained a huge screen that could be lowered by the push of a button, on which Lucy could view films or some of the 85,000 feet of home movies she had. She spent much of her post-*Here's Lucy* time in this room playing backgammon.

Barbara Walters gave television viewers a tour of Lucy and Gary Morton's Roxbury Drive home in this December 6, 1977 *Barbara Walters Special.*

In back of the main residence was a guesthouse, where Desi was obliged to stay at the end of the Arnazes' marriage. When Lucy returned to Beverly Hills following the demise of *Wildcat,* future husband Gary Morton made it his temporary quarters, while Desi Jr. and fiancée Liza Minnelli lived there for a period in the early seventies. Next to the guesthouse was the pool house, which, in later years, was decorated with photographs from *Mame.* On July 17, 1971, Lucie Arnaz married Phil Vandervort in the backyard of the Roxbury Drive house, where once her mother had created a playhouse with a stage and a spotlight so young Lucie could put on shows with her friends.

In front of the house, young Lucie and Desi Jr. would sell genuine Lucille Ball memorabilia and charge for tours. Unbeknownst to his mother, one of Desi Jr.'s favorite things to do was to tell motorists carrying maps of the stars' homes that the maps were inaccurate. He would then, for a fee, get in their car with them and point out who lived in each house and the unknowing tourist had no idea he was completely making these facts up.

In 1977, Lucy and Gary were interviewed by Barbara Walters for one of her ABC television specials, and a tour of their home was featured as part of the segment. The exterior was seen again as Lucille Ball's house in her 1980 special *Lucy Moves to NBC* for a sequence in which she takes a bus tour of the stars' homes to her own residence; a bit her neighbor Jack Benny had also done on his program years earlier. Not too much had changed in the Roxbury house from 1955 to 1989; Lucy still had rotary phones and many of her magazine subscriptions were still addressed to "Mrs. Desi Arnaz." In March 1989, Lucy was presented with the key to the City of Beverly Hills. The city council also proclaimed 1989 "Lucille Ball Year." Lucy passed away one month later. Her will stipulated the house be sold after her death, with the proceeds going to the trust she established for her children. The house that Lucy paid $85,000 for in 1955 sold in 1992 for $3.7 million.

Lucy's neighbors on Roxbury Drive included:

James Stewart 918

Academy Award winner James Stewart and his wife Gloria lived at 918 North Roxbury Drive, which was the next house to Lucy's left, although Lexington Road ran between them. The Stewarts had bought the place shortly after they were married in 1949. At the time the Arnazes moved in, however, there was another house situated between them and the Stewarts. In the nineteen-sixties, James and Gloria bought the house next door, tore it down, and created a magnificent garden in its place. As a result, all the rats on the

Lucy kids around with longtime neighbor Jack Benny.

property scurried over to Lucy's yard, which did not please her, to say the least.

A favorite story of the Ball-Arnaz-Morton family involved James Stewart coming over to their house with vegetables grown in his garden. The couple who worked in the Mortons' house did not know who the actor was and thought he was nothing more than a vegetable salesman. They told him they had their own vegetables and slammed the door in his face. When Gary was told by the couple, he knew exactly who the vegetable salesman in question really was and told them the next time the man came to the door with vegetables to take them and give him a dollar. When Stewart returned, he was indeed given a dollar for his vegetables.

Although Stewart never appeared in an episode of one of Lucy's series, the two did work together on television on occasion. The Mortons and the Stewarts (along with Steve Lawrence and Eydie Gorme) appeared together on a 1976 episode of *Dinah!* James Stewart presented Lucy with a plaque at the conclusion of *CBS Salutes Lucy: The First 25 Years,* and Lucy was one of the stars who participated in Stewart's 1978 *Dean Martin Celebrity Roast.* Stewart was also one of the speakers at *An All-Star Party for Lucille Ball*, in which he introduced an anniversary surprise to Lucy from Gary. In 1987, Lucy appeared alongside James Stewart in his TV special, *A Beverly Hills Christmas*. Gloria Stewart died in 1994, and James Stewart lived in the house until his death in 1997.

Jack Benny 1002

In 1937, Jack Benny and wife Mary Livingstone built a house at 1002 North Roxbury Drive. Contrary to his tightwad persona, Benny paid a quarter of a million dollars for the end result. One night, as a joke, he walked into Lucy's house while the family was eating dinner and, without saying a word, strolled around playing his violin, dressed as a gypsy. Going along with the gag, Gary tipped him a dollar, after which Jack walked back home, playing the violin all the way. When he reached his house, he discovered that he was locked out, just as a tour bus was pulling up, giving the spectators quite a sight. With Lucy's family next door, the comedian had some competition in the music department, fiddling that much louder on Sunday mornings, in order to drown out the noise that came from Desi Jr. practicing on his drum kit.

In 1965, Jack and Mary moved from their home on Roxbury to an apartment in Century City. The change of residence had been Mary's idea, and Jack forever regretted leaving behind his beloved house.

Lucy and Jack Benny worked together many times through the years. However, Jack only appeared in one *Lucy* episode while actually living next door to Lucille Ball: *The Lucy Show*'s "Lucy and the Plumber," which first aired on September 28, 1964. All of his other guest shots were done after he had moved away.

Peter Falk 1004

Peter Falk, another Emmy winner, made 1004 North Roxbury his home. While Lucy never appeared on his long-running *Columbo* series, her son-in-law Laurence Luckinbill did guest in an episode two years prior to his marriage to Lucie Arnaz. Falk did work on the Desilu lot, though, having appeared in a 1960 episode of *The Untouchables*.

Thomas Mitchell 1013

Oscar, Emmy, and Tony winner Thomas Mitchell (who was a frequent co-star of neighbor James Stewart) resided at 1013 North

Roxbury Drive. Although Lucy never worked with the actor, he did co-star with Desi in 1943's *Bataan*. Mitchell built the house in 1927 and lived there until his death in 1962.

Jeanne Crain 1017

Academy Award nominee (for 1949's *Pinky*) Jeanne Crain and her husband, actor-turned-business executive Paul Brinkman (who had acted under the name Paul Brooks), lived at 1017 North Roxbury. The Brinkmans had seven children in an eighteen-year period. Lucy and this other famous redhead never worked together.

Rosemary Clooney and José Ferrer 1019

Singer Rosemary Clooney and her husband, Academy Award winner José Ferrer, moved into 1019 North Roxbury Drive shortly after their 1953 marriage. They bought the house from Ginny Simms, who co-starred with Lucy in 1939's *That's Right—You're Wrong*. One of the house's previous occupants was singer Russ Columbo, who starred in one of Lucy's earliest films, *Broadway Thru a Keyhole*. Clooney would later claim the crooner haunted the house after being shot and killed there. Actually, he was accidently shot at the home of a friend, Lansing Brown, who lived at 584 Lillian Way in Beverly Hills. In fact, Columbo was no longer even living on Roxbury Drive at the time of his 1934 death. The Ferrers, who had five children together (including actor Miguel Ferrer), divorced in 1961, but remarried three years later. They divorced again in 1967. Rosemary Clooney lived in this house until her death in 2002. Lucy and Rosemary appeared together in several Bob Hope specials and alongside Hope, Jane Russell, Dorothy Lamour, and Rhonda Fleming on a 1977 episode of *Dinah!* saluting Hope.

Ira Gershwin 1021

Ira Gershwin, brother George, and wife Leonore (Lee) moved into 1019 North Roxbury Drive in 1936 after the brothers were hired by RKO to write the score of the Astaire-Rogers film *Shall We Dance*. Tragically, George would die the following year, at the age of thirty-eight. Ira could not bear the thought of staying in the house where he had lived with his late brother. When the elderly woman who lived next door at 1021 North Roxbury offered to sell her house to Ira and Lee, the Gershwins moved in there. Ira Gershwin lived there until his death in 1983.

Agnes Moorehead 1023

Lucy's friend Agnes Moorehead, who appeared with her in *The Big Street*, resided at 1023 North Roxbury Drive. *The Big Street* was only Moorehead's third film—the first two being the Orson Welles classics *Citizen Kane* and *The Magnificent Ambersons*. Agnes was known for her lavish holiday parties that coincided with her December 6th birthday. Lucy was a frequent attendee at these soirees. Lucy and Agnes found themselves as Emmy competitors when they were nominated against each other at the 1967 award ceremony. Agnes received six nominations for her famous role as Endora on *Bewitched*. This, however, was the only year she was nominated as a Lead Actress (other competition included her on-screen daughter, Elizabeth Montgomery). Lucy ended up winning the trophy, but Agnes did not go home empty-handed that night—she won her sole Emmy Award for guest starring on *The Wild, Wild West*.

Polly Bergen 1025

Actress/singer Polly Bergen and her husband, agent Freddie Fields, lived at 1025 North Roxbury Drive. Bergen appeared with fellow Roxbury residents Lucy and Jack Benny in 1967's *A Guide for the Married Man*, although none of them shared any scenes. Bergen was reportedly sought for the role of Ivy London, the ex-wife of Parker Ballantine (Bob Hope) in *Critic's Choice*. Marilyn Maxwell was eventually cast. (Lucy's character does not share any scenes with the character in the film.) Bergen was also a guest the night Dino, Desi & Billy performed on *The Ed Sullivan Show*, with Lucy, accompanied by Lucie and DeDe, taking a bow from the audience. Like Lucy, Polly loved backgammon, and the two often played together in tournaments.

150 East 69th Street. New York City

Lucy signed a three-year lease on two apartments on the sixteenth floor of the newly built Imperial House located at 150 East 69th Street. The two apartments were combined to make one big one. The rent was $1,300 a month. Lucy moved in during the summer of 1960 in anticipation of starring on Broadway in *Wildcat*, and was joined by Lucie, Desi Jr., DeDe, Lucy's maid Harriet, chauffeur Frank Gorey, and the children's nanny, Willie Mae. The building was so new that most of the lower floors were unfinished and the elevators were still being installed. Lucy was furious when she was informed that African Americans were prohibited from taking the front elevator. She got this rule changed.

Lucy said she chose the color, rugs, and furniture for the apartment in five hours. The apartment had a long gallery, featuring paintings by Calogera (one of Lucy's favorite artists), that led to the thirty-eight-foot terrace with a view of the East River. The apartment also featured paintings by friends and celebrities such as Russell Markert (creator of the Rockettes and the choreographer on Lucy's film *Moulin Rouge*), Claudette Colbert, Brooks West, Orson Welles, Claire Trevor, Jonathan Winters, and Orry-Kelly. After the closing of *Wildcat*, Lucy headed back to California in the summer of 1961, but briefly returned to Manhattan with Gary Morton that November. Lucy and Gary held their wedding reception at the Imperial House apartment on November 19, 1961.

Snowmass, Colorado

In 1970, Lucy purchased three condos, 9,800 feet up, in Snowmass, Colorado, situated on top of each other: one for her and Gary, one for Lucie and Desi Jr., and one for DeDe. Lucy's condo was on the third floor. Snowmass became a favorite location for DeDe, who, even after she had turned 80, would still go tobogganing and sledding there. Lucy loved doing her own cooking there and watching the skiers zip past her house. Gary, on the other hand, hated the cold weather, so he frequently escaped to the warmer climate of their Rancho Mirage home while Lucy went to Snowmass.

In the October 25, 1971 *Here's Lucy* episode "Someone's on the Ski Lift with Dinah," the Carter family goes on a ski trip to Snowmass. Lucille's real-life skiing instructor, Mike Howden, part-time actor, played an injured ski instructor in the episode. On January 6, 1972, while in Snowmass with Gary; DeDe; Lucie and her husband Phil Vandervort; and Desi Jr. and his fiancée Liza Minnelli, Lucy broke her leg. She was getting off the ski lift when a skier accidently ran into her. Rather than shut down production on *Here's Lucy*, the scriptwriters had Lucy Carter break her leg at Snowmass too. Although Lucy was unable to ski downhill as a result of her leg injury, she learned to love skiing cross-country on her visits to her winter retreat.

211 East 70th Street. New York City

Lucie, her husband Laurence Luckinbill, and their two sons were living in New York City, so Lucy and Gary decided to get an apartment of their own in Manhattan in 1983, taking up residence at 211 East 70th Street. They paid $2,500 a month for the two-bedroom, two-bathroom apartment, which Lucy asked her friend and former *Wildcat* co-star Paula Stewart to decorate. Paula eventually moved into an apartment in the building herself. Lucy's apartment received major coverage in the May 1984 issue of *Architectural Digest*.

7

"I Felt She Was Much Too Young for Henry Fonda."

The Other Men in Lucy's Life

In most people's minds it is hard to equate Lucille Ball with any man other than Desi Arnaz (with apologies to Gary Morton), so firmly ingrained in the pop culture consciousness is the team of "Lucy and Ricky," and therefore, Lucy and Desi. However, before Desi came into her life, Lucille, being an eligible and attractive young lady, found herself involved with her share of men; first in her pre-show business life and then once she found herself in the wild world of Hollywood, starting from 1933. Here is a list of those men known to have been linked to Lucy long enough to qualify as "dates," "affairs," "relationships," or perhaps something more.

Vinnie Myers

Vinnie Myers was Lucy's boyfriend in the eighth grade. When Lucy returned with Desi to Jamestown in 1956, she asked her friend Pauline Lopus to make sure Myers was in attendance at the party being held for Lucy's Celeron schoolmates. Trying to guess who each person at the party was, Lucille was able to recall select names or at least some memory of that person. The only one about whom she drew a complete blank was the last man introduced to her. Pauline gleefully informed Lucy that that man was none other than Vinnie Myers. Lucy and Desi both made a big fuss over Lucy's former boyfriend, and Lucy described this as a highlight of her trip back to her hometown.

In the premiere episode of *The Lucy Show*, "Lucy Waits Up for Chris," Lucy Carmichael reminisces about the first time she dated a guy who had a car, Vinnie Myers. In the third-season episode "Lucy Gets Amnesia," Max Showalter plays Lucy's boyfriend from when she was fourteen years old, Vinnie Myers. Showalter reprised the role in "Lucy and Arthur Godfrey."

Johnny DaVita

In the summer of 1926, Lucille Ball, nearly fifteen, began dating twenty-three-year-old Jamestown resident Johnny DaVita. Johnny came from a wealthy family and had aspirations of becoming a doctor, but his father was rumored to be a bootlegger with connections to the mob. Deeply displeased with this relationship, DeDe decided to send her daughter to drama school in New York, perhaps to keep the two apart. It was Johnny who drove Lucy to Buffalo, where she took the train to New York for the first time.

In February 1930, Johnny's father was shot to death outside of church, which put an end to Johnny's plans to become a doctor. Despite her mother's objections, Lucy's relationship with Johnny continued whenever she was in Jamestown, right up until she moved to California. She saw him back home again in February 1937 while she was on the East Coast after the closing of her play, *Hey Diddle Diddle*. Because the DaVita family no longer had the fortune they had when Johnny first met Lucille, Johnny asked his one-time girlfriend if she could lend him some money to pay for his mother's insurance, which she gladly did.

Roger Furse

One of Lucy's steady beaux in New York was British artist Roger Furse. Furse was the son of the distinguished Lieutenant General Sir William Furse and a descendent of the famous Kemble and Siddons acting families. Furse, who was nearly eight years older than Lucy, was credited with giving her her nickname at the time, "Two Gun," which is believed to have referred either to the time a bullet went through Lucy's bathtub in the Hotel Kimberly or to her adopted Montana birthplace. Lucille and Roger reportedly nearly eloped together. A painting of Lucy done by Furse later hung in her Rancho Mirage home.

Furse, who later became known for his collaborations with Laurence Olivier and won an Oscar for his art direction of Olivier's *Hamlet*, died in 1972.

Ralph Forbes

British actor Ralph Forbes was one of Lucy's first boyfriends in Hollywood. He had appeared on screen in such pictures as the silent version of *Beau Geste* (as Ronald Colman's brother) and the George Arliss melodrama *The Green Goddess*. Nearly fifteen years older than Lucille and recently divorced from actress Ruth Chatterton, Forbes proposed to Lucy, but she turned him down, saying that she thought she would never fit in with his cultured, British family. Almost immediately after Lucy ended her relationship with Forbes, he married actress Heather Angel. Angel and Forbes both appeared in 1935's *The Three Musketeers*, with Lucy featured as an extra. Two years later, Lucy's screen time surpassed Forbes's in *Stage Door*, but they did not share any scenes. The two would officially appear together in Lucy's 1938 starring vehicle *Annabel Takes a Tour*, with Forbes cast as her potential romantic interest, the Viscount River-Clyde. He died in March 1951 at the age of fifty-four.

Mack Gray

Another steady boyfriend for Lucy in her early Hollywood days was Mack Gray, assistant to George Raft and an occasional bit player. Lucille and Mack both appeared in Raft's 1933 film *The Bowery*. Raft was dating Lucy's friend Virginia Peine (who acted under the surname "Pine"), and the foursome would frequently go out together. Gray, whom many in Hollywood considered a shady character, was nicknamed "Killer." This colorful moniker had come from Carole Lombard, at the time *she* was involved with Raft. When Gray had a hernia operation, he explained to Lombard that the Yiddish word for hernia was "killah," prompting Lombard to call him "Killer." The nickname stuck for the rest of his life. Mack left Raft's employ in 1952 and went to work in the same capacity for Dean Martin, attending the crooner until Gray's death in 1981. In the mid sixties, Gray also served as the manager for Lucy's son's pop group, Dino, Desi & Billy.

Pandro S. Berman

When Lucille Ball arrived at RKO in 1935, the studio's supervising producer was thirty-year-old Pandro S. Berman, who produced her first film for the company, *Roberta*. Pan Berman had wed Viola Newman in 1927 and was still very much married to her when he supposedly fell in love with Lucy and proposed to her. Although Lucy wrote about this in her memoirs, she was careful not to identify the producer by name, as he was very much alive at the time. (Berman would outlive Lucille by seven years, dying in 1996 at the age of ninety-one.) She did, however, mention Berman several times in the book, saying that he was not impressed with her when she first came to the studio and later nearly fired her.

Lucy was encouraged by her friends to pursue this relationship with Berman. In addition to being one of the highest-paid men in Hollywood, he was Lucy's "type" and certainly talented. Berman drew comparisons to

MGM's mastermind Irving Thalberg, whose wife, Norma Shearer, was the Queen of the Metro lot and always received the best material. If Lucy married Pan Berman, her friends theorized, there was no doubt she could receive the same specialty treatment. However, Berman had a newborn baby boy at home and, having grown up without a father herself, Lucy, despite her ambitions, did not want to be the one responsible for breaking up a marriage and leaving a child fatherless. Mr. and Mrs. Berman remained married until 1959.

In 1940, Berman moved over to MGM and, eventually produced Lucy and Desi's 1954 film *The Long, Long Trailer.*

Lucille Ball with (left to right) future Academy Award winners Henry Fonda, Ginger Rogers, and James Stewart on their much talked about double date.

Henry Fonda

Having separated from husband Lew Ayres sometime in the summer of 1936, Lucy's close friend Ginger Rogers began dating James Stewart. It was Ginger's idea to set Lucille up with Stewart's best friend, Henry Fonda, with whom he was sharing a house in Brentwood at the time. (Fonda had already gone through his first marriage and divorce, to actress Margaret Sullavan.) Just the year before, Fonda (in his third Hollywood credit) had starred in *I Dream Too Much,* in which Lucy had a small role.

For their double date, the ladies went to the Brentwood house where Henry cooked for the group. After dinner, Ginger taught the boys to dance, while Lucy stayed in the kitchen washing all the dishes the bachelors had accumulated. This was followed by a trip to the Coconut Grove, where they danced to the music of the Freddy Martin Orchestra and then a stop at Barney's Beanery on Santa Monica Boulevard. By the time the women were ready to leave, it was daylight. Both Fonda and Stewart were startled by how heavy their dates' makeup appeared without the camouflage of the evening, prompting an ungallant Fonda to look at Lucy and declare "Yuk!" Not surprisingly, they never went out again. Fonda later joked, "If I'd behaved myself, they might have named that studio Henrylu not Desilu." Nearly forty years later, in 1975, Fonda told this story at Lucy's *Dean Martin Celebrity Roast,* which also featured Ginger Rogers among the guests.

Lucille Ball and Henry Fonda continued their relationship on a strictly professional basis in the following years, when they were paired in 1942's *The Big Street,* Lucy's favorite film, and 1968's *Yours, Mine and Ours,* her most financially successful. They also teamed up for the 1962 TV special *The Good Years* and roasted their pal Jimmy Stewart (by then Lucy's neighbor) on a 1978 *Dean Martin Celebrity Roast.* Lucy also appeared on Fonda's American Film Institute tribute that same year where she spoke about their work together in *The Big Street.*

Broderick Crawford

Future Academy Award winner Broderick Crawford (Best Actor for 1949's *All the King's Men*) dated Lucille in 1936, one year before he started working in movies. Unlike her other beaus at the time, Crawford was actually younger than Lucy, albeit by a mere four months. It was Crawford's mother, actress Helen Broderick (a co-star in *Top Hat,* one of the films in which Lucy did a bit part), who introduced her son to Lucy. Although Lucy later said, "There was never any love affair or anything," the two made the Hollywood columns in the summer of 1936 with stories that they were engaged to be married.

Lucy and Broderick Crawford later appeared together as guests on *The Tonight Show Starring Johnny Carson* in 1971. Crawford died on April 26, 1986, exactly three years to the day before Lucille's death.

Milton Berle, who dated Lucy in the 1930s, was forced to disguise himself as "Mildred," in *The Lucille Ball – Desi Arnaz Show* episode "Milton Berle Hides Out at the Ricardos."

Milton Berle

The future "Mr. Television" and "The First Lady of Television" actually dated a decade before Milton Berle became the new medium's first superstar. Lucy later said that nothing ever came of her romance with Milton because "Mama was around all the time," referring to Berle's famously possessive mother, Sarah (who preferred the name Sandra).

At one point, it looked as if Lucy and Milton would appear on screen together in *Having Wonderful Time*. Milton was seen as the front-runner for the role of camp social director Itchy, but Richard (Red) Skelton ended up being cast instead, thereby making his film debut.

Lucy and Milton remained friends and even attended the opening night of the Broadway show *Sim Sala Bim,* starring Dante the Magician, together in September 1940. At the time, Lucy was in New York promoting *Dance, Girl, Dance* and in the middle of her courtship with Desi Arnaz, who was starring in the Chicago production of *Too Many Girls.* Lucy and Milton would perform together many times on each other's television productions. Milton and Gary Morton would work together prior to Gary meeting and marrying Lucy. Lucy would also become close friends with Berle's wife Ruth, who died at Cedars-Sinai Hospital on April 18, 1989, the same day Lucy entered the hospital where she would pass away eight days later.

Lucy with her longtime boyfriend Al Hall at the premiere of *My Favorite Chickadee* in 1940.

Alexander Hall

Director Alexander Hall was Lucy's most serious boyfriend prior to meeting Desi Arnaz. Among his directorial credits was the 1934 version of *Little Miss Marker*, the remake of which, *Sorrowful Jones*, Lucille would co-star in fifteen years later. Seventeen years older than Lucille (less than a year and a half younger than her mother) and recently divorced from singer/actress Lola Lane, Hall started dating Lucy in 1937. Al introduced Lucy to such people as director Ed Sedgwick, who later became godfather to her two children, and his wife Ebba; and Marc and Marcella Rabwin (David O. Selznick's secretary), who would become lifelong friends. Lucy reportedly moved into Hall's Beverly Hills home, but would write in her memoirs, "I enjoyed his company, his advice and guidance, but was not in love with him." The gossip columns saw it otherwise and frequently reported the two were engaged. The relationship ended when Lucy met Desi, so she never did become Lucille Ball Hall. A few years after they parted company, Al Hall reached his career peak when he received an Oscar nomination for directing 1941's *Here Comes Mr. Jordan*. Fifteen years after his romance with Lucy ended, the Arnazes hired Hall to direct *Forever, Darling*, which was his final work as director.

8

"Two People Who Live Together and Like It"

Lucy on the Radio

Although Lucille Ball has become known as "The First Lady of Television," she worked extensively in radio prior to embarking on her career on the small screen.

Like most movie stars, Lucy was a frequent radio guest, appearing on such shows as *The Campbell Playhouse, The Lux Radio Theater, The Old Gold Comedy Theater, Screen Directors' Playhouse,* and *Screen Guild Theater.* It was on such programs that Lucy was able to reprise roles she had already played on film in radio adaptations of the stories. These included:

A Girl, a Guy, and a Gob (*Screen Guild,* Oct. 9, 1944, with George Murphy, and on *Old Gold,* Feb. 11, 1945, also with Murphy)

The Dark Corner (*Lux,* Nov. 10, 1947, with Mark Stevens)

The Big Street (*Ford Theater,* Dec. 3, 1948, with John Garfield)

Her Husband's Affairs (*Screen Directors,* May 22, 1949, with Elliott Lewis)

Sorrowful Jones (*Lux,* Nov. 21, 1949, with Bob Hope)

Miss Grant Takes Richmond (*Screen Directors,* May 19, 1950, with Stephen Dunne)

Fancy Pants (*Lux,* Sept. 10, 1951, with Bob Hope)

She also acted in radio adaptations of films in which she did not appear, in roles originated by such actresses as:

Ginger Rogers (*Bachelor Mother*—*Screen Guild,* Apr. 28, 1949, with Joseph Cotten, and then on *Screen Directors,* Mar. 8, 1951, with Robert Cummings; *Tom, Dick, and Harry*—*Ford Theater,* Oct. 22, 1949, with

Eddie Albert; *Lucky Partners—Lux,* Sept. 5, 1944, with Don Ameche; *It Had to Be You—Screen Guild,* Apr. 26, 1948, with Cornel Wilde)

Jean Harlow (*Dinner at Eight—Campbell,* Feb. 18, 1940, with Orson Welles; *China Seas—Screen Guild,* Dec. 4, 1944)

Jean Arthur (*A Foreign Affair—Screen Directors,* Mar. 1, 1951; *Too Many Husbands—Screen Guild,* Apr. 21, 1947, with Bob Hope)

Barbara Stanwyck (*Ball of Fire—Old Gold,* Nov. 5, 1944; *You Belong to Me—Screen Guild,* Jan. 19, 1950, with Don Ameche)

Loretta Young (*A Night to Remember—Screen Guild,* May 1, 1944, with Brian Donlevy)

Rosalind Russell (*Hired Wife—Screen Guild,* Aug. 19, 1946, with Brian Aherne)

Bette Davis (*The Man Who Came to Dinner—Lux,* Mar. 27, 1950, with Clifton Webb)

Marie McDonald (*Getting Gertie's Garter—Screen Guild,* Mar. 4, 1946, with Dennis O'Keefe)

Ida Lupino (*They Drive by Night—Lux,* June 2, 1941, with George Raft and Lana Turner)

These programs also gave Lucy the chance to act with people she never did otherwise like Gary Cooper (*Ball of Fire*), Clark Gable (*China Seas*), Frank Sinatra (*Too Many Husbands*), and Marlene Dietrich (*A Foreign Affair*). Lucy was also a popular guest on variety series like *The Kraft Music Hall* (with Bing Crosby), *The Jimmy Durante Show,* and *The Martin and Lewis Show* and was seen on the dramatic anthology series *Suspense* five times, including two episodes co-starring with Desi ("The Red-Headed Woman," Nov. 17, 1949 and "Early to Death," Apr. 12, 1951). Her career on radio was not limited to guest appearances, however. She was also a regular on several of her own series.

The Gulf Headliner (CBS, 1937–38)

Lucy's earliest radio series as a regular was *The Gulf Headliner* starring comedian Phil Baker. Patsy Kelly was the show's resident comedienne. Lucy would later recall nearly half a century later that Kelly had an epileptic fit before a show, and Lucy was drafted into taking her place even though she was not a member of the American Federation of Radio Artists. Subsequently, Lucy was made a regular on the program, which aired Sundays on CBS. Lucy's role on the show landed her on the cover of *Radio News* magazine in April 1938, where she was billed as "Phil Baker's heckler."

The Wonder Show (1938–39)

In the fall of 1938, Lucy joined the cast of *The Wonder Show,* which was headlined by Jack Haley. The previous season Haley hosted *The Log Cabin Jamboree* on NBC. *The Wonder Show* was a continuation of this series under the sponsorship of Wonder Bread. Other regulars on the Log Cabin incarnation were Jack Oakie, who, the same year (1938), starred with Lucy in the films *The Affairs of Annabel* and *Annabel Takes a Tour;* and Wendy Barrie (who would co-star with Lucy in *Five Came Back* the following year). They did not, however, make the transition to the new show. Those who did make the move from NBC to the new show on CBS were singer Virginia Verrill and bandleader Ted Fio Rito. Also among the series regulars was Artie Auerbach, who played a variety of funny and eccentric characters and who married Lucy's cousin Cleo.

The most significant cast member on *The Wonder Show,* however, at least where Lucille was concerned, was the program's announcer, Gale Gordon. Although neither could have guessed it at the time, this would mark the beginning of a six-decade-long working relationship.

The Wonder Show premiered on CBS on Friday, October 14, 1938. The very day before had marked the start of filming on a picture that initially had nothing whatsoever to do with Jack Haley, *The Wizard of Oz.* Several weeks later, however, Haley was asked if he could take over the role of the Tin Man when the original choice for the part, Buddy Ebsen, became critically ill due to the aluminum dust in the makeup he wore. Haley agreed and was loaned out to MGM from his home studio of 20th Century-Fox to play what would become his signature role, all the while continuing his duties on the radio show. Lucy stayed with *The Wonder Show* until the end of the season on April 7, 1939.

Let's Talk to Lucy (1964–65)

In 1964, CBS cancelled *The Garry Moore Show,* an hour-long variety show that had aired on their television network since 1958 (Lucy appeared in an episode in 1960). Moore was also the host of the popular panel show *I've Got a Secret* on the network and the host of his own daily CBS radio show. Moore was so displeased with CBS for cancelling his series that he completely left the network and embarked on a yearlong trip around the world with his wife. Steve Allen succeeded Moore in the hosting duties for *I've Got a Secret,* but this still left CBS with an opening in their radio schedule. Busy as she was with her own show, Lucy was interested in returning to radio, and was selected as Moore's replacement. The program would be a daily, ten-minute talk show, with husband Gary and cousin Cleo serving as producers. This would be their first time serving in this capacity for Lucille; Gary also did double duty as the show's announcer. Lucy said she loved interviewing people and thought it was great fun, but at the same time admitted that asking questions of celebrities also made her nervous no matter how close she was personally to the interview subject.

The series premiered on September 6, 1964 with Bing Crosby as her first guest. *Let's Talk to Lucy* lasted a single season. Some of the biggest stars in show business chatted with Lucy on the radio show including Julie Andrews, Dean Martin, Ginger Rogers, Frank Sinatra, Barbra Streisand, and Dick Van Dyke. Lucy typically went to wherever the celebrities were working with her tape recorder in hand to conduct the interview (one of her two separate interviews with Martin was on the set of his film *Marriage on the Rocks*; she dropped by backstage to talk with Rogers during the run of *Hello, Dolly!*, et al.). Lucy also chatted on air with people she saw on a daily basis, like Vivian Vance, Gale Gordon, and her own children.

My Favorite Husband

Background

In 1940, Isabel Scott Rorick published a book, *Mr. and Mrs. Cugat: The Record of a Happy Marriage*. This led to a 1942 Paramount film version entitled *Are Husbands Necessary?* with Ray Milland as George Cugat and Betty Field as Mary Elizabeth Cugat. In 1945, Cugat published a sequel to the Cugats' story, *Outside Eden*. Shortly afterwards, CBS approached Lucille Ball about starring in a radio series based on the first of Rorick's novels. Lucy was interested, but she wanted Desi to play her husband on the show. CBS balked at this, saying that her Cuban bandleader spouse would be completely unbelievable as a Midwestern banker. Lucy eventually relented and signed on.

A one-shot show was aired on July 5, 1948, and CBS was pleased enough with the result that they picked it up as a series without a sponsor being found at the time. Entitled *My Favorite Husband*, it featured Lucy as housewife Liz Cugat, while Lee Bowman, who previously appeared opposite Lucy in the films *Having Wonderful Time*, and *Next Time I Marry*, was cast as her husband George. This would be the only time Bowman would fill this role. Once *Husband* got the go-ahead to become a weekly series, Richard Denning took over the part. Ruth Perrott was cast as the couple's maid, Katy. Bob LeMond served as the series' announcer. The series was produced and directed by

Gordon Hughes and written by Frank Fox and Bill Davenport. The two writers, however, were already on the writing staff of *The Adventures of Ozzie and Harriet* and would have to return to that series when the summer hiatus ended. Meanwhile, their friends, Madelyn Pugh and Bob Carroll Jr. were writing for a show heard only on the West Coast entitled *It's a Great Life*, with Steve Allen. They were anxious, however, to write for a national radio show, specifically *My Favorite Husband*. To this end, Pugh and Carroll wrote a script for the series and were able to "sell" it (for no money). Bob and Madelyn were offered full-time jobs on *My Favorite Husband* and paid Steve Allen to write his own script that week (Allen would later guest in the *My Favorite Husband* episode "Speech for Civic Organization"). At the same time, veteran comedy writer Jess Oppenheimer found himself suddenly out of work when his series *Baby Snooks* ended because star Fanny Brice refused to take a cut in salary. Oppenheimer was approached to pen a script for *My Favorite Husband*. He very soon became the series' head writer. Gordon Hughes quickly left the series, and Oppenheimer replaced him as the show's producer/director.

Oppenheimer was pleased to have a job but was unhappy with the format of the show. He felt that the socially prominent Cugats were not accessible to the mass audience. To rectify this, he decided to make Liz more childlike, a la Baby Snooks. Effective with the January 7, 1949 episode, well-to-do Liz and George Cugat became the more average class Liz and George Cooper. This was also the first episode to be sponsored by General Foods, who used the show to advertise Jell-O. The sponsor wanted Lucille to appear in the commercials for their product. Lucy felt extremely ill at ease doing this, so the writers created a variety of characters for the star to play so she would not have to play herself in the commercials. Some of the things that came out of these commercials later reappeared on television. When Lucy played Little Miss Muffet in one of the commercials, she made a noise (an elongated "ewww!") when the spider came and sat down beside her. The writers loved this exclamation and her facial contortion that went with it, so they had Lucy repeat it many times over the years. All they had to write in the script was "SPIDER" and Lucy would know just what to do.

Jess Oppenheimer felt that Lucy needed to be less stiff when acting on the radio show and therefore gave her tickets to see *The Jack Benny Program* being performed. Lucy observed how comfortably Benny played the show to the studio audience and, taking a cue from one of the medium's most masterful comics, she really began to loosen up in her own role. Lucy's broader portrayal of Liz Cooper was exactly what Oppenheimer wanted.

The writers also decided that the Coopers needed another couple with whom to interact. Rather than simply have Rudolph Atterbury be George's boss at the bank, they introduced his wife Iris and made them the Coopers' best friends as well. Early on, when he was strictly the boss, Atterbury had been portrayed first by Hans Conried and then Joseph Kearns. With the friendship angle now added, Gale Gordon and Bea Benaderet, both of whom had been on the show before in different roles, were cast as the Atterburys.

Although he had vacated the Atterbury role, hardly an episode went by without Hans Conried in the show. The versatile actor frequently played multiple characters in a single episode using a variety of dialects, including next-door neighbor Benjamin Wood and Liz's music teacher Professor Krausmeyer. Another performer who was a ubiquitous presence on the series was Frank Nelson. He and Conried were among the many actors who lent their voices to the series who would later appear on *I Love Lucy*. These included Doris Singleton, Shirley Mitchell, Jerry Hausner, Robert Jellison, Elvia Allman, Herb Vigran, and Jay Novello.

The final episode of *My Favorite Husband* aired on March 31, 1951, by which time Lucille was heavily pregnant. The pilot for *I Love Lucy* had already been completed, but had yet to sell. By year's end Lucille would make the transition from radio to television in a big way. She and her creative team did not, however, completely leave *My Favorite Husband* behind as several of the scripts from that show were reworked for *I Love Lucy*. Plotlines, dialogue, and sometimes entire scenes were reused nearly verbatim on the television show. Just in the first several weeks on the air, *Husband* fans could spot elements of "Be Your Husband's Best Friend" in *Lucy*'s "Be a Pal" and pieces of "Iris and Liz's Easter" in "The Diet," to name but two.

In 1953, CBS began a television version of *My Favorite Husband*. Although it was originally announced that Richard Denning would be reprising his radio role opposite actress Martha Stewart as Liz, neither ended up in the series. Instead, Joan Caulfield played Liz and Barry Nelson was George. When the show came back for its third season, Vanessa Brown replaced Caulfield and *Husband* was done on film rather than live. At this time, the series was shot at Desilu. The television incarnation was cancelled in 1955, midway through its third season.

Storyline

1948

Debutante Elizabeth Elliot, the former hockey star at the Westover School for Girls, married George Cugat, "man about town and best catch of 1938." The couple's lavish wedding that December made all the society columns. George was the fifth vice president of Sheridan Falls Bank; the president was Rudolph Atterbury. Liz and George had a maid, Katy. Katy had gone through seven husbands: Clarence, Peter, Harold, Oscar, Orville, Egelburt, and Yancy. George's best friend was womanizing bachelor Cory Cartwright (originally Hal March, later John Hiestand). Liz's mother's name was Louise. Like Lucy, Liz's birthday was in August.

1949–51

In the newly revamped version of the show Elizabeth Elliot was no longer an August baby, but was born on June 12, 1917, the daughter of Bob and Adele Elliot (Sara Selby). Liz was one of several children, including a brother named Bill. She attended Shortridge High School and was the president of the school Scroll and Quill Club. George Cooper was a graduate of State University. (Some episodes mention that Liz and George went to college together.) Liz and George reside at 321 Bundy Drive in Sheridan Falls (state unnamed), although the house was actually owned by Mr. Curry (Jay Novello), who rented it to them. Their telephone number was PLaza 9970.

George eventually worked himself up from fifth vice president to executive third vice president at the Sheridan Falls Bank. George's mother, Leticia (Eleanor Audley, in the role that Bea Benaderet originated), never cared for her daughter-in-law. The Coopers' maid, Katy, eventually got engaged to the mailman, Harrison Q. Negley (another role for Jay Novello). Rudolph Atterbury was the President of the Sheridan Falls Bank and in addition to being George's boss, he was also his best friend. Rudolph's wife was Iris. Although the Coopers always called Rudolph "Mr. Atterbury," Rudolph and Iris usually called the Coopers "Liz-Girl" and "George-Boy." Rudolph's term of endearment for Iris was "Lotus Bud." Like George and Liz, Rudolph went to State University. Although Liz and Iris (whose birthday is given as May 12) were both members of the sorority Delta Upsilon Delta, in the episode "College Homecoming" Iris claimed to have gotten no farther than graduating from high school. Living next door to the Coopers were Benjamin and Gertrude Wood, who had eleven children. Seven of the children were Robert, Madelyn, Adele, Lucille, Jess, Estelle, and Joanne (they were named after the show's writers Robert Carroll Jr.,

Madelyn Pugh, and Jess Oppenheimer; Oppenheimer's wife, Estelle, and their daughter, Joanne; the show's script supervisor Adele Sliff; and, of course, the series' star).

Note that the earliest episodes of the series were not assigned titles.

July 5, 1948: Pilot
George's old girlfriend, Myra Ponsonby, might ruin the Cugats' tenth wedding anniversary.

Season One:
July 23, 1948: #1: *My Favorite Husband* Show #1
    Liz invites a big-game hunter who spoke at her literary club home to dinner.
July 30, 1948: #2: *My Favorite Husband* Show #2
    A photographer from a magazine comes to the Cugat house while George is sick. This episode was directed by CBS executive Harry Ackerman.
August 6, 1948: #3: *My Favorite Husband* Show #3
    George becomes jealous of the artist who is painting Liz's portrait, so he feigns an illness.
August 13, 1948: #4: *My Favorite Husband* Show #4
    Liz and George both run kissing booths at a charity bazaar.
August 20, 1948: #5: "Liz Teaches the Samba"
    This was Madelyn Pugh and Bob Carroll Jr.'s first script for Lucille Ball.
August 27, 1948:#6: *My Favorite Husband* Show #6
    The book *Is Your Ship of Matrimony on the Rocks?* makes Liz think about her own marriage.
September 3, 1948: #7: *My Favorite Husband* Show #7
    Liz's mother's engagement to an oil tycoon may be called off when Mrs. Elliot has second thoughts.
September 10, 1948: #8: *My Favorite Husband* Show #13
    A swami tells Liz an old beau will return.
September 17, 1948: #9: *My Favorite Husband* Show #9
    Liz tries to strike up a friendship with eccentric neighbor General Timberlake.
September 24, 1948: #10: *My Favorite Husband* Show #10
    George jumps to the conclusion that Liz is expecting when she begins knitting baby booties.
October 2, 1948: #11: "Young Matron League Tryouts"
    This was Jess Oppenheimer's first script for Lucille Ball.

October 3, 1948: #12: *My Favorite Husband* Show #12
   George's old girlfriend, Myra Ponsonby, might ruin the Cugats' tenth wedding anniversary.

October 9, 1948: #13: *My Favorite Husband* Show #13
   Unbeknownst to Liz, George will be playing opposite her in the Young Matrons' League play.
   This is the first collaboration between Jess Oppenheimer, Madelyn Pugh, and Bob Carroll Jr. This is also the last episode produced and directed by Gordon Hughes. Jess Oppenheimer takes over his duties with the next episode.

October 16, 1948: #14: "Liz Sells Dresses"

October 23, 1948: #15: "Quiz Show"

October 30, 1948: #16: "The Election"

November 6, 1948 #17: "Katy and Roscoe"

November 13, 1948: #18: "Learning to Drive"

November 20, 1948: #19: "George Attends a Teen-Age Dance"

November 27, 1948: #20: "Is There a Baby in the House?"

December 4, 1948: #21: "Be Your Husband's Best Friend"

December 11, 1948: #22: "Respective Mustaches"

December 18, 1948: #23: "Liz's New Dresses"

December 25, 1948: #24: "Numerology"

December 26, 1948: #25: "Young Matrons' League Tryouts"

January 7, 1949: #26: "Over Budget—Beans"
   Effective with this episode, the Cugats are now the Coopers. This was the first episode sponsored by Jell-O.

January 14, 1949: #27: "Piano and Violin Lessons"

January 21, 1949: #28: "Marriage License"

January 28, 1949: #29: "Absolute Truth"

February 4, 1949: #30: "Speech for Civic Organization"

February 11, 1949: #31: "Valentine's Day"
   Gale Gordon appears on the series for the first time.

February 18, 1949: #32: "Secretarial School"

February 25, 1949: #33: "Absentmindedness"

March 4, 1949: #34: "Mother-in-Law"

March 11, 1949: #35: "Charity Review"
   Gale Gordon's first show as Rudolph Atterbury.

March 18, 1949: #36: "Giveaway Program"

March 25, 1949: #37: "Old Jokes and Stories"
   Bea Benaderet plays Iris Atterbury for the first time.

April 1, 1949: #38: "April Fool's Day"

April 8, 1949: #39: "Gum Machine"

April 15, 1949: #40: "Horseback Riding"
April 22, 1949: #41: "Time Budgeting"
April 29, 1949: #42: "Vacation Time"
May 6, 1949: #43: "Overweight"
May 13, 1949: #44: "Anniversary Presents"
May 20, 1949: #45: "Getting Old"
May 27, 1949: #46: "Liz in the Hospital"
June 3, 1949: #47: "Budget—Mr. Atterbury"
June 10, 1949: #48: "Hair Dyed"
June 17, 1949: #49: "Television"
June 24, 1949: #50: "Liz Changes Her Mind"

> This episode had the distinction of being the only one of the series to be rebroadcast on CBS during the original run of the series. It re-aired on September 30, 1950.

July 1, 1949: #51: "Reminiscing"

> During the credits, Lucy interrupts Bob LeMond and thanks writer/producer/director Jess Oppenheimer, writers Bob Carroll Jr. and Madelyn Pugh, musical director Marlin Skyles, conductor Wilbur Hatch, and Richard Denning, Ruth Perrott, Gale Gordon, Bea Benaderet, Hans Conried, and Frank Nelson, and others connected to the series.

Season Two:
September 2, 1949: #52: "The Elves"
September 9, 1949: #53: "The Auction"
September 16, 1949: #54: "Baseball"
September 23, 1949: #55: "The Attic"
September 30, 1949: #56: "Women's Club Election"
October 7, 1949: #57: "George Tries for a Raise"
October 14, 1949: #58: "Television"
October 21, 1949: #59: "Superstition"
October 28, 1949: #60: "Halloween Surprise Party"
November 4, 1949: #61: "Mother-in-Law"
November 11, 1949: #62: "Baby-Sitting"
November 18, 1949: #63: "Katy and Mr. Negley"
November 25, 1949: #64: "Quiz Show"
December 2, 1949: #65: "College Homecoming"

> Gracie Allen joined Lucille and Bob LeMond in the Jell-O commercial for this episode.

December 9, 1949: #66: "The French Lessons"
December 16, 1949: #67: "George's Christmas Present"

December 23, 1949: #68: "The Sleigh Ride"
December 30, 1949: #69: "Liz and George Handcuffed"
January 6, 1950: #70: "The Question of Another Woman"
January 13, 1950: #71: "Liz Teaches Iris to Drive"
January 20, 1950: #72: "Liz and the Green Wig"
January 27, 1950: #73: "Liz Writes a Song"
February 3, 1950: #74: "The Country Club Dance"
February 10, 1950: #75: "Mrs. Cooper's Boyfriend"
February 17, 1950: #76: "Liz Teaches the Samba"
February 24, 1950: #77: "Liz Redecorates the House"
March 5, 1950: #78: "Women's Rights, Part One"
March 12, 1950: #79: "Women's Rights, Part Two"
March 19, 1950: #80: "The Wills"
March 26, 1950: #81: "Liz's Radio Script"
    Mary Jane Croft works with Lucille Ball for the first time in this episode.
April 2, 1950: #82: "April Fool"
April 9, 1950: #83: "Hobbies"
April 16, 1950: #84: "Anniversary"
April 23, 1950: #85: "Liz Appears on Television"
April 30, 1950: #86: "Spring Housecleaning"
May 7, 1950: #87: "The Health Farm"
May 14, 1950: #88: "Numerology"
May 21, 1950: #89: "Mrs. Cooper Thinks Liz Is Pregnant"
May 28, 1950: #90: "Selling Dresses"
June 4, 1950: #91: "George Is Messy"
June 11, 1950: #92: "Liz Learns to Swim"
June 18, 1950: #93: "Be a Pal"
June 25, 1950: #94: "Dancing Lessons"

Season Three:
September 2, 1950: #95: "Husbands Are Sloppy Dressers"
September 9, 1950: #96: "Gossip"
September 16, 1950: #97: "Movies"
September 23, 1950: #98: "Fuller Brush Show"
    This episode was written to promote Lucy's film *The Fuller Brush Girl,*
    which had been released on September 15, 1950.
October 7, 1950: #99: "Liz Becomes a Sculptress"
October 14, 1950: #100: "Liz Cooks Dinner for Twelve"
October 21, 1950: #101: "Safety Drive"
October 28, 1950: #102: "The Football Game"
November 4, 1950: #103: "The Two Mrs. Coopers"

November 11, 1950: #104: "Vacation from Marriage"
November 18, 1950: #105: "Liz Goes to Night School"
November 25, 1950: #106: "Liz's Birthday"
December 2, 1950: #107: "Trying to Marry Off Peggy Martin"
December 9, 1950: #108: "Trying to Cash the Prize Check"
December 16, 1950: #109: "The Christmas Cards"
December 23, 1950: #110: "The Christmas Stag"
December 30, 1950: #111: "Liz Has the Flimjabs"
January 6, 1951: #112: "Liz Substitutes in a Club Play"
January 13, 1951: #113: "The Cuckoo Clock"
January 20, 1951: #114: "Liz Stretches the Truth"
January 27, 1951: #115: "George Is Drafted—Liz's Baby"
February 3, 1951: #116: "Liz's Inferiority Complex"
February 10, 1951: #117: "The Misunderstanding of the Black Eye"
February 17, 1951: #118: "Renewal of Driver's License"
February 24, 1951: #119: "The Two Mothers-in-Law"
March 3, 1951: #120: "The Passports"
March 10, 1951: #121: "The Surprise Party"
March 17, 1951: #122: "Liz Hires a New Secretary for George"
March 24, 1951: #123: "Iris and Liz's Easter"
March 31, 1951: #124: "The April Fool Joke"

9

"The Lucy Ricardo Show"

I Love Lucy

Background

ucille Ball and Desi Arnaz had been married for ten years and were looking for a way to work together; the new medium of television seemed like the best idea. Since July 1948, Lucy had been starring in *My Favorite Husband,* a radio situation comedy for CBS. Although CBS was interested in having Lucy move over to television, they did not want Desi. Their belief that the American people would not buy the redhead and the Cuban as a married couple led the Arnazes to do a stage act to show the network that the public would indeed go for them. CBS still had no interest.

Lucy and Desi were advised that they should produce their own audition show, so they could cultivate interest from other networks. This meant, however, that they could not use Lucy's radio team who were under exclusive contract to CBS. A script in which Lucy and Desi would play fictionalized versions of themselves was nixed because the Arnazes thought the public believed Hollywood showbiz couples have no problems. NBC became interested in the Ball-Arnaz teaming, and that was all CBS had to hear to get interested again. A deal was reached in which the *Husband* team of Jess Oppenheimer, Madelyn Pugh, and Bob Carroll Jr. could create a situation comedy pilot for the Arnazes for CBS.

Oppenheimer came up with the concept of a bandleader married to a woman who wants a career in show business, even though he wants a wife who is just a wife. Along with Pugh and Carroll, Oppenheimer wrote the script for the audition show. They originally named the characters Lucy and Larry Lopez, but changed Desi's name to Ricky Ricardo to avoid confusion with another Latin American bandleader, Vincent Lopez. Ralph Levy directed the pilot, which was done on kinescope at CBS Columbia Square on Sunset Boulevard, where they did *My Favorite Husband.* Several weeks later, the show was sold to the Milton Biow agency whose client, Philip Morris Cigarettes, would sponsor the series.

In the meantime, the writers decided to place the focus of the program on the marriage of the Ricardos rather than on Ricky's show business career. The original concept was to make Ricky's agent, Jerry, a regular character (Jerry Hausner played him in the pilot), but with the change in direction, he would only show up intermittently during the early years of the show. Instead, the writers decided to create an older married couple for the Ricardos to be friends with, similar to the characters of the Atterburys on *My Favorite Husband*. They would be the Ricardos' landlords, Fred and Ethel Mertz, the surname coming from a family Madelyn Pugh knew growing up in Indiana. The idea was to hire the same actors who had played the Atterburys, Gale Gordon and Bea Benaderet, but both had to pass on the offer.

CBS expected *I Love Lucy* to be done live from New York, which came as a shock to the Arnazes and everyone else associated with the show. This was a time prior to the creation of the coaxial cable that allowed a program to be aired from coast to coast. Only part of the country could see the show live, while the others were obliged to wait for a lower quality kinescope. CBS was adamant that the show had to be done from Manhattan because the majority of television viewers were on the East Coast. Lucy and Desi, however, refused to move to New York. Instead, Desi suggested that the show be done on film so that the technical quality of the episodes would be the same no matter what part of the country it was being shown. Because it would cost an additional $3,000 an episode to film the show, Lucy and Desi agreed to cut their joint salary of $5,000 a week to $3,000, asking CBS to pick up the difference. Desi also asked for complete ownership of *I Love Lucy*. CBS agreed to all of this, so Desilu ended up owning 80 percent of the series, with Jess Oppenheimer having 20 percent per an earlier agreement with the network. Oppenheimer then gave his two fellow writers 5 percent out of his share.

Desi and Jess Oppenheimer knew that Lucy worked best in front of an audience, so it was decided to film the show in front of a live studio audience. This was a revolutionary idea, as it had never done by a situation comedy before. Karl Freund—the cinematographer on two of Lucy's MGM films, *Du Barry Was a Lady* and *Without Love*, and an Oscar winner for 1937's *The Good Earth*—was approached to become the show's directory of photography. He accepted the job for the challenge and certainly not for the money. (Once he came onboard, he worked exclusively on the small screen from that point on.) It was decided to film it with three cameras to get different shots that could be edited together. Four cameras were actually used

Lucy and Ethel announce to their husbands that they will be taking up golf in the *I Love Lucy* episode "The Golf Game."

for the first show. The original idea was to film the show straight through like a play. The first episode was done this way, with actors wearing one costume over another, so they did not have to stop, instead doing quick changes off set. After the first filming, it was evident that this approach was unfeasible, as it would prevent the writers from coming up with outlandish situations. It was decided that the audience would understand if they had to stop filming in order to change scenes. To keep them engaged, the Desi Arnaz Orchestra would entertain them during the breaks.

Marc Daniels, a director who had a good deal of television experience, was hired to helm the show. Jess Oppenheimer would serve as producer in addition to being head writer. William Frawley was cast as Fred Mertz after he called up Lucy and asked if there was a part for him on her show. Vivian Vance won the role of Ethel based on her performance in the play *The Voice of the Turtle*, which Marc Daniels took Desi and Jess Oppenheimer to see during its run in La Jolla.

CBS placed *I Love Lucy* on their Monday night schedule at 9:00 right after the number one show in the country, *Arthur Godfrey's Talent Scouts*. Godfrey's enthusiastic endorsement of the new show was extremely helpful, and Lucy's series quickly became a ratings smash. By the end of the season, *I Love Lucy* was ranked third after Godfrey and Milton Berle's *Texaco Star Theatre*.

As the first season came to a close, Lucy discovered she was pregnant again. The Arnazes feared that they would have to end the show, but Jess Oppenheimer thought it would be a terrific plotline if Lucy Ricardo had a baby too. CBS was afraid that viewers might be offended, so Desilu had each of the scripts dealing with Lucy's pregnancy looked over by a rabbi, a priest, and a minister to see if they thought there was anything that might be construed as offensive. They passed with flying colors, and Lucy's television pregnancy became a worldwide phenomenon. The writers decided to have Lucy Ricardo have a boy for several reasons. The Arnazes thought their real child, little Lucie, would be hurt if they had a daughter on the show that was not her; Desi believed having a boy on television might be his only chance of having a son; and the writers thought a male child would lead to funnier possibilities. On January 19, 1953, Lucille Ball gave birth to her son, Desi Jr., in the morning, and Lucy Ricardo gave birth to her son, Ricky Jr., that night. That episode, "Lucy Goes to the Hospital," was viewed by a record 44 million people. This number is even more impressive when just nine months earlier, the episode "The Marriage License" became the first television show to be viewed by over 10 million people. More people watched *I Love Lucy* on that January night than saw Dwight Eisenhower's inauguration as President of the United States the following day. Little Ricky was played by James John Ganzer in "Lucy Goes to the Hospital," but beginning with "No Children Allowed," Richard Lee and Ronald Lee Simmons played the role.

William Asher replaced Marc Daniels as the show's director after the first 38 shows were filmed. Five episodes shot earlier in the season were aired after the birth of the baby while Lucy was on maternity leave. Episodes from the first season with newly filmed flashback openings were re-aired throughout the season before and after the baby's arrival. A feature film version of *I Love Lucy* was created that strung together three first-season episodes ("The Benefit," "Breaking the Lease," and "The Ballet") with new footage (including part of a musical number that was actually from the second season's "The Anniversary Present"). In order to solve the problem of the studio audience laughter being heard throughout the show, which would sound out of place in a movie, it was decided that the film would be bookended by sequences involving the audience seeing an *I Love Lucy* episode being filmed. This new footage was shot the same night as the episode "The Handcuffs." The movie version of *I Love Lucy* was shelved, however, when the Arnazes signed with MGM to do a genuine theatrical feature, *The Long, Long Trailer*, since Metro did not want the other film to compete with theirs.

The fourth season brought a fresh outlook to the series when the Ricardos and the Mertzes went to Hollywood. With the start of the fifth season, Bob Schiller and Bob Weiskopf were added to the writing staff, joining Oppenheimer, Pugh, and Carroll, who had already written 127 episodes by themselves. James V. Kern also joined the company as director. When Jess Oppenheimer announced he was leaving at the end of season five to accept an executive position at NBC, Desi assumed his producer responsibilities for season six. During the fifth season, *I Love Lucy* found itself *not* in first place for the first time since the first season. Quiz shows were sweeping the nation, putting *The $64,000 Question* in the number one Nielsen spot and *I Love Lucy* in second.

For the sixth season, the writers decided to expand Little Ricky's role and make him slightly older than he would actually be, based on his 1953 date of birth. Twins Michael and Joseph Mayer had been playing the role since the beginning of the third season. Five-year-old Keith Thibodeaux auditioned to take over the part. Keith had been drumming since he was a year old and took up the instrument professionally at the age of three. Everyone loved the idea of having Little Ricky be a drummer, and they also thought Keith looked like he could be Desi's son, which secured him the part. For a change of scenery, the writers eventually had the Ricardos and the Mertzes move from their Manhattan digs to Westport, Connecticut. William Asher returned to the show and directed the final thirteen episodes.

Lucy and Desi decided to end the show at the close of the sixth season, but agreed to come back for the following season in the occasional hour-long special. *I Love Lucy* ended its run as the number one show in the nation.

Storyline

Lucille Esmeralda McGillicuddy was born in West Jamestown (there is no actual *West* Jamestown), New York on August 6, 1921. Of Scottish descent, her ancestors came from the village of Kildoonan, Scotland. She was raised in Jamestown, New York and attended Celeron High School, where she played saxophone in the school band because she was in love with a football player and the band got to go on trips with the team. Lucy later said she graduated from Jamestown High School. Lucy lived in Jamestown until she was seventeen. She then went to New York and worked as a stenographer.

The Lucille Ball-Desi Arnaz Show episode "Lucy Takes a Cruise to Havana" shows how Lucy and her co-worker Susie McNamara (Ann Sothern) took a cruise to Havana, where Lucy met Ricky Ricardo, who owned a taxi service with his friend Carlos Garcia (Cesar Romero). Ricky and Carlos ended up being hired by Rudy Vallee as members of his "Connecticut Yankees" after Lucy introduced them to Vallee. Ricky, however, was traded to Xavier Cugat for a xylophone player because Vallee claimed Ricky could not be understood when he sang "The Whiffenpoof Song." This storyline, however, is negated in the *I Love Lucy* episode "Don Juan and the Starlets," where Lucy claims that she met Ricky on a blind date arranged by her friend Marion Strong.

Ricardo Alberto Fernando Ricardo y de Acha III (also given as Enrique Alberto Ricardo y de Acha III) was born in Havana, Cuba, one of six brothers. Ricky began his career in show business when he was twelve years old. Lucy and Ricky married at the Byram River Beagle Club in Greenwich, Connecticut. Ricky served in the army during World War II and earned the Good Conduct medal. Shortly after their marriage, the Ricardos moved to 623 East 68th Street in New York City (although it is implied that they married years earlier, Ricky gives the date of their move as August 6, 1948 in "The Fur Coat") into an apartment building owned by Fred and Ethel Mertz. As seen in "Lucy Takes a Cruise to Havana," the Mertzes were on the same boat as Lucy and the foursome met then. The Ricardos' phone number is alternately given as MUrray Hill 5-9975, CIrcle 7-2099, and MUrray Hill 5-9099.

Frederick Hobart Mertz was from Steubenville, Ohio, where he grew up on a farm. He had a brother, and his mother later lived in Indiana. During World War I, he was stationed in France. Fred was a vaudeville performer, where he had an act with Barney (originally known as Ted) Kurtz. (Charles Winninger played him in the episode "Mertz and Kurtz.") He later had an act with his wife, Ethel.

Ethel Potter (whose middle name was alternately given as Louise, Roberta, and Mae) was from Albuquerque, New Mexico. Her father, Will Potter, owned a sweet shop and soda fountain in the town. Ethel was named "Miss Albuquerque" and frequently performed at the Albuquerque Little Theatre. In New York, Lucy and Ethel were members, and later served as co-presidents, of the Wednesday Afternoon Fine Arts League. The Mertzes' apartment number alternated as 3A, 3B, and 3C. Their telephone number was given as both PLaza 5-6098 and SChuyler 4-8098.

Lucy and Ricky lived in apartment 4A. Other residents of 623 East 68th Street were Matilda Trumbull (Elizabeth Patterson), who would become the Ricardos' permanent babysitter; Bill and Grace Foster (Richard Reeves and Gloria Blondell); Miss Lewis (Bea Benaderet); and Mrs. Benson (Norma Varden) and her husband (mentioned but never seen).

Ricky's earlier career highlights included the Broadway production of *Too Many Girls* and performing at the Copacabana. He was held over indefinitely at the Tropicana Club and eventually became the club's manager.

After eleven years of marriage, Lucy discovered that she was pregnant and gave birth to Ricky Ricardo Jr. Following the baby's birth, the Ricardos switched apartments with downstairs neighbors the Bensons. The larger apartment was originally 3B, but later changed to 3D. (This allowed for a joke about the then-current craze for 3-Dimensional movies in the episode "Lucy Tells the Truth," when Lucy informs a casting director—played by frequent Lucy guest Charles Lane—that she "was in 3D.")

Ricky was selected for the title role in Metro-Goldwyn-Mayer's $3 million Technicolor spectacle *Don Juan*. The Ricardos and the Mertzes, joined by Lucy's mother (whose first name is never given), went to Hollywood, where they stayed at the Beverly Palms Hotel. (The Ricardos took up residence in room 315. The Mertzes had room 317, but after feuding with the Ricardos and checking out in "Ricky Sells the Car," they had room 372.) *Don Juan* was shelved, but MGM found another picture to star Ricky in (the nameless film would eventually open at the Radio City Music Hall).

The Ricky Ricardo Orchestra went on a European tour, stopping in London, Paris, Switzerland, Italy, and the French Riviera. Fred Mertz served as Ricky's band manager, having managed his own vaudeville career. An engagement at the swanky Eden Roc Hotel in Miami Beach followed, where Ricky and the band were featured in the documentary *The Florida Story*. Ricky bought a controlling interest in the Tropicana and renamed it Ricky Ricardo's Club Babalu, after his signature song. Little Ricky became a fine drummer in his own right.

For their sixteenth wedding anniversary, Ricky bought Lucy a house in Westport, Connecticut that was owned by Joe and Eleanor Spaulding (Frank Wilcox and Eleanor Audley). The Ricardos had visited their friends Harry and Grace Munson, who lived in the same town, and Lucy fell in love with the house. Fred rented the Ricardos apartment to a newlywed couple, the Taylors (Gene Reynolds and Mary Ellen Kaye). The Mertzes soon made Mrs. Trumbull's (unseen) sister manager of their apartment house and moved into the Ricardos' guesthouse. The two couples went into the egg business together. Living next door to the Ricardos were Ralph and Betty Ramsey (Frank Nelson and Mary Jane Croft), who had a son, Bruce (Ray Farrell), the same age as Little Ricky. Ralph was an advertising executive at the firm of Burton, Washman, and Ramsey. Ethel initially disliked Betty Ramsey, but the two hit it off when they discovered that they were both raised in Albuquerque, attended Albuquerque Elementary School, and their fathers, Leslie Foster and Will Potter, were members of the same lodge. Betty was a member of the Westport Historical Society, which Lucy later joined as well.

(The episodes are listed in the order in which they aired, while the numbers correspond to the order in which they were produced.)

Season One: Nielsen Ratings Rank: #3
October 15, 1951: #2: "The Girls Want to Go to a Nightclub"
October 22, 1951: #3: "Be a Pal"
October 29, 1951: #4: "The Diet"
November 5, 1951: #1: "Lucy Thinks Ricky Is Trying to Murder Her"
November 12, 1951: #5: "The Quiz Show"
　　On October 21, 1952, this would be the first episode of the series to
　　be rerun.
November 19, 1951: #6: "The Audition"
November 26, 1951: #7: "The Séance"
December 3, 1951: #8: "Men Are Messy"
December 10, 1951: #10: "The Fur Coat"
December 17, 1951: #11: "Lucy Is Jealous of a Girl Dancer"
December 24, 1951: #9: "Drafted"
December 31, 1951: #12: "The Adagio"
January 7, 1952: #13: "The Benefit"
January 14, 1952: #14: "The Amateur Hour"
January 21, 1952: #15: "Lucy Plays Cupid"
January 28, 1952: #16: "Lucy Fakes Illness"
February 4, 1952: #17: "Lucy Writes a Play"
February 11, 1952: #18: "Breaking the Lease"
February 18, 1952: #19: "The Ballet"
February 25, 1952: #20: "The Young Fans"
March 3, 1952: #21: "New Neighbors"
March 10, 1952: #22: "Fred and Ethel Fight"
March 17, 1952: #23: "The Moustache"
March 24, 1952: #24: "The Gossip"
March 31, 1952: #25: "Pioneer Women"
April 7, 1952: #26: "The Marriage License"
　　The first television program to be viewed by over 10 million people.
April 14, 1952: #27: "The Kleptomaniac"
April 21, 1952: #28: "Cuban Pals"
April 28, 1952: #29: "The Freezer"
May 5, 1952: #30: "Lucy Does a TV Commercial"
May 12, 1952: #31: "The Publicity Agent"

May 19, 1952: #32: "Lucy Gets Ricky on the Radio"
May 26, 1952: #33: "Lucy's Schedule"
   Gale Gordon appears in a *Lucy* show for the first time with this episode.
June 2, 1952: #34: "Ricky Thinks He's Getting Bald"
June 9, 1952: #35: "Ricky Asks for a Raise"

Season Two: Nielsen Ratings Rank: #1
September 15, 1952: #39: "Job Switching"
September 22, 1952: #40: "The Saxophone"
September 29, 1952: #36: "The Anniversary Present"
October 6, 1952: #37: "The Handcuffs"
   Scenes for the *I Love Lucy* feature film were filmed the night of this
   episode.
October 13, 1952: #38: "The Operetta"
October 27, 1952: #41: "Vacation from Marriage"
November 10, 1952: #42: "The Courtroom"
November 24, 1952: #43: "Redecorating"
December 1, 1952: #44: "Ricky Loses His Voice"
December 8, 1952: #50: "Lucy Is Enceinte"
December 15, 1952: #51: "Pregnant Women Are Unpredictable"
December 22, 1952: #52: "Lucy's Show Biz Swan Song"
December 29, 1952: #53: "Lucy Hires an English Tutor"
January 5, 1953: #53: "Ricky Has Labor Pains"
January 12, 1953: #55: "Lucy Becomes a Sculptress"
January 19, 1953: #56: "Lucy Goes to the Hospital"
   The highest-rated television event up to that time.
January 26, 1953: #45: "Sales Resistance"
February 2, 1953: #46: "The Inferiority Complex"
February 16, 1953: #47: "The Club Election"
   Doris Singleton's first show, here as Lillian Appleby. Her name will later
   be changed to Caroline.
March 9, 1953: #48: "The Black Eye"
March 30, 1953: #49: "Lucy Changes Her Mind"
April 20, 1953: #57: "No Children Allowed"
   The first of Elizabeth Patterson's ten appearances as Mrs. Trumbull.
April 27, 1953: #58: "Lucy Hires a Maid"
May 4, 1953: #59: "The Indian Show"
May 11, 1953: #60: "Lucy's Last Birthday"
May 18, 1953: #61: "The Ricardos Change Apartments"
May 25, 1953: #62: "Lucy Is Matchmaker"
June 1, 1953: #63: "Lucy Wants New Furniture"

June 8, 1953: #64: "The Camping Trip"
June 22, 1953: #66: "Ricky and Fred Are TV Fans"
June 29, 1953: #67: "Never Do Business with Friends"

Season Three: Nielsen Ratings Rank: #1
October 5, 1953: #65: "Ricky's *Life* Story"
   This episode was originally supposed to air on June 15, 1953, but was rescheduled because of *The Ford 50th Anniversary Show*, which was telecast on both CBS and NBC.
October 12, 1953: #68: "The Girls Go Into Business"
   This episode was filmed during Lucy's "Red Scare."
October 19, 1953: #69: "Lucy and Ethel Buy the Same Dress"
October 26, 1953: #70: "Equal Rights"
November 2, 1953: #71: "Baby Pictures"
November 9, 1953: #72: "Lucy Tells the Truth"
November 16, 1953: #73: "The French Revue"
November 23, 1953: #74: "Redecorating the Mertzes' Apartment"
November 30, 1953: #75: "Too Many Crooks"
December 7, 1953: #76: "Changing the Boys' Wardrobe"
December 14, 1953: #77: "Lucy Has Her Eyes Examined"
December 21, 1953: #78: "Ricky's Old Girlfriend"
January 11, 1954: #79: "The Million-Dollar Idea"
January 18, 1954: #80: "Ricky Minds the Baby"
January 25, 1954: #81: "The Charm School"
February 1, 1954: #82: "Sentimental Anniversary"
February 8, 1954: #83: "Fan Magazine Interview"
February 15, 1954: #84: "Oil Wells"
February 22, 1954: #85: "Ricky Loses His Temper"
March 1, 1954: #86: "Home Movies"
March 8, 1954: #87: "Bonus Bucks"
March 22, 1954: #88: "Ricky's Hawaiian Vacation"
March 29, 1954: #89: "Lucy Is Envious"
   This marks Mary Jane Croft's first appearance on a *Lucy* show.
April 5, 1954: #90: "Lucy Writes a Novel"
April 12, 1954: #91: "Lucy's Club Dance"
April 19, 1954: #93: "The Black Wig"
April 26, 1954: #92: "The Diner"
May 3, 1954: #94: "Tennessee Ernie Visits"
May 10, 1954: #95: "Tennessee Ernie Hangs On"
May 17, 1954: #96: "The Golf Game"
May 24, 1954: #97: "The Sublease"

Season Four: Nielsen Ratings Rank: #1

October 4, 1954: #100: "The Business Manager"

October 11, 1954: #102: "Mertz and Kurtz"

October 18, 1954: #98: "Lucy Cries Wolf"

October 25, 1954: #99: "The Matchmaker"

November 1, 1954: #101: "Mr. and Mrs. TV Show"
> This episode was preempted for a message from the Republican Party and did not air in a majority of places until April 11, 1954.

November 8, 1954: #103: "Ricky's Movie Offer"

November 15, 1954: #104: "Ricky's Screen Test"

November 22, 1954: #105: "Lucy's Mother-in-Law"
> William Asher received a Directors' Guild of America Award nomination for this episode.

November 29, 1954: #106: "Ethel's Birthday"

December 6, 1954: #107: "Ricky's Contract"

December 13, 1954: #108: "Getting Ready"

January 3, 1955: #109: "Lucy Learns to Drive"

January 10, 1955: #110: "California, Here We Come"
> Kathryn Card makes her first appearance as Lucy's mother, Mrs. McGillicuddy.

January 17, 1955: #111: "First Stop"

January 24, 1955: #112: "Tennessee Bound"

January 31, 1955: #113: "Ethel's Home Town"

February 7, 1955: #114: "LA at Last!"
> Writers Jess Oppenheimer, Madelyn Pugh, and Bob Carroll Jr. received an Emmy nomination for this episode.

February 14, 1955: #115: "Don Juan and the Starlets"

February 21, 1955: #116: "Lucy Gets in Pictures"

February 28, 1955: #117: "The Fashion Show"

March 14, 1955: #118: "The Hedda Hopper Story"

March 21, 1955: #119: "*Don Juan* Is Shelved"

March 28, 1955: #120: "Bull Fight Dance"

April 4, 1955: #121: "Hollywood Anniversary"

April 18, 1955: #122: "The Star Upstairs"

April 25, 1955: #123: "In Palm Springs"

May 2, 1955: #125: "The Dancing Star"

May 9, 1955: #124: "Harpo Marx"

May 16: 1955 #126: "Ricky Needs an Agent"

May 30, 1955 #127: "The Tour"

Season Five: Nielsen Ratings Rank: #1
October 3, 1955: #128: "Lucy Visits Grauman's"
    The first episode with Bob Schiller and Bob Weiskopf as part of the
    writing team.
October 10, 1955: #129: "Lucy and John Wayne"
October 17, 1955: #130: "Lucy and the Dummy"
October 24, 1955: #131: "Ricky Sells the Car"
October 31, 1955: #132: "The Great Train Robbery"
November 7, 1955: #133: "Homecoming"
November 14, 1955: #134: "The Ricardos Are Interviewed"
November 28, 1955: #135: "Lucy Goes to a Rodeo"
December 5, 1955: #136: "Nursery School"
December 12, 1955: #137: "Ricky's European Booking"
December 19, 1955: #138: "The Passports"
January 2, 1956: #139: "Staten Island Ferry"
January 16, 1956: #140: "Bon Voyage"
January 23, 1956: #141: "Second Honeymoon"
January 30, 1956: #142: "Lucy Meets the Queen"
February 6, 1956: #143: "The Fox Hunt"
February 20, 1956: #144: "Lucy Goes to Scotland"
February 27, 1956: #145: "Paris At Last"
March 5, 1956: #146: "Lucy Meets Charles Boyer"
March 19, 1956: #147: "Lucy Gets a Paris Gown"
March 26, 1956: #148: "Lucy in the Swiss Alps"
April 9, 1956: #149: "Lucy Gets Homesick in Italy"
April 16, 1956: #150: "Lucy's Italian Movie"
April 23, 1956: #151: "Lucy's Bicycle Trip"
May 7, 1956: #152: "Lucy Goes to Monte Carlo"
May 14, 1956: #153: "Return Home from Europe"
    The final episode with Jess Oppenheimer as producer and head writer.

Season Six: Nielsen Ratings Rank: #1
October 1, 1956: #154: "Lucy and Bob Hope"
    Keith Thibodeaux's first appearance as Little Ricky.
October 8, 1956: #157: "Little Ricky Learns to Play the Drums"
October 15, 1956: #155: "Lucy Meets Orson Welles"
October 22, 1956: #156: "Little Ricky Gets Stage Fright"
October 29, 1956: #158: "Visitor from Italy"
November 12, 1956: #159: "Off to Florida"
November 19, 1956: #160: "Deep Sea Fishing"
November 26, 1956: #161: "Desert Island"

December 3, 1956: #162: "The Ricardos Visit Cuba"
December 17, 1956: #163: "Little Ricky's School Pageant"
December 24, 1956: "Christmas Show"
    This episode was not included in the later syndication package.
January 7, 1957: #164: "Lucy and the Loving Cup"
January 14, 1957: #166: "Lucy and Superman"
January 21, 1957: #165: "Little Ricky Gets a Dog"
January 28, 1957: #167: "Lucy Wants to Move to the Country"
February 4, 1957: #168: "Lucy Hates to Leave"
February 11, 1957: #169: "Lucy Misses the Mertzes"
February 18, 1957: #170: "Lucy Gets Chummy with the Neighbors"
March 4, 1957: #171: "Lucy Raises Chickens"
March 11, 1957: #172: "Lucy Does the Tango"
March 18, 1957: #173: "Ragtime Band"
March 25, 1957: #174: "Lucy's Night in Town"
April 1, 1957: #175: "Housewarming"
April 8, 1957: #176: "Building a Bar-B-Q"
April 22, 1957: #177: "Country Club Dance"
April 29, 1957: #178: "Lucy Raises Tulips"
May 6, 1957: #179: "The Ricardos Dedicate a Statue"
    Desi Jr. appears as an extra in the final scene. Lucie Arnaz, however,
    does not.

10

"Cook the Meals, Do the Dishes, Make the Beds, Dust the House"

The Lucille Ball-Desi Arnaz Show

Background

L ucy and Desi were tired of the grind of a weekly television series and decided to instead continue in their beloved personas in an occasional hour-long format. Desi had considered the idea for a couple of years, but CBS continually pressed for more half-hour *I Love Lucy* shows. The Ford Motor Company agreed to sponsor five, large-budget hour-long shows for the 1957–58 season. Bert Granet, who had written several of Lucy's early RKO vehicles, was hired to produce the show. Former *I Love Lucy* assistant director Jerry Thorpe was promoted to director. Hedda Hopper, Ann Sothern (in her *Private Secretary* role of Susie McNamara), Cesar Romero, and Rudy Vallee were slated to be guest stars for the premiere installment, which would be a flashback showing how Lucy and Ricky first met.

During rehearsals for "Lucy Takes a Cruise to Havana," it was realized that the show was running longer than the intended hour-long slot, but Desi felt it was simply too good to cut. Desi called up CBS head William S. Paley and told him that they had a seventy-five minute show. Paley said they had to either cut or add fifteen minutes, but Desi was certain either way would louse up the show. The series that would follow the premiere Lucy-Desi show was the low-rated *The United States Steel Hour,* so Desi asked if he could have fifteen minutes of *their* time. Paley opted to stay out of the matter, but told Desi he was free to contact US Steel himself. Explaining the situation, Desi asked if they could have the first fifteen minutes of the *Steel Hour* time slot (which Ford would pay for). At the end of the Lucy show, Desi would tell the audience to stay tuned to an outstanding install-ment of *The United States Steel Hour,* thereby guaranteeing them high ratings. US Steel acquiesced. "Lucy Takes a Cruise to Havana" received tremen-dous ratings, and the *Steel Hour* garnered its highest ratings ever. (That epi-sode, "The Locked Door," starred one of Lucy's *Dance, Girl, Dance* co-stars, Ralph Bellamy.)

Desilu created an anthology series to be sponsored by Westinghouse, *The Westinghouse Desilu Playhouse,* with five Lucy-Desi shows scheduled to air on the program for the 1958–59 season. Bob Carroll Jr. and Madelyn Martin announced that they would not be returning to write more shows; Madelyn had a new baby at home (she had married Desilu film editor and future producer Quinn Martin), and Bob wanted to move to Europe. For the first Lucy-Desi show of the new season, Bob Schiller and Bob Weiskopf brought in fellow comedy writer Everett Freeman to help them out. Freeman soon realized that he wasn't needed and left. Bob and Madelyn decided to come back by the time the first episode had finished production. Bob was not as content living in Europe as he was visiting there, and Desi had a nursery built off of Madelyn's office for her son. Bob and Madelyn were credited as "script consultants" for the remaining shows.

Around this time, Lucy and Desi popped up on several other programs as Lucy and Ricky Ricardo to pay back the guest stars who appeared on their shows. The two were seen as the Ricardos in *The Danny Thomas Show* episode "Lucy Upsets the Williams Household" (January 5, 1959). On October 5, 1959, Lucy Ricardo appeared for the first and only time without Ricky when Lucille guest starred on *The Ann Sothern Show* in an episode entitled "The Lucy Story." On November 1, 1959, Lucy and Desi played Lucy and Ricky on NBC's *The Sunday Showcase: The Milton Berle Special.*

As time went on, the live studio audience, which had been so important during the early days, was phased out. In addition to his duties as execu-tive producer, Desi directed the three hour-long shows produced for the 1959–60 season. "Lucy Meets the Mustache," guest starring Ernie Kovacs and Edie Adams, was the last time the Ricardos and the Mertzes were seen. Lucy filed for divorce the day after the show was filmed. When the show went into reruns, it carried the title *The Lucy-Desi Comedy Hour.*

Storyline

The Ricardos and the Mertzes continued to live in Westport, Connecticut, while Ricky and his orchestra performed in such places as Las Vegas, Alaska, and Japan. Lucy Ricardo finally achieved success in show business as the Girl Friday on *The Paul Douglas "Early Bird" Show,* only to realize that she was happier as a wife and mother. She returned to her normal home life.

Lucy and Ethel's plan to catch a glimpse of Bob Cummings did not go as smoothly as they had hoped in "The Ricardos Go to Japan," the penultimate *Lucille Ball – Desi Arnaz Show.*

Season One:

November 6, 1957: #1: "Lucy Takes a Cruise to Havana"

   This episode originally ran seventy-five minutes.

December 3, 1957: #2: "The Celebrity Next Door"

January 3, 1958: #3: "Lucy Hunts Uranium"

February 3, 1958: #4: "Lucy Wins a Racehorse"

April 14, 1958: #5: "Lucy Goes to Sun Valley"

   Lucie and Desi Arnaz Jr. are visible as extras in this installment.

Season Two:

October 6, 1958: #6: "Lucy Goes to Mexico"

December 1, 1958: #7: "Lucy Makes Room for Danny"

   Bert Granet received the Producers Guild of America Award for this installment.

February 9, 1959: #8: "Lucy Goes to Alaska"

April 13, 1959: #9: "Lucy Wants a Career"

June 8, 1959: #10: "Lucy's Summer Vacation"

Season Three:
September 25, 1959: #11: "Milton Berle Hides Out at the Ricardos"
    The first episode in which Desi Arnaz is credited as director.
November 27, 1959: #12: "The Ricardos Go to Japan"
April 1, 1960: #13: "Lucy Meets the Mustache"

"Impersonating a Secretary"

The Lucy Show

Background

I n 1962, Desilu, of which Lucy was still the vice president, was in trouble. Apart from *The Untouchables*, the company had no weekly series that would be picked up from the previous season to air during 1962–63. The obvious solution to placing Desilu back in the winners' circle was to have Lucille Ball star in another show. The announcement that she would possibly return to television made headlines in January 1962, a few short weeks after Lucy's poorly received CBS "comeback," *The Good Years*, a special teaming her with Henry Fonda.

In 1961, writer Irene Kampen wrote her first book, *Life without George*, based on her real life following her divorce from her husband. The mother of a teenage daughter, Christine, Irene decided to share her Ridgefield, Connecticut house with another divorced friend, Evelyn, and her son, Eric, in order to save on expenses. Desilu purchased the rights to the book shortly after publication. In February 1962, rumors floated about that Lucy and Ann Sothern might possibly star in a television series based on Kampen's book. However, by April, it was confirmed that Vivian Vance would be joining her old co-star on her new show.

The old *Lucy* writing team of Madelyn Martin, Bob Carroll Jr., Bob Schiller, and Bob Weiskopf were engaged to write the new series. Several changes were made from Kampen's story. Lucy would play a widow since her writers were certain viewers would not accept Lucy in the role of a divorcée, believing that confused audiences might think that Lucy Ricardo had divorced Ricky. Vivian would be a divorcée. The show was set in Danfield, New York rather than Kampen's Ridgefield, Connecticut (it was mentioned that the next town over was Ridgebury).

Candy Moore was cast as Lucy's daughter, Chris. Although Irene Kampen did not have any other children, the writers created a young son

Lucy with her two most frequent collaborators, Vivian Vance and Gale Gordon, in a scene from *The Lucy Show* episode "Lucy, the Stockholder."

for Lucy Carmichael and seven-year-old Jimmy Garrett won the role. For the part of Vivian's son, Sherman, Ralph Hart was selected. Dick Martin, of the successful comedy team of Rowan and Martin, who had starred in a sitcom pilot for Desilu, *My Wife's Brother*, was cast as Lucy's airline pilot neighbor, Harry Conners. Rowan and Martin were in great demand at the time, so Desilu needed to schedule the filming of Martin's episodes around his nightclub dates. He only appeared in eleven episodes before being written out of the show altogether. Frequent Lucy co-star Charles Lane was cast as Mr. Barnsdahl, the executor of Lucy's trust, but the character was only seen in four episodes, early in the first season. Jack Donohue, who had been the choreographer on some of Lucy's MGM films, was hired to direct. Elliott Lewis was the producer, and Desi was executive producer. Desi only performed in this capacity for the first fifteen episodes before he sold his stake in Desilu to his ex-wife.

For the second season, *The Lucy Show* started filming in color, although CBS continued to air the series in black and white. (It was assumed that the show would be more valuable in reruns if it was filmed in color.) Gale Gordon joined the cast as Theodore J. Mooney, who replaced Mr. Barnsdahl at the Danfield Bank. At the close of the second season, the series' original writing team departed. Bob Schiller and Bob Weiskopf left to write for *The Red Skelton Show*, and Madelyn Martin and Bob Carroll Jr. bowed out when Madelyn married Dr. Dick Davis and moved to Indiana. Lucy announced that the show would end after the second season, but CBS convinced her to return. This pattern would be repeated at the end of nearly every subsequent season. Milt Josefsberg, who had been Jack Benny's longtime head writer, was hired to take over the writing department. Among those joining him were Bob O'Brien, Garry Marshall and Jerry Belson, and Fred S. Fox and Iz Ellison (who had written several second-season episodes with Carroll and Martin).

Vivian returned for the third season on the condition that she would not appear every week; as a result, she was not featured in six of the twenty-six episodes produced. Ann Sothern was brought in for four episodes of the season as Countess Rosita Harrigan Framboise. At the end of the season Lucy yet again announced that she would be ending the show, but once again gave in. Vivian, however, was definitely not going to return.

The key factor in persuading Lucy to return was a change in format. Camera coordinator Maury Thompson and associate producer Tommy Thompson (no relation) approached her with a story outline they wrote about Lucy moving to California. Lucy loved the idea and saw this as a viable reason for the show to continue. Although the initial idea had Lucy portraying a new character, the owner of a magazine managed by a character played by Gale Gordon, it was decided to just continue with *The Lucy Show* characters after all. Lucy Carmichael moved to Los Angeles and discovered that Mooney had been transferred there. She eventually went to work as his secretary. The children were written out of the show (Jimmy Garrett appeared in the fourth-season premiere and one other episode, "Lucy, the Choirmaster," before leaving for good) and were thereafter rarely referenced. Mary Jane Croft appeared in the second episode of the new format as Lucy's neighbor, Mary Jane Lewis. Joan Blondell played another neighbor, Joan Brenner, in two episodes, and Ann Sothern returned as Rosie in three shows during season four. Mary Jane remained on the show as Lucy's sidekick for the rest of the series. Tommy Thompson would become the show's producer and Maury Thompson the director. Jack Donohue would return as director for the sixth season.

When Lucy sold Desilu in 1967, she sold the series as well. At the end of the sixth season, Lucy was ready yet again for a change. She had more than enough episodes to put into syndication and wanted to own her own show. It was decided that Lucy would come back for the 1968–69 season in a brand new series. *The Lucy Show* ended its six-year run at number two in the ratings. It was closely behind *The Andy Griffith Show,* which followed it on the CBS Monday lineup and was also ending. In January 1968, former series regular Dick Martin debuted *Rowan & Martin's Laugh-In,* which aired on NBC directly opposite *The Lucy Show.* Martin's new show would soon become a national phenomenon.

Storyline

Lucy Carmichael was from Jamestown, New York. Her maiden name is given as Taylor in "Lucy's College Reunion," but she later says it is McGillicuddy in "Lucy and John Wayne." Lucy is of Irish and Scottish descent. She has a brother, Fred, whose wife's name is Zo, and two sisters: Cleo, whose husband's name is Cecil, and Marge (Janet Waldo), who is married to Hughie (Peter Marshall). Lucy learned to play "Glow Worm" on an E flat alto sax when she was in the eighth grade. She attended Jamestown High School and won a silver cup as the nineteenth runner-up in a baton twirling competition. One of Lucy's close friends in high school was Rosita "Rosie" Harrigan (Ann Sothern), who invited Lucy to go to Paris with her. Lucy chose to go to Poughkeepsie instead, while Rosie met and married a count while in France.

According to the episode "Lucy's College Reunion," Lucy graduated from (fictitious) Milroy University. This would be contradicted in later seasons. In "Lucy, the Babysitter," she says she has had two years of business college, while in "Lucy Gets Her Diploma," she says she never graduated from high school because she got the mumps right before her final examinations senior year. Lucy graduated top of her class in secretarial school; there was only one other student in the class. During World War II, Lucy served in the WAVES. It was there she met best friend Vivian.

Vivian Tuttle (Vivian Vance) graduated from Shortridge High School and went to Kansas State University. She and Lucy worked as typists in the Navy purchasing department. Lucy married Mr. Carmichael (because the title of Irene Kampen's book, *Life without George,* was seen in the end credits, it might be assumed that he was called George, but no name was ever given) and had two children, a daughter, Chris, and son, Jerry. Vivian married Ralph Bagley and had a son, Sherman. After the Bagleys divorced and Lucy's husband died, Viv and Sherman moved into Lucy's house at 321 Post Road, Danfield, New York (telephone number KL 5-4320). Danfield (the only fictional town Lucy would "live in" on any of her series) is located in Westchester County by New Rochelle and (the also fictitious) Ridgebury.

Lucy and Viv served as den mothers for Jerry and Sherman's Cub Scout troop (troop 57, den 8). Chris, who attended Danfield High School, was a drum majorette cheering on the Danfield Bears. Chris had her first job as a soda jerk at Wilbur's Ice Cream Parlor alongside her best friend Cynthia (Lucie Arnaz).

Living next door to Lucy and Viv was Harry Conners (Dick Martin), an airline pilot. Lucy and Harry dated frequently, but not steadily. Due to his job, Harry was regularly out of town. Viv's regular boyfriend was business-man Eddie Collins (Don Briggs).

Lucy's late husband left her a trust fund, which was overseen by Mr. Barnsdahl (Charles Lane). Her husband's will stated that Mr. Barnsdahl was not permitted to advance Lucy even small amounts of money no matter what tricks she pulled. Mr. Barnsdahl eventually left his position as pres-ident of the Danfield Bank and was succeeded by Theodore J. Mooney. Mooney and his wife, Irma (spoken of but never seen), had three chil-dren—a daughter Rosemary, who was married and lived in Trenton, New Jersey; a teenage son Bob (Eddie Applegate), whose name was changed to Ted (Michael J. Pollard); and another son, Arnold (Barry Livingston, later Teddy Eccles). The Mooney family lived only a couple of blocks away from Lucy, at 429 Elm Street.

Lucy was the captain of the all-female Danfield Volunteer Fire Department with Viv serving as her lieutenant. Other members includ-ed Audrey Simmons (Mary Jane Croft), Thelma Green (Carole Cook), Dorothy Boyer (Dorothy Konrad), and Frances (Mary Wickes). Apart from Harry Conners, Lucy's boyfriends in Danfield included athletic Bill King (Keith Andes), golf enthusiast Gary Stewart (Gary Morton), attorney Howard McClay (Philip Carey), and Doctor Sam Eastman (Frank Aletter). Vivian eventually married Vern Bunson (another unseen character) and remained in Danfield.

Lucy moved to California and took up residence at the Glen Hall Apartments (apartment 2B) located at 780 North Gower Street, Los Angeles. Chris went to a college in Northern California, while Jerry went to Los Angeles Military Academy. As it turns out, Mr. Mooney had also gone west, having been transferred from the Danfield Bank to the Westland Bank in Los Angeles to serve as a vice president. Lucy quickly became good friends with her next-door neighbor, Mary Jane Lewis (Mary Jane Croft), who worked at Mammoth Studios (she was originally a script girl and then later secretary to one of the secretaries to producer Nelson Penrose, played by Lew Parker). In addition to Lucy and Mary Jane, other residents of the Glen Hall Apartments included actress Joan Brenner (Joan Blondell), songwriter Mel Tinker (Mel Tormé), airline pilot Brad Collins (Keith Andes), and the musical group the Vagabonds. Lucy eventually went to work as Mooney's sec-retary. The president of the Westland Bank was Mr. Cheever (Roy Roberts).

Season One: Nielsen Ratings Rank: #5
October 1, 1962: #1: "Lucy Waits Up for Chris"
    The highest rated episode of the series.
October 8, 1962: #3: "Lucy Digs Up a Date"
October 15, 1962: #4: "Lucy Is a Referee"
    Desi Jr. and Lucie make un-credited appearances in this episode.
October 22, 1962: #5: "Lucy Misplaces $2,000"
October 29, 1962: #2: "Lucy Buys a Sheep"
November 5, 1962: #6: "Lucy Becomes an Astronaut"
November 12, 1962: #7: "Lucy Is a Kangaroo for a Day"
November 19, 1962: #8: "Lucy, the Music Lover"
November 26, 1962: #9: "Lucy Puts Up a TV Antenna"
December 3, 1962: #11: "Vivian Sues Lucy"
    The last of Charles Lane's four appearances as Mr. Barnsdahl.
December 10, 1962: #10: "Lucy Builds a Rumpus Room"
December 17, 1962: #15: "Lucy and Her Electric Mattress"
December 24, 1962: #12: "Together for Christmas"
December 31, 1962: #13: "Chris's New Year's Eve Party"
January 7, 1963: #14: "Lucy's Sister Pays a Visit"
January 14, 1963: #16: "Lucy and Viv Are Volunteer Firemen"
January 21, 1963: #17: "Lucy Becomes a Reporter"
January 28, 1963: #18: "Lucy and Viv Put in a Shower"
February 4, 1963: #20: "Lucy's Barbershop Quartet"
February 11, 1963: #19: "Lucy and Viv Become Tycoons"
February 18, 1963: #21: "No More Double Dates"
February 25, 1963: #22: "Lucy and Viv Learn Judo"
    The final episode featuring Dick Martin as neighbor Harry Conners.
March 4, 1963: #23: "Lucy Is a Soda Jerk"
    Lucie Arnaz's first speaking role in her mother's series.
March 11, 1963: #24: "Lucy Drives a Dump Truck"
March 25, 1963: #25: "Lucy Visits the White House"
April 1, 1963: #26: "Lucy and Viv Take Up Chemistry"
April 8, 1963: #27: "Lucy Is a Chaperone"
April 15, 1963: #28: "Lucy and the Little League"
April 22, 1963: #29: "Lucy and the Runaway Butterfly"
April 29, 1963: #30: "Lucy Buys a Boat"

Season Two: Nielsen Ratings Rank: #6
September 30, 1963: #35: "Lucy Plays Cleopatra"
    The series begins to be filmed in color, although it will be broadcast in
    black and white until season four.

October 7, 1963: #36: "Kiddie Parties, Inc."

October 14, 1963: #32: "Lucy and Viv Play Softball"

October 21, 1963: #33: "Lucy Gets Locked in the Vault"

> Gale Gordon's first episode as Theodore J. Mooney.

October 28, 1963: #37: "Lucy and the Safe Cracker"

November 7, 1963: #31: "Lucy Goes Duck Hunting"

November 11, 1963: #34: "Lucy and the Bank Scandal"

November 18, 1963: #38: "Lucy Decides to Redecorate"

December 2, 1963: #41: "Lucy Puts Out a Fire at the Bank"

December 9, 1963: #42: "Lucy and the Military Academy"

December 16, 1963: #43: "Lucy's College Reunion"

December 23, 1963: #40: "The Loophole in the Lease"

> This episode was scheduled to air on November 25, 1963, but was pre
> empted by the ongoing coverage of President John F. Kennedy's assas-
> sination the previous day.

December 30, 1963: #39: "Lucy Conducts the Symphony"

January 6, 1964: #45: "Lucy Plays Florence Nightingale"

January 13, 1964: #46: "Lucy Goes to Art Class"

January 20, 1964: #47: "Chris Goes Steady"

January 27, 1964: #49: "Lucy Takes Up Golf"

> Features Gary Morton in his first guest role on a *Lucy* series.

February 3, 1964: #44: "Lucy Teaches Ethel Merman to Sing"

February 10, 1964: #48: "Ethel Merman and the Boy Scout Show"

February 17, 1964: #50: "Lucy and Viv Open a Restaurant"

February 24, 1964: #51: "Lucy Takes a Job at the Bank"

March 2, 1964: #52: "Viv Moves Out"

March 9, 1964: #53: "Lucy Is Her Own Lawyer"

March 16, 1964: #54: "Lucy Meets a Millionaire"

> Last episode scripted by the Martin/Carroll/Schiller/Weiskopf writing
> team.

March 23, 1964: #55 "Lucy Goes into Politics"

March 30, 1964: #56: "Lucy and the Scout Trip"

April 20, 1964: #57: "Lucy Is a Process Server"

April 27, 1964: #58: "Lucy Enters a Baking Contest"

> The final episode written by Madelyn Martin and Bob Carroll Jr.

Season Three: Nielsen Ratings Rank: #8

September 21, 1964: #59: "Lucy and the Good Skate"

September 28, 1964: #66: "Lucy and the Plumber"

> The first of six episodes during the third season not featuring Vivian.

October 5, 1964: #61: "Lucy Tries Winter Sports"

October 12, 1964: #65: "Lucy Gets Amnesia"
October 19, 1964: #62: "Lucy and the Great Bank Robbery"
October 26, 1964: #64: "Lucy, the Camp Cook"
November 2, 1964: #60: "Lucy the Meter Maid"
November 9, 1964: #68: "Lucy Makes a Pinch"
November 16, 1964: #67: "Lucy Becomes a Father"
November 23, 1964: #69: "Lucy's Contact Lenses"
November 30, 1964: #74: "Lucy Gets Her Maid"
December 7, 1964: #73: "Lucy Gets the Bird"
December 14, 1964: #71: "Lucy, the Coin Collector"
December 21, 1964: #70: "Lucy and the Missing Stamp"
December 28, 1964: #63: "Lucy Meets Danny Kaye"
January 11, 1965 #76: "Lucy and the Ceramic Cat"
January 18, 1965: #77: "Lucy Goes to Vegas"
January 25, 1965: #75: "Lucy and the Monsters"
February 1, 1965: #78: "Lucy and the Countess"
> The first of seven appearances by Ann Sothern as the Countess.

February 8, 1965: #79: "My Fair Lucy"
February 15, 1965: #80: "Lucy and the Countess Lose Weight"
March 1, 1965: #84: "Lucy and the Old Mansion"
> The final episode featuring Candy Moore as Chris and Ralph Hart as Sherman.

March 8, 1965: #81: "Lucy and Arthur Godfrey"
March 22, 1965: #83: "Lucy the Beauty Doctor"
March 29, 1965: #82: "Lucy the Stockholder"
April 12, 1965: #72: "Lucy and the Disc Jockey"
> The final episode with Vivian as a regular and the final episode set in Danfield. This episode was originally supposed to air on January 4, 1965, but was preempted by Lyndon Johnson's State of the Union Address. It was rescheduled for March 15, only to be preempted by another speech by the President.

Season Four: Nielsen Ratings Rank: #3
September 13, 1965: #86: "Lucy at Marineland"
> The first episode set in California and the first one aired in color.

September 20, 1965: #85: "Lucy and the Golden Greek"
> The first appearance of Mary Jane Croft as Mary Jane Lewis.

September 27, 1965: #89: "Lucy in the Music World"
October 11, 1965: #87: "Lucy and Joan"
October 18, 1965: #88: "Lucy the Stunt Man"
October 25, 1965: #93: "Lucy and the Countess Have a Horse Guest"

Features a cameo by Bill Frawley; his final television appearance.

November 1, 1965: #92: "Lucy Helps Danny Thomas"

Lucy gets her job as Mooney's secretary in this episode.

November 8, 1965: #90: "Lucy Helps the Countess"

November 15, 1965: #91: "Lucy and the Sleeping Beauty"

November 22, 1965: 94: "Lucy the Undercover Agent"

Ann Sothern's final appearance as Rosie Harrigan, the Countess Framboise.

November 29, 1965: #95: "Lucy and the Return of the Iron Man"

December 6, 1965: #96: "Lucy Saves Milton Berle"

December 13, 1965: #98: "Lucy the Choirmaster"

Jimmy Garrett's final episode as Jerry Carmichael.

December 27, 1965: #99: "Lucy Discovers Wayne Newton"

January 3, 1966: #101: "Lucy the Rain Goddess"

January 10, 1966: #100: "Lucy and Art Linkletter"

January 17, 1966: #97: "Lucy Bags a Bargain"

January 24, 1966: #102: "Lucy Meets Mickey Rooney"

January 31, 1966: #103: "Lucy and the Soap Opera"

February 7, 1966: #104: "Lucy Goes to a Hollywood Premiere"

February 14, 1966: #105: "Lucy Dates Dean Martin"

February 21, 1966: #106: "Lucy and Bob Crane"

February 28, 1966: #107: "Lucy the Robot"

March 7, 1966: #108: "Lucy and Clint Walker"

March 14, 1966: #109: "Lucy the Gun Moll"

Lucille plays a dual role in this episode: Lucy Carmichael and nightclub singer Rusty Martin.

March 21, 1966: #110: "Lucy the Superwoman"

Season Five: Nielsen Ratings Rank: #4

September 12, 1966: #111: "Lucy and George Burns"

September 19, 1966: #116: "Lucy and the Submarine"

September 26, 1966: #112: "Lucy the Bean Queen"

October 3, 1966: #118: "Lucy and Paul Winchell"

October 10, 1966: #113: "Lucy and the Ring a Ding Ding"

October 17, 1966: #120: "Lucy Goes to London"

This set up the storyline for the special *Lucy in London* that aired on October 24.

October 31, 1966: #114: "Lucy Gets a Roommate"

November 7, 1966: #115: "Lucy and Carol in Palm Springs"

November 14, 1966: #117: "Lucy Gets Caught in the Draft"

November 21, 1966: #119: "Lucy and John Wayne"

November 28, 1966: #121: "Lucy and Pat Collins"
December 5, 1966: #122: "Mooney the Monkey"
December 12, 1966: #123: "Lucy and Phil Silvers"
January 2, 1967: #124: "Lucy's Substitute Secretary"
January 9, 1967: #125: "Viv Visits Lucy"
January 16, 1967: #126: "Lucy the Baby Sitter"
January 23, 1967: #127: "Main Street U.S.A."
January 30, 1967: #128: "Lucy Puts Main Street on the Map"
February 13, 1967: #129: "Lucy Meets the Law"
February 20, 1967: #130: "Lucy the Fight Manager"
February 27, 1967: #132: "Lucy and Tennessee Ernie Ford"
March 6, 1967: #131: "Lucy Meets Sheldon Leonard"

Season Six: Nielsen Ratings Rank: #2
September 11, 1967: #137: "Lucy Meets the Berles"
September 18, 1967: #133: "Lucy Gets Trapped"
September 25, 1967: #134: "Lucy and the French Movie Star"
October 2, 1967: #136: "Lucy, the Starmaker"
October 9, 1967: #140: "Lucy Gets Her Diploma"
October 16, 1967: #138: "Lucy and Jack Benny's Account"
     Writers Milt Josefsberg and Ray Singer received an Emmy nomination
     for this episode.
October 23, 1967: #135: "Little Old Lucy"
October 30, 1967: #139: "Lucy and Robert Goulet"
November 6, 1967: #141: "Lucy Gets Mooney Fired"
November 13, 1967: #147: "Lucy's Mystery Guest"
November 20, 1967: #144: "Lucy the Philanthropist"
November 27, 1967: #142: "Lucy Sues Mooney"
December 4, 1967: #148: "Lucy and the Pool Hustler"
December 11, 1967: #145: "Lucy and Carol Burnett, Part One"
December 18, 1967: #146: "Lucy and Carol Burnett, Part Two"
January 1, 1968: #149: "Lucy and Viv Reminisce"
     A clip show featuring Vivian.
January 15, 1968: #143: "Lucy Gets Involved"
January 22, 1968: #151: "Mooney's Other Wife"
January 29, 1968: #152: "Lucy and the Stolen Stole"
February 5, 1968: #150: "Lucy and Phil Harris"
February 19, 1968: #153: "Lucy Helps Ken Berry"
February 26, 1968: #154: "Lucy and the Lost Star"
March 4, 1968: #155: "Lucy and Sid Caesar"
March 11, 1968: #156: "Lucy and the 'Boss of the Year' Award"

12

"Unusual Jobs For Unusual People"

Here's Lucy

Background

L ucy knew that a new format had to be created for her when she returned for the 1968–69 television season. One thing that was certain was that Gale Gordon would once again be her co-star, only this time his character would be related to Lucy's. More unexpectedly, Lucy decided to include her own children as her character's children on the series. Lucy knew her kids were talented and saw that they had an interest in the business. (Indeed, Desi Jr. had already been on the pop charts as part of Dino, Desi & Billy.) Lucy was not pleased with the school system at the time and thought that it would be beneficial if her children worked on her show and had a private tutor instead. Initially, Lucie and Desi Jr. were not sure if they wanted to participate. Lucy did not want them to give her an answer right away and told them to think about it while she went to Monaco for the next month to judge the International Television Festival of Monte Carlo. She explained to them up front that they would be paid scale and not be given any preferential treatment just because they were her children. When she returned from her trip, the children informed her that they wanted to do the show.

The original premise of the series had Lucy working part-time for her brother-in-law Harry at his employment agency. Harry had another secretary, Carole Elkins, who worked for him in the morning and was extremely efficient, a distinct contrast to the often unreliable Lucy. When Doris Singleton was cast in the role, the character was actually renamed "Doris Singleton." However, it was decided to place more emphasis on Lucy's home life with the children than on her time spent at the office, so Miss

Singleton only appeared in the premiere episode, "Mod, Mod Lucy." *Rowan & Martin's Laugh-In*, which aired opposite *Here's Lucy* and was unlike any show on television, shot to the top of the ratings. However, by the season's end, *Here's Lucy* was also firmly in the top ten.

Director Jack Donohue left the series after the first season and various directors helmed *Here's Lucy* over the next two years. Coby Ruskin was hired at the start of the fourth season to direct and was responsible for every episode after that until Jack Donohue replaced him on the last six episodes of the series. Lucy's cousin Cleo replaced Tommy Thompson as producer at the beginning of the second season, while Gary Morton served as executive producer for the show's entire run.

Here's Lucy received its highest ratings ever for its third-season premiere. The premise for the episode came about after Lucy and Gary met Elizabeth Taylor and Richard Burton at a party given for David Frost at the British Consulate. Burton told Lucy that he would love to do her show, and a deal was eventually struck. The Burtons, the most publicized couple in America, would appear on *Here's Lucy* in an episode revolving around the equally publicized 69-carat diamond ring Burton had recently purchased for his

The Carter family in a Gay Nineties scene from one of their many musical productions in *Here's Lucy*, from the episode "Lucy and the Generation Gap."

wife. Madelyn Davis and Bob Carroll Jr. were approached to write a script and ended up returning to Lucy's employ, writing a third of the series' scripts for its last three seasons. The Burton-Taylor episode would become one of the most publicized of Lucy's career, no doubt helped by the fact that a dozen of the top entertainment reporters in the country appeared in it as themselves. "Lucy Meets the Burtons" proved to be a ratings smash and was instrumental in the series ending up the third highest-rated program of the season. *Here's Lucy* was the highest-rated sitcom on television for the 1970–71 season and CBS's number one show.

Desi Jr. was written out of several episodes during the third season so he could make the film *Red Sky at Morning*. He officially left the series when that season ended. After Lucille broke her leg skiing, the writers incorporated the mishap into the series. Lucy was shown in bed for the first three episodes of season five, then in a motorized wheelchair in three installments, followed by a walking cast in six more (one of which, "Goodbye, Mrs. Hips," aired months after the rest of the episodes featuring Lucy's broken leg).

Milt Josefsberg, who was the series' script consultant, left prior to the fifth season. Outside writers were no longer used. Every script from that point forward was written by Madelyn Davis and Bob Carroll Jr., Fred S. Fox and Seaman Jacobs, or Bob O'Brien. Lucy wanted to wrap up the series at the end of the fifth season. The final episode of that season, "Lucy and Harry's Memoirs," was a clip show with the plotline that Harry had sold the employment agency. This was intended to be the series finale, but CBS talked Lucy into one more year. At the end of season six, *Here's Lucy* called it quits for real.

Lucie Arnaz accepted the lead in the national tour of the musical *Seesaw* and, for that reason, would not be returning if the series continued. Lucy had just completed *Mame,* and a cross-country publicity tour was planned to promote the film. These were reasons enough to end the show, although it was reported in later years that CBS had no intention of renewing *Here's Lucy* for the 1974–75 season. The network had already eliminated all the rural programs that made their network so popular with audiences in the nineteen-sixties and had cancelled all of the other stars from the Golden Age of Television who were still on the network, such as Jackie Gleason, Ed Sullivan, and Red Skelton. The network was going for a younger audience and did not think that sixty-two- year-old Lucille Ball fit that image. Lucy, however, would continue to do specials for CBS.

Storyline

Lucy Carter was born in Jamestown, New York, and spent part of her childhood in Montana. Her maiden name is implied to be Hinkley in "Kim Finally Cuts You-Know-Who's Apron Strings," but she later says it is McGillicuddy in "Lucy and the Professor." She has a brother, Herb Hinkley (Alan Oppenheimer). Her grandmother, Flora Belle Orcutt, was the first female sheriff in Carriage Belt, Montana. Lucy's childhood best friend from kindergarten through high school was Vivian Roberta Jones (Vivian Vance). Lucy attended Jamestown High School and played the saxophone in the school band. She also boasts that she was named Miss Cheerleader of Nineteen Th— ("I was a darn good one," she says.). Lucy married at the age of seventeen. The Carters (Mr. Carter's first name was never given) had two children, Kim and Craig. After the death of her husband, Lucy took a job as secretary to her brother-in-law (having had only two-and-a-half weeks of business college), Harrison Otis Carter IV, at Carter's Unique Employment Agency ("Unusual jobs for unusual people"). Carter's Unique Employment Agency was office number 1506 in the Bradshawe Building in Los Angeles.

Harry was a graduate of Bullwinkle University, class of 1928. He had a sister (Mary Wickes) who became a nun, Sister Paula. It is also implied that he has another brother, as Lucy's niece, Patricia Carter (Eve Plumb), appears in the episode "Lucy and Donny Osmond."

Lucy, Kim, and Craig resided at 4863 Valley Lawn Drive (originally given as 5780 Cherry Blossom Lane) in Encino, in California's San Fernando Valley. Their telephone number was 865-8221, later given as KL5-8231. Kim and Craig attended Angeles High School. Kim's first job was as a salesgirl at Lady Vogue Dress Shop (Kim's social security number was 554-60-0676), while Craig briefly worked as a stock boy at a local supermarket.

Kim was later a student at a local (unspecified) college, while Craig went away to school (also unspecified). Kim pursued a teaching degree and worked part-time for a public relations company and later as a receptionist at a talent agency. She also had a strong interest in theater. Kim's first home away from her mother was next door to her mother's house over the garage of their neighbors, the Thompsons. Kim later moved to an apartment by the marina that was run by her Uncle Herb.

Although Craig was a third-string substitute quarterback on his high school football team, he later shifted his interest to another sport, becoming a championship tennis player in college. He was also a fine drummer and aspired to be a rock 'n' roll musician and composer. One song he penned, "Country Magic," he performed with Ann-Margret on a television special. Craig had a rock 'n' roll group, and Kim served as the band's vocalist.

Lucy's best friend was Mary Jane Lewis (Mary Jane Croft), who worked as a secretary to a trial lawyer in the same office building as the employment agency. Their other close friend was Vanda Barra (Vanda Barra), another secretary in the building. Vanda had a steady romance with Sam (Sid Gould), who ran the coffee shop located downstairs from their office. Lucy, Mary Jane, and Vanda were members of the Canary Club, a choral group, and the Girl Friday Association, an organization for secretaries.

While skiing down Fanny Hill in Snowmass, Colorado, Lucy fell and broke her leg.

Lucy's boyfriends through the years included cosmetics company executive Bob Collins (Bob Cummings); antiques dealer Bob Henning (Bob Cummings; apparently Lucy Carter had a *very* specific "type" she wanted to date); Prince Phillip Gregory Hennepin, ruler of the Principality of Montalbania (Ricardo Montalban); and mechanic Jack Scott (Robert Rockwell).

The Carters of *Here's Lucy*: Desi Arnaz Jr., Lucie Arnaz, Lucille Ball, and Gale Gordon.

Season One: Nielsen Ratings Rank: #9
September 23, 1968: #1: "Mod, Mod Lucy"
September 30, 1968: #6: "Lucy Visits Jack Benny"
October 7, 1968: #7: "Lucy the Process Server"
October 14, 1968: #9: "Lucy and Miss Shelley Winters"
October 21, 1968: #4: "Lucy the Conclusion Jumper"
October 28, 1968: #8: "Lucy's Impossible Mission"
November 11, 1968: #5: "Lucy and Eva Gabor"
November 18, 1968: #2: "Lucy's Birthday"
November 25, 1968: #13: "Lucy Sells Craig to Wayne Newton"
December 2, 1968: #3: "Lucy's Working Daughter"
December 9, 1968: #12: "Guess Who Owes Lucy $23.50?"
December 16, 1968: #14: "Lucy the Matchmaker"
    Vivian Vance's first of six appearances as Vivian Jones.
December 30, 1968: #10: "Lucy and the Gold Rush"
January 6, 1969: #15: "Lucy the Fixer"
January 13, 1969: #17: "Lucy and the Ex-Con"
January 20, 1969: #16: "Lucy Goes on Strike"
January 27, 1969: #21: "Lucy and Carol Burnett"
February 3, 1969: #11: "Lucy and the Great Airport Chase"
February 10, 1969: #18: "A Date for Lucy"
    Mary Jane Croft's first appearance as Mary Jane Lewis.
February 17, 1969: #20: "Lucy the Shopping Expert"
February 24, 1969: #19: "Lucy Gets Her Man"
March 3, 1969: #22: "Lucy's Safari"
March 10, 1969: #23: "Lucy and Tennessee Ernie's Fun Farm"
March 17, 1969: #24: "Lucy Helps Craig Get a Driver's License"

Season Two: Nielsen Ratings Rank: #6
September 22, 1969: #25: "Lucy and the Air Force Academy, Part One"
September 29, 1969: #26: "Lucy and the Air Force Academy, Part Two"
October 6, 1969: #27: "Lucy and the Indian Chief"
October 13, 1969: #28: "Lucy Runs the Rapids"
October 20, 1969: #29: "Lucy and Harry's Tonsils"
October 27, 1969: #32: "Lucy and the Andrews Sisters"
November 3, 1969: #30: "Lucy's Burglar Alarm"
November 10, 1969: #31: "Lucy and the Drive-In Movie"
November 17, 1969: #33: "Lucy and the Used Car Dealer"
November 24, 1969: #34: "Lucy the Cement Worker"
December 1, 1969: #35: "Lucy and Johnny Carson"
December 8, 1969: #36: "Lucy and the Generation Gap"

December 15, 1969: #37: "Lucy and the Bogie Affair"
December 22, 1969: #40: "Lucy Protects Her Job"
December 29, 1969: #39: "Lucy the Helpful Mother"
January 5, 1970: #42: "Lucy and Liberace"
January 12, 1970: #38: "Lucy the Laundress"
January 19, 1970: #43: "Lucy and Lawrence Welk"
January 26, 1970: #44: "Lucy and Viv Visit Tijuana"
February 2, 1970: #45: "Lucy and Ann-Margret"
February 9, 1970: #46: "Lucy and Wally Cox"
February 16, 1970: #41: "Lucy and Wayne Newton"
February 23, 1970: #47: "Lucy Takes Over"
March 2, 1970:   #48: "Lucy and Carol Burnett"

Season Three: Nielsen Ratings Rank: #3
September 14, 1970: #58: "Lucy Meets the Burtons"
> The highest-rated episode of the series and the first to be written by Madelyn Davis and Bob Carroll Jr., who received an Emmy nomination for their efforts.
September 21, 1970: #52: "Lucy the Skydiver"
September 28, 1970: #53: "Lucy and Sammy Davis, Jr."
October 5, 1970: #57: "Lucy and Buddy Rich"
October 12, 1970: #51" "Lucy the Crusader"
October 19, 1970: #65: "Lucy the Coed"
October 26, 1970: #62: "Lucy, the American Mother"
November 2, 1970: #63: "Lucy's Wedding Party"
November 9, 1970: #49: "Lucy Cuts Vincent's Price"
November 16, 1970: #54: "Lucy the Diamond Cutter"
November 23, 1970: #55: "Lucy and Jack Benny's Biography"
November 30, 1970: #68: "Lucy and Rudy Vallee"
December 7, 1970: #50: "Lucy Loses Her Cool"
December 14, 1970: #67: "Lucy, Part-Time Wife"
December 21, 1970: #56: "Lucy and Ma Parker"
December 28, 1970: #59: "Lucy Stops a Marriage"
January 4, 1971: #69: "Lucy's Vacation"
January 11, 1971: #64: "Lucy and the 20-20 Vision"
January 18, 1971: #72: "Lucy and the Raffle"
January 25, 1971: #70: "Lucy's House Guest, Harry"
February 1, 1971: #66: "Lucy and Aladdin's Lamp"
February 8, 1971: #71: "Lucy and Carol Burnett"
February 15, 1971: #60: "Lucy Goes Hawaiian, Part One"

February 22, 1971: #61: "Lucy Goes Hawaiian, Part Two"
    The final episode with Desi Jr. as a regular.

Season Four: Nielsen Ratings Rank: #11
September 13, 1971: #81: "Lucy and Flip Go Legit"
September 20, 1971: #80: "Lucy and the Mountain Climber"
September 27, 1971: #75: "Lucy and the Italian Bombshell"
October 4, 1971: #73: "Lucy and Mannix Are Held Hostage"
October 11, 1971: #77: "Lucy and the Astronauts"
October 18, 1971: #76: "Lucy Makes a Few Extra Dollars"
October 25, 1971: #79: "Someone's On the Ski Lift with Dinah"
November 1, 1971: #78: "Lucy and Her All-Nun Band"
November 8, 1971: #85: "Won't You Calm Down, Dan Dailey?"
November 15, 1971: #82: "Lucy and the Celebrities"
November 22, 1971: #84: "Ginger Rogers Comes to Tea"
November 29, 1971: #87: "Lucy Helps David Frost Go Night-Night"
December 6, 1971: #88: "Lucy in the Jungle"
December 13, 1971: #74: "Lucy and Candid Camera"
December 20, 1971: #83: "Lucy's Lucky Day"
December 27, 1971: #86: "Lucy's Bonus Bounces"
January 3, 1972: #92: "Lucy and the Little Old Lady"
January 10, 1972: #89: "Lucy and the Chinese Curse"
January 17, 1972: #93: "Lucy's Replacement"
January 24, 1972: #90: "Kim Moves Out"
January 31, 1972: #91: "Lucy Sublets the Office"
February 7, 1972: #95: "Lucy's Punctured Romance"
February 14, 1972: #94: "With Viv As a Friend, Who Needs an Enemy?"
    The last episode with Vivian Vance guest starring as Vivian Jones.
February 21, 1972: #96: "Kim Finally Cuts You-Know-Who's Apron Strings"
    The pilot for a proposed Lucie Arnaz spin-off.

Season Five: Nielsen Ratings Rank: #15
September 11, 1972: #98: "Lucy's Big Break"
    The first episode featuring Lucy's broken leg.
September 18, 1972: #97: "Lucy and Eva Gabor Are Hospital Roomies"
September 25, 1972: #99: "Harrison Carter, Male Nurse"
October 2, 1972: #100: "A Home Is Not an Office"
October 9, 1972: #101: "Lucy and Joe Namath"
    Desi Jr. guest stars as Craig; his final appearance on the series.
October 16, 1972: #104: "The Case of the Reckless Wheelchair Driver"

October 23, 1972: #103: "Lucy, the Other Woman"
October 30, 1972: #102: "Lucy and Petula Clark"
November 6, 1972: #110: "Lucy and Jim Bailey"
November 13, 1972: #108: "Dirty Gertie"
November 20, 1972: #106: "Lucy and Donny Osmond"
November 27, 1972: #111: "Lucy and Her Prince Charming"
December 11, 1972: #114: "My Fair Buzzi"
December 18, 1972: #105: "Lucy and the Group Encounter"
January 1, 1973: #112: "Lucy Is Really in a Pickle"
January 8, 1973: #116: "Lucy Goes on Her Last Blind Date"
January 15, 1973: #113: "Lucy and Her Genuine Twimby"
January 22, 1973: #115: "Lucy Goes to Prison"
January 29, 1973: #118: "Lucy and the Professor"
February 5, 1973: #117: "Lucy and the Franchise Fiasco"
February 12, 1973: #119: "Lucy and Uncle Harry's Pot"
February 19, 1973: #109: "The Not-So-Popular Mechanics"
February 26, 1973: #107: "Goodbye, Mrs. Hips"
March 5, 1973:   #120: "Lucy and Harry's Memoirs"

> A clip show that Lucy originally intended to be the final episode. She was coaxed back for another season.

Season Six: Nielsen Ratings Rank: #29
September 10, 1973: #126: "Lucy and Danny Thomas"
September 17, 1973: #123: "The Big Game"
September 24, 1973: #122: "Lucy the Peacemaker"
October 1, 1973: #124: "Lucy, the Wealthy Widow"
October 8, 1973: #125: "The Bow-Wow Boutique"
October 15, 1973: #128: "Lucy Gives Eddie Albert the Old Song and Dance"
October 22, 1973: #127: "Lucy's Tenant"
October 29, 1973: #129: "Lucy and Andy Griffith"
November 5, 1973: #130: "Lucy and Joan Rivers Do Jury Duty"
November 12, 1973: #131: "Tipsy Through the Tulips"
November 19, 1973: #132: "The Carters Meet Frankie Avalon"
December 3, 1973: #133: "Harry Catches Gold Fever"
December 17, 1973: #135: "Lucy and Chuck Connors Have a Surprise Slumber Party"
December 31, 1973: #121: "Lucy Plays Cops and Robbers"
January 7, 1974: #134: "Lucy Is a Bird Sitter"
January 14, 1974: #136: "Meanwhile, Back at the Office"
January 21, 1974: #137: "Lucy Is N.G. as an R.N."

January 28, 1974: #138: "Lucy the Sheriff"

Lucille receives director credit alongside regular director Coby Ruskin.

February 11, 1974: #139: "Milton Berle is the Life of the Party"

February 18, 1974: #140: "Mary Jane's Boy Friend"

The last episode featuring Mary Jane Croft.

February 25, 1974: #142: "Lucy and Phil Harris Strike Up the Band"

March 4, 1974: #141: "Lucy Carter Meets Lucille Ball"

Lucy plays a dual role in this episode that was used to promote the upcoming film *Mame*.

March 11, 1974: #143: "Where Is My Wandering Mother Tonight?"

March 18, 1974: #144: "Lucy Fights the System"

13

"World's Greatest Grandma"

Life with Lucy

Background

Although Lucy was asked in nearly every interview she had done since the end of *Here's Lucy* if she would ever do another television series, she always responded with a very definite "no." As far as she was concerned, she could never top what she had done. Furthermore, after Vivian Vance's death in 1979, she said she would *never* do another series because Vivian was no longer around. Against all odds, Lucy was finally persuaded to do another sitcom in 1986.

Aaron Spelling, who, in his acting days, had appeared as Ernie Ford's cousin Zeke in the *I Love Lucy* episode "Tennessee Bound" thirty-one years earlier, was now the most successful producer on television. He had signed a deal with ABC to do a sitcom, and the deal was near expiration. After Spelling ran into Lucy and Gary at a restaurant, he became very intrigued at the idea of asking the most successful sitcom star of them all to return to television. To this end, he first called up his and Gary's mutual friend and business associate Marvin Davis to ask Gary if Lucy would be willing to do another series. Lucy, of course, gave her usual "no" answer. To further woo the television legend, the network offered Lucy a full season, twenty-two episode commitment, with no pilot or testing necessary. Gary contacted Bob Carroll Jr. and Madelyn Davis to ask if they would be interested in creating another show for Lucy and Gale Gordon, whom Lucy always said she would never do another series without. Lucy was then presented the whole idea. With so many elements to her liking, Lucy agreed to do the series. The new show was announced in March 1986 with filming scheduled to begin in July for a September airdate. *Life with Lucy* was a joint venture between Lucille Ball and Aaron Spelling's production companies. Spelling, Gary, and Douglas S. Cramer served as the series' producers.

Ann Dusenberry was cast as Lucy's daughter, Margo; Larry Anderson as Margo's husband, Ted; Jenny Lewis as Becky, Lucy's granddaughter; and Philip J. Amelio II as Lucy's grandson, Kevin. However, during production of the first episode, eight-year-old Amelio had trouble remembering his lines. The producers wanted to replace him immediately, but Lucy demanded he not be fired because she could not bear to see such a young performer lose his job. Lucy was insistent that the boy do the first show, and if he did not reach the producers' expectations, then they could discuss dismissing him. It was no longer a problem when Amelio performed perfectly at the first filming. Rounding out the cast was Donovan Scott as Leonard Stoner, an employee of the hardware store Lucy and Gale's characters co-owned. Marc Daniels, who directed the first thirty-eight episodes of *I Love Lucy* and also her 1977 special *Lucy Calls the President*, directed the pilot and several subsequent episodes.

ABC's lowest-rated night was Saturday, so they scheduled *Life with Lucy* for 8:00 to kick off their all-new Saturday night lineup and hopefully draw audiences. When the episodes were filmed, the studio audience was so thrilled to see the legendary Lucille Ball, their idol, in person that they laughed and applauded at everything she did. This warm reception no doubt was instrumental in clouding the judgment of those behind the scenes, who failed to consider the possibility of there being any problems

Lucille Ball and Gale Gordon together again, in "One Good Grandparent Deserves Another," the premiere episode of *Life with Lucy* (1986).

with the show's quality. If the studio audience loved it so much, there was every reason to believe the home viewers would feel the same way.

Over the next few months, excitement and anticipation grew regarding the show. Skeptical critics eventually began to wonder what the quality of the show actually was when they were not supplied with a customary preview tape to review. Those involved with the series were optimistic that the premiere would be number one in the ratings because of the public's great love of Lucy. They were shocked when the show only came in at twenty-third place. This ended up being *Life with Lucy*'s highest-rated episode. Reviewers savaged the show, criticizing every aspect of it. They and audiences said that they were afraid for seventy-five-year-old Lucille Ball's safety when she did physical comedy. Lucy saw that she was in a no-win situation. The TV movie *Stone Pillow* had taught her that the public wanted to see her as "Lucy," but now she saw that the public only wanted to see her as a *young* Lucy. She was deeply hurt by the reviews and the tepid ratings.

The twelfth episode filmed, "Mother of the Bride," featured Audrey Meadows as Lucy's sister, leading to the possibility of her becoming a series regular. However, *Life with Lucy* was constantly in the bottom ten shows of the week. The day the thirteenth episode, "World's Greatest Grandma," was to be filmed, ABC notified Aaron Spelling that the series was being cancelled. Spelling had his assistant tell Gary Morton, but Gary kept the news to himself. It was not until their drive home from that night's filming that Gary told Lucy the sad news. The following day, ABC announced that they would be removing *Life with Lucy* and the series that followed it, *The Ellen Burstyn Show* (which received even lower ratings), from their Saturday night schedule, but assured viewers that both sitcoms would be back on the network in some capacity. Although ABC did burn off the remaining episodes of *The Ellen Burstyn Show* in the summer of 1987, *Life with Lucy* was never seen on the network again, leaving five episodes unaired. Lucy felt awful that so many people were out of work and blamed herself for the show's failure. She had always said that the only time she had ever been fired in Hollywood was when she was laid off from Columbia in 1934, but then got a job at RKO a few hours later. But now she, "The First Lady of Television," was fired, and she was devastated.

Storyline

Lucy Barker was from Pasadena, California. Born Lucille Everett, she attended Pasadena High School. Lucy's high school sweetheart was Ben Matthews (Peter Graves), but their yearlong romance ended when his family moved to the East Coast. Lucy played the saxophone in the school marching band

The cast of *Life with Lucy*: (l – r) Donovan Scott (on the floor), Larry Anderson, Jenny Lewis, Lucy, Gale Gordon, Philip J. Amelio II, and Ann Dusenberry.

and even performed during the Rose Bowl one year, but younger sister Audrey (Audrey Meadows) overshadowed her when she was chosen to be a Rose Princess and rode on a float. In the band, Lucy met flugelhorn player Sam Barker, who would become her husband. Sam opened up M&B Hardware with partner Curtis McGibbon (Gale Gordon). Lucy and Sam would have a daughter, Margo. Curtis and his wife, Josephine, had a son named Ted. Ted and Margo would marry and have two children, Becky and Kevin.

After Sam died, Lucy inherited his half of the hardware store, much to Curtis's dismay. M&B Hardware was located at 7207 Hill Street, Pasadena, California 91106 and had only one other employee, Leonard Stoner. Lucy, who was a health food and exercise aficionado, moved into Ted and Margo's house in order to help with the kids and assist the couple financially (Ted was a law student). Curtis was not pleased with this arrangement at all, certain that Lucy could not be trusted with his grandchildren. Curtis announced he was moving in as well and then had to deal with Lucy at both work and home.

Season One: Nielsen Ratings Rank: #78
September 20, 1986: #1: "One Good Grandparent Deserves Another"
September 27, 1986: #4: "Lucy Makes a Hit with John Ritter"
October 4, 1986: #6: "Love Among the Two-By-Fours"
October 18, 1986: #3: "Lucy Gets Her Wires Crossed"
October 25, 1986: #5: "Lucy Is a Sax Symbol"
November 1, 1986: #8: "Lucy Makes Curtis Byte the Dust"
November 8, 1986: #10: "Lucy, Legal Eagle"
November 15, 1986: #12: "Mother of the Bride"
Unaired: #2: "Lucy and the Guard Goose"
Unaired: #7: "Lucy and Curtis Are Up a Tree"
Unaired: #9: "Lucy's Green Thumb"
Unaired: #11: "Breaking Up Is Hard to Do"
Unaired: #13: "World's Greatest Grandma"

14

"His, Hers, and Somebody Else's"

Inside Jokes on the Lucy Series

Most of them flew over the heads of even the most ardent fans of Lucille Ball's series, but for those who committed the names of the behind-the-scenes folks to memory or delved into the personal lives of Lucy and her co-stars, there might have been an occasional smile of recognition when certain names and places were mentioned in passing.

Here is a sample list of some of the inside jokes that appeared on *I Love Lucy* (ILL), *The Lucille Ball-Desi Arnaz Show* (LD), *The Lucy Show* (TLS), and *Here's Lucy* (HL). Of course the entire *Here's Lucy* episode "Lucy Carter Meets Lucille Ball" is one long in-joke and speaks for itself, so it is not included here.

Harry Ackerman: In *ILL:* "Charm School," Ricky mentions an article he read about color television written by Harry Ackerman. Ackerman was a CBS executive who was instrumental in getting *I Love Lucy* on the air. He appeared in the episode "The Audition."

Mary Ackerman: In *ILL:* "Ricky Asks for a Raise," Ethel, disguising herself as Mrs. Miriam Chumley, supposedly calls up her friend Mary Ackerman to tell her Ricky Ricardo is no longer appearing at the Tropicana. Mary Ackerman was named after Mary Shipp Ackerman, the wife of Harry Ackerman. In *ILL:* "Too Many Crooks," the Ackermans across the street are victims of burglar Madame X.

Jack Aldworth: In *ILL:* "Ricky's Screen Test," assistant director Jack Aldworth's name is listed as the name of the director of Ricky's test. In *LD:* "Lucy Meets the Mustache," Mr. Aldworth is the name of Ernie Kovacs's sponsor. In *HL:* "Lucy and Jim Bailey," Lucy says that Mr. and Mrs. Jack

Aldworth contributed a lot of money and wants Mary Jane to give them a good table at the Chamber of Commerce benefit.

Lillian Appleby: Lucy's favorite schoolteacher, Lillian Appleby, inspired the name of Doris Singleton's character on *I Love Lucy.* Doris played Lillian Appleby in her first appearance on the series, "The Club Election." Her character was renamed Caroline Appleby for subsequent episodes, although she is again referred to as Lillian Appleby in "Lucy Gets in Pictures."

Billy, Dani, and Jerry Asher: In *ILL:* "Bon Voyage," the Ricardos receive a fruit basket from Billy, Dani, and little Jerry Asher. They were named after former series director William Asher, his wife Dani Sue Nolan (who played Mr. Sherman's secretary in "LA at Last!"), and their son Jerry.

Fred Ball and Zo Ball: In *TLS:* "Lucy's Sister Pays a Visit," Lucy Carmichael mentions her brother Fred and his wife Zo, named after Lucille Ball's real-life brother and sister-in-law.

Lucille Ball: The writers enjoyed sneaking in inside jokes about the real Lucille Ball. In *HL:* "Guess Who Owes Lucy $23.50," Kim tells Van Johnson that she loved him in "His, Hers, and Somebody Else's." Van replies, "Thanks, but the name of the picture was *Yours, Mine and Ours.*" Van also says, "I loved working with that kooky redhead." Lucy replies, "Personally, I felt she was much too young for Henry Fonda." In *HL:* "Lucy and the Andrews Sisters," Kim decorates her bedroom with posters of movie stars of the thirties and forties. Lucy Carter holds up a poster of Lucille Ball to put on the wall, but changes her mind and takes it down. In *HL:* "Lucy and the Generation Gap," in a sketch set in the time of Julius Caesar, Lucy is shown reading *Roman Scandals* magazine, a nod to Lucille's film debut. In the *My Favorite Husband* episode "Hair Dyed," Liz Cooper's hair is accidently dyed black, and she is told she looks like "that movie star, Lucille Ball." Liz thinks she's pretty, but her friend Iris (Bea Benaderet) tells her, "Lucille Ball never saw the day she looked as young as you." Liz replies, "Thanks . . . I think."

Ray Beal: Ray Beal, *Here's Lucy*'s art director, is mentioned as a friend of Harry's in "Someone's on the Ski Lift with Dinah."

Ben Benjamin: Writers Bob Carroll Jr. and Madelyn Pugh used their agent's name for Frank Nelson's talent scout character in *ILL:* "Ricky's Movie Offer."

Fred Bigelow: In *ILL:* "The Passports," it is mentioned that, as a child, Lucy was bitten on the ear by Fred Bigelow's cat. Fred Bigelow was a real-life department store owner in Jamestown.

Vivian Bowman: *Here's Lucy* production coordinator Vivian Bowman had her name dropped in "Lucy Is a Birdsitter." Kim says she got her used new car from her friend Vivian Bowman.

Ralph S. Bowyer: In *ILL:* "The Girls Go into Business," Lucy and Ethel sell their dress shop to a Mr. Ralph S. Bowyer. This was the name of Vivian Vance's real-life brother-in-law. He was married to Viv's younger sister, Maxine (nicknamed "Mickey").

Jack and Paula Carter: In *TLS:* "Lucy's Sister Pays a Visit," Lucy mentions friends Jack and Paula Carter are practically family. The Carters were named after Jack Carter and Paula Stewart, who introduced Lucy to Gary Morton and served as best man and matron of honor at their wedding. Jack would later guest star in *TLS:* "Lucy Sues Mooney" and direct two episodes from the third season of *HL:* "Lucy and the 20-20 Vision" and "Lucy and Carol Burnett." Paula, who co-starred in *Wildcat*, would later appear in *HL:* "Lucy and Harry's Tonsils."

Barbara Cushing: In *TLS:* "Lucy's Barbershop Quartet," Viv suggests they add Barbara Cushing to their quartet, but she is out of the running because she's not a member of the Danfield Volunteer Fire Department. In real life, Barbara Cushing was better known as Babe Paley, wife of CBS chairman William S. Paley. Paley received a mention of his own in "Lucy Meets Danny Kaye."

Tony DiBello: The writers used the name of their secretary Elaine DiBello's father, Tony, as the name of Danfield's Italian restaurateur on *The Lucy Show*. In "No More Double Dates," Harry Conners suggests going to dinner at Tony DiBello's. In "Lucy Meets a Millionaire," Lucy and her date, Umberto Fabrini (Cesare Danova), go to Tony DiBello's. Jay Novello plays Tony in that installment.

John R. Dodds: In *TLS:* "Lucy and Viv are Volunteer Firemen," Lucy writes to Senator John R. Dodds about the lack of a fire department in Danfield. John R. Dodds was Vivian Vance's husband.

Jack Donohue: In *TLS:* "Lucy and the Runaway Butterfly," Carl Benton Reid plays Jack Donohue, Lucy's boyfriend Howard McClay's boss, named after the series' director.

Jack Foley: Series film editor Jack Foley received multiple mentions on *Lucy* shows. Lucy receives a letter about her G.I. Loan from John Foley Jr. in *TLS:* "Lucy and Viv Open a Restaurant." In *HL:* "Kim Moves Out," it is mentioned that Jack Foley is casting Kim's school show.

Gertrude Foote: Lucy's Jamestown friend and New York roommate, Gertrude Foote, was mentioned as a Connecticut neighbor in *ILL:* "Ragtime Band."

Fred S. Fox: *Lucy* scriptwriter Fred S. Fox's name appears in two *Here's Lucy* episodes. In "Lucy's Wedding Party," Lyle Talbot played Harry's college chum Freddy Fox. In "Lucy and the Chinese Curse," the fight Harry is watching on television is between "Freddie the Fox" and "Kid Jacobs," named after the writing team of Fred S. Fox and Seaman Jacobs. Fox had a local San Francisco children's show called *Freddie the Fox* early in his career.

Bennett Green: The name of producer Bennett Green in *ILL:* "Home Movies" was from Desi's stand-in and frequent bit player and extra Bennett Green.

Lee Greenway: *Here's Lucy* makeup artists Hal King and Lee Greenway both have characters named after them in "My Fair Buzzi." Hal England plays Kim's community theater director, Mr. Greenway.

Lou Ann Hall: In *I Love Lucy*, Wednesday Afternoon Fine Arts League member Lou Ann Hall was named after Vivian Vance's youngest sister. Lou Ann is mentioned in "Lucy and Ethel Buy the Same Dress" and is featured in "Charm School," played by Vivi Janiss. In the latter, Tyler McVey plays Lou Ann's husband, Bill, named after the real Lou Ann's husband.

Betty Jo Hansen: In *The Lucy Show*, Lucy Carmichael's college classmate Betty Jo Hansen, played by Carole Cook in "Lucy's College Reunion," was named after writer Madelyn Martin's college friend.

Andrew Hickox: The Arnazes' business manager and business director of Desilu was immortalized by Charles Lane in *ILL:* "The Business Manager."

Annie Hinsche: In *HL:* "Guess Who Owes Lucy $23.50," Kim mentions neighbor Annie Hinsche. Annie Hinsche was the name of a real-life friend of the Arnaz children and the sister of Billy Hinsche of Dino, Desi & Billy.

Ed Holly: Desilu Senior Vice President Ed Holly found his name worked into the script of *TLS:* "Lucy Gets in Politics" as Mooney's opponent in the race for Danfield comptroller.

Flora Belle Emeline Orcutt Hunt & Frederick C. Hunt: Lucille Ball's maternal grandparents' names were used as Lucy Carter's great-grandparents in *HL* "Lucy Takes Over." Flora Belle Orcutt was also used as the name of Lucy's sheriff great-grandmother in "Lucy, the Sheriff."

Seaman Jacobs: In *HL:* "Lucy and the Chinese Curse," Harry watches a televised fight between "Freddy the Fox" and "Kid Jacobs," named after show writers Fred S. Fox and Seaman Jacobs. The episode was not written by the duo, however. Martin A. Ragaway penned the installment.

Venus Jones: In *ILL:* "Mertz and Kurtz," Ethel mentions Venus Jones, whom the Mertzes knew in their vaudeville days. Venus Jones was Vivian's real-life sister.

Hal King: Lucille's longtime makeup man Hal King has his name appear in two *Lucy* episodes. In *ILL:* "Ricky Asks for a Raise," Fred borrows the wardrobe trunk of his quick change artist friend Hal King. On *HL:* "My Fair Buzzi," the object of Annie Whipple's (Ruth Buzzi) affection is fellow theater club member Hal King.

Ron Knox: In *TLS:* "Lucy and Carol in Palm Springs," *Lucy Show* gaffer Ron Knox's name is featured on the board of golfers.

Joe Lombardi: In *TLS:* "Lucy and the Runaway Butterfly," Lucy's boyfriend Howard McClay works for the law firm Donohue, Pomerantz, Lombardi, and McClay. Lombardi is taken from Joe Lombardi, the show's special effects man.

Francis and Marion Lederer: In *ILL:* "Visitor from Italy," Lucy thinks visitor Mario is a friend of the Lederers whom they met in Europe. This is a reference to the Arnazes' close friends, actor Francis Lederer (who was one of the stars of the film *A Woman of Distinction*, in which Lucy made a cameo appearance) and his wife, Marion.

Pauline Lopus: Lucy's next-door neighbor and best friend in Celeron, Pauline Lopus, was mentioned many times on the *Lucy* series. Reggy Rea portrayed Wednesday Afternoon Fine Arts League member Pauline Lopus in *ILL* "The Club Election." In "Tennessee Ernie Visits," Mrs. McGillicuddy writes to Lucy about Flo Pauline Lopus (her real name), her club's recording secretary. In *TLS:* "Lucy's Barbershop Quartet," fellow volunteer firefighter Pauline Lopus is mentioned. In *HL:* "Lucy and the Bogie Affair," Lucy calls up her friend Pauline Lopus and tries to pawn off one of her new puppies on her. Lucy Ricardo, Lucy Carmichael, and Lucy Carter all had friends named Pauline Lopus.

Howard McClay: The name of Lucy's longtime publicist, Howard McClay, was utilized in several installments. In *TLS:* "Lucy and Her Electric Mattress," Lucy mentions Mr. McClay at the hardware store. In *TLS:* "Lucy and the Runaway Butterfly," Philip Carey portrays Lucy's boyfriend Howard McClay. In "Lucy and Carol in Palm Springs," Howie McClay is listed as one of the players in the Palm Springs Golf Classic. In *HL:* "Lucy Goes Hawaiian, Part One" and "Lucy Goes Hawaiian, Part Two," Robert Alda plays Captain McClay.

Warren Magenetti: *Here's Lucy*'s associate producer, Warren Magenetti, lent his name to two law enforcers on the series. In "Lucy and Mannix Are Held Hostage," Harry hits Officer Magenetti on the head with a flower pot. In "Lucy Goes to Prison," Roy Roberts plays Warden Magenetti.

Steve March: In *HL:* "Lucy, the Crusader," Kim and Craig mention their friend Steve March. March (the son of Mel Tormé and stepson of Hal March, each of whom showed up in three *Lucy* episodes) was a real-life friend of the Arnazes and appeared in "Lucy and the Bogie Affair" and "Lucy and Sammy Davis Jr."

George Marshall: In *HL:* "Lucy and the Generation Gap," Kim's character in the show-within-a show mentions a boy by the name of Georgy Marshall, named after series director George Marshall. Marshall appeared in the *Here's Lucy* episode "Lucy Runs the Rapids."

Dick Martin: In *TLS:* "Lucy and Carol in Palm Springs," Dick Martin's name was listed as one of the players in the Palm Springs Golf Classic. Martin had played Harry Conners during the series' first season and was the comedy partner of Dan Rowan, who appears in the episode as Colin Grant.

Michael Martin: Series writer Madelyn Pugh Martin used her own son's name as a little league player in *TLS:* "Lucy and the Little League."

Denni Massey: The *Lucy* writing team twice worked their secretary's name into a Lucy script both times as secretaries. Doris Packer played Miss Massey, Paul Douglas's secretary in *LD:* "Lucy Wants a Career," while Majel Barrett played Miss Massey, the secretary Lucy was replacing in *TLS:* "Lucy Is a Kangaroo for a Day."

Helen and Bob Mauer: Gary Morton's sister, Helen, and her husband, Bob Mauer, Lucy's in-laws, were mentioned in *TLS:* "Lucy, the Good Skate." "Mr. and Mrs. Robert Mauer" are announced as guests at the country club dance. In *HL:* "Milton Berle Is the Life of the Party," Joyce McNeal and John Calvin play Lucy's friends Helen and Bob Mauer.

Cleo Mandicos/Cleo Morgan: Lucy's cousin Cleo Morgan was mentioned by name in *ILL:* "Ricky's Hawaiian Vacation" as a contestant on *Be a Good Neighbor.* In *TLS:* "Lucy's Sister Pays a Visit," Lucy mentions her sister Cleo and her husband Cecil, who was named after Cleo's new husband, Cecil Smith. Cleo would later become producer of *Here's Lucy,* where her maiden name of Cleo Mandicos was the name of the bride played by Cynthia Hull in *HL:* "Lucy's Wedding Party." In addition to producing several Lucille Ball projects, Cleo also appears as an extra in the final scene of *I Love Lucy's* "Lucy's Last Birthday."

Gary Morton: After Lucy married Gary Morton, her husband's name was frequently used on her programs. In *TLS:* "Lucy and the Countess Have a Horse Guest," Bill Quinn plays stable owner Mr. Morton (but is billed in the credits as "Mr. Frink") and Lucy gets a telephone call from her downstairs neighbor, Mrs. Goldaper. Gary's real name was Morton Goldaper. In *HL:* "Lucy the Shopping Expert," Kim buys gefilte fish after grocer Mr. Goldaper tells her it is delicious. In *HL:* "Lucy's Burglar Alarm," Harry wants to dictate a letter to the firm of Goldaper and Russ. In *HL:* "Lucy, the Cement Worker," Harry's car is being repaired at the Morton Service Station. In *HL:* "Lucy and Carol Burnett" (second season), Carol Krausmeyer works for Horton, Gorton, Norton, and Morton. In *HL:* "Lucy and Aladdin's Lamp" and "The Not-So-Popular Mechanics," Mary Jane invites Lucy to go to Morton's Department Store. In *HL:* "Lucy and the Celebrities," Lucy goes to the Morton Pictures studio. Gary Morton's name used as an inside joke was not limited to his wife's series. When Gary's friend Jack Carter appeared in *The Dick Van Dyke Show* episode "Stretch Petrie Vs. Kid Schenk," his character, Neil Schenk, mentions his friend Morty Goldaper.

Grace Munson: Grace Munson, a friend of Lucy's mother, DeDe, from Jamestown, was a Wednesday Afternoon Fine Arts League member played by Hazel Pierce in *ILL:* "The Club Election." Grace Munson, now a resident of Westport, Connecticut, was mentioned in several sixth-season episodes: "Lucy Wants to Move to the Country," "Lucy Misses the Mertzes," "Ragtime Band," "Housewarming," and "Lucy Raises Tulips." When the character of Grace Munson appears on camera again in "Country Club Dance," she is now played by Ruth Brady. Grace is mentioned again in *LD:* "Lucy Wins a Racehorse." Grace Munson appears once again in a Lucy-related program when Doris Singleton played her in the 1971 *Make Room for Granddaddy* episode "Lucy Carter, Houseguest."

Argyle Nelson: In *TLS:* "Lucy Becomes a Reporter," John Vivyan plays Vivian's high school boyfriend Argyle Nelson, named after the series' production manager.

Louis Nicoletti: Desi's former band manager and series frequent bit player, Louis Nicoletti, had his name used as hotel proprietor Señor Nicoletti, in *ILL:* "Lucy Gets Homesick in Italy."

Duke Niles: In *TLS:* "Lucy Takes Up Golf," Gary's ill golf partner whom Lucy ends up replacing is named Duke Niles, after a real-life music publisher friend of Gary Morton.

DeDe Peterson: Lucy Carter's alias when she goes undercover in *HL:* "Lucy Goes to Prison" is DeDe Peterson, Lucy's mother's second married name.

Charlie Pomerantz: Lucy's publicist Charlie Pomerantz found his name worked into several *Lucy* installments. Ruth Perrot played society matron Mrs. Pomerantz in *ILL:* "Pioneer Women." Hy Averback played Ricky's publicity man Charlie Pomerantz in *ILL:* "The Hedda Hopper Story." In *TLS:* "Lucy and the Runaway Butterfly," Lucy's boyfriend Howard McClay works for the law firm Donohue, Pomerantz, Lombardi, and McClay.

Marc Rabwin: Ricky's physician, Dr. Rabwin, played by Lou Merrill, in *ILL:* "Ricky Has Labor Pains," was named after Lucy and Desi's close friend Dr. Marc Rabwin.

Louisa Mae Ragan: In *TLS* "Lucy and Viv Become Tycoons," Viv says that her caramel corn recipe came from her Grandmother Ragan. Vivian Vance's real-life maternal grandmother was named Louisa Mae Ragan.

Ralph and Betty Ramsey: The Ricardos' Westport, Connecticut neighbors, Ralph and Betty Ramsey (Frank Nelson and Mary Jane Croft), were named after writer Bob Weiskopf's actual Westport neighbors.

Howard Rayfiel: Lucille Ball Productions Vice President Howard Rayfiel has a mention in *HL:* "Lucy and Flip Go Legit." Flip Wilson's secretary (Kim Hamilton) speaks to Mr. Rayfiel on the telephone.

Bob O'Brien: In *TLS:* "Lucy and Carol in Palm Springs," "Bobby O'Brien," named after episode scriptwriter Bob O'Brien, is one of the golfers listed as playing in the tournament.

Jane Sebastian: Vivian Vance's real-life friend Jane Sebastian found her name worked into several *I Love Lucy* scripts. In "Lucy Becomes a Sculptress," Ethel tells Lucy that Jane Sebastian's overdue baby turned out to be twins. In real life, Vivian was godmother to Jane's son, songwriter John Sebastian ("Welcome Back, Kotter"). In "Lucy and Ethel Buy the Same Dress," Lucy says that Jane Sebastian will want to recite "Trees" on the Wednesday Afternoon Fine Arts League television show. In "The Fashion Show," Lucy and Ethel discuss how Jane Sebastian will be green with envy because of Lucy's Don Loper dress.

Don Sharpe: The name of Lucy's longtime agent, Don Sharpe, was used in *ILL:* "Lucy Meets Charles Boyer" as Ricky's agent. It reappears in *TLS:* "Lucy Drives a Dump Truck," as the name of the Danfield salvage man.

Hank Speer: One of Ethel's former boyfriends mentioned in *ILL:* "Ethel's Hometown" is Hank Speer. In reality, Hank Speer was Vivian's brother-in-law, married to her elder sister Venus.

Adele Sliff: *I Love Lucy* script supervisor Adele Sliff was the subject of a lengthy story told by Rock Hudson in "In Palm Springs." In *ILL:* "Lucy Is Envious," Cynthia Harcourt mentions schoolmates of hers and Lucy's, Renita, Adele, and Hazel. These names came from Vivian Vance's stand-in (and later Lucy series costumer) Renita Reachi, Adele Sliff, and Hazel Pierce, Lucy's stand-in.

June Havoc and Bill Spier: In *ILL:* "Homecoming," Betty Ramsey lists Bill and June Spier among the people that have to be invited to the Ricardos' housewarming party. The couple was named after Lucy's friends June Havoc and Bill Spier. June had appeared with Desi in the 1941 film *Four Jacks and a Jill* and starred in the Desilu sitcom *Willy,* which was produced by her husband, Bill Spier. Spier wrote, produced, and directed "radio's theater of thrills" *Suspense,* which Lucy (and Desi) appeared on several times.

Maury Thompson: Maury Thompson started as the script supervisor on *I Love Lucy,* moving up to camera coordinator and eventually to the director of *The Lucy Show.* In *ILL:* "Drafted," Ricky receives a letter from Maurice A. Thompson from the War Department. In *TLS:* "Lucy Is a Disc Jockey," Lucy announces a baseball game that includes a player named Maury Thompson.

Tommy Thompson: Associate producer and (later producer) of *The Lucy Show* Thompson was mentioned in "Lucy and Viv Play Softball." Lucy wears the uniform usually worn by Art Thompson, nicknamed "Moose." Art Thompson was Tommy Thompson's real name. In "Lucy, the Camp Cook," Viv asks if Tommy Thompson put his pet snake in the chef's bed.

Tommy Tucker: The name of Lucy's cue card man Tommy Tucker was featured in *HL:* "Lucy Sublets the Office," when Wally Cox plays "Little Tommy Tucker, the Toy Tycoon."

Charlie Van Tassel: Duck hunter Charlie Van Tassel, played by Gordon Jones, in *TLS:* "Lucy Goes Duck Hunting," was named after the husband of Madelyn Martin's college friend Marge. Marge and Chuck Van Tassel were names that appeared several times in *My Favorite Husband* scripts as well.

Marion Strong Van Vlack: Lucille's best friend from high school and former New York roommate received many mentions on Lucy's series. Marion Strong was frequently mentioned on *I Love Lucy* as a member of the Wednesday Afternoon Fine Arts League. She is played by Margie Liszt in "The Club Election" and later by Shirley Mitchell in "Lucy and Ethel Buy the Same Dress," "Lucy Tells the Truth," and "Lucy's Club Dance." Lucy Ricardo also frequently mentions her friend Marion Van Vlack, which was the Jamestown resident's real-life married name. Both the real-life Marion and her television counterpart were married to Norman Van Vlack (a character never actually seen on screen). Lucy mentioned Jamestown friend Marion Van Vlack in "California, Here We Come." Van Vlack's name comes up again in *LD:* "Lucy Wins a Racehorse." In *TLS* "Lucy Gets Her Maid," Lucy's employer is named Mrs. Van Vlack (played by Norma Varden).

Vivian Vance: In *Here's Lucy,* Vivian Vance's character was named Vivian Roberta Jones, which was the actress's name at birth. (Originally, the name Vivian Dodds was considered, which was Viv's married name at the time.) In "Lucy, the Matchmaker," Vivian Jones is living in Santa Fe, New Mexico, which is where Vance was actually living at the time. The following season, in "Lucy and Viv Visit Tijuana," Vivian says she lives in North Salem, New York, where Viv lived at that time. In "Lucy and Lawrence Welk," Viv says she is from Cherryvale, Kansas, which was the actress's birthplace.

Charles Walters: In *HL:* "Lucy and Carol Burnett" (third season), Carol points out unemployed singer Chuck Walters. Charles Walters had directed two episodes of the series that season, "Lucy's House Guest, Harry" and "Lucy and Aladdin's Lamp." Walters worked on the dances of many of Lucy's nineteen-forties films and would go on to direct *Three for Two* and *What Now, Catherine Curtis?* later in the nineteen-seventies.

Bernard Weitzman: In *TLS:* "Lucy Is Her Own Lawyer," Mooney's lawyer's name is Mr. Weitzman, after Desilu attorney Bernard Weitzman.

Kenneth Westcott: *The Lucy Show's* prop man Kenneth Westcott's name was utilized as the principal of Danfield High School played by Hanley Stanford in *TLS:* "Lucy Is a Chaperone." Westcott's daughter's name in the episode is Debbie, like the real-life Westcott's offspring. Debbie Westcott herself would later play a character named Debbie Westcott in *HL:* "Lucy and the Bogie Affair." Ken Westcott's name reappears as one of the players in the Palm Springs Golf Classic in "Lucy and Carol in Palm Springs."

Mary Wickenhauser: In *TLS:* "Lucy and the Runaway Butterfly," Mary Wickes plays Mrs. Wickenhauser, which was the actress's birth name.

Howdy Wilcox: Madelyn Martin's high school friend Howdy Wilcox got his name mentioned in the script of *TLS:* "Lucy's College Reunion" and was played by Lyle Talbot.

Places

780 North Gower Street: Lucy Carmichael's California home at the Glen Hall Apartments is said to be located at 780 North Gower Street. This was the actual address of *The Lucy Show*'s Desilu Studios filming location. North Gower Street pops up again as the site of a record company in *HL:* "Lucy and Ann-Margret."

Borrego Springs, California: Gale Gordon actually resided in Borrego Springs, California during his long stint on the *Lucy* series and was even the town's honorary mayor. The town received mention in two *Here's Lucy* episodes. In "Someone's on the Ski Lift with Dinah," Harry, boasting of his skiing ability, referred to himself as "the Jean-Claude Killy of Borrego Springs." In "The Not-So-Popular Mechanics," Lucy remarks, while watching Harry drool over his new Rolls Royce, "I haven't seen anything like this since you judged the Miss Borrego Springs beauty contest."

Hunt Road: In *ILL:* "California, Here We Come," Lucy asks her mother about Jamestown resident Marion Van Vlack. Mrs. McGillicuddy tells Lucy that she moved "way up on the old Hunt Road." Hunt Road was named after Lucy's maternal family.

Old Long Ridge Road: In *TLS* "Kiddie Parties, Incorporated" Viv says that Lucy, who floated away holding a bunch of helium balloons, was last spotted over Old Long Ridge Road. That was the name of the street Vivian actually lived on in Stamford, Connecticut at the time.

Shortridge High School: Writer Madelyn Martin used the name of her Indiana high school, Shortridge, as Vivian's high school in *TLS:* "Lucy Becomes a Reporter." Viv's principal, Mr. Hadley, was the name of the real-life principal. Madelyn also worked the school name into a *My Favorite Husband* script, "Liz's Radio Script," as Liz Cooper's alma mater.

15

"Hello, Clark! Hello, Walter! Hello, Hedy!"

Pop Culture References on Lucille Ball's Series: People

lthough situation comedies dwell predominantly within their own universe, Lucy's series always kept one foot in the real world, with cultural and topical references in abundance. Indeed, Ball made sure that her shows were rampant with celebrity appearances, most famously the Ricardos' and Mertzes' 1955 trip to Hollywood, which stretched from season four into season five, so prominent was it a part of *I Love Lucy*. Outside of these and other direct star appearances, here is a major sampling of some of the famous names and places in show business, sports, politics, and beyond that were referenced on the various Lucy series. (*ILL: I Love Lucy; LD: The Lucille Ball-Desi Arnaz Show; TLS: The Lucy Show; HL: Here's Lucy; LWL: Life with Lucy*)

Singers/Musicians/Composers

Herb Alpert and the Tijuana Brass. In *HL*: "Lucy and the Bogie Affair," Kim puts a picture of a sheepdog on top of a picture of Herb Alpert in her locker. In *HL*: "Lucy's House Guest, Harry," Harry brings his John Philip Sousa records over to Lucy's house, and Lucy tells a confused Kim, "Sousa was the Tijuana Brass of his generation."

Wee Bonnie Baker. In *TLS*: "Lucy's Barbershop Quartet," Lucy tells Chris that Viv is always saying she could have been another Wee Bonnie Baker. Chris doesn't know who she is, so Lucy sings "Oh, Johnny, Oh, Johnny, Oh!"

Beatles. In *TLS*: "Lucy and the Plumber," Lucy says that a trained dog howls like the Beatles. In *TLS*: "Lucy and the Great Bank Robbery," Lucy says she doesn't like the music Jerry is listening to. She likes 'long hair' music. Jerry tells her it *is* long hair music; it's the Beatles. In *TLS:* "Lucy, the Camp Cook," Lucy promises Jerry she will bring all his Beatles records to camp. In *TLS:* "Lucy's Contact Lenses," when Lucy hears Mooney's dog bark, she asks, "Was that Nelson?," to which Vivian responds, "It ain't the Beatles giving a concert." In *TLS:* "Lucy and the Return of Iron Man," according to Mooney, "A banker at a racetrack is as conspicuous as Yul Brynner standing among the Beatles." In *HL:* "Mod, Mod Lucy," Harry needs a band to play at a sixteenth birthday party. He suggests that "English group that's so popular . . . the Grasshoppers . . . the Caterpillers . . . the Centipedes . . . ?" Lucy tells him it's the Beatles. Harry says, "I knew it was some kind of a bug." Lucy tells him that the $100 payment wouldn't keep the Beatles in hairspray. In *HL:* "Lucy and Lawrence Welk," Welk claims to be writing a song for the Beatles. In *HL:* "Lucy and Rudy Vallee," Kim tries to teach Rudy "She Came in Through the Bathroom Window." Rudy says, "The Beatles wrote that? . . . No wonder they broke up." Also mentioned is "Mean Mr. Mustard," "Polythene Pam." and "Octopus's Garden." In *HL:* "Lucy Helps David Frost Go Night-Night," Harry says to Lucy, "One day in London and you think you're one of the Beatles!"

Harry Belafonte. In *HL:* "Lucy and Sammy Davis Jr.," when Lucy first meets Sammy, she thinks he is Harry Belafonte.

Leonard Bernstein. In *HL:* "Lucy, the Cement Worker," Harry can't believe the price to tune his car motor. He asks, "Who tuned it? Leonard Bernstein?"

Pat Boone. In *ILL:* "Country Club Dance," while talking about Diana Jordan (Barbara Eden), Ralph Ramsey (Frank Nelson) says, "It's amazing how little I have in common with a twenty-year-old. Who's Pat Boone?" In *HL:* "Harrison Carter, Male Nurse," when trying to coax Lucy into drinking her milk, Harry says, "Dear Abby likes milk. Pat Boone likes milk. Vida Blue likes milk."

Boswell Sisters. In *HL:* "Lucy and the Andrews Sisters," Lucy lists the Mills Brothers, the Boswell Sisters, and the Andrews Sisters as some of her favorite groups when she was a teenager. (The Boswells were featured in one of Lucy's early movie credits, *Moulin Rouge.*)

Ray Charles. In *HL:* "Lucy and Flip Go Legit," in the *Gone with the Wind* skit, Flip Wilson, as Prissy, wears an Abraham Lincoln T-shirt. Scarlett asks,

"Is that a picture of President Lincoln?," to which Prissy replies, "It ain't Ray Charles." (Lucy and Ray Charles received the Kennedy Center Honor together in 1986.)

Perry Como. In *ILL:* "Lucy Does the Tango," Ricky hears a hidden chicken cluck and says, "It doesn't sound like Perry Como."

Xavier Cugat. In *ILL:* "The Marriage License," Lucy tells Ricky she wouldn't marry him even if he was Xavier Cugat. In *ILL:* "Tennessee Ernie Visits," Lucy's mother's letter begins, "Dear Lucy, How are you and how is Xavier?" Lucy tells Ricky that her mother knows she's married to a Latin American bandleader, she just doesn't know which one. In *ILL:* "Lucy Goes to Scotland," Lucy gives Scotty MacTavish MacDougal MacArdo a Xavier MacCugat record. In *ILL:* "Lucy Gets Chummy with the Neighbors," an angry Ralph Ramsey tells Ricky they will get instead Xavier Cugat for the guest shot on his television program that he asked Ricky to do. In *LD:* "Lucy Takes a Cruise to Havana," Ricky tells Hedda Hopper that after one night with Rudy Vallee he was traded to Xavier Cugat's orchestra because Rudy couldn't understand him when he sang "The Whiffenpoof Song." In *LD:* "Lucy Wants a Career," after Lucy tells Paul Douglas she is Ricky Ricardo's wife, he tells her he wouldn't care if she was Xavier Cugat's wife.

Bobby Darin. In *TLS:* "Lucy, the Music Lover," Lucy goes to the music shop to buy Bobby Darin latest album for Chris.

Dave Brubeck Quartet. In *TLS:* "Chris Goes Steady," Chris says she and Ted Mooney both listen to the Dave Brubeck jazz combo when they do their homework.

Nelson Eddy. In *LD:* "Lucy Takes a Cruise to Havana," Rudy Vallee recalls when he was forced to stump the nation to stem the rising tide of Nelson Eddy.

Skinnay Ennis. In *TLS:* "Lucy the Referee," Viv doesn't know who Ricky Nelson or Frankie Avalon are, but doesn't feel too bad because she's sure Chris doesn't know who Skinnay Ennis is.

Larry Funk. In *HL:* "Lucy and Her All-Nun Band," band booker Mr. Adams tells Lucy that he goes as far back as Larry Funk and His Band of a Thousand Melodies.

Jan Garber. In *TLS:* "Lucy the Disk Jockey," radio announcer Gordon Feldsen announces "the swingin' sounds of Jan Garber."

Benny Goodman. In *ILL:* "The Publicity Agent," Lucy reads that the Shah of Persia has a standing order for all of Benny Goodman's records. In *LWL:* "One Good Grandparent Deserves Another," Ted asks Lucy if she's listening to Benny Goodman or Glenn Miller on her walkman. She's actually listening to Top Jimmy and the Rhythm Pigs.

Horace Heidt. In *ILL:* "Little Ricky Learns to Play the Drums," Ethel calls Ricky "Havana Horace Heidt."

Jascha Heifetz. In *ILL:* "Ragtime Band," Ethel calls violinist Fred "Jascha." In *HL:* "Lucy and Jack Benny's Biography," Jack Benny's mother (played by Lucy) answers a phone call from a neighbor complaining about young Jack's violin playing. Jack's mother says, "You're just jealous because my Jackie plays the violin a lot better than your Jascha, Mr. Heifetz."

Skitch Henderson. In *TLS:* "Lucy and the Plumber," Lucy suggests that Harry Tuttle grow a beard like fellow musician Skitch Henderson so he won't look so much like Jack Benny.

Don Ho. In *HL:* "Lucy and Carol Burnett" (second season), in Carol's speech about American history, she says the U.S. acquired Hawaii because of Don Ho. In *HL:* "Lucy Goes Hawaiian, Part Two," Craig imitates Don Ho and sings "Tiny Bubbles." (Lucy appeared as a guest on Don Ho's talk show in 1977 during Lucie's three week stint as co-host.)

Engelbert Humperdinck. In *HL:* "Lucy and Ann-Margret," Lucy says Craig could be a big star like "Engelbert Pumpernickel." In *HL:* "Lucy Gives Eddie Albert the Old Song and Dance," after being told they need a big name for their show, Mary Jane suggests Engelbert Humperdinck because "he's got the biggest name I know."

Mahalia Jackson. In *HL:* "Mod, Mod Lucy," when Lucy finds out that Kim is out surfing before she is supposed to sing with Craig's band, Lucy asks, "Does Mahalia Jackson go surfing before she sings?"

Mick Jagger. In *LWL:* "Lucy and the Guard Goose," Margo says she had a dream in which Mick Jagger wanted her to join his group, to which she said, "Mick, you can't always get what you want."

Jack Jones. In *TLS*: "Lucy Dates Dean Martin," Lucy tells her date, who is actually Dean Martin, that she has records of Frank Sinatra, Jack Jones, and Andy Williams.

Spike Jones. In *TLS*: "Lucy, the Disk Jockey," Mooney walks in on Lucy and Viv making different noises for a radio contest and says, "I didn't expect to interrupt a Spike Jones rehearsal."

Sammy Kaye. In *LWL*: "Lucy, the Legal Eagle," Curtis sells his copy of "Swing and Sway with Sammy Kaye" at the family garage sale.

King Family. In *HL*: "Lucy and Liberace," Liberace tells the auditioning Carter family that they're "about 83 short of the King Family." (The King Sisters appeared in Lucy's 1944 film *Meet the People* and were also featured in Desi Arnaz's 1946 movie *Cuban Pete*. King Family member Tina Cole was in *The Lucy Show* episode "Lucy's College Reunion.")

Wayne King. In *TLS*: "Lucy and Pat Collins," insomniac Mooney says that he tried to listen to Wayne King records to get to sleep.

Gene Krupa. In *LD*: "Lucy Meets the Mustache," Ernie Kovacs calls Ricky "the Cuban Krupa."

Frankie Laine. In *LWL*: "Lucy and the Guard Goose," when Lucy calls to return the guard goose, all she gets is a message that has Frankie Laine singing "The Cry of the Wild Goose."

Guy Lombardo. In *HL*: "Lucy and Buddy Rich," Harry says that Guy Lombardo is his favorite musician. Kim and Craig don't know who he is, so Lucy says, "he was the Lawrence Welk of his generation."

Glenn Miller. In *LWL*: "One Good Grandparent Deserves Another," Ted assumes Lucy is listening to Benny Goodman or Glenn Miller on her walkman.

Mitch Miller. In *TLS*: "Lucy Puts Up a TV Antenna," Lucy says before they had a TV they used to have community sings. Jerry asks if they did it with Mitch Miller. In *TLS*: "Lucy and the Plumber," Lucy suggests to Jack Benny look-alike violinist Harry Tuttle that he grow a beard like Mitch Miller.

Mills Brothers. In *HL:* "Lucy and the Andrews Sisters," Lucy lists the Mills Brothers, the Boswell Sisters, and the Andrews Sisters as some of her favorite groups when she was a teenager.

Ricky Nelson. In *TLS:* "Lucy the Referee," Chris's new love is Frankie Avalon, and she promises to be true to him for as long as she lives. When asked what happened to Ricky Nelson, she dismissively replies, "That was *last* week." (Although Lucy never appeared on film with Ricky Nelson, she appeared with his mother Harriet Hilliard in *Follow the Fleet;* his father, Ozzie Nelson, in *The Big Street;* and his daughter Tracy Nelson in *Yours, Mine and Ours.*)

Elvis Presley. In *ILL:* "Lucy Misses the Mertzes," Ethel couldn't use a pay phone because "some teenager was talking to her girlfriend about that Elvis what's-his-name." In *TLS:* "Lucy's Barbershop Quartet," when Chris can't believe Wee Bonnie Baker's "Oh, Johnny, Oh, Johnny, Oh!" was a hit song, Lucy says that one day Chris'll have to explain to *her* daughter what was so hot about Elvis Presley singing "Hound Dog." In *TLS:* "Lucy Goes to a Hollywood Premiere," a little old lady riding a motorcycle wants to buy a map to the movie stars' homes so she can see where Elvis Presley lives. In *HL:* "Lucy and Donny Osmond," Kim compares Cousin Patricia's crush on Donny Osmond to hers on Elvis Presley. In *HL:* "Harry Catches Gold Fever," Lucy says that when Harry pans for gold he looks like "a fat Elvis Presley."

Richard Rodgers & Oscar Hammerstein III. In *ILL:* "Redecorating," Ricky says he got tickets to the "new Rodgers and Hammerstein show." In *ILL:* "Sentimental Anniversary," Lucy wants to spend her anniversary alone with Ricky, so she tells the Mertzes that they have a business meeting with Rodgers and Hammerstein. In *ILL:* "Ricky Needs an Agent," Lucy tells MGM executive Walter Reilly that a famous team of producers want to star Ricky in a big Broadway musical. She can't reveal their names, but "Oscar and Dick are just wild about the boy." In *LD:* "The Celebrity Next Door," Lucy says that the PTA was fawning over everything Tallulah Bankhead said like she was "Oscar Hammerstein or somebody."

Paul Simon & Art Garfunkel. In *HL:* "Lucy and Ann-Margret," Lucy says that Craig could be as a big a songwriter as "Simon & Carbuncle." Kim and Craig tell her that the correct name is "Garfunkel." Later on, Ann-Margret tells them she has discovered a new songwriting team named "Simon & Carbuncle."

Kate Smith. In *TLS:* "Lucy and Phil Harris," Lucy, who has been singing at a piano bar, asks Mooney what he would like to hear. Mooney replies, "Kate Smith." (Lucy appeared with Smith on a 1966 episode of *The Dean Martin Show.*)

Sonny and Cher. In *HL:* "Mod, Mod Lucy," Lucy is going to replace Kim as the vocalist in Craig's band. Lucy to Craig: "Sonny, meet Cher." In *HL:* "Lucy Stops a Marriage," Harry refers to Kim and Craig as "Sonny and Cher." In *HL:* "The Carters Meet Frankie Avalon," Kim and Frankie Avalon play Sonny and Cher and sing "I've Got You, Babe" in a talent contest. (Lucy would appear in Cher's 1978 television special *Cher . . . and Other Fantasies.* Cher's mother, Georgia Holt, played a Jacques Marcel model in *I Love Lucy*'s "Lucy Gets a Paris Gown.")

Phil Spitalny. In *ILL:* "Lucy Is Jealous of a Girl Dancer," Ricky says the first member of his band that sounds like he is playing in his sleep will be traded to (all-girl orchestra leader) Phil Spitalny.

Ringo Starr. In *TLS:* "Lucy and the Monsters," in Lucy's nightmare, Mooney the Vampire's gorilla butler is named Ringo. In *HL:* "Lucy's Birthday," Kim and Craig are thinking of a date for Lucy. Craig suggests someone Kim would go out with. Kim says, "I don't think Mother would be happy with Ringo Starr," so Craig offers Lawrence Welk instead.

Tiny Tim. In *HL:* "Lucy and Miss Shelley Winters," when Harry discovers Lucy singing into a tape recorder, he says, "Thank you, Tiny Tim!" In *HL:* "Lucy and Rudy Vallee," Rudy Vallee refers to himself as "the Tiny Tim of the Roaring '20s."

Top Jimmy and the Rhythm Pigs. In *LWL:* "One Good Grandparent Deserves Another," after Lucy dances into the house while listening to her walkman, Ted asks what she's listening to: "Benny Goodman? Glenn Miller?" Lucy replies, "No, Top Jimmy and the Rhythm Pigs!"

Andy Williams. In *TLS:* "Lucy Dates Dean Martin," Lucy tells her date, who is actually Dean Martin, that she has records of Frank Sinatra, Jack Jones, and Andy Williams. In *HL:* "Lucy and Flip Go Legit," when Lucy wears a *Three Musketeers* costume that is for a sketch on Flip's show, Flip thinks she must be one of the show's guest stars. He rules out Rock Hudson and asks her to sing something to prove she's his other guest, Andy Williams. Lucy sings a line of "Moon River" and Flip says, "Definitely not Andy Williams."

Actors/Performers/Celebrities

Bud Abbott and Lou Costello. In *HL:* "The Bow-Wow Boutique," after Harry and his employee Mr. Dinwitty (Jonathan Hole) argue, Lucy states, "I haven't heard anything like this since Abbott and Costello!" (Lucy had a cameo in the 1945 film *Bud Abbott and Lou Costello in Hollywood* and also guest starred on a 1943 episode of their radio series.)

June Allyson. In *ILL:* "Hollywood Anniversary," June Allyson and Dick Powell are among those supposedly invited to the Ricardos' anniversary party. (Allyson appeared with Lucy in *Best Foot Forward* and *Meet the People*. It was on the set of the latter film that Lucy introduced June to Dick Powell, who would become her husband.)

Don Ameche. In *HL:* "Lucy's Tenant," Mary Jane tells Lucy about an old movie she saw on television in which Jack Oakie and Mary Astor were about to be married, but Don Ameche, playing Mary's long-lost husband, returns from being missing at sea. (Ameche co-starred with Lucy in the 1944 *Lux Radio Theatre* adaptation of the 1940 Ronald Colman- Ginger Rogers film *Lucky Partners* and in the 1950 *Screen Guild Theater* version of the 1941 movie *You Belong to Me* playing the roles originated by Henry Fonda and Barbara Stanwyck on film.)

Eddie "Rochester" Anderson. In *TLS*: "Lucy Gets Jack Benny's Account," Lucy points out a picture of "Rochester" in Benny's living room.

Julie Andrews. In *HL:* "Lucy and the Andrews Sisters," Lucy can't think of Patty Andrews's name. Patty says, "Try 'Andrews,'" to which Lucy responds, "You're Julie Andrews!"

Fred Astaire. In *ILL:* "The Adagio," Lucy needs a dance partner and says, "I wonder what Fred Astaire is doing." Ethel later says that she found Lucy a partner: Fred. Lucy excitedly says, "Astaire!" then Fred Mertz comes out. In *TLS:* "Lucy and George Burns," Lucy tells George Burns about a Fred Astaire-Ginger Rogers movie she saw on television. In *HL:* "Lucy's Lucky Day," when Lucy sees Jackie the chimp dancing, she says, "someone call Fred Astaire, we've got another Ginger Rogers." In *HL:* "Ginger Rogers Comes to Tea," Lucy tells Ginger that she's seen every picture she did with Fred Astaire (three of them up close, since Lucy was featured in *Roberta, Top Hat,* and *Follow the Fleet*).

Mary Astor. In *HL:* "Lucy's Tenant," Mary Jane describes an old movie with Jack Oakie, Mary Astor, and Don Ameche that gives Lucy the idea to pretend she has a long-lost husband who returns after being lost at sea in order to scare off tenant Kermit Boswell (Jackie Coogan).

Lauren Bacall. In *ILL:* "Lucy and John Wayne," a poster of Wayne and Lauren Bacall in *Blood Alley* is displayed.

Vilma Banky. In *ILL:* "Lucy Does the Tango," Ethel says that when Lucy and Ricky tango, they look just like Vilma Banky and Rudolph Valentino. (Actually, Valentino's partner in the tango that made him famous in *The Four Horsemen of the Apocalypse* was not Banky but Beatrice Dominguez, but that name hardly conjures up silent movie mystique.)

Theda Bara. In *TLS:* "Lucy Plays Cleopatra," Theda Bara's version of *Cleopatra* is mentioned. In *HL:* "Lucy and Miss Shelley Winters," Harry tells Lucy, who is not too subtly auditioning for a movie producer, "That will be all, Theda Bara."

Brigitte Bardot. In *TLS:* "Lucy Dates Dean Martin," Eddie Feldman (Dean Martin) compares his date, Lucy, to Brigitte Bardot.

Ethel Barrymore. In *HL:* "Lucy, the Cement Worker," Harry says that he has been told he looks like one of the Barrymores. It doesn't matter which one. Lucy says it does because "one of them was Ethel."

Lionel Barrymore. In *ILL:* "Lucy and Ethel Buy the Same Dress," Lucy says that Caroline Appleby will want to do her impersonation of Bette Davis on their TV program. Ethel tells her that it isn't Bette Davis, it's Lionel Barrymore.

Ingrid Bergman. In *TLS:* "Lucy Gets Mooney Fired," Lucy describes to Mary Jane the plot of *Gaslight* with Charles Boyer and Ingrid Bergman. In *HL:* "Lucy Carter Meets Lucille Ball," Lucy says, "I may look like Lucille Ball now, but when I was young, I looked like Ingrid Bergman."

Shelley Berman. In *TLS:* "Lucy Saves Milton Berle," Berle, posing as a skid row bum, tells Lucy his name is Berman. Lucy says, "Like the comedian Shelley Berman!" (Shelley Berman served as a guest panelist on the January 1, 1961 episode of *What's My Line?* with mystery guest Lucille Ball.)

Sarah Bernhardt. In *ILL:* "Ricky's Movie Offer," after Lucy tries to give him line readings, Ricky asks her, "Who do you think you are, Sarah Bernhardt?" In *HL:* "My Fair Buzzi," Harry describes Annie Whipple (Ruth Buzzi) as "a budding Sarah Bernhardt."

Humphrey Bogart. In *ILL:* "Ricky's Movie Offer," Lucy says that, for his movie, Ricky has to develop a distinctive way of speaking, like Humphrey Bogart. Later, Fred guesses that Lucy, in her Marilyn Monroe guise, is "Humphrey Bogart in a wig." In *HL:* "Lucy and the Bogie Affair," Kim names their dog "Bogie" because she thinks he looks like Humphrey Bogart at the end of *Casablanca. HL:* "Lucy and Carol Burnett" (third season), Lucy, Kim, and Carol see one of Humphrey Bogart's costumes in their musical.

Marlon Brando. In *ILL:* "The Dancing Star," Lucy says that Marlon Brando was one of the stars she told Caroline Appleby she has met in Hollywood. Lucy: "Did you see *On the Waterfront?* Wonderful! He won the Academy Award, you know." In *ILL:* "Lucy Visits Grauman's," Ricky's cake says, "To my darling, another Marlon." Ricky says, "I guess Brando and I do have a lot in common." In *TLS:* "Lucy Dates Dean Martin," Marlon Brando's undershirt from *A Streetcar Named Desire* is one of the sale items for the bank's charity ball.

Yul Brynner. In *ILL:* "Country Club Dance," Fred thinks that the "Yul Brynner influence" is what made Diana Jordan (Barbara Eden) interested in him. In *TLS:* "Lucy and the Return of Iron Man," Mooney claims that "a banker at a racetrack is as conspicuous as Yul Brynner standing among the Beatles." In *TLS:* "Lucy Meets the Law," robbery victim Mr. Trindle (Byron Foulger) says he did not think there would be so many redheads in the police lineup. Lieutenant Finch (Claude Akins) asks, "What did you expect? A bunch of Yul Brynners?"

John Bunny. In *ILL:* "Ricky's Screen Test," after Lucy talks about her chance of being discovered during Ricky's screen test, Fred says she might be "a second John Bunny," referring to the silent screen comedian.

Francis X. Bushman. In *ILL:* "The Hedda Hopper Story," Mrs. McGillicuddy asks Lucy if while in Hollywood she's seen her favorite stars, Ramon Novarro and Francis X. Bushman.

Champ Butler. In *ILL:* "Lucy Gets in Pictures," Bobby the bellboy informs Lucy that country western singer Champ Butler was discovered parking cars.

James Cagney. In *TLS*: "Lucy the Disc Jockey," Viv was up late watching "The Late, Late Show" because the best movie James Cagney ever made, the one where he shoves the grapefruit in his girlfriend's face, was on. In *HL*: "Lucy and Sammy Davis Jr.," Sammy does a Cagney impression. In *HL*: "Lucy and Carol Burnett" (third season), one of Cagney's costumes is on display and Kim says she once saw him get the electric chair five nights in a row on "The Late, Late Show." In *HL*: "Lucy and Mannix Are Held Hostage," bank robber Vernon (John Doucette) says Cagney is his idol. In *HL*: "The Carters Meet Frankie Avalon," Frankie impersonates Cagney in *Yankee Doodle Dandy*.

Eddie Cantor. In *ILL*: "LA at Last!," Lucy points out a caricature of Eddie Cantor at the Brown Derby. In *HL*: "Someone's On the Ski Lift with Dinah," Harry tells Dinah Shore that he used to listen to her on Eddie Cantor's radio show. (Cantor starred in Lucy's first film *Roman Scandals* as well another one of Lucy's Goldwyn assignments, *Kid Millions*.)

Richard Chamberlain. In *TLS*: "Lucy and John Wayne," Lucy thinks she sees Richard Chamberlain in the studio commissary.

Lucy as Carol Channing, supported by Mr. Mooney (Gale Gordon) and the Countess (Ann Sothern) in *The Lucy Show* episode "Lucy, the Undercover Agent."

Marge & Gower Champion. In *ILL:* "Lucy and Bob Hope," a dancing Bob Hope jokes, "If Marge sees this, Gower's finished!"

Carol Channing. In *TLS:* "Lucy, the Undercover Agent," Lucy disguises herself as Carol Channing. (Carol Channing and Lucy appeared together on *Super Password* in 1988, Lucy's final game show appearance.)

Charlie Chaplin. In *TLS:* "Chris's New Year's Eve Party," Lucy plays Charlie Chaplin. In *TLS:* "Lucy and Mickey Rooney," Lucy plays Chaplin with Rooney as The Kid (Jackie Coogan).

Claudette Colbert. In *TLS:* "Lucy, the Camp Cook," hitchhikers Lucy and Viv are having no luck stopping passing cars, so Viv suggests they give them "the Claudette Colbert bit" and hike up their skirts to show off their leg like Colbert did in *It Happened One Night*.

Joan Collins. In *LWL:* "Lucy Makes a Hit with John Ritter," the director of *A Soldier's Song* tells John he might be able to get Joan Collins to be his leading lady. (Joan Collins was one of the speakers at *An All-Star Party for Lucille Ball* in 1984.)

Ronald Colman/Benita Hume Colman. In *ILL:* "Harpo Marx," Lucy tells Caroline Appleby that "Ronnie and Benita" will be at her party, but then remembers that they were at last week's party, so they won't be in again.

Gary Cooper. In *ILL:* "Ricky Asks for a Raise," the gang goes out to see Gary Cooper in *High Noon*. In *ILL:* "The Dancing Star," Lucy tells Caroline that Gary will be at her party the following day. In *ILL:* "Harpo Marx," Lucy wears a Cooper mask and answers with Cooper's trademark "Yup" to fool Caroline.

Bill Cosby. In *HL:* "Lucy and Flip Go Legit," Flip thinks Lucy wants a second autograph so she can trade two of his for one of Bill Cosby's.

Bing Crosby. In *ILL:* "Ricky's Screen Test," Lucy imagines talking to Bing Crosby at a famous Hollywood restaurant. In *ILL:* "Ricky's Contract," Hollywood bound Ricky says, "I'm going to make that Crosby look like a bum." In *ILL:* "LA at Last!," William Holden says he has just finished making *The Country Girl* with Bing Crosby and Grace Kelly. In *LD:* "Lucy Takes a Cruise to Havana," Lucy tells Rudy that she and her friends are all officers of the Rudy Vallee Fan Club and they're having great difficulty with Susie, who is trying to swing everybody over to the Bing Crosby Fan Club. Rudy later calls Susie "Crosby Lover." In *TLS*: "Lucy, the Disc Jockey," Lucy gets a request to play "Bing Crosby Sings Stephen Foster." In *HL*: "Lucy and the Andrews Sisters," Craig plays Bing Crosby's part in the Andrews Sisters numbers that featured the singer. In *HL*: "Lucy and Rudy Vallee," Lucy says that some kids today do not know who Bing Crosby is. Rudy asks, "Who's Bing Crosby?"

Arlene Dahl. In *ILL*: "Ricky's Screen Test," Arlene is one of the rumored leading ladies to play opposite Ricky in *Don Juan*.

Bette Davis. In *ILL*: "Lucy and Ethel Buy the Same Dress," Lucy says that Caroline Appleby will want to do her impersonation of Bette Davis on their TV program. Ethel tells her that it isn't Bette Davis, it's Lionel Barrymore. In *HL*: "Lucy, the American Mother," Kim imitates Bette Davis by saying, "Petah! Petah! You read the letter, didn't you?" and pretending a stalk of celery is a cigarette.

Doris Day. In *TLS*: "No More Double Dates," Lucy says she heard that the new Doris Day picture is "cute" but Viv doesn't feel like seeing something with Doris Day. In *TLS*: "Lucy Is a Soda Jerk," Chris wonders if Doris Day started out as a soda jerk. In *TLS*: "Lucy Goes to a Hollywood Premiere," Lucy buys a nightgown worn by Doris Day in *Pillow Talk*. In *HL*: "Lucy and Lawrence Welk," on the Universal Studio tour, Viv says she saw Doris Day's bicycle. In *HL*: "Lucy's Bonus Bounces," Lucy says that if they ever made a movie about Harry's life, he could be played by Doris Day.

Yvonne de Carlo. In *ILL*: "Ricky's Screen Test," Yvonne is one of the rumored leading ladies to play opposite Ricky in *Don Juan*.

Frances Dee. In *ILL*: "The Fashion Show," Mrs. Joel McCrea is scheduled to be in the Don Loper fashion show, but cancels because she is going to Europe. Lucy takes her place in the show. (Dee starred in one of Lucy's earliest films, *Blood Money*.)

Marlene Dietrich. In *HL*: "Lucy and Carol Burnett" (third season), Lucy imitates Marlene Dietrich singing her signature song "Falling in Love Again." (Lucy co-starred with Dietrich in 1951's *Screen Director's Playhouse* radio adaptation of the Billy Wilder comedy *A Foreign Affair*. Dietrich and John Lund recreated the roles they played in the 1948 film with Lucy taking over the part originated by Jean Arthur.)

Phyllis Diller. In *HL:* "Lucy and Jim Bailey," Phyllis Diller is supposed to be the entertainment at the Chamber of Commerce banquet, but gets laryngitis, so Jim Bailey impersonates her. In *HL:* "Meanwhile, Back at the Office," Lucy's new employer, Mr. Richards (Don Porter) tells Lucy that if he wanted a funny secretary, he would have hired Phyllis Diller. (Diller appeared in Lucy's *Dean Martin Celebrity Roast* that aired in 1975. The two would team up for several Bob Hope specials.)

Alfred Drake. In *ILL:* "Lucy Tells the Truth," Lucy says that she starred in a musical comedy—*Oklahoma!* Ethel says, "What was your maiden name? Alfred Drake?"

Clint Eastwood. In *HL:* "Lucy and the Group Encounter," Lucy says that if she was stuck on a desert island, she would like Clint Eastwood to be there. In *HL:* "Lucy's Tenant," Lucy asks why men like Clint Eastwood don't go around renting rooms. Mary Jane says, "If they did, I'd open a boardinghouse." In *HL:* "Milton Berle Is the Life of the Party," Harry, who claims he doesn't care about celebrities, names Clint Eastwood as one of the people Lucy could have at her party and it would not interest him.

Ralph Edwards. In *HL:* "Lucy and Candid Camera," Lucy thinks Allen Funt is Ralph Edwards.

Faye Emerson. In *ILL:* "Lucy Does a TV Commercial," Fred says he hopes Faye Emerson will be on television. (Lucy appeared as mystery guest on *What's My Line?* with friend Faye Emerson on the panel in 1961. On one occasion in 1956, Lucy replaced Emerson in her most famous panelist gig on *I've Got a Secret.*)

Maurice Evans. In *ILL:* "Lucy Meets Orson Welles," Lucy tells Orson she thinks he's even better than Maurice Evans.

Alice Faye. In *HL:* "Lucy and Carol Burnett" (third season), Lucy and Carol come across costumes worn by Betty Grable and Alice Faye, which leads to a musical medley. In *HL:* "Lucy and Phil Harris Strike Up the Band," Lucy says that she was at the Wilshire Bowl the night Alice and Phil met.

W. C. Fields. In *HL*: "Lucy and the Bogie Affair," Lucy says, "It isn't a fit night out for man nor beast," but can't remember if it was Shakespeare or W. C. Fields who said it first. In *HL*: "Lucy, the Wealthy Widow," banker Ed McAllister (Ed McMahon) quotes W. C. Fields.

Henry Fonda. In *HL*: "Guess Who Owes Lucy $23.50," in an inside joke, Van Johnson discusses his movie *Yours, Mine, and Ours* and his kooky redhead co-star. Lucy says, "Personally, I thought she was much too young for Henry Fonda." In *HL*: "Lucy and Joan Rivers Do Jury Duty," Lucy is the lone hold-out and Joan describes her as "Henry Fonda in *12 Angry Men*." Later, Lucy and Joan must share a hotel room and Joan says, "I wish you were Henry Fonda." (Although Fonda and Lucy co-starred in the films *The Big Street* and *Yours, Mine and Ours*, as well as the special *The Good Years*, he never guest starred on any of her series.)

Jane Fonda and Peter Fonda. In *HL*: "Lucy and Carol Burnett" (third season), their version of "Hooray for Hollywood" contains the lyrics: "Even a big star like Henry Fonda begins to wonder how Jane and Peter make good."

Annette Funicello. In *TLS*: "Lucy, the Star Maker," bank employee Tommy (Frankie Avalon) tells Lucy that not everyone can be an Annette Funicello. In *HL*: "Guess Who Owes Lucy $23.50," Craig tells Van Johnson that he's the biggest star he's met outside of Annette Funicello.

Clark Gable. In *ILL:* "The Benefit," Ethel says getting Lucy for a show instead of Ricky is like expecting Clark Gable and getting Hubert Grimset (Lucy: "I never heard of him." Ethel: "Neither did I."). In *ILL:* "The Business Manager," Lucy asks Mr. Hickox (Charles Lane) if anyone ever told him he looked like Clark Gable. In *ILL:* "Ricky's Screen Test," Lucy reads in *Modern Screen* that there is a vacant lot next door to Clark Gable's house. Lucy plans to move there and borrow butter from him. In *ILL:* "The Dancing Star," Lucy wrote to Caroline Appleby that she had lunch with Clark Gable. It wasn't a lie. She was at Perino's and Clark was there and they ate lunch together . . . at different tables. Later, Lucy tells Caroline that Clark Gable, Walter Pidgeon, and Hedy Lamarr are all down by the pool. When Caroline wants to go down to see them, Lucy tells her they're off to the races. In *ILL:* "Harpo Marx," Lucy impersonates Clark Gable. In *ILL:* "The Tour," Lucy wants to sit on the left side of the bus because Clark Gable's house is on that side. *LD:* "Milton Berle Hides Out at the Ricardos" Lucy says that "Clark Gable" is a nice name. In *HL:* "Lucy and Carol Burnett" (third season), Lucy, Kim, and Carol see the costumes that Clark Gable and Vivien Leigh wore in *Gone with the Wind*. (Lucy starred opposite Clark Gable in a 1944 *Gulf Screen Theater* radio adaptation of the 1935 Gable-Jean Harlow film *China Seas*.)

Zsa Zsa Gabor. In *ILL*: "Ricky Asks for a Raise," a framed photo of Zsa Zsa is prominently displayed in the entranceway of the Tropicana. In *HL*: "Lucy and Eva Gabor Are Hospital Roomies," Lucy tries to tell Harry who her new roommate is without Eva hearing. Lucy gives Harry several clues and he guesses Zsa Zsa Gabor. (Lucy was a guest on *The Zsa Zsa Gabor Show*, an unsold talk show pilot in 1969. Zsa Zsa appeared on a 1975 installment of *Dinah!* saluting Lucy.)

Greta Garbo. In *ILL*: "The Saxophone," Lucy shows Ethel the hat she wore during her "Greta Garbo period." In *ILL:* "The Dancing Star," while singing "How About You?," Van Johnson sings, "Greta Garbo's looks give me a thrill." In *TLS*: "Lucy Waits Up for Chris," Lucy and Viv want to watch Greta Garbo in *Camille* on television. Jerry asks Sherman, "Who's Greta Garbo?" Sherman says she's before his time and asks Viv. Viv insists, "She's before my time too."

Ava Gardner. In *ILL*: "LA at Last!," Fred is sick of Lucy and Ethel gawking at the Brown Derby and tells them that movie stars are "just people like you and me." Ava Gardner is paged, and Fred jumps right up. After Ethel reminds him what he just said to them, Fred says, "She might be people, but she's not like you and me." In *ILL:* "The Tour," Lucy and Ethel see Gardner's house on their bus tour. Lucy's conversation with Ethel about Ava Gardner becomes so involved that the exasperated bus driver holds the microphone up to Lucy's face just as she says, "And I understand she wears nothing but black lace lingerie." In *ILL:* "Lucy Visits Grauman's," when everyone is listing the Hollywood sights they have yet to see, Fred names Ava Gardner. (Frawley was featured in the 1949 Gardner film *East Side, West Side*. A pre-fame Ava Gardner appeared in an unbilled role in Lucy's movie *Du Barry Was a Lady*.)

Judy Garland. In *HL*: "Lucy and Carol Burnett" (third season), as part of the show-within-a show, Lucy, Kim, and Carol visit a Hollywood studio and see Judy Garland's costume from *The Wizard of Oz*. In *HL:* "Lucy and Jim Bailey," it is mentioned that Judy is one of the ladies Jim impersonates. (Lucy and Judy Garland both appeared in separate segments of *Thousands Cheer* and *Ziegfeld Follies*. Their children, Desi Arnaz Jr. and Liza Minnelli, would become engaged in the nineteen-seventies.)

Cary Grant. In *ILL:* "LA at Last!," Cary Grant is paged at the Brown Derby. In *ILL:* "Hollywood Anniversary," Cary and Betsy Grant are among the guests supposedly invited to the Ricardos' party. In *ILL:* "The Dancing Star," Lucy says she mentioned she met Cary Grant in her letters to Caroline Appleby. In *ILL:* "Lucy Visits Grauman's," Lucy saves a tin can that was squashed by Cary Grant's left rear wheel. In *TLS:* "No More Double Dates," Lucy wants to see the new Cary Grant picture. In *TLS:* "Lucy Decides to Redecorate," Viv wants to go to the movies, but Lucy would rather stay home and look at her new upholstery. Viv says she'd rather look at Cary Grant's upholstery. In *TLS:* "Lucy and Viv Open a Restaurant," Vivian says, "If I want to spend a thousand dollars on a meal, I'll rent a couple of togas and fly Cary Grant in for a Roman banquet." In *TLS:* "Lucy and Joan," Cary Grant is one of the celebrities expected to attend the charity event Lucy has tickets to. In *TLS:* "Lucy, the Babysitter," at an employment agency, Lucy is given a word association test. When given the word "carry," she says "Grant." Lucy remarks that Cary Grant could now use a babysitter (a reference to the birth of Grant's first child with Dyan Cannon a year earlier). In *HL:* "Lucy and Eva Gabor," in the screenplay Lucy dictates to Eva, the scene opens with her in Cary Grant's arms. In *HL:* "Lucy, the Helpful Mother," Lucy tells Irving the chimp that he's kind of cute, but no Cary Grant. In *HL:* "Lucy and Johnny Carson," Harry lies to Lucy and tells him that Cary Grant just walked into the Brown Derby so he, Johnny Carson, and Ed McMahon can escape from her. In *HL:* "Lucy Protects Her Job," upon meeting Harry, secretary "Shoiley Shopenhauer" (played by Kim) claims she had no idea she would be working for a man who is "so Cary Grant-ish." In *HL:* "Lucy and Carol Burnett" (third season), Carol is trying to con Harry and calls him "Cary," saying that she got confused because he looks so much like Cary Grant. Harry replies, "So do you." In *HL:* "Lucy Goes Hawaiian, Part One," the Matson Steamship Line is looking for a cruise director and Lucy says that the job description sounds like a cross between Cary Grant, Albert Einstein, Joe Namath, and Bob Hope. Harry selects himself for the job. In *HL:* "A Home Is Not an Office," while Lucy is convalescing after her skiing accident, Harry cannot find the file relating to his client, Mr. Bradshaw. Kim suggests he check the "G" file because her mother thinks Bradshaw looks like Cary Grant. She is right. (Grant spoke at 1984's *An All-Star Party for Lucille Ball.* Lucy and Cary both spoke at *An All-Star Party for Clint Eastwood* in 1986. The latter special ended up being aired on television on November 30, 1986, the night after Grant's death. It was his final television appearance.)

Alec Guinness. In *LD:* "Lucy's Summer Vacation," after Lucy drills holes in Ricky and Howard Duff's fishing boat, Ida Lupino tells Lucy that their husbands want to take them on a moonlight boat ride to a nearby island. Ida asks, "How do you expect us to get over there? Have Alec Guinness build us a bridge?," a reference to his Oscar-winning role in *The Bridge on the River Kwai*.

Cedric Hardwicke. In *ILL*: "Lucy Writes a Play," Ricky asks if Lucy is getting Sir Cedric Hardwicke to star in her play. (Hardwicke appeared opposite Lucy in the 1947 film *Lured*.)

Jean Harlow. In *HL*: "Lucy and Carol Burnett" (third season), Lucy, Carol, and Kim look at a portrait of Jean Harlow. (Lucy reprised the part Jean Harlow had played in *Libeled Lady* in the 1946 remake, *Easy to Wed*, as well as her roles in *Dinner for Eight* and *China Seas* on radio.)

Rex Harrison. In *HL*: "Lucy, the Wealthy Widow," Lucy compares banker Ed McAllister (Ed McMahon) to England's "Divine Mr. Harrison," "Sexy Rexy." In *LWL:* "World's Greatest Grandma," Lucy remembers that Rex Harrison talked all the lyrics in *My Fair Lady* and was brilliant without singing a note, so she decides to do the same thing in the grandmother talent show.

Laurence Harvey. In *TLS*: "Lucy Plays Cleopatra," Audrey Simmons (Mary Jane Croft) says that she thinks she might be able to get Harvey to play the part of Antony. Professor Gitterman (Hans Conried) asks, "Laurence Harvey?" Audrey replies, "My husband, Harvey."

Sessue Hayakawa. In *LD*: "The Ricardos Go to Japan," Lucy says that Fred in his kimono looks likes Japan's answer to Sessue Hayakawa.

Gabby Hayes. In *ILL:* "Lucy Goes to a Rodeo," Ricky inquires about Gabby Hayes's availability for his Western show.

Rita Hayworth. In *TLS:* "Lucy and Joan," Lucy wears a dress that Rita Hayworth wore in one of her pictures and later gave to Lucy's neighbor Joan (Joan Blondell).

Joey Heatherton. In *HL:* "Lucy and Johnny Carson," Ed McMahon hears Johnny Carson on the telephone say he can't do Joey's show (Ed presumes it is Joey Bishop, Johnny's competitor at the time). Johnny says, "Joey Heatherton drives me nuts." (Lucy and Joey Heatherton would later appear on the same installment of *The Tonight Show Starring Johnny Carson* in 1977.)

Lucy and Katharine Hepburn discuss a scene from *Stage Door* (1937) with director Gregory LaCava, who received an Oscar nomination for his efforts. Lucy had shown up as an extra in a previous La Cava credit, *The Affairs of Cellini* (1934), and would support Hepburn yet again, in *Without Love* (1945).

Paul Henried. In *ILL:* "The Adagio," Ricky lights two cigarettes and says he feels like Paul Henried, a reference to a scene in *Now, Voyager.*

Audrey Hepburn. In *TLS:* "Lucy Dates Dean Martin," Dean buys Lucy a jacket Audrey Hepburn once wore in one of her pictures. In *TLS:* "Lucy's Substitute Secretary," Mary Jane lends Lucy a wig that Audrey Hepburn wore in a movie. In *HL:* "Lucy's Working Daughter" Craig says, "I finally see a girl who looks like Audrey Hepburn and it has to be my sister."

Katharine Hepburn. In *ILL:* "Lucy's Italian Movie," Lucy says, "The calla lilies are in bloom again," echoing Hepburn's famous line from *Stage Door.* In *HL:* "Lucy, the American Mother," Kim says, "The calla lilies are in bloom again." In *HL:* "Ginger Rogers Comes to Tea," Having had her fill of devotion, Ginger asks Lucy to do her a favor: "Please, please become a Katharine Hepburn fan." (Both Rogers and Lucy appeared with Hepburn in the 1937 film *Stage Door.* Lucy also supported Hepburn in the 1945 film *Without Love.*)

Charlton Heston. In *HL:* "Lucy Is a Bird Sitter," Mary Jane invites Lucy to see Charlton Heston in a play at the Music Center. Harry asks Lucy if she thinks he's going to part the Los Angeles River. Lucy tells Harry that he is "not fit to touch the hem of his toga."

Judy Holliday. In *ILL:* "LA at Last!," Lucy and Ethel can't decide if one of the caricatures at the Brown Derby is Shelley Winters or Judy Holliday. It's Eve Arden.

Tab Hunter. In *TLS:* "Lucy Goes to a Hollywood Premiere," rising young star Road Block is compared to Tab Hunter and Rip Torn.

Jennifer Jones. In *HL:* "Lucy and Chuck Connors Have a Surprise Slumber Party," Chuck Connors is told that his old film *Good Morning, Miss Dove* starring Jennifer Jones is on TV. Chuck says that's one of the few times he got to nuzzle someone besides a horse.

Ruby Keeler. In *HL:* "Lucy and Carol Burnett" (third season), Carol imitates Ruby Keeler tap dancing. In *HL:* "Lucy Goes on Her Last Blind Date," Ben Fletcher (Don Knotts) says his grandfather came to Hollywood in the twenties to open a miniature golf course and marry Ruby Keeler.

Grace Kelly. In *ILL:* "LA at Last!," William Holden says he has just finished making *The Country Girl* with Bing Crosby and Grace Kelly. In *ILL:* "Country Club Dance," Lucy suggests that Ethel wear her glamorous hairdo that makes her look like Grace Kelly. "It worked for Grace Kelly." In *TLS:* "Lucy Gets Her Maid," Viv sarcastically refers to their new maid, Miss Putnam, as "Princess Grace."

Durwood Kirby. In *HL:* "Milton Berle Is the Life of the Party," Durwood Kirby is mentioned as one of the people that is supposed to be on the celebrity telethon.

Alan Ladd/Sue Carol Ladd. In *ILL:* "Getting Ready," Lucy points out where Alan Ladd lives on a map of the movie stars' homes in *Modern Screen.* In *ILL:* "The Fashion Show," Sue Carol, Mrs. Alan Ladd, is supposed to be in the Hollywood wives fashion show. (She is not seen on camera.) In *ILL:* "The Tour," when the tour boss passes by Alan Ladd's home, Lucy hopes Sue Carol will walk by.

Hedy Lamarr. In *ILL:* "The Dancing Star," Lucy tells Caroline that Clark Gable, Walter Pidgeon, and Hedy Lamarr are all down by the pool. When Caroline wants to go down to see them, Lucy tells her they're off to the races.

Dorothy Lamour. In *ILL:* "Lucy Gets in Pictures," Lucy hears that Dorothy Lamour was discovered in an elevator. In *HL:* "Lucy, the Coed," Lucy says Harry can get over his college flame Gloria Pendleton because he got over Dorothy Lamour.

Burt Lancaster. In *ILL:* "The Hedda Hopper Story," Ricky's publicist pretends to mistake a lifeguard for Burt Lancaster. In *TLS:* "Lucy and John Wayne," Lucy thinks she sees Burt Lancaster in the movie studio commissary, and later the director of John Wayne's movie suggests they send meddlesome Lucy over to Lancaster's film set next door.

Stan Laurel & Oliver Hardy. In *TLS:* "Lucy and Pat Collins," Lucy and Mooney are hypnotized into thinking they are Laurel & Hardy.

Gypsy Rose Lee. In *TLS:* "Lucy Gets Amnesia," after the sleeve comes off the rabbit coat Lucy is wearing, Viv asks if the coat was made for Gypsy Rose Lee.

Peggy Lee. In *HL:* "Lucy and Jim Bailey," it is mentioned that Peggy is one of the ladies Jim impersonates. (Lucy and Peggy Lee worked together on radio on *The Jimmy Durante Show* in 1948.)

Pinky Lee. In *HL:* "Milton Berle is the Life of the Party," Pinky Lee is mentioned as one of the people that is supposed to be on the celebrity telethon Lucy, Harry, and Mary Jane watch.

Vivien Leigh. In *HL:* "Lucy and Carol Burnett" (third season), Lucy, Kim, and Carol see the costumes that Clark Gable and Vivien Leigh wore in *Gone with the Wind.*

Jack Lemmon. In *TLS:* "Lucy Goes to a Hollywood Premiere," Lucy buys the nightgown that Doris Day wore in *Pillow Talk.* Mooney says he wouldn't pay money for "a nightie if it was worn by Jack Lemmon in *Some Like It Hot.*" In *HL:* "Lucy Visits Jack Benny," Lucy looks through Benny's guest registry and notes that Mr. and Mrs. Jack Lemmon stayed at the Benny residence. In *HL:* "Lucy Protects Her Job," after "Shoiley Shopenhauer" describes Harry as "Cary Grant-ish," he tells her most people think he looks like Jack Lemmon.

Jerry Lewis. In *TLS:* "Lucy Dates Dean Martin," Lucy tells her date Eddie Feldman, who unbeknownst to her is really Dean Martin, that the first time she saw Dean he was working with Jerry. Dean asks, "Jerry who?" Lucy: "Jerry Lewis." Dean: "Oh, I remember him." Lucy says that she was worried about Dean after they broke up. She didn't think Dean was going to make it. (Lucy guest starred on the first installment of *The Martin and Lewis Show* on radio in 1949. In addition, Lucy and Jerry appeared together in *Danny Thomas' Wonderful World of Burlesque* in 1965.)

Harold Lloyd. In *ILL:* "Lucy Visits Grauman's," Lucy and Ethel see Harold Lloyd's footprints and the prints of his trademark glasses at Grauman's Chinese Theatre. (Lloyd produced Lucy's 1941 film *A Girl, a Guy, and a Gob.*)

Gina Lollobrigida. In *ILL:* "Staten Island Ferry," Ethel has been studying Italian and tells Fred that he won't be able to tell the difference between her and Gina Lollobrigida. In *ILL:* "Lucy's Italian Movie," in order to wake a sleeping Fred up on the train, Ethel says, "Hey look, there goes Gina Lollobrigida!" In *TLS:* "Lucy Dates Dean Martin," Eddie Feldman (Dean Martin) compares his date, Lucy, to Gina Lollobrigida.

Carole Lombard. In *TLS*; "Lucy Goes to a Hollywood Premiere," Lucy holds up a magazine with Carole Lombard's picture on the cover.

Sophia Loren. In *HL:* "Guess Who Owes Lucy $23.50," Van Johnson tells Lucy, dressed as Italian sex symbol Gina Linguini, that he likes her even more than Sophia Loren. In *HL:* "Lucy and the Generation Gap," Lucy turns down a piece of pizza, saying that she has to watch her figure. She reconsiders when she's reminded what it did for Sophia Loren's figure.

Bela Lugosi. In *HL:* "Lucy Takes Over," Craig scares Kim in the attic by pretending to be Bela Lugosi.

Ali MacGraw. In *HL:* "Kim Finally Cuts You Know-Who's Apron Strings," Kim looks at herself in the mirror and says, "Ali MacGraw, eat your heart out!"

Marjorie Main. In *HL*: "Lucy Stops a Marriage," Lucy says Harry once got an autographed picture of Marjorie Main. (Main supported Lucy and Desi in the 1954 film *The Long, Long Trailer.*)

Jayne Mansfield. In *TLS*: "Lucy Is a Chaperone," one of Chris's friends, wearing a blonde wig, pretends to be Jayne Mansfield. (Lucy and Mansfield both appeared in separate vignettes in *A Guide for the Married Man,* the last movie the sex symbol would film before her death in 1967.)

Margo. In *ILL*: "Lucy Gives Eddie Albert the Old Song and Dance," Albert's wife, Margo, is mentioned several times. Eddie says he can't be in Lucy's show because it's the same night as Margo's birthday. (Margo starred in the 1936 film *Winterset,* which Lucy appeared in as an extra.)

Mary Martin. In *TLS*: "Lucy Teaches Ethel Merman to Sing," After Lucy tells Agnes Schmidlapp, who is really Ethel Merman, that she told her son that she was good friends with Merman, "Agnes" says that she once told her daughter that her best friend was Mary Martin.

The Marx Brothers. In *ILL*: "*Don Juan* is Shelved," Ricky says, "Maybe they'll use me in one of the Marx Brothers' pictures—Chico, Harpo, Groucho and Floppo. " Harpo later appeared in the episode "Harpo Marx" in which Ricky and Fred dressed up like Groucho and Chico. (Lucy appeared in the 1938 Marx Brothers' film *Room Service.*)

Butterfly McQueen. In *HL*: "Lucy and Carol Burnett" (third season), Lucy, Kim, and Carol see the costumes that Clark Gable and Vivien Leigh wore in *Gone with the Wind.* Lucy does an impression of Butterfly McQueen saying, "Please, Miss Scarlett, I don't know nothing about birthin' babies."

Steve McQueen. In *TLS:* "Lucy Goes to a Hollywood Premiere," Lucy yells to an elderly, motorcycle-riding lady who buys a map of the movie stars' homes, "Say hello to Steve McQueen!" In *HL:* "Lucy Visits Jack Benny," Lucy sees in Jack's guest registry that Mr. and Mrs. Steve McQueen were among those who stayed at the Benny residence. In *HL:* "Lucy the Skydiver," Lucy tells new motorcyclist Kim that she's raised a daughter, not Steve McQueen. In *HL:* "Lucy and Carol Burnett" (third season), Carol tells Lucy her Butterfly McQueen impression sounds more like Steve. In *HL:* "Lucy and the Astronauts," Harry gets Lucy out of the bathroom by pretending that Steve McQueen walked in.

Marilyn Monroe. In *ILL:* "Changing the Boys' Wardrobe," the gang goes to see a Marilyn Monroe movie. In *ILL:* "Ricky's Movie Offer," Lucy sees that one of the roles in *Don Juan* is supposed to be a "Marilyn Monroe type," so she dresses as Marilyn. In *ILL:* "Ricky's Screen Test," Marilyn is one of the rumored leading ladies for *Don Juan*. In *ILL:* "The Hedda Hopper Story," Ricky says he can't get his name in Hedda Hopper or Louella Parsons's columns. "All they talk about is Marilyn Monroe, Marilyn Monroe. What's Marilyn Monroe got that I haven't . . . don't answer that!" In *ILL:* "Harpo Marx," Lucy says that Caroline Appleby is so nearsighted she might think Ethel is Marilyn Monroe. Ethel puts her hair down over one eye and walks like Marilyn. Lucy says, "Nobody's *that* nearsighted." In *ILL:* "Lucy Visits Grauman's," Ricky's cake says, "To my darling, another Marlon." Fred asks who Marlon is. Ethel says, "Marlon Brando. Know anybody else named 'Marlon?' Fred replies, "Sure, Monroe." In *ILL:* "Lucy and Superman," Caroline Appleby describes the plot of a Marilyn Monroe movie she just saw. In *ILL* "Lucy Does the Tango," Lucy tells Ethel, who has eggs in her back pocket, not to walk like Marilyn Monroe.

Paul Newman. In *TLS:* "Lucy Is a Chaperone," Chris describes a boy as looking like Paul Newman. In *HL:* "Lucy and the Andrews Sisters," Patty Andrews says her home has a terrific view—on a clear day you can see Paul Newman. He lives next door. Unfortunately, you can also see his wife. In *HL:* "Won't You Calm Down, Dan Dailey?," Dan Dailey is producing a movie and thinks Paul Newman would be great in the lead. In *HL:* "Lucy, the Other Woman," the wife of Lucy's milkman, Mr. Butkis, thinks Lucy is having an affair with her husband and says Lucy can have him. Lucy later says giving up a Butkis isn't like giving up Paul Newman.

Mabel Normand. In *ILL:* "Baby Pictures," Charlie Appleby says that his TV station just bought some films and they are going to make television stars out of some of the actors. He tells them to remember their names: Conway Tearle and Mabel Normand. (Tearle had died in 1938 and Normand died in 1930.)

Ramon Novarro. In *ILL:* "The Hedda Hopper Story," Mrs. McGillicuddy asks Lucy if she's seen her favorite stars, Ramon Novarro and Francis X. Bushman.

Hugh O'Brian. In *ILL:* "Lucy Goes to a Rodeo," Ricky is looking for western acts for the rodeo he is performing in at Madison Square Garden. Ricky asks if "the fellow who plays Wyatt Earp . . . O'Brian" is available.

Lucy, Jack Oakie, Frank Jenks, and Lily Pons, with their "makes you want to stick your fingers in your ears" music, during production of *That Girl from Paris* in 1937.

Margaret O'Brien. In *ILL:* "Lucy Gets Ricky on the Radio," the gang can't figure out who the little girl is on TV; Lucy thinks it's Margaret O'Brien.

Maureen O'Hara. In *TLS:* "Lucy and John Wayne," Lucy says that the girl in John Wayne's pictures is usually Maureen O'Hara and she has beautiful red hair. (O'Hara was Lucy's co-star in the 1940 film *Dance, Girl, Dance.*)

Jack Oakie. In *HL:* "Lucy's Tenant," Lucy gets the idea to chase Kermit (Jackie Coogan) away by Mary Jane's description of an old movie with Jack Oakie, Mary Astor, and Don Ameche. (Lucy appeared with friend Jack

Oakie on film in *Murder at the Vanities, That Girl From Paris, The Affairs of Annabel,* and *Annabel Takes a Tour.*)

Laurence Olivier. In *ILL:* "Lucy Meets Orson Welles," Orson tells Lucy she left out Laurence Olivier when she listed the Shakespearean actors she thought Orson was better than.

Gregory Peck. In *ILL:* "The Girls Want to Go to a Nightclub," Ethel says it's her wedding anniversary. Lucy asks, "Yours and Fred's?" Ethel replies, "No, mine and Gregory Peck's." (This is the first celebrity mention on a Lucy show.) In *ILL:* "The Young Fans," Peggy describes Arthur as looking like Gregory Peck. Lucy thinks he sounds more like Lassie. In *ILL:* "Ricky's Screen Test," Lucy points out where Gregory Peck lives on a map in *Modern Screen.* *ILL:* "LA at Last!," Gregory Peck is paged at the Brown Derby. In *ILL:* "Little Ricky Gets a Dog," after seeing Lucy struggle with Little Ricky's fish, Ethel says, "Gregory Peck had less trouble with Moby Dick." In *HL:* "Lucy and Johnny Carson," Lucy sees that Gregory Peck is at the Brown Derby, jumps up, bumps into a waiter, and spills drinks all over Johnny Carson. In *HL:* "Lucy and the Celebrities," Peck is mentioned as one of the stars Rich Little imitates.

Mary Pickford. In *ILL:* "Lucy Gets Ricky on the Radio," the gang can't figure out who the little girl is on TV. Fred thinks it's Mary Pickford.

Walter Pidgeon. In *ILL:* "The Dancing Star," Lucy tells Caroline Appleby that Clark Gable, Walter Pidgeon, and Hedy Lamarr are all down by the pool. When Caroline wants to go down to see them, Lucy tells her they're off to the races.

Dick Powell. In *ILL:* "Hollywood Anniversary," June Allyson and Dick Powell are among those supposedly invited to the Ricardos' anniversary party. (Powell starred opposite Lucy in *Meet the People* in 1944.)

William Powell. In *HL:* "Lucy and the Andrews Sisters," Lucy lists William Powell as one of the movie stars she had a crush on when she was a teenager. (Powell portrayed Florenz Ziegfeld in the introductory sequence of Lucy's movie *Ziegfeld Follies.*)

Tyrone Power. In *ILL:* "Lucy Visits Grauman's," Ethel points out Tyrone Power's footprints. Later, a cop puts his feet in the footprints.

Dorothy Provine. In *TLS*: "Lucy and George Burns," George Burns mentions he had an act with Dorothy Provine, but she left and went into television.

Burt Reynolds. In *HL*: "Lucy and Joan Rivers Do Jury Duty," Lucy describes a ninety-one-year-old juror (Burt Mustin, who was a mere eighty-nine at the time) as "the Burt Reynolds of Sun City."

Debbie Reynolds. In *TLS*: "Lucy and Joan," Debbie is supposed to be at the Hollywood premiere Lucy is going to attend.

Jason Ritter. In *LWL*: "Lucy Makes a Hit with John Ritter," In a rare instance of an actor being mentioned *before* he became an actor, Lucy impresses John Ritter with her knowledge about his life. She knows his wife's name is Nancy and his children are Carly, Tyler, and Jason. (Jason was six years old at the time.)

Tex Ritter. In *ILL*: "Lucy Goes to a Rodeo," Ricky is looking for western acts for the rodeo he is performing in at Madison Square Garden. Ricky wants to know if Tex Ritter could do it. (Tex Ritter was the father of John Ritter and grandfather of Jason.)

Roy Rogers. In *ILL*: "Lucy Goes to a Rodeo," after Lucy pokes fun at Ricky's Western talk, he says, "I'd like to hear Roy Rogers sing 'Babalu.'"

Jane Russell. In *ILL*: "Lucy Visits Grauman's," Russell's name is on the Grauman's marquee advertising *The Tall Men*.

Lillian Russell. In *ILL*: "Desert Island," Ethel says Fred hasn't worn Eau de Cologne since Lillian Russell came to town. (One of Lucy's unfulfilled ambitions was to play Russell in a movie biopic.)

Soupy Sales. In *TLS*: "Chris's New Year's Eve Party," the kids think Charlie Chaplin is a stone age Soupy Sales. In *HL*: "Milton Berle Is the Life of the Party," Soupy Sales is mentioned as one of the people that is supposed to be on the celebrity telethon. (Although they shared no scenes, Sales had a bit part in Lucy's 1963 film *Critic's Choice*.)

Omar Sharif. In *HL*: "Lucy the Sheriff," Lucy calls the two outlaws in her custody "Little Richie Burton and Omar Sharif."

Frank Sinatra. In *ILL:* "*Don Juan* Is Shelved," Ricky wonders if he could borrow some bobbysoxers from Frank Sinatra. In *ILL:* "Lucy and the Dummy," At the MGM studio party, a clip is shown of Sinatra in *Guys and Dolls.* In *TLS:* "Lucy and Joan," Sinatra is one of the guests scheduled to attend the premiere Lucy plans on going to. In *HL:* "Lucy and Ann-Margret," Ann-Margret's accompanist suggests the singer get Frank Sinatra or Dean Martin to perform Craig's song on TV with her. In *HL:* "Lucy and Sammy Davis Jr.," Lucy asks Sammy what Frank Sinatra is really like. In *HL:* "Lucy and Eva Gabor Are Hospital Roomies," Eva has to cancel her dinner with Frank Sinatra because she's in the hospital. In *HL:* "Lucy and Donny Osmond," Kim recalls that she developed a crush on Frank Sinatra when she was eleven. Lucy asks when she got over it. "Soon, I hope," Kim replies. In *HL:* "Lucy Gives Eddie Albert the Old Song and Dance," the girls need a singer/dancer for their show. Lucy reads that Frank Sinatra is coming out of retirement. Mary Jane says he's a good singer, but he's not a very good dancer, so he's eliminated. In *HL:* "Milton Berle Is the Life of the Party," Harry names Frank Sinatra as one of the people Lucy could have at her party that he would not care about. (Lucy and Frank Sinatra co-starred in *The Screen Guild Theatre* production of *Too Many Husbands* with Bob Hope, on April 21, 1947.)

Smothers Brothers. In *TLS:* "Lucy and the Lost Star," Mooney calls Lucy and Viv "the Smothers Mothers." In *HL:* "Mod, Mod Lucy," Lucy says, "Suppose the Smothers Brothers didn't hire relatives, we'd only have one Smother."

Connie Stevens. In *TLS:* "Lucy and George Burns," George Burns mentions he had an act with Connie Stevens, but she left and went into pictures.

James Stewart. In *HL:* "Lucy and Sammy Davis Jr.," as part of Sammy's movie, he does an imitation of James Stewart playing cards at a casino. In *HL:* "Won't You Calm Down, Dan Dailey?," Dan Dailey drops the name Jimmy Stewart to show Lucy how overly excited she gets when he mentions a celebrity. In *HL:* "Lucy and the Celebrities," Lucy poses as Stewart's dietician and ballet instructor. Rich Little later does a Stewart impression. (Although he was Lucy's neighbor on Roxbury Drive, Stewart never guest starred on any of her series. He and Lucy both appeared together on several other television programs including *CBS Salutes Lucy: The First 25 Years,* Stewart's *Dean Martin Celebrity Roast, Dinah!, An All-Star Party for Lucille Ball,* and *A Beverly Hills Christmas.*)

Barbra Streisand. In *TLS:* "Lucy, the Babysitter," the chimpanzees aren't pleased with Lucy's singing. Lucy tells them that she isn't Barbra Streisand. In *HL:* "Lucy and the Bogie Affair," Kim puts a picture of a sheepdog on top of a picture of Streisand in her locker. In *HL:* "Lucy and Jim Bailey," it is mentioned that Barbra is one of the ladies Jim impersonates.

Gloria Swanson. In *ILL:* "Lucy Visits Grauman's," Lucy and Ethel see Gloria Swanson's footprints. Her feet are so small they guess she must be a size one-and-a-half shoe.

Robert Taylor. In *ILL:* "Don Juan and the Starlets," Robert Taylor is down by the hotel pool. Ethel points to his feet sticking out underneath an umbrella to Lucy. In *ILL:* "The Star Upstairs," Lucy has an orange Taylor squeezed at the Farmer's Market. In *ILL:* "The Tour," Lucy plans to steal a Richard Widmark grapefruit to go with her Robert Taylor orange. In *ILL:* "Lucy Visits Grauman's," Lucy's Robert Taylor orange has shriveled, and his signature now looks like it says "Wobert Tawlor."

Conway Tearle. In *ILL:* "Baby Pictures" Charlie Appleby says that his TV station just bought some films and they are going to make television stars out of some of the actors. He tells them to remember their names: Conway Tearle and Mabel Normand. (Lucy appeared in the Broadway-bound play *Hey Diddle Diddle* in 1937, but the play closed out of town due to Tearle's ill health.)

Shirley Temple. In *ILL:* "Lucy Gets Ricky on the Radio" The gang can't figure out who the little girl is on TV. Ricky thinks it's Shirley Temple. In *ILL:* "The Tour" on their bus tour, Lucy and Ethel see Shirley Temple's old home with a dollhouse in the backyard. Shirley doesn't live there anymore because she's married to Mr. Black. In *TLS:* "Ethel Merman and the Boy Scout Show." Vivian, dressed as Shirley, sings "On the Good Ship Lollipop."

Three Stooges. In *LWL:* "Lucy Is a Sax Symbol" Margo mentions when Lucy sat through a Three Stooges film festival with Becky. Becky calls Margo and Ted "Moe and Curly." (Lucy appeared in the 1934 Three Stooges short *Three Little Pigskins.*)

Rip Torn. In *TLS:* "Lucy Goes to a Hollywood Premiere," Hollywood's honorary mayor, Johnny Grant, compares rising young star Mr. Block to Tab Hunter and Rip Torn. (Rip Torn co-starred with Lucy in *Critic's Choice.*)

Lana Turner. In *ILL:* "Ricky's Screen Test," Lana is one of the rumored leading ladies for *Don Juan.* In *ILL:* "Lucy Gets in Pictures," Lucy hears that Lana Turner was discovered sitting on a stool at Schwab's Drug Store, so she tries to do the same thing. In *ILL:* "*Don Juan* Is Shelved," Fred is unhappy because he might have to leave Hollywood without having seen Lana Turner. In *ILL:* "Lucy Visits Grauman's," Fred saves Lana Turner's lipstick print. (Ball and Turner co-starred in a 1941 *Lux Radio Theater* adaptation of the 1940 film *They Drive By Night.* Turner also had a cameo in Lucy's first MGM Picture, *Du Barry Was a Lady.* Lucy got her follow-up assignment at Metro, *Best Foot Forward,* after original star Turner had to withdraw because of pregnancy.)

Robert Wagner. In *TLS:* "Lucy Meets the Berles," Milton Berle is producing a movie about a pilot and thinks Robert Wagner would be great in the lead.

Raquel Welch. In *HL:* "Lucy Visits Jack Benny," Jack rents Harry his old room, which he had to give up because of doctor's orders. It overlooks Raquel Welch's patio, and she sunbathes every day. In *HL:* "Lucy and Johnny Carson," Lucy says that Harry drools over seeing a panel show about the origin of money as if he was going to see Raquel Welch take a bubble bath. In *HL:* Lucy the American Mother," Lucy suggests Craig get Raquel Welch to play her in the movie he's making. In *HL:* "Lucy, the Crusader," when Lucy tells Craig that his birthday gift is something he always wanted, Craig excitedly asks, "Raquel Welch?" In *HL:* "Lucy and Carol Burnett" (third season), Carol claims that she's an actress working under a different name—Raquel Welch. "Somebody let the air out." In *HL:* "My Fair Buzzi," Harry jokes, "My only regret is that I'm already promised to Raquel Welch."

Esther Williams. In *ILL:* "The Hedda Hopper Story," Ricky's publicist tells a lifeguard that he would be perfect for the lead in Esther Williams's new picture. In *ILL:* "Hollywood Anniversary," Esther Williams is among those supposedly invited to the Ricardos' anniversary party. (Lucy appeared with Williams in the 1946 film *Easy to Wed,* and both actresses were among the all-star cast of *Ziegfeld Follies.*)

Monty Woolley. In *ILL:* "The Mustache," Ricky wants to talk to a bearded Lucy on the phone and asks for Monty Woolley.

Robert Young. In *HL:* "Won't You Calm Down, Dan Dailey?," Dan Dailey mentions he knows Robert Young, which excites Lucy.

Sports Figures

Eddie Arcaro. A jockey who held the record for winning more American Classic Races than anyone else. In *TLS:* "Lucy and the Countess Have a Horse Guest," new horse owner Rosie says that she will be in with the Longdens and the Arcaros. (Jockey Johnny Longden previously appeared in *ILL:* "Lucy and the Loving Cup.")

Patty Berg. Record-holding female golfer. In *TLS:* "Lucy Tries Winter Sports," Vivian describes Lucy in tennis clothes as "a regular Patty Berg."

Yogi Berra. The New York Yankee catcher (1946–65) was actually the team's manager when he was mentioned on *The Lucy Show* in 1964. In "Lucy, the Good Skate," Vivian says that she and Lucy, at a sporting goods store with curlers in their hair, look like Yogi Berra.

Jim Brown. American football player who, in his rookie year, held the record for most yards gained by rushing. In *TLS:* "Lucy Is a Referee," Lucy studies Brown's football card and then impresses Jerry and Sherman with her knowledge.

Jack Dempsey. The Heavyweight Champion of the World from 1919 to 1926. In *TLS:* "Lucy, the Fight Manager," Lucy overhears some fight managers talking about Jack Dempsey, "the Manassa Mauler."

Joe DiMaggio. Centerfielder for the New York Yankees (1936–51) was one of the great names in baseball. In *ILL:* "Lucy Is Enceinte," Fred gives Lucy a baseball signed by Joe DiMaggio for the baby. In *ILL:* "Lucy's Italian Movie" Fred says the Coliseum is smaller than Yankee Stadium and Joe DiMaggio "would have hit eighty home runs in that hat box." In *ILL:* "Lucy and Bob Hope," when Little Ricky accidently calls the athlete "Joe Maggio," Fred tells him that he's getting more like his father every day. True to form, Ricky later calls him "Joe Maggio."

A. J. Foyt. The racecar driver won numerous championships throughout the years. In *HL:* "Kim Finally Cuts You-Know-Who's Apron Strings," Uncle Herb (Alan Oppenheimer) tells Kim's date Ronnie Cumberland (Lloyd Batista) that he could have beat A. J. Foyt in Ontario if his engine hadn't conked out.

Gorgeous George. One of early television's novelty celebrities, wrestler "Gorgeous George" Wagner stood out because of his outrageously flamboyant persona, which included platinum blond hair and a flowing cape. In *ILL:* "Pioneer Women," Ethel says that their grandmothers, after churning butter, must have had arms like Gorgeous George. In *ILL:* "Ricky's Movie Offer," Fred says that Lucy dressed as Marilyn Monroe is supposed to be Gorgeous George.

Jean-Claude Killy. The French skier came to prominence by winning three events at the 1968 Winter Olympics. In *HL:* "Someone's on the Ski Lift with Dinah," Harry claims that he's "Borrego Springs' answer to Jean-Claude Killy." In *HL:* "Lucy's Big Break," the story of Lucy's broken leg gets so exaggerated that it becomes "Jean-Claude Killy had an accident and Lucy carried him down the slope on her back."

Sandy Koufax. Pitcher for the Dodgers (1955–66), Koufax was known for his ability to pitch a perfect game of no-hitters. In *TLS:* "Lucy, the Fight Manager," Lucy thinks Koufax is a boxer because Mooney said, "No one can hit him."

Mickey Mantle. He was the Yankees' center fielder (having joined the team in 1951) at the time he was mentioned in *ILL:* "Lucy and Bob Hope," when Fred tells Little Ricky he might be another Mickey Mantle. (William Frawley would later appear with Mantle in the 1962 film *Safe at Home!*)

Willie Mays. The centerfielder was best known for his long stint with the Giants in both New York and San Francisco. In *TLS:* "Lucy Tries Winter Sports," after Lucy repeatedly causes him harm during a skiing lesson, Mooney tells her, "Willie Mays would love your batting average."

Barney Oldfield. One of the first and most successful automobile racers in the early nineteen-hundreds. In *ILL:* "Lucy Learns to Drive," when new driver Lucy makes it seem like she knows so much more about cars than Ethel, Ethel says, "Pardon me, Barney Oldfield."

Arnold Palmer. Since establishing himself professionally in the mid fifties, Palmer's name became one of the most frequently mentioned when talking about the world of golf. In *TLS:* "Lucy Takes Up Golf," Lucy's boyfriend Gary (played by Gary Morton in his first appearance on a *Lucy* series episode) comes over to Lucy's house to watch Arnold Palmer play golf on TV.

Red Phillips. American football player who, one year, caught more passes than any other man in the National Football League. In *TLS:* "Lucy Is a Referee," Lucy studies Phillips's football card and then impresses Jerry and Sherman with her knowledge.

Al Rosen. Third baseman for the Cleveland Indians (1947–56). In *ILL:* "Lucy and Bob Hope," Lucy distracts Bob during a baseball game at Yankee Stadium, and he gripes, "Al Rosen hits a home run and I have to miss it."

Y. A. Tittle. Quarterback Y. A. Tittle had already wrapped up his professional career (with the New York Giants) five years before he was mentioned in *HL:* "Lucy the Fixer," in which Kim calls Craig in his football uniform "the Y. A. Tittle of the teenyboppers."

Johnny Unitas. He was the star quarterback for the Baltimore Colts at the time he was mentioned in *TLS:* "Lucy the Referee," when Jerry can't find his Johnny Unitas trading card.

Political Figures

Spiro Agnew. The Greek first name of Richard Nixon's vice president (1969–73) was always good for a laugh during his term in office. His name is heard in two *HL* episodes. In "Lucy's Wedding Party," Lucy says the only Greek she knows is Spiro. Mary Jane asks if that's Spiro Agnew. Lucy replies, "No, Spiro Shapiro. He owns a Greek restaurant down in Chinatown." In "Lucy and the Celebrities," Lucy finds out that one of the people Rich Little imitates is Spiro Agnew and wonders, "Who would want to be Spiro Agnew?"

Secretary General Leonid Brezhnev. Brezhnev served as the Soviet leader from 1964 until his death in 1982. In *HL:* "Lucy and Chuck Connors Have a Surprise Slumber Party," Chuck Connors picking up Secretary Brezhnev in his arms is referenced several times. This real-life incident happened earlier that same year (1973) at a party given for Brezhnev by President Nixon at the Western White House in San Clemente, California.

Dwight Eisenhower. The 34th President of the United States (1954–61), was referenced twice during his term in office on *ILL,* once along with his wife, Mamie. In "The Sublease," The Mertzes have turned down everybody who wants to sublet the Ricardos' apartment, to which Lucy cracks that the Mertzes "wouldn't even approve Ike and Mamie." In "The Star Upstairs,"

Cornel Wilde's newspaper was so wet he could see one page through another. Says Wilde: "I thought President Eisenhower was playing golf with Little Orphan Annie."

Mamie Eisenhower. The wife of 34th U.S. President Dwight Eisenhower was not a fan of exercise or physical activity. In *ILL*: "The Golf Game," Ricky tells Lucy that she shouldn't take up golf because "Mamie doesn't play."

Queen Elizabeth II. The ruler of Great Britain and its sovereign states since 1953 was the basis of an entire *I Love Lucy* episode, "Lucy Meets the Queen," when Ricky is scheduled to participate in a command performance for Her Royal Highness. Ricky calls his agent, Phil Wilcox, but Lucy thinks he's talking to the Queen's husband, Prince Philip. In *LD*: "Lucy Wants a Career," Ricky reads that Danny Kaye is going to England to do another command performance for Queen Elizabeth. Lucy wonders what the Queen is cooking for Phil that night. In *TLS*: "Lucy and the Ring-a-Ding Ring," Lucy pretends to talk to Elizabeth and Philip while wearing Mrs. Mooney's ring.

John Kennedy. The 35th President of the United States (1961–63) was not just referenced but heard (as played by an uncredited actor) on *TLS*: "Lucy Visits the White House." Lucy, Viv, and the Cub Scouts plan to take the replica of the White House they made out of sugar cubes to President Kennedy. Lucy ends up getting stuck in a rocking chair once owned by Tad Lincoln. The voice of "President Kennedy" is heard saying, "Come in, Mrs. Carmichael. Don't be bashful. I'm glad to see I'm not the only one who is attached to a rocking chair." (In order to alleviate the pain from a back injury, the President had several special rockers from the P&P Chair Company made for himself during his term in office.) Wife Jackie and daughter Caroline are also mentioned on this episode. In "Lucy Decides to Redecorate," Lucy mentions President Kennedy's fitness plan. Kennedy was assassinated four days after the episode aired.

Nikita Khrushchev. The leader of the Communist Party in the Soviet Union, who in 1959, had a planned visit to Disneyland cancelled for security reasons. In *HL*: "Lucy Meets the Burtons," Richard Burton bemoans that everybody has been to Disneyland except him and Khrushchev.

Lyndon Johnson. The 36th President of the United States (1963–69). In *TLS*: "Lucy the Stockholder," Lucy says she's going to send Lyndon a thank you note for her tax refund. Later, after Lucy says she invested the money in his bank, a distraught Mooney, wondering why his country would do such a thing to him, looks at a picture of President Johnson and cries, "Lyndon!" In *TLS:* "Lucy Goes to a Hollywood Premiere," when Lucy's neighbor, Tom Foley, has to miss a movie premiere because he is being inducted into the army, Lucy suggests, "Tell the army you're going to report tomorrow." Tom replies, "I don't think Lyndon would like that." The month before he was to hand over the office to his successor, Johnson was mentioned on *HL:* "Guess Who Owes Lucy $23.50," when Lucy says she can get Van Johnson to sing to a cow in Texas. Harry suggests "the other Johnson fellow . . . Lyndon . . . he's from Texas and he could use the work."

Princess Anne. The daughter of Queen Elizabeth II, she married Lt. Mark Phillips in November 1973. *HL:* "Milton Berle Is the Life of the Party." Harry says he does not care that Milton Berle is coming to Lucy's party and furthermore wouldn't care about any celebrity, including "Princess Anne and her new husband."

Princess Margaret. The younger sister of Queen Elizabeth II. In *ILL:* "Harpo Marx," Lucy sarcastically suggests they have Princess Margaret over for tea after Ethel suggests they invite Harpo Marx.

Richard Nixon. The 37th President of the United States (1969–74). In *IIL:* "Lucy and the Astronauts," Lucy talks to the president on the phone. His name, however, is never mentioned.

Ronald Reagan. The former movie star was a frequent point of reference by those in the industry he was once a part of, first when he served as the 33rd Governor of California (1967–75) and then later when he became the 40th President of the United States (1981–89). He rated three mentions on *HL.* In "Lucy Visits Jack Benny," Jack tells Lucy not to argue with him about state tax, but "go fight with Ronnie Reagan." In "Lucy and the Raffle," after Kim tells Lucy she will put a governor in her new car, Lucy says, "Ronald Reagan has enough things to do." In "Lucy and Carol Burnett" (third season), the unemployment agent (Richard Deacon) says, "I'm back in show biz, Ronnie. Don't you wish you were?" In *LWL:* "Mother of the Bride," Lucy invites Ron and Nancy Reagan to the wedding. Lucy: "They won't come, but can you imagine the gift they'll send?" (In 1977, Ronald and Nancy Reagan were guests on *The Merv Griffin Show* with Lucy and Gary.)

William H. Seward. Served as secretary of state under both Presidents (1861–69) Abraham Lincoln and Andrew Johnson. He was most famous for his purchase of Alaska from Russia, labeled "Seward's Folly" by many at the time. In *LD*: "Lucy Goes to Alaska," Lucy and Ethel are mad because their husbands buy a piece of land in Alaska sight unseen. In his defense, Ricky says Secretary of State Seward bought the entire territory of Alaska without ever having seen it.

Harry Truman. The 33rd President of the United States (1945–53) was still holding office when he and his wife, Bess, were mentioned in *ILL*: "Ricky Asks for a Raise." Lucy says that "Harry and Bess Truman" got the last table at the Tropicana.

Various Other Notable Names Referenced

Bonnie and Clyde. The notorious Depression-era bank robbers Bonnie Parker and Clyde Barrow were gunned down by the law on May 23, 1934. Thirty-three years later, Warren Beatty's hit movie *Bonnie and Clyde* made them famous all over again. In *HL*: "Lucy's Birthday," Harry says he always has trouble with Kim and Craig's names. He wished that Lucy listened to him and named them after his grandparents: Bonnie and Clyde; In *HL*: "Lucy Helps Craig Get a Driver's License," Lucy does not want Craig to be fingerprinted. The clerk says that the only other people who ever objected were Bonnie and Clyde.

Major Bowes. As the creator and host (1934–45) of radio's *Original Amateur Hour*, Major Edward Bowes became one of the medium's most instantly recognizable names and his program the forerunner of all similar media competitions. In *ILL*: "The Mustache," after the Mertzes and the Ricardos audition for him in the Ricardo apartment, talent scout Mr. Murdoch asks, "What is this? A stranded Major Bowes unit?"

Diamond Jim Brady. The millionaire and philanthropist was a key social figure in turn-of-the-century New York whose flamboyant habits exemplified high living and extravagant spending. In *ILL*: "The Business Manager," Ricky tells Fred that their business manager, Mr. Hickox, makes him look like Diamond Jim Brady. In *TLS*: "Lucy and Paul Winchell," Lucy says that the bank employees call her boss "Diamond Jim Mooney." In *TLS*: "Lucy Gets Involved," Lucy tells Mooney she's not exactly working for Diamond Jim Brady. In *HL*: "Lucy, the Shopping Expert," Kim tells Craig that Uncle Harry "makes Jack Benny look like Diamond Jim Brady." In *HL*: "Lucy Takes Over," Lucy tells Harry he "makes Scrooge look like Diamond Jim Brady." (A movie bio about Brady and his relationship with Lillian Russell was one of Lucy's unrealized dream projects for her and Jackie Gleason.)

Art Buchwald. One of America's most widely circulated columnists and humorists first came to prominence in 1949 when he joined the *New York Herald Tribune*. In *ILL:* "Lucy Meets Charles Boyer," Buchwald writes in his column that Ricky will be lunching with Charles Boyer.

Earl Carroll. Broadway showman Earl Carroll (who had died in 1948) was known for his opulent productions, most famously *Vanities*, which featured beautiful show girls. In *ILL:* "The Audition," Lucy claims that if Ziegfeld or Earl Carroll had seen her, they would have signed her in a minute. (Lucy appeared as an Earl Carroll girl in the 1934 film *Murder at the Vanities*.)

Bennett Cerf. The New York publisher and co-founder of Random House became a familiar face to television viewers as a regular panelist on *What's My Line?* In *ILL:* "Lucy Writes a Novel," while tearing up her manuscript, Lucy cries, "You had your chance, Bennett Cerf!" (Lucy held the record for being the mystery guest more times than any other star on the original *What's My Line?* Cerf, who was married to Lucy's friend Phyllis Frasier, cousin of Ginger Rogers, was a panelist for four of Lucy's stints.)

Florence Chadwick. The first woman to swim the English Channel in both directions; the event took place on August 8, 1950 and made her a media name for a brief period. In *ILL:* "Lucy's Bicycle Trip" After Lucy goes swimming in the Mediterranean, Fred calls her "the poor man's Florence Chadwick."

Howard Cosell. The opinionated sportscaster with the distinctively monotonous voice was best known as the announcer on *ABC's Monday Night Football*. In *HL:* "The Big Game" Mary Jane says she knows so much about football because she has a crush on Howard Cosell. His voice is what appeals to her.

Walter Cronkite. The anchorman of the CBS Evening News from 1962 to 1981, Cronkite, with his deep, authoritative voice, was often referred to as "the most trusted man in America." In *TLS:* "Lucy, the Disk Jockey," Mooney compares a voice contest between him and Lucy to one between Walter Cronkite and Donald Duck. In *HL:* "Lucy and the Mountain Climber," Lucy leaves Harry with a nonsensical message that she thinks Walter Cronkite will probably do ten minutes on. In *HL:* "Lucy Plays Cops and Robbers," after watching TV on his first color set, Harry asks, "Did you know Astroturf was green and not grey?" To which Lucy replies, "Yes, and you'll be glad to know that Walter Cronkite has baby blue eyes." In *HL:* "Lucy Is N.G. as an R.N.," Lucy tells Mary Jane Harry will not be eating with them for dinner because he spends every night at home watching Cronkite do the news during dinner.

"Dear Abby." The advice column founded in 1956 by Pauline Phillips (pen name Abigail Van Buren). The name was used both to identify the writer herself and to describe any similar means of dispensing advice. In *TLS*: "Lucy, the Superwoman," Mooney tells Lucy they will be getting a computer, not Dear Abby, when Lucy wants to ask the machine dating advice. In *HL*: "Harrison Carter, Male Nurse," when trying to coax Lucy into drinking her milk, Harry says, "Dear Abby likes milk. Pat Boone likes milk. Vida Blue likes milk." In *HL*: "Mary Jane's Boyfriend," Harry says, "In affairs of the heart, 'Dear Abby' always comes to me."

Phil Donohue. The host of daytime television's influential, long-running tabloid talk show. In *LWL*: "Lucy and Curtis Are up a Tree," after Lucy tells Curtis that by buying their grandchildren lots of gifts, they are actually competing for their love. Curtis replies, "Uh-oh, you've been watching Phil Donohue again."

Albert Einstein. The physicist whose theory of relativity and involvement in the eventual development of nuclear weaponry made him one of the most famous scientists in history. His name became synonymous with genius. In *ILL*: "Harpo Marx" Ethel says, "If Einstein can't handle a problem, you don't hand it to Mortimer Snerd." (Einstein died three weeks before the airing of this episode.) *HL*: "Lucy Goes Hawaiian, Part One" Lucy says that the job description for a cruise director sounds like a cross between Cary Grant, Albert Einstein, Joe Namath, and Bob Hope. The only person Harry thinks can fill that part is himself.

Jack Entratter. The entertainment director at Las Vegas' Sands Hotel. In *LD*: "Lucy Hunts Uranium," the Ricardos, Mertzes, and Fred MacMurray stayed at the Sands, and Ricky remarks that Entratter cancelled all shows because of the pandemonium involving the discovery of uranium. This episode aired on January 3, 1958. Later that month, Entratter was made president of the Sands.

Irving Fein. Show business manager best known for his long association with Jack Benny. In *HL*: "Lucy and Jack Benny's Biography," Harry gets a call from Irving Fein asking for a secretary for one of his clients. Lucy is hired and Jack Benny is the celebrity client. (Fein actually published a book about his friend, *Jack Benny: An Intimate Biography*, in 1976.)

John Ford. The filmmaker who worked in many genres but was most associated with westerns, held the record for winning the most directorial Oscars (four) and helped turn John Wayne into a star when he directed him in *Stagecoach.* They would collaborate on thirteen additional films. In *TLS:* "Lucy and John Wayne," Lucy says that John Ford directs most of John Wayne's pictures. (Ford directed the 1935 Edward G. Robinson-Jean Arthur film *The Whole Town's Talking,* in which Lucy was an extra.)

Billy Graham. The Christian evangelist cultivated a huge following via his radio and television sermons. In *HL:* "Lucy and Johnny Carson," Lucy tells Johnny that she loves how he closes each of his shows by saying, "Bless you." Carson tells her "that's Billy Graham."

Sheilah Graham. A Hollywood columnist who, in 1958, wrote the book *Beloved Infidel* about her long affair with F. Scott Fitzgerald (who had been Lucy's neighbor during that time). In *ILL:* "The Star Upstairs," Ethel reads in Sheilah Graham's column about a star who might possibly be hiding out in their hotel.

Mata Hari. The stage name of Margaretha MacLeod, this exotic Dutch dancer was accused of spying for the Germans during World War I and subsequently executed by firing squad in 1917. Her made-up name became a byword for female spies. In *LD:* "Lucy Makes Room for Danny," Danny Williams claims that Lucy only keeps coming over to the house to spy on them. When Lucy walks in, he exclaims, "Here comes Mata Hari now!"

Ernest Hemingway. The revered author of such books as *For Whom the Bell Tolls* and *The Old Man and the Sea* lived part of the time in Cuba during the nineteen-thirties and forties. In *LD:* "Milton Berle Hides Out at the Ricardos," Berle's publisher, Mr. Watson (Larry Keating), suggests that Milton stay at his house until he completes his book. Milton turns him down, claiming that his mother-in-law caused Ernest Hemingway to flee to Cuba.

Victor Herbert. The Irish-born, German-raised composer was known for such operettas as *Babes in Toyland* and *Naughty Marietta.* In *ILL:* "The Operetta," Ricky asks who wrote the operetta they are performing. Lucy asks, "Have you ever heard of Victor Herbert?"

Conrad Hilton. A hotelier who started with one establishment in Texas that led to a chain of hotels around the world bearing his name. In *ILL:* "Lucy

Gets Homesick in Italy," at the rundown Hotel Grande in Nice, Lucy tells Fred to "ring for Conrad Hilton."

Alfred Hitchcock. Cinema's master of suspense was known for directing such thrillers as *Notorious* and *Rear Window*, though the knitting needle ploy in the following episode appears to be Lucy's own invention. In *LD:* "Lucy Meets the Mustache," Lucy gets a letter Ricky wrote to his uncle in Cuba out of its envelope by rolling it out with a knitting needle. Lucy claims she saw a housewife do it in an Alfred Hitchcock picture.

J. Edgar Hoover. The head of the Federal Bureau of Investigation from its inception in 1935 until 1972. In *ILL:* "The Great Train Robbery," Lucy says, "Anything for J. Edgar!" after she thinks she is helping to catch a jewel thief. In *TLS:* "Lucy Makes a Pinch," Viv calls overzealous meter maid Lucy "J. Edna Hoover."

Howard Hughes. The reclusive and eccentric billionaire's name became synonymous with extravagant wealth. He was in charge of RKO from 1948 to 1954; three years later, the studio was sold to Desilu. In *HL:* "Lucy Visits Jack Benny," Benny says that Howard Hughes stayed at his house on business—he wanted to borrow some money. In *HL:* "Lucy and Wayne Newton," Lucy says Harry came to Las Vegas to kiss Howard Hughes's ring. In *HL:* "Lucy, the American Mother," Craig tells Harry that he plans to lose money on the film he is making. Harry says, "A Howard Hughes you'll never be."

Huntley & Brinkley. Chet Huntley and David Brinkley were the anchors of NBC's evening news show, *The Huntley-Brinkley Report,* from 1956 to 1970. In *TLS:* "Lucy and Bob Crane," the movie director replies, "Has Huntley ever heard of Brinkley?" after Mooney asks him if he has ever heard of Iron Man Carmichael. In *HL:* "Lucy and the Great Airport Chase," Harry says that Huntley and Brinkley were talking on their newscast about the secret formula Lucy has been given. In *HL:* "A Date for Lucy," after Lucy tells Harry she does not know who to take to her party, Harry says, "When you do, be sure to notify Huntley and Brinkley."

Alfred Kinsey. The professor whose reports on human sexuality made him a controversial figure in the late nineteen-forties and early fifties, his last name became a household word in his day, customarily used to evoke frankness. In *ILL:* "Fan Magazine Interview," Lucy and Ethel pretend to be pollsters in order to meet Minnie Finch (Kathryn Card), whom they think

Ricky might be having an affair with. When Lucy tells her that she is conducting a poll and would like to ask her some questions, a skeptical Minnie asks, "Your name ain't Kinsey, is it?"

Joseph E. Levine. The Hollywood producer and founder of Embassy Pictures brought attention to himself by heavily ballyhooing his movies. In *TLS*: "Lucy Saves Milton Berle," Berle tells his agent he can do a dramatic role since he just played one in Levine's new picture. The picture in question, *The Oscar*, is not mentioned.

Charles Lindbergh. His solo flight from Long Island to Paris in May 1927 made Lindbergh an American hero and became one of the defining events of that decade. In *ILL*: "Homecoming," after the neighborhood makes a big deal out of the gang returning from Hollywood, Mrs. Trumbull says that she hasn't seen anything like it since Lindbergh came home in '27.

Frank Loesser. The Hollywood and Broadway songwriter whose credits in the latter field include *The Most Happy Fella*. In *ILL*: "Lucy's Night in Town," during intermission from *The Most Happy Fella*, Ethel says the Frank Loesser music is great.

Clare Boothe Luce. The journalist, one-time *Vanity Fair* managing editor, and playwright (including *Kiss the Boys Goodbye*, which featured Vivian Vance) eventually segued into politics, serving in the House of Representatives. In *TLS:* "Lucy Becomes a Reporter," Lucy says that she was called "Clare Boothe Lucy" in high school because she was the star reporter on the school paper.

Sam Lutz. Lawrence Welk's personal manager and producer of *The Lawrence Welk Show*. In *HL:* "Lucy and Lawrence Welk," Lucy calls up Mr. Lutz to inquire about how much Welk is paid for one night's work.

Elsa Maxwell. The gossip columnist became famous for the many parties she hosted for royalty and the social elite. In *ILL:* "Housewarming," Ethel refers to Betty Ramsey as "the Elsa Maxwell of Westport."

Mary Margaret McBride. The popular radio host-interviewer-writer was a fixture in the medium for some 40 years. In *ILL:* "Job Switching," Fred calls Ricky "a regular Mary Margaret McBride." In *ILL:* "The Million Dollar Idea," Ethel plays Mary Margaret McMertz, spokesperson for Aunt Martha's Old Fashioned Salad Dressing.

Rod McKuen. Perhaps best known as a poet, he also achieved great success as a composer and singer. In *HL:* "Lucy and the Celebrities," after Rich Little gives a poetic testimonial on behalf of Carter's Unique Employment Agency as Jack Benny, Harry says, "Rod McKuen, eat your heart out."

David Merrick. The noted producer was responsible for some of Broadway's longest-running shows, including *Hello, Dolly!* and *42nd Street.* In *HL:* "Ginger Rogers Comes to Tea," Ginger stops by Lucy's house to pick up her missing purse on the way to New York, where she has a meeting with David Merrick to discuss her appearing in his newest musical. Rogers had been the first replacement Dolly Levi in Merrick's *Hello, Dolly!* when Carol Channing left the Broadway production.

Vincente Minnelli. During his twenty-two years as one of MGM's top film-makers, Vincente Minnelli directed Lucy and Desi in the 1954 comedy *The Long, Long Trailer.* In *ILL:* "Lucy Gets in Pictures," Ricky tells Lucy he has to leave to have lunch with "Mr. Minnelli."

"Minnie the Moocher." Cab Calloway first recorded what would become his signature song (with the "Hi-De-Hi-De-Hi" refrain) in 1931. The word "moocher" thereafter became invariably linked to the name Minnie. In *ILL:* "The Fox Hunt," when Lucy wants to wangle an invitation to the country estate of Sir Clive Richardson, Ricky says, "You don't want to be a moocher." Lucy replies, "Just call me 'Minnie.'"

Grandma Moses. Anna Mary Robertson Moses first gained fame as a painter when she was in her seventies, therefore earning the nickname "Grandma." In *ILL:* "Nursey School," Lucy says that Little Ricky, who did a finger paint-ing at school, might be another "Grandpa Moses." In *HL:* "Lucy and Danny Thomas," Harry says aspiring painter Lucy reminds him of Grandma Moses.

Arthur Murray. The famed dancer lent his name to a dance studio fran-chise. He became even better known to television viewers when he host-ed his own series, *The Arthur Murray Party* (1950–60). In *ILL:* "The Young Fans," Lucy tells Ricky that she gave dance lessons to Arthur and it wasn't Arthur Murray. In *ILL:* "Little Ricky Gets a Dog," Lucy hides Fred the dog under a Mexican hat. She dances around the hat and says that she's been taking dance lessons from Arthur Murray.

Edward R. Murrow. The outspoken radio and television journalist-host was best known for the series *See It Now* and *Person to Person.* Because of strained relations with the powers that be at CBS, Murrow announced in February 1959 that he would be taking a leave of absence. In *LD:* "Lucy Wants a Career," an exasperated Paul Douglas questions his decision to go into television, saying, "No wonder Ed Murrow's taking a year off!"

Jacqueline Kennedy Onassis. The First Lady of the United States married billionaire Greek shipping magnate Aristotle Onassis in 1968 after the death of her first husband, President John F. Kennedy. In *TLS:* "Lucy Visits the White House," Lucy says she hopes Jackie can find a place on the mantle for their cub scout troop's sugar cube White House. In *HL:* "Lucy and Andy Griffith," Kim, posing as a runaway, asks youth camp director Andy Johnson (Andy Griffith), "Who do I look like? Jackie Onassis?"

William S. Paley. The founder and chairman of CBS, the Paley Center for Media is named after him. In *TLS:* "Lucy Meets Danny Kaye." Danny Kaye calls up William S. Paley to request tickets for his show for Lucy.

Bert Parks. A former radio and television host-announcer, Parks became an American institution when he served as emcee of the Miss American Pageant from 1955 to 1979. In *HL:* "Lucy and Carol Burnett" (second season), stressed-out pageant host Robert Alda asks, "I wonder if Bert Parks ever had days like this?"

Louella Parsons. The reigning Hollywood gossip columnist for decades, she wielded a surprising degree of power in the movie industry. Her closest competitor in the field was Hedda Hopper. In *ILL:* "The Gossip," Lucy says "Thank you, Hedda and Lolly" to gossiping Ricky and Fred. In *ILL:* "Ricky's Screen Test," Lucy imagines running into Louella at a famous Hollywood restaurant. In *ILL:* "The Hedda Hopper Story," Ricky says he can't get his name in Hedda Hopper or Louella Parsons's columns because all they talk about is Marilyn Monroe. In *TLS:* "Lucy Becomes a Reporter," Viv calls Lucy "Louella."

General George S. Patton. The controversial World War II commander became even better known to the American public as the subject of the 1970 Best Picture Oscar-winner *Patton.* In *HL:* "Lucy, the Part-Time Wife," Harry says that, in college, they called his girlfriend Gertrude Krebs (Jean Wills) "Blood and Guts Gertie," after General Patton. She and Patton looked alike except Patton did not have a mustache.

Cole Porter. Known for his sophisticated lyrics, Porter became one of Broadway and Hollywood's best-known songwriters. In *ILL:* "Lucy and Ethel Buy the Same Dress," Lucy and Ethel decide to sing Cole Porter's "Friendship" for their television appearance. (Porter wrote *Friendship* for the Broadway production of *Du Barry Was a Lady*, which Lucy sang in the film version. Vivian Vance appeared in the original Broadway productions of Porter's *Anything Goes; Red, Hot, and Blue;* and *Let's Face It!*)

Grantland Rice. The sports columnist was known for the poetic way he wrote about his field. (His daughter, actress Florence Rice, starred in the films *Fugitive Lady* and *Carnival*, which Lucy had bit parts in.) In *ILL:* "The Camping Trip," while reading the sports pages with Lucy, Ricky calls his confused wife "Grantland Rice" and then asks her, "Surely, you've heard of Grantland Rice?" Lucy replies, "Sure, I've heard of it, but I've never tasted it."

Morley Safer. The *60 Minutes* correspondent joined the long-running series in 1970. In *LWL:* "Lucy's Green Thumb," Curtis thinks Lucy's Gigantagrow would be an excellent story for Morley Safer on *60 Minutes.*

Mickey Spillane. The best-selling author wrote a series of hard-boiled detective novels that were considered pretty racy in their day for their emphasis on sex and violence. In *TLS:* "Lucy Gets Her Maid," Lucy hides all the detective novels in her house before their new maid arrives because she doesn't want her to know they don't read anything besides Mickey Spillane.

Dr. Seuss. The pen name of children's author and illustrator Theodor Geisel, many of his books became classics in this field; his name also becoming shorthand for writing aimed at the very young. In *HL:* "Lucy Is N.G. as an R.N.," Lucy says that she heard the book Mary Jane is reading "makes Jacqueline Susann look like Dr. Seuss." After Lucy catches Harry reading the book, she remarks, "It sure beats *How the Grinch Stole Christmas!*"

Benjamin Spock. Pediatrician who became known as one of the world's foremost authorities on childcare. In *ILL:* "Nursey School," Lucy quotes from one of Dr. Spock's books.

Jacqueline Susann. The best-selling author of salacious potboilers, her most famous book was *Valley of the Dolls*. In *HL:* "Lucy Is N.G. as an R.N.," Lucy says that she heard the book Mary Jane is reading "makes Jacqueline Susann look like Dr. Seuss."

Tennessee Williams. The author of such works as *The Glass Menagerie* and *A Streetcar Named Desire,* Williams became one of the most important playwrights of the postwar era. In *ILL:* "Lucy Writes a Play," playwright Lucy says that she may become another Tennessee Ernie. Ricky corrects her and tells her she means Tennessee Williams.

Walter Winchell. The outspoken commentator and columnist's name became synonymous with newspaper gossip for decades. His familiar voice was also used on occasion to narrate films including *Broadway Thru a Keyhole* and *Sorrowful Jones,* both of which featured Lucy. In *ILL:* "Lucy Is Enceinte," when Ricky sings "We're Having a Baby," the lyrics include the line, "You'll read it in Winchell that we're adding a limb to our family tree." This comes true. In *ILL:* "Ricky Has Labor Pains," Winchell has an item saying that Lucy is "infanticipating." (Although he never appeared on camera in a Lucy episode, Winchell did do the voice-over narration for *TLS* "Lucy, the Gun Moll.")

Sergeant Alvin York. This World War I Presidential Medal of Honor recipient had a 1941 film based on his life, which earned Gary Cooper an Oscar. In *TLS:* "Lucy and the Sleeping Beauty," Lucy asks how she looks in a hard-hat. Mooney responds, "Like Sergeant York."

Darryl F. Zanuck. As one of the founders of 20th Century-Fox, he served as producer and head of that studio until 1971. In *ILL.* "Getting Ready," Ricky talks in his sleep, saying "My price is a million dollars, Mr. Zanuck." Lucy doesn't want to wake him until he makes the deal.

Florenz Ziegfeld. The Broadway impresario was known for his lavish *Ziegfeld Follies,* which featured beautiful showgirls. In *ILL:* "The Audition," Lucy claims that if Ziegfeld or Earl Carroll had seen her, they would have signed her in a minute. (Lucy appeared as a Ziegfeld girl in MGM's 1946 release, *Ziegfeld Follies.*)

Fictional Characters

Andy Gump. Sidney Smith's comic strip, *The Gumps,* about an average American family, ran in newspapers from 1917 to 1959, and even was heard on radio for a time in the nineteen-thirties. As drawn by Smith, patriarch Andy Gump appeared to have no chin. In *ILL:* "The Adagio," Ricky complains about shaving and says he's liable to wear his chin away. Lucy says, "Okay, Andy Gump."

Andy Hardy. Mickey Rooney played the role of Andy Hardy in sixteen films for MGM from 1937 to 1958, beginning with *A Family Affair.* In *ILL:* "Ricky Needs an Agent," Lucy proposes that MGM make "Andy Hardy Meets a Conga Player" with Ricky.

Baby Snooks. Comedian-singer Fanny Brice's character of the inquisitive, mischievous little girl first appeared in her vaudeville act but became nationally famous when she made the transition to radio. *The Baby Snooks Show* ran from 1944 until May 1951, the last episode airing only two days before Brice died. In *ILL:* "Ricky Loses His Voice," Lucy asks Ethel if Fred acts like a child when he gets sick. Ethel replies, "You mean Baby Snooks?" (Jess Oppenheimer previously wrote *Baby Snooks* with Fanny Brice; Brice appeared with William Frawley in the "Sweepstakes Ticket" sequence of *Ziegfeld Follies,* while Lucille showed up in the opening number.)

Brenda Starr. The glamorous reporter created for comic strips by Dale Messick first appeared in newspapers in June 1940. In *TLS:* "Lucy Becomes a Reporter," news editor Mr. Foley (Roscoe Karns) refers to Lucy as Brenda Starr.

Bugs Bunny. The undisputed superstar of Warner Bros.' series of *Looney Tunes* and *Merrie Melodies* cartoons, the carrot-chomping, smart aleck rabbit first appeared on screen in 1938. Two years later, he first uttered the immortal line that became not only his catchphrase, but one of the great wiseacre queries of all time, "What's up, doc?" Not surprisingly in *ILL:* "Oil Wells," after Ethel calls Fred "a dumb bunny," Fred replies with Bugs's signature line, "What's up, doc?" In *TLS:* "Lucy Gets Amnesia," Vivian says Lucy's new coat couldn't be more rabbit if it wrinkled its nose and said "What's up, doc?" Later, when Lucy tries on the coat, she gets stuck with a pin and thinks "Bugs Bunny bit me."

Buster Brown. First a comic strip created (in 1902) by Richard Fenton Outcault, then, two years later, the logo for a shoe company, Buster was known for his pageboy haircut and his wide-collar suit, complete with bowtie, wide-brimmed hat, and short pants. In *ILL:* "Lucy Hires an English Tutor," Fred shows up for their tutoring session dressed as Buster Brown. In *LD,* "The Celebrity Next Door," Fred refers to the wig he's wearing as a "Buster Brown bob."

Captain Kangaroo. The gentle children's show, hosted by Bob Keeshan as the title character, ran on CBS from 1955 to 1984. In *TLS:* "Chris's New

Year's Eve Party," Viv describes Lucy, who takes control of planning Chris's parties with her friends, as "Captain Kangaroo." In *TLS:* "Lucy Teaches Ethel Merman to Sing," Jerry and Sherman want Ethel Merman to be the star of their Boy Scout show because she would be easier to get than Captain Kangaroo. In *TLS:* "Lucy and Bob Crane," Lucy tells Bob Crane (who played Colonel Hogan on *Hogan's Heroes*) he is her favorite soldier since Captain Kangaroo.

Charlie Chan. The soft-spoken, epigram-spouting Chinese American detective was created by author Earl Derr Biggers in 1923. His exploits were subsequently dramatized on radio, in films, and for television. In *HL:* "Lucy and the Chinese Curse," Harry calls launderer Mr. Wong (Keye Luke) "a starch happy Charlie Chan." (Keye Luke had previously played "Number One Son" in the Charlie Chan films.)

Charlie Brown/Snoopy. Charles M. Schulz created the characters of good-hearted Charlie Brown and his independent dog for his syndicated newspaper comic strip *Peanuts* in 1950. They also appeared in films, television specials, and stage musicals. In *HL:* "Ginger Rogers Comes to Tea," after Lucy gives Ginger all the things that were in the purse she lost and Lucy found, Lucy points out that Ginger's driver's license is soon to expire. Ginger remarks, "Apparently, Charlie Brown isn't the only one who has a Snoopy."

Cho-Cho-San. Cho-Cho-San is the name of the main character in Puccini's opera *Madama Butterfly*. In *LD:* "The Ricardos Go to Japan," Ethel calls Fred, dressed in a kimono, "Cho-Cho-San."

Donald Duck. Walt Disney's feisty animated bird with the garbled speaking voice had been a constant point of reference since his 1934 screen debut, often in a playfully cheeky way, to indicate anyone with a volatile temper or as a representative of mainstream cartoon fare in general. In *ILL:* "The Black Wig," when Fred complains that he couldn't understand the Italian movie they just saw, Ethel explains, "If it isn't Donald Duck, it's over his head." In *TLS:* "Lucy, the Disk Jockey," Mooney compares a voice contest between him and Lucy to one between Walter Cronkite and Donald Duck.

Dr. Jekyll and Mr. Hyde. The characters of a scientist and his evil alter ego originated in Robert Louis Stevenson's 1886 novella *Strange Case of Dr. Jekyll and Mr. Hyde*. It has been adapted for many mediums including the 1931 film *Dr. Jekyll and Mr. Hyde* for which Fredric March won an Oscar for playing the two roles. In *HL:* "Lucy Cuts Vincent's Price," Craig writes a book report about the story, and he and Kim worry about their mother going over to Vincent Price's house because they think he is a Dr. Jekyll and Mr. Hyde type. In *HL:* "Lucy Goes on Her Last Blind Date," Lucy scares away unwanted suitor Ben (Don Knotts) by showing him that she is a Jekyll and Hyde type herself.

Dr. Kildare. Although he first was seen in the person of Joel McCrea in Paramount's 1937 release *Internes Can't Take Money* (adapted from a Max Brand story) it was MGM's series of low-budget dramas starring Lew Ayres that made Dr. James Kildare the fictional physician of reference for years to come. (For a subsequent generation it was the 1961–66 ABC series starring Richard Chamberlain that was the *Kildare* point of reference, but that, of course, did not air until *after* this particular Lucy reference.) In *ILL:* "Little Ricky Learns to Play the Drums," Lucy wants Little Ricky to be a doctor and buys him, what Ricky calls, "a junior Dr. Kildare kit."

Ellery Queen. The fictional detective first appeared in a series of novels by Frederic Dannay and Manfred Bennington Lee that inspired radio, television, and movie adaptations. In *ILL:* "The Matchmaker," Fred says that if missing Ricky does not come back, they will send for Ellery Queen.

Francis the Talking Mule. David Stern's novel about a loquacious mule inspired a series of highly profitable Universal comedies starring Donald O'Connor during the early nineteen-fifties. In *ILL:* "Ethel's Birthday," Ricky and Fred describe their wives as stubborn mules, prompting Fred to call Ethel "Francis."

Gidget. Created by writer Frederick Kohner for his 1957 novel (subtitled "The Little Girl with Big Ideas"), this fictional teen came to symbolize the California beach culture of the era, and was played the following year on screen by Sandra Dee. In *TLS:* "Lucy Is a Chaperone," after Lucy attempts to fit in with her daughter's teen friends at a beach party, one of them (played by *My Three Son*'s Don Grady) dismisses her as "that overgrown Gidget." At the time the line was delivered, Gidget had returned to screens in the person of Deborah Walley in *Gidget Goes Hawaiian* (1961) and was about take a third trip in *Gidget Goes to Rome* (1963; played by Cindy Carol). It was, however, two years before the TV adaptation with Sally Field premiered.

Howdy Doody. Television's first puppet superstar, the freckle-faced, plaid-shirted marionette, as audiences came to know him, debuted on *Puppet*

Playhouse in 1948 and became a dominant figure throughout the nineteen-fifties thanks to the seminal children's series *Howdy Doody*. In *ILL*: "Mr. and Mrs. TV Show," Lucy tells Ethel that wives are puppeteers pulling the strings of their husbands. When Ricky enters, Ethel says, "Here's Howdy Doody now."

Ironside. Because NBC's crime series *Ironside* (1967–75) offered the unusual premise of having its sleuth (Raymond Burr, Ball's co-star in *The Magic Carpet*) be confined to a wheelchair, it prompted many a handicap joke in its day. In *HL*: "Lucy and Joe Namath," Kim calls wheelchair-bound Lucy "little Ironside."

James Bond. Once novelist Ian Fleming's debonair spy made the transition from page to screen in a series of hit movies starting in 1962, pretty much everyone made references to or spoofed the intrepid Agent 007. In *TLS*: "Lucy, the Undercover Agent," after seeing a James Bond movie (exactly which one is never specified), Lucy, Mooney, and the Countess (Ann Sothern) think a suspicious man (Jack Cassidy) is a spy. In *HL*: "Lucy's Impossible Mission," Kim compares government agent Mr. Geller (Richard Derr) to Bond, and Craig remarks that the situation is "real 007." In *HL*: "Lucy and the Great Airport Chase," Harry, after being chased by enemy agents, says, "I have had enough of this James Bond movie."

Lassie. First seen in Eric Knight's 1940 novel, *Lassie Come-Home*, the loyal and lovable collie became a canine sensation after starring in the 1943 film adaptation and MGM's subsequent series of movies. Even before Lassie made the transition to television in 1954, she was referenced in *ILL*: "The Young Fans," in which teenager Peggy (Janet Waldo) describes Arthur (Richard Crenna) as looking like Gregory Peck, while Lucy thinks he sounds more like Lassie. The dog received later mention in *ILL*: "Hollywood Anniversary," when Ricky, upon reading the list of celebrities scheduled to attend his and Lucy's anniversary party, says "I guess Lassie couldn't make it." In *ILL*: "Little Ricky Gets a Dog," Lucy tries singing to the new pooch, only to apologize with "I'm sorry I'm no Dinah Shore. You're no Lassie either." In *TLS*: "Lucy and the Countess Have a Horse Guest," when naming stars she has met in Hollywood, Lucy lists Lassie's hairdresser.

Little Lord Fauntleroy. The hero of Frances Hodgson Burnett's 1886 novel was famous for his precious and somewhat sissified appearance, sporting ringlet curls, knee pants, and a velvet cutaway jacket with a ruffled collar. In *ILL*: "Changing the Boys' Wardrobe," Fred calls formally dressed Ricky "Little Lord Fauntleroy."

Li'l Abner. A naïve hillbilly who had a self-titled comic strip by Al Capp. In *ILL:* "Tennessee Ernie Visits," when Fred brings over his rollaway bed for Ernie, he tells the Ricardos to "say goodnight to Li'l Abner."

Little Orphan Annie. Harold Gray's adventurous little girl with the curly red hair and the blank eyes had been a comic strip staple in newspapers since 1924, and inspired several references on *Lucy* series. In *ILL:* "Lucy Wants New Furniture," when Lucy walks in with her botched home permanent, Fred greets her with, "Well, Little Orphan Annie!" In *ILL:* "Ricky's Old Girlfriend," when Lucy asks what Ethel doesn't want her to see in the newspaper, Ethel says, "Daddy Warbucks left Little Orphan Annie again." In *ILL:* "The Star Upstairs," after Cornel Wilde's newspaper becomes wet, he points out that he could see one page through another, "I thought President Eisenhower was playing golf with Little Orphan Annie." In *TLS:* "Lucy Gets Trapped," when Mooney inquires about his newspaper that Lucy doesn't want him to see, Lucy fills him in about the news, saying, "The temperature's up, the stock market's down, and Little Orphan Annie's lost again."

Lone Ranger. The masked Texas ranger was a favorite character of radio and 1950s' television. His signature line, as he departed on his trusty horse, Silver, was "Hi-yo, Silver, away!" In *HL:* "Lucy and Rudy Vallee," Kim does not know who Rudy Vallee is. When he says, "Hi ho, everybody!," she guesses he is the Lone Ranger.

Mickey Mouse. Disney's most famous animated creation and company mascot was equally well known for the wristwatch on which he first appeared in 1933, his arms made to point toward the appropriate numbers on the dial. In *TLS:* "Lucy, the Coin Collector," Lucy offers Mooney her watch as collateral for a loan. Mooney remarks, "Mickey Mouse is one of my favorites." Lucy realizes that she accidently put on Jerry's watch. In *TLS:* "Lucy Gets Jack Benny's Account," Lucy suggests the bank try to get Mickey Mouse as a client, so they could use the slogan "Put your money where your mouse is." In *HL:* "Lucy the Skydiver," after Lucy arrives late and breaks Harry's watch by hitting him with the door, she looks at the damaged item and laments, "Look at poor little Mickey Mouse," to which Harry adds, "You broke his tail."

Mr. Ed. Sort of an un-credited cousin of *Francis the Talking Mule,* Mr. Ed was a talking horse who starred in his own CBS series for five seasons during the sixties and therefore became a punchline of many equestrian barbs. In

TLS: "Lucy Meets Danny Kaye," when Lucy asks Mooney to help her meet Danny Kaye, he informs the ever-meddlesome redhead that "I'd be reluctant to put you in touch with Mr. Ed." Even years after *Ed's* cancellation, the chatty Palomino was referenced in *HL*: "Lucy and Carol Burnett," when, in response to Lucy describing beauty contestants as horses exhibiting their bodies at a horse show, Carol says, "Comb out my tail and call me Mr. Ed."

Mr. Magoo. The befuddled, nearsighted cartoon character first appeared in the 1949 short "Ragtime Beer." In *ILL*: "Lucy Has Her Eyes Examined," Ethel calls visually impaired Lucy "Miss Magoo."

Mortimer Snerd. The dim-witted dummy was ventriloquist Edgar Bergen's second most famous creation, after Charlie McCarthy. In *ILL*: "Harpo Marx," Ethel says, "If Einstein can't handle a problem, you don't hand it to Mortimer Snerd."

Peter Pan. James M. Barrie's classic creation of the boy who refused to grow up became synonymous with being airborne or youthful, as witnessed by it being referenced on three *Lucy* series: In *ILL*: "Return Home from Europe," when Ricky says he's trying to find out if he can fly home from Europe, Lucy assures him, "You'll make it, Peter Pan." In *TLS*: "Lucy Tries Winter Sports," Lucy skis off her roof and lands on top of Mooney, who groans, "I just bent down to tie my shoe and Peter Pan came in for a landing." In *HL*: "Lucy's Tenant," when Mary Jane implies that Lucy is old, Lucy replies, "Well, listen to Peter Pan!"

Rin-Tin-Tin. A heroic German Shepherd dog who found success starring in films, radio, and television, beginning in the nineteen-twenties. In *TLS*: "Lucy Goes to a Hollywood Premiere," Lucy says, as a child, she had a pet named Rin-Tin-Tin, a canary. In *HL*: "Won't You Calm Down, Dan Dailey?," Dan Dailey explains to Harry his problem of Lucy getting overly excited whenever he mentions a movie star's name. Harry says, "She even makes a fool of herself over Rin-Tin-Tin."

Rip Van Winkle. The lead character of Washington Irving's 1819 eponymous short story became synonymous with extensive sleeping for having stayed in slumber for a twenty-year stretch. In *LD*: "Lucy Wants a Career," Ethel calls a sleeping Fred "Rip Van Mertz." In *TLS*: "Lucy Gets Involved," Mooney says, "What in the name of Rip Van Winkle?" after Lucy says she cannot sleep because her TV set is broken.

Simon Legree. The barbaric slave owner created by Harriet Beecher Stowe for her seminal 1852 novel *Uncle Tom's Cabin* became a byword for cruel employers. In *ILL:* "Lucy's Schedule," Mr. Littlefield (Gale Gordon) refers to Ricky, who has Lucy operating on a time schedule, as "a Simon Legree." In *ILL:* "The Ricardos Dedicate a Statue," Lucy calls Ricky "Señor Simon Legree." In *TLS:* "Lucy and the Countess Lose Weight," Rosie (Ann Sothern) refers to health farm trainer Mooney as "the Simon Legree of the concentration camps." In *TLS:* In "Lucy Gets Caught in the Draft," Mary Jane, on the telephone, calls Mooney "Simon Legree." In *TLS:* "Lucy Gets Involved," Lucy calls her new boss "an upholstered Simon Legree."

Trigger. The dependable golden Palomino owned and ridden on screen by Roy Rogers was so well known in his own right that when Roy was invited to place his footprints in the forecourt of Grauman's Chinese Theatre in 1949, Trigger added his hoof-prints alongside him. In *ILL:* "Lucy Visits Grauman's," after Ethel complains that her feet are bigger than all the star footprints she tries to match, Fred suggests she try Trigger's. In *HL:* "Lucy Goes on Her Last Blind Date," Ben Fletcher (Don Knotts) says he got his feet stuck in the hoof prints of Roy Rogers's horse at Grauman's Chinese Theater.

Mr. Whipple. This grocer, played by Dick Wilson, urged people "please don't squeeze the Charmin," in a long-running series of toilet paper commercials. In *LWL:* "Lucy Gets Her Wires Crossed," Curtis mentions that a lot of people have told him he bears a strong resemblance to Mr. Whipple.

Winnie-the-Pooh. The sweet-natured, honey-loving bear appeared in a series of short stories written by A. A. Milne, starting in 1926. In *LWL:* "Lucy, Legal Eagle," after a woman (Nora Boland) attempts to pass off a stuffed rabbit as Kevin's missing teddy bear for the reward money, she asks, "What did you expect for fifty bucks? Winnie-the-Pooh?"

16

"That Story's Had More Performances Than South Pacific"

Pop Culture References on Lucille Ball's Series: Entertainment

Radio Shows

"Mrs. Hush." A radio guessing contest that ran on *Truth or Consequences* in 1947. Listeners had to guess who an unnamed woman was by clues in a cryptic jingle. The answer was twenties "It Girl" Clara Bow. In *TLS:* "Lucy, the Disc Jockey," when Lucy tells Mooney about the sound radio contest she is participating in, he says, "I haven't heard of anything so ridiculous since Mrs. Hush."

Queen for a Day. The shamelessly manipulative radio (1945–57) and television (1956–64) giveaway show allowed average women to be treated like royalty for a day, provided they told a sob story about themselves potent enough to rate the honor. In *ILL:* "The Publicity Agent," Lucy asks Ethel if she knows any royalty, to which she replies, "My aunt was Queen for a Day once."

Television Shows

The Ed Sullivan Show. Because his variety show was the one by which all others were measured in the medium for twenty-three years, Ed Sullivan's Sunday night series was constantly referenced in the medium, including Lucy's shows. Ed was often kidded for his grim countenance and stiff manner of introducing guests. In *ILL:* "The Ricardos Are Interviewed," Ricky's agent tells him that he might get him a spot on *The Ed Sullivan Show*, which is never mentioned again. In *ILL:* "Lucy Meets the Queen," Lucy tells a stone-faced palace guide that he "makes Ed Sullivan look like Laughing Boy." In *LD:* "Milton Berle Hides Out at the Ricardos," the comedian suggests that they could be on *The Ed Sullivan Show* billed as "The Flying Ricardos." In *LD:* "Lucy Meets the Mustache," Lucy says that Ricky is depressed because he hasn't had any recent job offers, not even being asked to stand from the audience on *The Ed Sullivan Show*, a reference to that show's venerable tradition of acknowledging stars in attendance. In *TLS*: "Ethel Merman and the Boy Scout Show," Lucy imitates a juggler on *The Ed Sullivan Show*. In *HL*: "Lucy and Johnny Carson," Lucy gets Johnny and Ed Sullivan mixed up because, according to her, they "have the same type of personality."

The Flying Nun. The ABC sit-com (1967–70) had the bizarre central character of a novice (Sally Field) who was able to fly because of her small size and the shape of her starched habit. In *HL:* "Lucy's Working Daughter," Craig says if Kim's heels were any higher, she'd look like the Flying Nun. In *HL:* "Lucy, the Skydiver," skydiver Lucy, who has just crashed through a glass roof, says, "I don't know how the Flying Nun did this every week." In *HL:* "Lucy, the Crusader," Harry says that the channels are getting mixed up on his new television set. He just watched the Flying Nun self-destruct in ten seconds.

Gunsmoke. CBS's longest-running western, which shared the Monday night lineup with Lucy for seven of its twenty seasons, *Gunsmoke* featured James Arness as Marshal Matt Dillon and Amanda Blake as saloon keeper Kitty Russell. In *TLS*: "Lucy and Viv Take Up Chemistry," Lucy says their idea of an interesting conversation is sitting around talking about whether Marshal Dillon will ever marry Kitty. (They never did.) In *HL:* "Lucy and the Bogie Affair," Lucy compares Bogie, the large sheepdog, to a horse and calls the dog "Matt Dillon's last mount."

The Life and Legend of Wyatt Earp. Hugh O'Brian came to prominence playing real-life lawman Wyatt Earp on this ABC series that ran from 1955 to 1961. In *ILL:* "Lucy Goes to a Rodeo," Ricky is looking for western acts for the rodeo he is performing in at Madison Square Garden and wonders if "the fellow who plays Wyatt Earp . . . O'Brian" is available.

Life with Luigi. From September to December 1952, this CBS comedy (adapted from a popular radio series) followed *I Love Lucy* on the Monday schedule, before its extreme ethnic stereotyping ran into sponsorship troubles, causing it to be cancelled. In *ILL:* "The Black Wig," Fred tells Ethel that the wig she's wearing makes her look like *Life with Luigi.*

The Lineup. Basing its storylines on files from the San Francisco Police Department, this CBS series (1954–60) starring Warner Anderson was a Desilu production. In *ILL:* "Lucy Wants to Move to the Country," Mrs. Spaulding (Eleanor Audley) frisks Ricky and, after making sure he is not carrying a gun, says, "He's clean . . . that's what they say on *Lineup.*"

Mannix. This detective series (1967–75) starring Mike Connors, began life as a Desilu production. In *HL:* "Lucy Gives Eddie Albert the Old Song and Dance," Eddie's secretary says she feels like she's on *Mannix.* Drawing attention to the program being a fictional creation is an inconsistency since Mannix appeared as a character in the fourth-season episode "Lucy and Mannix Are Held Hostage."

Mission: Impossible. The CBS series (1966–73) that sent its intrepid agents to solve their cases after hearing their instructions on a self-destructing tape recorder began as a Desilu production while Lucy was studio head. In *HL:* "Lucy and Liberace," Lucy tells Harry that he would be a goofball on *Mission: Impossible.*

My Friend Flicka. Mary O'Hara's 1941 novel was adapted into a weekly series on CBS (1956–57). Previously it had been a 1943 Fox film starring Roddy McDowall. In *LD:* "Lucy Wins a Racehorse," Lucy tries to coax Whirling Jet up the stairs by telling the horse that there's a television set in the guest room and he can watch *My Friend Flicka.*

Naked City. The television adaptation (1958–63) of the 1948 Manhattan-shot movie thriller followed its lead by actually being filmed on location in New York. In *TLS:* "Lucy, the Rain Goddess," Lucy says Mooney could not have gone to a nudist colony because he used to blush when he watched *Naked City.*

Perry Mason. Erle Stanley Gardner's mystery-solving attorney, Perry Mason, became so popular with television viewers when his eponymous series debuted on CBS in 1957 (with Lucy's *The Magic Carpet* co-star Raymond Burr in the lead) that the name became a byword for the legal profession. In *TLS:* "Lucy and the Bank Scandal," Lucy wonders what Perry Mason would do their situation. In *TLS:* "Lucy, the Meter Maid," Lucy refers to court opponent Viv as a "bleached blonde Perry Mason." In *HL:* "Lucy and Sammy Davis Jr.," Lucy asks Craig if he's been ditching his homework and watching *Perry Mason* reruns.

Person to Person. Instead of a reference to the real thing, *I Love Lucy* parodied Edward R. Murrow's famous CBS interview show *Person to Person*, in the episode "The Ricardos Are Interviewed." The Ricardos and the Mertzes appear on the fictitious *Face to Face*, with actor Elliott Reid doing a send-up of Murrow's deadly serious, clipped speech pattern, as host "Ed Warren."

Peyton Place. Grace Metalious's red-hot 1956 best seller became a smash hit movie in 1957 and then a twice-weekly ABC series (1964–69), bringing soap operas to sixties prime-time television. In *TLS:* "Lucy and Joan," Lucy says that her life isn't exactly like the lives they live on *Peyton Place.* In *TLS:* "Lucy the Babysitter," Lucy won't let the chimps she's babysitting watch *Peyton Place.* In *TLS:* "Lucy's Substitute Secretary," Lucy calls her replacement, Audrey Fields (Ruta Lee), a "one woman Peyton Place." In *HL:* "Lucy, the Shopping Expert," Craig tells Harry he has known all about the facts of life since he was seven because he watched *Peyton Place.* In *HL:* "Lucy, the Other Woman," Harry says he hasn't seen a situation like the one Lucy's in since *Peyton Place.*

Rowan & Martin's Laugh-In. For four seasons, this one-of-a-kind NBC comedy-variety series offered Lucy serious ratings competition for the 8:30 p.m. slot. (The "Martin" of its title was Dick Martin, Lucy's on-again, off-again boyfriend, Harry Conners, on the first two seasons of *The Lucy Show.* "Rowan" referred to Dan Rowan who guest starred on *The Lucy Show* episodes "Lucy and Carol in Palm Springs" and "Lucy Puts Main Street on the Map.") Its occasional, affectionate ribbing of Lucy and her show was answered in kind by many *Here's Lucy* references to its various catchphrases. In "Lucy, the Conclusion Jumper," Lucy tells Harry that Kim went to the courthouse and didn't go to sing "here come da judge." In "Lucy's Burglar Alarm," the thief who only comes away with $1.19 beefs, "For this I missed *Laugh-In.*" In "Lucy and the Andrews Sisters," Lucy tells Harry she would like to "sock it to him." In "Lucy and Johnny Carson," Kim asks Craig, "Which one are you today? Rowan or Martin?" In "Lucy and Wally Cox" Moose Manley (Alan Hale Jr.) says, "You bet your bippy!" In "Lucy and Sammy Davis Jr.," Sammy says, "Here come da judge," which he had been the first celebrity to utter on *Laugh-In.* In "Won't You Calm Down, Dan Dailey?," Harry says, "Verrrry interesting!," *Laugh-In*'s immortal sign-off line. Most intriguingly, that line was almost featured in the famous "Lucy Meets the Burtons" episode, which was supposed to conclude with Elizabeth Taylor purring, "Verrrry interesting! Goodnight, Lucy," but was cut before airing. (Although Lucy never appeared on *Laugh-In*, ex-husband Desi did on the November 23, 1970 episode, which aired against the *Here's Lucy* episode "Lucy and Jack Benny's Biography." Lucie Arnaz guest starred after the series was no longer aired opposite her own program in 1973.)

60 Minutes. CBS's long-running news magazine series welcomed Morley Safer to its team of correspondents in 1970. In *LWL:* "Lucy's Green Thumb," while Curtis is on the phone with the *Los Angeles Times*, he asks if they have a connection with *60 Minutes* because he thinks Lucy's Gigantagrow would be an excellent story for Morley Safer.

Sesame Street. This children's show featuring the Muppets began in 1969 and became one of the longest-running continuing shows on television. In *HL:* "Lucy and Donny Osmond," when Kim realizes she has to put a stop to 14-year-old Donny Osmond's crush on her, she says, "I feel like the femme fatale of *Sesame Street.*"

Star Trek. The most famous and enduring non-Lucy series to come from Desilu, the sci-fi classic *Star Trek* was not referenced during its 1966–69 prime-time run but after its cancellation. In *HL:* "Lucy's Replacement," Lucy says that Harry's new computer looks like "a leftover from *Star Trek.*"

The Untouchables. Although *The Untouchables* was a Desilu production, rather than actually use the program's real name, *The Lucy Show* episode "Lucy, the Gun Moll" instead features cast members Robert Stack, Bruce Gordon, and Steve London playing parodies of their characters, three years after the series' cancellation. As with the real thing, Walter Winchell is on hand as narrator. At the end of the episode, Stack and Gordon say that they're really "touched," to which Lucy cleverly responds, "So you see, nobody is really *untouchable.*"

What's My Line? This long-running quiz show, on which a celebrity panel was asked to guess the occupation of its contestants, had a title that itself became a catchphrase of sorts. In *TLS:* "Lucy and Viv Put in a Shower," Lucy thinks a plumber is a doctor; when informed of his actual profession, Lucy tells him, "You could fool the panel on *What's My Line?*" In *HL:* "A Date for Lucy," when Lucy tells Harry to ask her what her date does for a living, an impatient Harry replies, "This is no time to play *What's My Line?*." (Unlike other shows referenced, Lucy had an actual association with this series, having appeared as the celebrity "mystery guest" on six occasions, a record.)

Wild Kingdom. Television's most famous wildlife series ran alternately in syndication and prime time for twenty-five years (1963–88). In *LWL:* "Lucy Makes Curtis Byte the Dust," Lucy tells Curtis he's been watching too much *Wild Kingdom.*

Theater

Arsenic and Old Lace. Joseph Kesselring's 1941 black comedy became one of the longest-running shows in Broadway history (1,444 performances). In *ILL:* "Ricky Needs an Agent," Lucy suggests that MGM remake one of their big hits and tailor it for Ricky. One suggestion is "Arsenic and Old Ricky." (The film version of the play was actually a Warner Bros. release.) In *HL:* "Lucy and the Little Old Lady," Harry is suspicious of Lucy's houseguest Mrs. Brady (Helen Hayes) and says she might poison people with elderberry wine like the little old ladies in *Arsenic and Old Lace.* (Hayes had actually played one of those lethal old ladies, Abby Brewster, in both the 1955 and 1969 television presentations of the play.)

The Caine Mutiny Court-Martial. Herman Wouk's 1951 Pulitzer Prize-winning novel *The Caine Mutiny* was first adapted (or at least a portion of its plot) into the 1953 Broadway play *The Caine Mutiny Court-Martial*, a year before it became an Oscar-nominated movie. In *ILL:* "Lucy Meets Orson Welles," Lucy's former drama teacher Miss Hannah (Ellen Corby) cannot come to New York to see Lucy perform with Orson Welles because the Jamestown High School is doing *The Caine Mutiny Court-Martial.* One of the boys has the chickenpox and she may have to play Captain Queeg.

Fiddler on the Roof. The 1964 Broadway musical by Jerry Bock and Sheldon Harnick about a Jewish milkman and his family was at one point the longest-running Broadway show. In *HL:* "Lucy Plays Cops and Robbers," Lucy calls the police when she thinks she hears a burglar, but it turns out to be Harry fixing the TV antenna for Kim. After the police catch him, Harry angrily tells Lucy that he "wasn't The Fiddler on the Roof!" (Gino Conforti, who played the real burglar in this episode, originated the role of the titular fiddler in the Broadway show.)

Hello, Dolly! Jerry Herman's musical based on *The Matchmaker* became a sensation from the time of its opening in January 1964, giving Carol Channing her signature role. In *TLS*: "Lucy, the Undercover Agent," Lucy disguises herself as Carol Channing and sings a variation of "Hello, Dolly!" At the end, she is told "Goodbye, Dolly!" In *HL*: "A Home Is Not an Office," Lucy's friends sings "Hello, Lucy!" while Lucy is recovering from her broken leg. Kim says "it sounds a lot like 'Hello, Dolly!'."

I Remember Mama. In 1944 Kathryn Forbes's autobiographical book *Mama's Bank Account*" became a long-running play retitled *I Remember Mama,* by John Van Druten; and, subsequently, a hit film with Irene Dunne; and, finally, a popular television series, the title shortened to *Mama,* which ran on CBS for seven seasons. In *HL:* "Where Is My Wandering Mother Tonight?," Kim doesn't have time for Lucy anymore. One of her activities is a show she is doing with a local theater group. Hurt, Lucy asks, "What play are they doing? *I DON'T Remember Mama?*"

The Most Happy Fella. The 1956 Frank Loesser musical version of Sidney Howard's play *They Knew What They Wanted* is unique among pop culture references on the Lucy shows because in *ILL*: "Lucy's Night in Town," rather than it merely being talked about, the Ricardos and Mertzes actually go to see the show, during its run at the Imperial Theatre. Or rather, each of them sees *some* of the show, as the plot involves the four theater-goers having to share two tickets. During the episode, bits of the songs "Big D," "Standing on the Corner," and "Don't Cry" are heard. The reason for all this attention is simple; Desilu had some money invested in the show.

The Man Who Came to Dinner. Kaufman & Hart's 1939 hit comedy (and subsequent 1941 film adaptation) starred Monty Woolley as Sheridan Whiteside, an acid-tongued radio commentator whose leg injury forces him to spend an extended period of time at the house of a beleaguered midwestern couple. The premise soon turned the play's title into shorthand for unwanted houseguests. In *TLS*: "Lucy and Viv Reminisce," Vivian stays with Lucy to care for her after she breaks her leg. Viv ends up breaking her leg as well, and says she "feels like the female version of *The Man Who Came to Dinner.*" In *HL*: "Lucy's House Guest, Harry," Harry stays with Lucy and Kim and drives them crazy. When he's about to leave, Lucy remembers what happened to Whiteside in *The Man Who Came to Dinner* and is afraid the same thing will happen to Harry. It does; while leaving, he falls and breaks his leg. Lucy starred in a *Lux Radio Theatre* adaptation of *The Man Who Came to Dinner* on March 27, 1950, with Clifton Webb as Whiteside.

Oklahoma! Rodgers & Hammerstein's landmark 1943 musical starring Alfred Drake had become the longest-running Broadway musical of all time when it closed on May 29, 1948. In *ILL:* "Lucy Tells the Truth," when Lucy gets tired of Ricky and the Mertzes telling their show business stories, she insists that she starred in a musical comedy—*Oklahoma!* A skeptical Ethel asks, "What was your maiden name? Alfred Drake?" Lucy says it's not a lie, she really was once in Oklahoma—she spent two weeks in Tulsa.

Pygmalion. The Greek legend of a sculptor named Pygmalion who falls in love with the statue he has created provided the name for George Bernard Shaw's 1912 play, which, in turn, was the basis for the 1956 musical *My Fair Lady.* In *TLS:* "My Fair Lucy," Mrs. Dunbar (Reta Shaw) tells the Countess that she will never make a Pygmalion out of her Galatea (Liza Lumpwhomper, played by Lucy). In *HL:* "My Fair Buzzi" Kim tells her friend Annie (Ruth Buzzi) she will give her the Pygmalion treatment.

Rio Rita. The 1927 Florenz Ziegfeld production of Harry Tierney and Joseph McCarthy's musical was one of the big hits of its decade. In *TLS:* "Lucy's Barbershop Quartet," Lucy says her friend Thelma Green (Carole Cook) was in the third road company of *Rio Rita.* In real life, Lucille was, but she was fired during rehearsals.

South Pacific. The 1949 Rodgers & Hammerstein musical commenting on racism during World War II was one of the most acclaimed and highly attended shows of its era, winning the Pulitzer Prize. It would run a total of 1,925 performances making it the fifth-longest-running show in Broadway history by the time of its closing in January 1954. In *ILL:* "No Children Allowed," Ethel repeatedly tells the story of how she defended the Ricardos to Mrs. Trumbull. After Ethel insists she's only told a couple of people, Lucy, wearied of hearing her tale, snaps "A couple of people? Ethel, that story's had more performances than *South Pacific!*" Since the show was still running at the time the episode aired on April 20, 1953, it made sense to use this as an example of a stage work that ran a lengthy amount of time and not the four that had out-run it (including Rodgers & Hammerstein's *Oklahoma!,* which held the number four position; it, and the other three, had all since closed).

Movies

Angels with Dirty Faces. In one of Warner Bros.' seminal gangster dramas, hoodlum James Cagney and priest Pat O'Brien fought over which of them would influence the neighborhood youths, portrayed by the "Dead End" Kids. In *HL:* "Lucy and Mannix Are Held Hostage," Lucy and one of the bank robbers bond over their love of James Cagney movies. The robber informs Lucy that *Angels with Dirty Faces* will be on "The Late, Late Show" next week; but unfortunately Lucy won't be alive to watch it. Lucy assures him she's already seen it.

Animal Crackers. The Marx Brothers' second starring vehicle was an adaptation of their stage hit. (The title, like all early Marx films, is deliberately meaningless, as no actual crackers are seen or consumed.) In *HL:* "Good Bye, Mrs. Hips," a dieting Lucy complains that "I tried to take my mind off food by watching television. There were only three old movies on: *Breakfast at Tiffany's, Guess Who's Coming to Dinner,* and *Animal Crackers!*" (The Marx comedy was the one movie in the trio of titles that could qualify as being "old," having debuted 43 years earlier at the time of the episode's airing.)

The Barretts of Wimpole Street. This 1934 American film about the love affair between poets Elizabeth Barrett and Robert Browning received a Best Picture Oscar nomination. In *ILL:* "Ricky Needs an Agent," when Lucy says MGM should take one of their big properties and remake it with Ricky, she suggests "The Ricardos of Wimpole Street." (MGM did remake the movie two years later, in 1957, starring Jennifer Jones.)

Beach Blanket Bingo. The fifth of seven silly "beach party" frolics released by American International Pictures in the mid sixties, most of them featuring the team of Frankie Avalon and Annette Funicello. In *HL:* "Ginger Rogers Comes to Tea," Lucy fights with a fellow audience member at a Ginger Rogers Film Festival who, unbeknownst to her, is actually Ginger Rogers. Ginger says that she's not going to stay to see *Tender Comrade* because "I've seen it and I don't want to see it again!" Lucy replies, "Well, that shows what kind of taste you have in movies. Why don't you come back next week; they might be showing *Beach Blanket Bingo!*"

***Ben-Hur* (1925).** MGM's first adaptation of the Lew Wallace novel was one of the mightiest epics of the silent era, its key sequence being a chariot race between Ramon Novarro (as Ben-Hur) and Francis X. Bushman. In *ILL:* "The Handcuffs," Lucy complains that it's been a long time since Ricky took her to the movies. She can't remember the last movie they saw, but "there was a guy named Ben who won a chariot race."

Ben-Hur **(1959).** MGM's second, even more lavish version of the biblical tale starred Charlton Heston and became perhaps the defining epic of its era. In *TLS:* "No More Double Dates," Lucy, Viv, Harry, and Eddie can't decide what movie to see. Eddie suggests *Ben-Hur* as an alternative to *Two for the Seesaw* because it has a cast of 30,000—that's 200 actors a penny.

Bob & Carol & Ted & Alice. Paul Mazursky's 1969 couple-swapping comedy had the sort of distinctive title that people loved to utilize for jokes, whether the subject was related to the movie's theme or not. In *HL:* "Lucy Fights the System," waitress Kim calls two couples out to dinner "Bob & Carol & Ted & Alice."

Breakfast at Tiffany's. This 1961 adaptation of the Truman Capote novel about a free-spirited New Yorker named Holly Golightly gave Audrey Hepburn one of her most enduring roles. In *HL:* "Good Bye, Mrs. Hips," a dieting Lucy explains that "I tried to take my mind off food by watching television. There were only three old movies on: *Breakfast at Tiffany's, Guess Who's Coming to Dinner,* and *Animal Crackers!*" (*Tiffany's* was the only one of the trio in which its consumptive title was carried out on screen, as Hepburn starts the film by munching a pastry in front of the Fifth Avenue jewelry store.)

Camille. The 1936 Greta Garbo melodrama, in which she portrays a nineteenth-century French courtesan who succumbs to consumption, gave the legendary actress one of her greatest roles and an Oscar nomination. In *ILL:* "Lucy Gets in Pictures," Ricky says Lucy, who has a bit part in a movie, thinks she's playing Camille. In *TLS:* "Lucy Waits Up for Chris," Lucy and Viv express interest in watching *Camille* on television but none of their children know who Greta Garbo is. In *HL:* "Lucy's Birthday," having to fake a sickness to get out of paying their restaurant bill, Lucy says, "You're about to see an Academy Award performance that will make the dying scene in *Camille* look like a love-in."

Casablanca. Among the many unforgettable scenes of this Oscar-winning wartime classic is Humphrey Bogart and Ingrid Bergman's emotional farewell at a fog-shrouded airport. In *HL:* "Lucy and the Bogie Affair," Kim names their dog "Bogie" because she thinks he looks like Humphrey Bogart at the end of *Casablanca.*

Cleopatra. Fox's gargantuan epic about the Queen of the Nile was the most publicized and expensive movie of its day when it opened in the summer of

1963. Elizabeth Taylor had the title role, with her off-screen lover Richard Burton portraying her on-screen squeeze, Marc Antony. In *TLS*: "Lucy Plays Cleopatra," Lucy says she should play the Egyptian ruler because she's seen the movie twelve times (which would total a staggering 48 hours, if she'd seen the complete, road show engagement of the picture!). In *HL*: "Lucy and Her Genuine Twimby," Mr. Kincaid (William Lanteau) tells his boss Bob Henning (Bob Cummings), "Marc Antony would have gotten the job done in Egypt if he hadn't bumped into Elizabeth Taylor." In *HL*: "Lucy Plays Cops and Robbers," Harry buys a color TV set and rushes home to see Elizabeth Taylor in *Cleopatra*. His TV set is stolen, so he ends up watching it with Lucy at her house.

Father of the Bride. The popular 1950 comedy starred Spencer Tracy and Elizabeth Taylor. In *TLS:* "Lucy's Sister Pays a Visit," Viv tries to cheer up Lucy's sister Marge (Janet Waldo), who has left her husband, by inviting her to watch the movie playing on TV that night, *Father of the Bride*. Marge only cries more.

Gaslight. Although it started life as the long-running play *Angel Street*, the renamed 1944 film adaptation starring Ingrid Bergman as a wife being driven insane by husband Charles Boyer made such an impact that the title *Gaslight* could be used as shorthand to explain the premise. In *TLS*: Lucy Gets Mooney Fired," after watching *Gaslight* on television with her pal Mary Jane, Lucy gets the idea to give Mr. Cheever (Roy Roberts), the president of the bank, the "Gaslight treatment."

Gone with the Wind. David O. Selznick's much-heralded and acclaimed adaptation of Margaret Mitchell's Pulitzer Prize-winning novel became *the* movie event of 1939; indeed of the entire Hollywood studio era, becoming the most widely attended motion picture of all time and the winner of eight Academy Awards. Its fame was such that it was a frequent "go to" title when a very well-known motion picture or novel needed to be mentioned. In *ILL*: "Lucy Writes a Novel," Lucy says the book she's writing could be another *Gone with the Wind* and tells Ethel she would be Scarlett O'Hara. Lucy titles her novel *Real Gone with the Wind*. In *ILL*: "Ricky Needs an Agent," one of the film remakes Lucy suggests MGM tailor for Ricky is *Gone with the Cuban Wind*. In *TLS*: "Lucy and the Monsters," Viv says she hasn't seen a movie with a monster since *Gone with the Wind*. Lucy: "There was no monster in *Gone with the Wind*." Viv: You didn't see my date." In *TLS*: "Lucy and Robert Goulet," Mooney says about taking the picture of Chuck Willis (Robert Goulet), overseen by Lucy, that they didn't have that much trouble making *Gone with the Wind*. In *HL:* "Lucy and Carol Burnett" (third season), Lucy, Kim, and Carol come across the costumes Clark Gable and Vivien Leigh wore in the movie. Lucy does a Butterfly McQueen impression. In *HL:* "Lucy and Flip Go Legit," Harry's community theater group puts on a capsule production of *Gone with the Wind* with him as Rhett Butler, Lucy as Scarlett O'Hara, Kim as Melanie, and Flip Wilson as Prissy. In *HL:* "Lucy's Lucky Day," Lucy gets a notice from the library saying that her copy of *Gone with the Wind* is overdue. Lucy borrowed it when it first came out.

Guess Who's Coming to Dinner. This famous 1967 social comedy-drama about a white, liberal couple coping with their daughter's decision to marry a black man led up to the title meal, which was never actually seen on screen. In *HL:* "Good Bye, Mrs. Hips," a dieting Lucy says, "I tried to take my mind off food by watching television. There were only three old movies on: *Breakfast at Tiffany's, Guess Who's Coming to Dinner,* and *Animal Crackers!*" (*Dinner* was a mere six years in the past at the time the episode aired, which hardly qualified it as "old.")

Guys and Dolls. The 1955 Samuel Goldwyn-produced adaptation of Frank Loesser's Broadway hit starred Marlon Brando, Frank Sinatra, Jean Simmons, and Vivian Blaine. In *ILL:* "Lucy and the Dummy," a clip from the film, featuring Frank Sinatra singing "Adelaide," is shown at the MGM studio party. (This is the only instance of an actual film clip being shown on any of the Lucy series.)

High Noon. This 1952 Gary Cooper western became one of the landmarks of the genre and a cross-over, award-winning success. In *ILL:* "Lucy's Schedule," the Ricardos and the Mertzes go out to see *High Noon*, which is a bit premature. The episode aired on May 12, 1952, but the picture did not actually open for the public until late July of that year.

I Am Curious (Yellow). This scandalous Scandinavian movie became a media sensation in the late nineteen-sixties, resulting in all kinds of jokes about its X-rated content and its unforgettable, oddball title. In *HL:* "Lucy and Jack Benny's Biography," Benny titles his autobiography *I Am Curious Jell-O*.

It Happened One Night. This 1934 Frank Capra comedy starring Clark Gable and Claudette Colbert was the first film to win the "Grand Slam" at the Academy Awards: Best Picture, Actor, Actress, Director, and Screenplay. In *ILL:* "Ricky Needs an Agent," Lucy proposes an MGM remake entitled "It Happened One Noche." (*It Happened One Night* was a Columbia film.)

Jonathan Livingston Seagull. This 1973 film, based on the best seller by Richard Bach, featured no human actors on screen. The title character was an actual seagull. In *HL:* "Lucy Is a Birdsitter," Sir Osbird Place (Arte Johnson), says his bird, Floyd, a "weewawk," enjoyed the plane ride from Africa because they played *Jonathan Livingston Seagull* on the flight.

Lawrence of Arabia. The 1962 Oscar winner for Best Picture starred Peter O'Toole as the enigmatic British officer T. E. Lawrence. In *TLS:* "Lucy, the Disc Jockey," Lucy, trying to guess the mystery sound in a radio contest, holds up an hourglass to Viv's ear and asks her if she hears anything. Viv replies, "Laurence of Arabia calling for help." In *TLS:* "Lucy, the Stunt Man," Lucy as Iron Man Carmichael says "he" has been out of the country working on *Lawrence of Arabia* and was kicked in the throat by a camel.

Mary Poppins. The title character of Walt Disney's phenomenally popular 1964 musical fantasy about a magical nanny soon entered the cultural lexicon because of her ability to fly. In *TLS:* "Lucy's Mystery Guest," Mooney says that Lucy looks like a "grounded Mary Poppins." In *HL:* "Kim Finally Cuts You-Know-Who's Apron Strings," Kim's amorous date tells her that she's *not* dressed like Mary Poppins. In *HL:* "Lucy's Tenant," renter Kermit Boswell (Jackie Coogan) calls Lucy "Mary Poppins."

Meet Me In St. Louis. This Judy Garland musical about a family in the early nineteen-hundreds was MGM's biggest hit of 1944. In *ILL:* "Ricky Needs an Agent," Lucy suggests a remake, "Meet Me in St. Ricky."

Moby Dick. Gregory Peck portrayed the obsessive, one-legged Captain Ahab in John Huston's 1956 adaptation of the Herman Melville novel. In *ILL:* "Little Ricky Gets a Dog," after seeing Lucy struggle with Little Ricky's fish, Ethel says, "Gregory Peck had less trouble with Moby Dick. "In *ILL:* "Lucy Hates to Leave," Fred calls Little Ricky's fish "Moby."

On the Waterfront. Directed by Elia Kazan, this 1954 drama about corruption on the New Jersey docks became one of Marlon Brando's seminal credits and one of the most acclaimed films of the nineteen-fifties, winning eight Academy Awards. In *ILL:* "The Dancing Star," Lucy says that Marlon Brando was one of the stars she told Caroline Appleby she has met in Hollywood. Says Lucy: "Did you see *On the Waterfront?* Wonderful! He won the Academy Award, you know."

One Hundred Men and a Girl. A major hit for Universal's popular song-bird Deanna Durbin in 1937, its title was a reference to her performing with Leopold Stokowski and his orchestra. In *LD*: "Lucy Takes a Cruise to Havana," this flashback episode dramatizes when Ricky and Lucy first met. Ironically, since Lucy's ship is filled with women and no single men, the movie she goes to see onboard is *One Hundred Men and a Girl.*

Pillow Talk. This 1959 Rock Hudson-Doris Day box-office success set the standard for battle-of-the-sexes comedies for years to come. In *TLS*: "Lucy Goes to a Hollywood Premiere," after Lucy buys the nightgown that Doris Day wore in *Pillow Talk*, Mooney says he wouldn't pay money for "a nightie if it was worn by Jack Lemmon in *Some Like it Hot.*"

Robin Hood. In 1973 the Disney Studio released their all-animal, animated version of the legend. In *HL*: "Where Is My Wandering Mother Tonight?," when Kim invites Lucy to see an R-rated (fictitious) movie entitled *The Great Struggle,* Lucy says she doesn't want to see that racy picture and suggests instead something that will get their minds off the troubles of the world, "like *Robin Hood.*"

Sabrina. Humphrey Bogart, Audrey Hepburn, and William Holden were the stars of this 1954 romantic comedy. In *ILL*: "Getting Ready," Lucy asks her friend Marion Van Vlack on the phone if she has anything she wants Lucy to tell a star when they're in Hollywood. Marion's response is to "Tell Bill Holden Marion Van Vlack saw *Sabrina* five times." (Holden would indeed be one of the first celebrities spotted once the Ricardos and the Mertzes arrived in Hollywood, appearing on the episode "LA at Last," less than two months after this one aired.)

Sayonara. Adapted from James Michener's novel, this highly popular 1957 Marlon Brando film made a statement against racism toward the Japanese. In *LD*: "The Ricardos Go to Japan," Lucy says she sat through *Sayonara* twice.

Seven Brides for Seven Brothers. MGM's rousing 1954 musical about a family of backwoods brothers who abduct the women they want to be their brides starred Howard Keel and Jane Powell. In *ILL*: "Ricky Needs an Agent," Lucy suggests MGM remake it as "Seven Brides for Seven Cubans" (despite the fact the original film was released less than a year before). In *ILL*: "Lucy in the Swiss Alps," Lucy is afraid that the gang will get stuck in an avalanche like in *Seven Brides for Seven Brothers.* When an avalanche does occur, Fred says he could get through the ordeal if they had five more brides. Lucy points out that the characters in the movie had to wait until the spring thaw.

Some Like It Hot. So popular was this 1959 farce featuring Tony Curtis and Jack Lemmon as a pair of musicians who dress in drag to escape gangland killers, that it became synonymous with cross-dressing. In *TLS:* "Lucy Goes to a Hollywood Premiere," when Lucy buys the nightgown that Doris Day wore in *Pillow Talk,* Mooney says he wouldn't pay money for "a nightie even if Jack Lemmon wore it in *Some Like It Hot.*"

Stage Door. RKO's 1937 adaptation of the stage hit by Edna Ferber and George S. Kaufman featured among its stellar cast Katharine Hepburn, Ginger Rogers, Eve Arden, Ann Miller, and, of course, Lucille Ball. It was Hepburn, however, who uttered the script's most famous and oft-repeated line, "The calla lilies are in bloom again," as part of the play in which her character is appearing. The line shows up in *ILL:* "Lucy's Italian Movie," where Lucy says it, and then again in *HL:* "Lucy, the American Mother," with Kim giving her best Hepburn interpretation.

A Streetcar Named Desire. This 1951 adaptation of the sensational play by Tennessee Williams turned Marlon Brando into a star. In *ILL:* "Ricky Needs an Agent," one of Lucy's suggestions for an MGM remake to tailor for Ricky is "A Streetcar Named Ricardo" (*A Streetcar Named Desire* was actually a Warner Bros release.) In *TLS:* "Lucy Dates Dean Martin," the undershirt Marlon Brando wore in *A Streetcar Named Desire* is among the memorabilia up for purchase at the bank's charity ball.

The Tall Men. This 1955 20th Century-Fox western paired Clark Gable with Jane Russell. In *ILL:* "Lucy Visits Grauman's," *The Tall Men* is the film advertised on the fabled movie theater's marquee.

Three Coins in the Fountain. A notable 1954 film about three young American woman finding romance in Rome. In *ILL:* "Ricky Needs an Agent," Lucy proposes a remake "Three Cubans in a Fountain." (*Three Coins in the Fountain* was actually a 20th Century-Fox film.)

Thunderhead—Son of Flicka. Roddy McDowell reprised his role from the 1943 film *My Friend Flicka,* about a boy and his horse in this 1945 sequel. In *ILL:* "Ricky Needs an Agent," one of the titles Lucy suggests for an MGM remake to be tailored for Ricky is "Ricky—Son of Flicka." (*Thunderhead—Son of Flicka* was actually a 20th Century-Fox film.)

12 Angry Men. The 1957 drama starred Henry Fonda as the sole juror to holdout from declaring a murder suspect guilty. In *HL*: "Lucy and Joan Rivers Do Jury Duty," the plotline of Lucy being the lone holdout juror was so clearly paying tribute to the film that Joan even describes Lucy as "Henry Fonda in *12 Angry Men*."

Two for the Seesaw. The 1962 film version of William Gibson's 1957 Broadway play was mentioned in *TLS*: "No More Double Dates," when Harry suggests it as the movie he, Lucy, Viv, and Eddie see. After Harry informs her that there are only two actors in the film, Lucy refuses to buy the $1.50 ticket because that means seventy-five cents per actor. In reality, while the play featured only two actors onstage throughout, Robert Mitchum and Shirley MacLaine shared the screen with a few other added characters. (Lucie Arnaz would later play the lead in the national touring company of the play's musical adaptation, *Seesaw*.)

Valley of the Dolls. Jacqueline Susann's all-time best-selling 1966 novel about the ups and downs of some show business ladies was quickly made into a movie that was just as popular and just as critically reviled. *HL*: "Lucy and Eva Gabor" contains a spoof of the book. Eva von Gronyitz is the author of the controversial *Valley of the Puppets*.

What Ever Happened to Baby Jane? The 1962 gothic chiller about a pair of one-time performing sisters going mad while living out their later years together in Hollywood starred Bette Davis and Joan Crawford in the most famous latter-day roles of their careers. It was twice referenced on *TLS*: "No More Double Dates," Lucy, Viv, Harry, and Eddie can't decide what movie to see. Vivian wants to see *What Ever Happened to Baby Jane?*, but Lucy refuses because it's too scary. The following week, Viv wants to see it alone with Eddie, but he tells her he saw it without her. In "Lucy and the 'Boss of the Year' Award," Mooney mistakenly calls Mary Jane "Baby Jane."

Who's Afraid of Virginia Woolf? The controversial 1966 film adaptation of Edward Albee's landmark play starred Elizabeth Taylor and Richard Burton in their greatest screen pairing. In *HL*: "Lucy Cuts Vincent's Price," Price's new film is called *Who's Afraid of Virginia's Wolfman?*

Winning. This 1969 racing opus was one of the many cinematic pairings of real-life couple Paul Newman and Joanne Woodward. In *HL*: "Won't You Calm Down, Dan Dailey?," Dan Dailey thinks Paul Newman would be great in the lead of a movie he is producing. Lucy agrees and says that she saw him in *Winning*, prompting her to imitate Newman as a race car driver.

The Wizard of Oz. Arguably the most widely viewed movie of them all, the 1939 classic fantasy musical might also be the most frequently referenced within all media. In *HL*: "Lucy and Carol Burnett" (third season), as part of the show-within-a show, Lucy, Kim, and Carol visit a Hollywood studio where they see Judy Garland's costume from *The Wizard of Oz*; Kim imitates a Munchkin; and the three women sing a bit of "We're Off to See the Wizard."

Yankee Doodle Dandy. Warner Bros.' 1942 salute to showman George M. Cohan gave James Cagney one of his signature roles and brought him an Academy Award. In *HL*: "The Carters Meet Frankie Avalon," Frankie does impressions of what some famous actors would sound like auditioning for the role of George M. Cohan, among them John Wayne, before doing a Cagney impersonation.

Books/Stories/Publications

Agatha Christie, *Nemesis*. This Miss Marple murder mystery was the latest Agatha Christie novel to have been published (in November 1971) at the time it was mentioned in *HL*: "Harrison Carter, Male Nurse," in which Lucy asks Harry if he's read the book; he hasn't.

Alice's Adventures in Wonderland. Lewis Carroll's classic fantasy was published in 1865 and has been adapted by many different mediums. One of its most famous set pieces is a nonsensical tea party. In *HL*: "Ginger Rogers Comes to Tea," Lucy invites Rogers over to her house to pick up her lost purse that Lucy found. After Lucy tells her that she actually does not have the purse (Harry is getting it repaired after they tore it), Ginger asks, "If you don't have my purse, then why am I playing Alice in Wonderland at this mad tea party?"

Black Beauty. Anna Sewell's 1877 story of the various owners and adventures in the life of a horse, as told from its point of view, was one of the first novels to address the mistreatment of animals, and has come to be thought of as a children's book over the years. In *HL*: "Harrison Carter, Male Nurse," Lucy asks Harry if he's read it; unlike the others in question (*The Moon's a Balloon* and *Nemesis*), he has. Lucy asks if he thought it was exciting when the barn caught fire. Harry says he hasn't gotten that far yet. (The chapter in question is #16: "The Fire.")

The Caine Mutiny. The 1951 Pulitzer Prize winner by Herman Wouk. In *HL:* "Lucy and Eva Gabor," Lucy's friends want controversial novelist Eva's autograph. The book given to Eva from Lucy's friend Dolores (Gail Bonney) is *The Caine Mutiny* because, she says, "I'm president of the PTA, and I couldn't have your book in my house."

A Christmas Carol. Charles Dickens's enduring 1843 novella of miserly Ebenezer Scrooge's redemption has probably been referenced in pop culture more than any other story. In *TLS*: "Together for Christmas," Lucy says her father always read her *A Christmas Carol.*

David Niven, *The Moon's a Balloon.* Niven's first autobiography was considered one of the most enjoyable of all movie star memoirs when it was published in 1971. In *HL:* "Harrison Carter, Male Nurse," Lucy asks Harry if he's read it; he hasn't. Despite her plug for his book, Niven is one luminary who never appeared on any of Ball's series. The editor of this book was John Dodds, who was married to Vivian Vance at the time.

Field & Stream. The periodical covering the world of outdoor sports was first seen in 1895. *ILL:* "The Camping Trip," Lucy, showing off her camping outfit, asks Ethel, "Does it look like I just stepped out of *Field & Stream?*" Ethel replies, "Looks more like you fell in."

How the Grinch Stole Christmas! Dr. Seuss's 1957 children's classic about a Scrooge-like creature's Yuletide reformation became even better known after it was turned into a 1966 animated television special. In HL: "Lucy Is N.G. as an R.N.," Lucy catches Harry reading Mary Jane's spicy book, to which she remarks, "It sure beats *How the Grinch Stole Christmas!*"

Life. Launched by Henry Luce in 1936, this photo-journal chronicling news, sports, culture, and entertainment was a weekly staple in American homes until it ceased regular publication in 1972. In *ILL:* "Ricky's *Life* Story," Ricky has a feature in *Life*. Only Lucy's elbow makes it in the issue. Earlier in the same year this episode aired, Lucy and Desi were seen on the cover of the April 6, 1953 issue, along with their children, Lucie and Desi Jr.

Look. Very much akin to *Life* in its photojournalistic approach to culture and news, *Look* was published from 1937 to 1971. In *ILL:* "Men Are Messy," Lucy, who has turned the apartment into a junkyard, thinks she is being photographed for a musician's magazine, *The Half Beat*, but it is actually

Look. Much to her horror she makes the cover, looking like a hillbilly. In *ILL:* "Lucy Gets Ricky on the Radio," Ricky is seen reading the June 3, 1952 issue of *Look* with Lucille Ball and Marilyn Monroe among those on the cover.

Playboy. Hugh Hefner started this gentleman's magazine, famous for its provocative glimpses of skin, in 1953. In *HL:* "Lucy Loses Her Cool," Lucy finds Craig reading *Playboy* and says she wants Uncle Harry to have a talk with him. Lucy asks Craig where he got the magazine, to which he replies, "From Uncle Harry." In *HL:* "Lucy and Donny Osmond," when Kim mentions the possibility of not letting Donny Osmond down until after he appears in the show she is putting on, she tells her shocked mother, "Don't look at me like I just made the centerfold in *Playboy*."

Portnoy's Complaint. With its explicit sexuality, Philip Roth's satirical 1969 novel became one of the most widely read and notorious books of its day. It was thereafter difficult not to associate the word "complaint" with the protagonist's last name, Portnoy. In *HL:* "Lucy, the Crusader," Lucy asks a member of her consumer group, "What is your complaint, Mrs. Portnoy?"

TV Guide. The medium's invaluable directory to weekly television made its national debut on April 3, 1953, with Lucy sharing the cover with her newborn son, Desi Arnaz Jr. It appeared three times on *ILL:* in "Breaking the Lease," a pre-national *TV Guide* with Lucy and Desi is glimpsed on the coffee table; in "Ricky and Fred are TV Fans," Ricky is seen reading the May 29, 1953 issue with Queen Elizabeth on the cover; and in "Lucy's Club Dance," many copies of *TV Guide* are seen on the newsstand. In *HL:* "Won't You Calm Down, Dan Dailey?," Lucy is surprised to learn that Dan Dailey is married. She said she read in *TV Guide* that he was a widower, unaware that they were referring to his character in his sitcom *The Governor & JJ*.

A Visit from St. Nicholas. Clement C. Moore's 1923 poem has become even better known by its opening line, "'Twas the night before Christmas . . ." In *TLS*: "Together for Christmas," Vivian says her father always read her "'Twas the Night Before Christmas."

Tom Swift and His Electric Rifle. Launched in 1910, this series of adventure books was created by Edward Stratemeyer and continued on and off for decades, written by various authors. A new series of books was published years *after* the character was mentioned on *Here's Lucy* as an example of literature of a bygone era: In "Lucy Helps Craig Get a Driver's License," Harry gives Craig a copy of this particular book in the series (first published in 1911) for his sixteenth birthday because it was his favorite book when he was Craig's age.

17

"Us Show Folk Who Eat There All the Time, We Just Call It 'the Derby'"

Pop Culture References on Lucille Ball's Series: Places

Places

Brown Derby Restaurant. Although the name brings to mind the most famous branch of the Los Angeles-based eateries, the one shaped like a hat, it was the Hollywood locale, at 1628 North Vine Street, that was recreated for *ILL*: "LA at Last!," in which Lucy and the Mertzes go to the Brown Derby and encounter Eve Arden and William Holden. This incident is later referenced in "The Tour," when Richard Widmark asks Ricky if Lucy actually hit William Holden with a pie at the Brown Derby; and in "Homecoming," when Lucy tells her New York friends that they went to "the Derby . . . you all probably know it as the Brown Derby, but us show folk who eat there all the time we just call it 'the Derby'." In *HL*: "Lucy and Johnny Carson," Lucy wins a dinner at the Brown Derby on *The Tonight Show,* and she and Harry bump into Johnny Carson and Ed McMahon there. (This branch closed in 1987 after fifty-eight years of operation.)

Carnegie Hall. Located in New York at Seventh Avenue and 57th Street, it is one of the most prestigious concert halls in the world. In *TLS*: "Lucy, the Music Lover," Lucy and Sam Eastman (Frank Aletter) go see the symphony at Carnegie Hall. *TLS:* "Lucy and the Plumber," Harry Tuttle (Jack Benny) says he made his debut at the age of four at Carnegie Hall.

During their trip to the Brown Derby Restaurant, a star-struck Lucy is determined to get a glimpse of William Holden in the next booth, while Ethel (Vivian Vance) and Fred (William Frawley) once again wait patiently to see where her latest scheme will end up; from the *I Love Lucy* episode "L.A. at Last" (1955).

Churchill Downs. This racetrack, located in Louisville, Kentucky, became famous for hosting the Kentucky Derby, starting in 1875. In *ILL:* "The Camping Trip," Lucy, reading the sports pages, is horrified to read that they are racing little girls at Churchill Downs—a race was won by "a three-year-old maiden." Ricky tells her not to worry, "she's as strong as a horse."

Ciro's. Opened in 1940, this nightclub located at 8433 Sunset Boulevard, became a popular spot for Hollywood stars. In *ILL:* "Lucy Visits Grauman's," Lucy saves match covers from Ciro's among her Hollywood souvenirs.

Coconut Grove. This famous Hollywood nightclub was located in the Ambassador Hotel. In *ILL:* "Lucy Visits Grauman's," it is mentioned as one of the Hollywood sites the gang has yet to go to. In *HL:* "Lucy and Wayne Newton," the Carters remind Wayne Newton that they met him when he performed at the Coconut Grove. In *HL:* "Lucy and Her All-Nun Band," Lucy tells Freddy Martin she used to see him at the Coconut Grove. Martin says he was there so long he "started to look like a coconut."

The Colony. This eatery located at 667 Madison Avenue in Manhattan was called "the most expensive restaurant in the world." In *TLS:* "Lucy Goes Duck Hunting," Lucy and Viv hope their dates Bill and Eddie take them there.

Copacabana. The fabled Manhattan night spot, which opened in 1940, was located at 10 East 60th Street for its first 52 years of existence. Its name (often shortened to the Copa) is the likely inspiration for Ricky's fictional Tropicana club. In *ILL:* "The Girls Want to Go to a Nightclub," Lucy and Ethel want to go to the Copacabana for the Mertzes' anniversary. In *ILL:* "Sentimental Anniversary," Lucy and Ricky look at a picture of themselves at the Copa when they were first married (the photo was actually taken at the Stork Club). In *TLS:* "Viv Moves Out," Lucy's new tenant, Roberta, gets a job singing at the Copa.

Disneyland. Walt Disney's trend-setting and world-famous amusement park opened in Anaheim, California in 1955. In *TLS:* "Lucy, the Bean Queen," bean company owner Colonel Bailey (Ed Begley) says that the chart marking how his beans are selling goes up and down like a ride at Disneyland. In *HL:* "Lucy and Lawrence Welk," Lucy hopes that Viv will spend so much time at Disneyland and Knott's Berry Farm that she will forget that Lucy promised her a date with Welk. In *HL:* "Lucy Meets the Burtons," Richard Burton bemoans that everybody has been to Disneyland except him and Khrushchev. In *LWL:* "Lucy and Curtis Are up a Tree," Margo is angry because she feels that her children are being spoiled by their grandparents. Among their extravaganzas was a trip to Disneyland. In *LWL:* "Lucy, Legal Eagle," Lucy, claiming to be the owner of grandson Kevin's teddy bear, says she took the bear to Disneyland and he especially loved Country Bear Jamboree.

Don the Beachcomber. A popular tiki bar/restaurant chain that began in Los Angeles in the thirties. In *ILL:* "Lucy Visits Grauman's," Lucy keeps chopsticks from the Beachcomber as a souvenir. In *TLS:* "Lucy Goes to a Hollywood Premiere," Lucy thinks "Will Power" is a star discovered washing dishes at the Beachcomber.

El Morocco. The famed Manhattan nightclub with the zebra-striped banquets opened in 1931 and remained at its 154 East 54th Street address until 1960. In *TLS:* "Lucy Goes Duck Hunting," Lucy and Viv hope that their dates will take them to a club like El Morocco or The Colony.

Grauman's Chinese Theatre. The Asian-styled Hollywood movie palace, which opened on Hollywood Boulevard in 1927, was and is best known for its forecourt featuring the hand- and footprints of movie stars. In *ILL:* "Ricky's Screen Test," Lucy imagines Ricky putting his footprints in the forecourt of Grauman's Chinese Theatre. In *ILL:* "Lucy Learns to Drive," Lucy says if it is discovered she and Ethel were responsible for the car cash, "Ricky and Fred will be planting their footprints somewhere and it won't be Grauman's Chinese Theatre." In *ILL:* "Lucy Visits Grauman's," Lucy, Ethel, and Fred visit the theater and end up stealing John Wayne's footprints. In *ILL:* "Lucy and John Wayne," the gang gets John Wayne to replace his destroyed footprints before the premiere of his new movie at Grauman's. In *HL:* "Lucy the Laundress," Lucy claims Mr. Wong, whose car she destroyed, is actually an interior decorator who previously decorated Grauman's Chinese.

Hollywood Bowl. The shell-like amphitheater, located near the Hollywood Freeway, opened in 1922. In *ILL:* "Lucy Visits Grauman's," it is mentioned as a Hollywood site the gang has not yet seen. In *TLS:* "Viv Visits Lucy," Vivian says she would rather sing at the Hollywood Bowl than at the Sunset Strip's Hairy Ape.

Knott's Berry Farm. This still-active amusement park in Buena Park, California expanded over the years from Walter and Cordelia Knotts's popular Chicken Dinner Restaurant, which served a pie filled with the berry first cultivated in the area by Rudolph Boysen, the Boysenberry. In *ILL:* "Don Juan and the Starlets," Fred asks Lucy if she wants to go to Knott's Berry Farm with them. In *HL:* "Lucy and Lawrence Welk," Lucy hopes that Viv will spend so much time at Disneyland and Knott's Berry Farm that she will forget that Lucy promised her a date with Lawrence Welk.

Imperial Theatre. Located at 249 West 45th Street, this Broadway theater opened on Christmas Day, 1923. The exterior of the theater, where *The Most Happy Fella* opened in 1956, was shown in *ILL:* "Lucy's Night in Town." Desi Arnaz made his Broadway debut in this theater in *Too Many Girls* in 1939, and his daughter Lucie made her Broadway debut in the same venue forty years later in *They're Playing Our Song.* Lucie would later return there in 2006 when she co-starred in *Dirty Rotten Scoundrels.* Lucy proved to be the only one of the *I Love Lucy* quartet not to work on the Imperial stage. William Frawley appeared in the show *Sons O' Guns* in 1929, and Vivian Vance took the stage in 1941's *Let's Face It!* The theater appears to have been good luck for everybody in the *Lucy* cast because those shows were the longest running productions Frawley and Vance appeared in. It was at the Imperial Theatre that Lucy first laid eyes on Desi Arnaz when she saw him in *Too Many Girls*.

Lindy's. Established by Leo "Lindy" Linderman in 1921, the deli/restaurant stayed in its original 1626 Broadway location until 1949, while its companion branch, at 1655 Broadway, operated from 1930 to 1959. In *LD:* "Milton Berle Hides Out at the Ricardos," Milton Berle says Lindy once promised to name a sandwich after him if he gave him his seat by the window.

Movieland Wax Museum. Located in Buena Park, California, the museum exhibited wax likenesses of famous stars in settings recreating scenes from their movies and television shows. It was open from 1962 to 2005. In *HL:* "Lucy and Lawrence Welk," to fool Viv, Lucy and Mary Jane get a wax figure of Lawrence Welk from the Movieland Wax Museum, where Mary Jane's friend is the manager. (In 1963, a wax figure of Lucille Ball became the first addition to the TV Hall of Fame section at the Movieland Wax Museum.)

NY World's Fair. Held in Flushing Meadows-Corona Park in the borough of Queens, this was New York City's third such event, taking place during two six-month periods, April–October 1964 and April–October 1965. In *TLS:* "Lucy and the Scout Trip," the winning scout team gets a trip to the World's Fair. In *TLS:* "Lucy, the Good Skate," Lucy is supposed to take Jerry and his scout troop to "Sitting Bull Day" at the Fair. In *TLS:* "Lucy and the Great Bank Robbery," Lucy sees an ad asking people to rent rooms to visitors in town for the World's Fair.

Ohrbach's. This department store opened in Manhattan's Union Square in 1923 before rapidly expanding after World War II. In *ILL:* "The Adagio," Ethel asks Lucy if she saw a polka dot dress at Ohrbach's. (Ohrbach's supplied the wardrobe for the first two seasons of *I Love Lucy*.)

Palace Theatre. This movie and vaudeville theater opened in Jamestown, New York in 1923. In *ILL:* "Ricky Loses His Voice," Fred tells Lucy that he and Ethel performed *The Flapper Follies of 1927* at the Palace Theatre, which was "the best theater in Jamestown, New York." Lucy makes no mention that she is from Jamestown. In real life, Lucille Ball performed on the stage of the Palace Theatre in her early years. The premiere of the Arnazes' film *Forever, Darling* would be held here in 1956.

Perino's. A Los Angeles restaurant open from 1932 to 1986 that was frequented by Hollywood's biggest names. In *ILL:* "The Dancing Star," Lucy says that she had lunch with Clark Gable. "I was at Perino's and Clark was there and we ate lunch together. At different tables." In *ILL:* "Homecoming," Ricky says he had lunch with Richard Widmark at Perino's (in "The Tour," Ricky and Widmark actually went to lunch at Romanoff's).

Romanoff's. A Beverly Hills eatery patronized by movie stars from the Golden Age of Hollywood from 1941 to 1962. In *ILL:* "Ricky's Screen Test," Lucy imagines "dropping in on the gang" at Romanoff's. In *ILL:* "The Tour," Ricky is having lunch with Richard Widmark at Romanoff's and won't let Lucy come along.

Roosevelt Raceway. Located in Westbury, New York, this horse track hosted harness racing starting in 1940. In *LD:* "Lucy Wins a Racehorse," the Ricardos, Mertzes, and Betty Grable and Harry James go to Roosevelt Raceway.

Roseland Ballroom. The venerable Manhattan dance hall was originally located on Broadway before moving to its current 52nd Steet location. In *HL:* "Lucy and Jack Benny's Biography," a flashback shows Jack Benny turning down an invitation to go to Roseland because he would have to pay ten cents a dance.

Sands Hotel. This Las Vegas hotel was in business from 1952 to 1996. In *LD:* "Lucy Hunts Uranium," the Ricardos, Mertzes, and Fred MacMurray all stay at the Sands.

Santa Anita. After opening in Arcadia, California in 1934, this track became the favorite destination for Hollywood's horse racing aficionados. In *ILL:* "Ricky Minds the Baby," Fred jokingly asks Little Ricky, "Who do you like in the fifth at Santa Anita?" In *HL:* "Lucy and Carol Burnett" (second season), in Lucy's ad-libbed recitation about Christopher Columbus, she says, "Columbus sailed in three ships: the Nina, the Pinta, and . . . the Santa Anita."

Schrafft's. The Boston-based candy company once ran a chain of restaurants, several of which were located in Manhattan. They are mentioned in two *ILL* episodes: in "Lucy Does the Tango," Lucy says that if Ricky and Fred stop being friends, she and Ethel can meet secretly at Schrafft's; while in

"Housewarming," Lucy invites Ethel over for a luncheon like they used to have a Schrafft's.

Schwab's Pharmacy. Located on Sunset Boulevard in Hollywood, this drug store was a frequent hangout for those in the movie business. In *ILL:* "Lucy Gets in Pictures," Lucy hears that Lana Turner was discovered at Schwab's, so she decides to go there and try to get discovered too. In *HL:* "The Case of the Wreckless Wheelchair Driver," Kim goes down to Schwab's to see if Lucy's accident victim, Billy Joe Jackson, is really injured.

Starlight Roof. Located in Manhattan's mighty Waldorf-Astoria Hotel on Park Avenue, this was the go-to nightclub for New York's elite from the early thirties into the fifties. It got its name from its retractable roof. In *ILL:* "The Girls Want to Go to a Nightclub," Lucy and Ricky call up their friend Ginny Jones, who sings at the Starlight Roof.

"21" Club. A former speakeasy, this swank Manhattan eatery moved to its present location at 21 West 52nd Street in 1929. In *ILL:* "Vacation from Marriage," Lucy and Ethel claim to have gone to "21" four times in one week. Ethel: "That's 84!" In *ILL:* "Mr. and Mrs. TV Show," Lucy comes back from lunch at "21" with Caroline Appleby.

Yankee Stadium. The home ballpark of the New York Yankees, the original stadium opened in the Bronx in 1923. In *ILL:* "Lucy's Italian Movie," Fred is surprised by the size of the Coliseum and says it is smaller than Yankee Stadium. He claims Joe DiMaggio "could have hit fifty home runs out of that hat box." In *ILL:* "Lucy and Bob Hope," Fred takes Lucy, Ethel, and Little Ricky to Yankee Stadium because it's Ladies Day ("Ladies and little boys get in free"). Lucy encounters Bob Hope there. In *ILL:* "Lucy Raises Tulips," Harry Munson has some extra tickets to the baseball game, so Ricky, Fred, and Little Ricky go to Yankee Stadium, with Ricky leaving the lawn only half mowed. In *TLS:* "Lucy Is a Referee," after causing a riot at Jerry and Sherman's football game, Lucy plans to take both teams to a football game at Yankee Stadium, but a blizzard intervenes.

18

"We're Going to Be on the Stage with the Alabama Foghorn."

People Who Almost Guest Starred on Lucy Shows

Bette Davis

Two-time Academy Award winner Bette Davis, who was the star pupil at the John Murray Anderson–Robert Anderson School during Lucy's short tenure there, twice was signed to guest star on a Lucy series, but never actually ended up appearing. For the second, hour-long *Lucille Ball-Desi Arnaz Show,* Madelyn Martin, Bob Carroll Jr., Bob Schiller, and Bob Weiskopf wrote a script with Davis in mind. The title of the episode, "The Celebrity Next Door," came from real life, as Davis and her fourth husband, actor Gary Merrill, had actually lived next door to Bob Weiskopf in Connecticut. For her appearance, Davis demanded equal billing with Lucy and Desi, her round-trip travel expenses from her home in Maine paid for, and the exorbitant salary of $20,000. Surprisingly, Desilu agreed to all of Davis's stipulations. However, before production could get underway, Davis badly injured her back in a fall. She also filed for divorce from Merrill, who was scheduled to appear in the show as well. These setbacks led to Davis leaving the production. Tallulah Bankhead replaced her. Having no celebrity husband of her own to fill the Gary Merrill part, Tallulah was given a butler named Winslow in the revised script, the role played by Richard Deacon.

In 1971, Davis was approached to guest star in an episode of *Here's Lucy,* although this time she was not the first choice. However, after the appearance was agreed upon, Davis said she was not pleased with the $5,000 every guest star was paid on the show, instead demanding twice the amount. Not wanting to set a new precedent, Lucille Ball Productions was forced to turn Bette down. At the eleventh hour, Lucy asked her close pal Ginger Rogers to appear in the episode that was planned for Bette. Nobody mentioned to Ginger that she was not their first choice. Instead, she was told that she was approached so close to production because of an impending technical strike about to hit Hollywood. Amazingly, "Ginger Rogers Comes to Tea" was produced in only two days. All the scripts for the Bette Davis version were destroyed, and Ginger never knew the real reason why she was asked so late.

Jean Arthur

Lucy hoped to get screen veteran Jean Arthur to guest star on *The Lucy Show,* during the fall of 1964. Lucy had been a big fan of Jean Arthur's in the nineteen-thirties and wanted to be an actress of her "type." Arthur had co-starred in the 1935 Columbia film *The Whole Town's Talking,* in which Lucy had a background role. Getting Arthur to appear before the cameras again would have been a major coup, as she had not been seen on film since the 1953 western *Shane,* and worked infrequently in theater. Nor had she ever accepted television offers of any kind, being one of the select motion picture luminaries to have stayed away from the medium since its inception. So intent was Lucy on landing Arthur that she even spoke of her desire to coax the actress into doing her show during an appearance on *Password.*

It was reported that a script was written for Jean Arthur and that the actress spent time observing the set. In the end, Arthur decided against appearing on the series. Due to Lucy's proposal, Arthur was intrigued by television, and her interest in venturing into the medium might have been one reason she hired a manager for the first time in her career. Jean's new representative, Eddie Dukoff, was happy his client wanted to go into television, but thought she should make her debut in a dramatic program instead. He therefore lined up a guest starring role on the western *Gunsmoke,* where she finally made her small screen debut in March 1965. The following year, Arthur began a sitcom of her own, *The Jean Arthur Show,* which, like *The Lucy Show,* was part of CBS's Monday night lineup. The series only lasted twelve episodes, and Arthur never acted on television again.

Ingrid Bergman

Ingrid Bergman, who by 1971 had already won two Academy Awards (a third would be in her future), had seen the "Lucy Meets the Burtons" episode of *Here's Lucy* and thought that she would like to be a guest on the series as well. Bergman always liked to do comedy, although she was never given many opportunities to do so. Her most notable foray into this area was the 1969 film *Cactus Flower,* in a role originally offered to Lucy.

Madelyn Davis and Bob Carroll Jr. wrote a *Here's Lucy* script for Ingrid. Lucy even publicly announced when they started work on the season that Ingrid Bergman would likely be appearing on the show. It looked like everything was all set, but Bergman was forced to drop out, reportedly because of tax problems. Bette Davis, who Lucy also mentioned would be a probable guest star, was then signed to do the episode only to back out as well. The rewritten episode eventually became "Ginger Rogers Comes to Tea."

People Lucy Did Not Like Working With

Desi receives kisses from his wife and "The Celebrity Next-Door," Tallulah Bankhead, in this posed shot from *The Lucille Ball-Desi Arnaz Show.*

Tallulah Bankhead

Years after working with her, when speaking of Tallulah Bankhead, Lucy said, "There's a lady who I did not know was *not* a lady." Bankhead was not the first choice for the role of "The Celebrity Next Door" on the second installment of *The Lucille Ball-Desi Arnaz Show*. The show was originally written for Bette Davis, who dropped out. In an ironic twist, Bankhead, who twice saw roles she had originated on Broadway taken over by Davis when the plays were adapted for the screen (*Dark Victory, The Little Foxes*), was signed on as her replacement. However, Lucy and Desi soon regretted hiring Bankhead once rehearsals began.

According to several Desilu staffers, Tallulah returned from her daily lunch break visibly intoxicated. She also crashed a production meeting that guest stars were never invited to. When Lucy complimented Tallulah on the sweater she was wearing, Tallulah took it off and gave it to her. Following this exchange, Vivian Vance jokingly said she liked Tallulah's pants. In response, Tallulah removed them and handed them to the startled actress, revealing that she was not wearing anything underneath. During rehearsals, Tallulah could not remember her lines in certain scenes and kept consulting her script. Lucy was terrified that she would do this during the filming and became more and more nervous while they were doing the actual show. During the scene Tallulah had her biggest trouble with, Lucy was so worried about Tallulah's lack of preparation that she forgot her own lines. Bankhead turned to her in front of the audience and sniped, "What's the matter, dahling, can't you remember your lines?" Lucy was thrilled that the filming ended with no major problems, but later admitted she never liked watching the episode because of Tallulah's on-set behavior.

Joan Crawford

Joan Crawford was hired to guest star in one of the last installments of *The Lucy Show*. The episode, "Lucy and the Lost Star," was Vivian's final appearance on the series. In the show, Lucy and a visiting Viv stop at the first house they see to use the telephone after their car breaks down. They are greeted by a lady in a house that is devoid of any furniture. Lucy and Viv realize that the lady is Joan Crawford ("Mildred Pierce!," says Viv) and think that the shabbily dressed woman in the empty house is broke. Lucy, Viv, and Mooney put on a nineteen-twenties speakeasy revue starring Miss Crawford to raise money for her. Unbeknownst, to them Crawford is not penniless but not working by her own choice. Crawford had just sent her own furniture out to be cleaned, which mirrors her real life in which she was obsessed with cleanliness. Lucy reportedly found Crawford on the floor of her dressing room scrubbing the floor and did not even realize who it was.

The rehearsal week for this episode rivaled that of the Tallulah Bankhead fiasco. Lucy caught Joan drinking vodka out of her purse during rehearsals, which infuriated her. When Joan showed up late for rehearsal, Lucy told her she better be sure she was on time the following day. The next day, when Joan did not show up or get in touch with them, Lucy called her on the phone and told her if she was late the following day, she would be fired. Lucy telephoned Kaye Ballard to see if she knew Greer Garson and if she would be interested in replacing Crawford. Crawford, who said she had never been fired before, was on time the next day for rehearsal. According to Kaye Ballard, as the filming began, Joan became panic stricken and refused to go on. Frequent *Lucy* player Vanda Barra talked Crawford into going through with it, and filming went smoothly. Lucy never really liked to talk badly about fellow performers, but made an exception for Crawford.

Lucy's Favorite Guest Stars

Dean Martin

Lucy considered her favorite episode of all her series to be "Lucy Dates Dean Martin" from the fourth season of *The Lucy Show*. Lucy loved this episode because she got to work with Dean Martin. Gale Gordon also considered it to be his favorite of the series, and his reason was the same as Lucy's: Dean Martin. Martin's work ethic was the complete opposite of Lucy's. He hated to rehearse. Martin was in Hawaii and did not come to the set until the day before the show was to be filmed. (This was akin to the arrangement on Dean's weekly variety show, when he would not report to work until the day of filming.) Lucy later said, "He did it in two days. He wouldn't even give us four days and he was better than anyone."

In the episode, Dean played a dual role. Mary Jane fixes Lucy up on a blind date for a charity ball with Dean's stunt double, "Eddie Feldman." When Eddie has to work in Dean's place, Dean takes Eddie's place on the date, so Lucy is not disappointed. Unbeknownst to Lucy, she is out on the town with the real Dino. Lucy would frequently screen this episode for guests at her home. She described Martin as "a living doll."

John Wayne

When John Wayne agreed to guest star on *I Love Lucy*, the writers decided to do a two-part episode about the action-western superstar to kick off the fifth season of the series. This would be the first script written by Bob Schiller and

Lucy loved working with Dean Martin on *The Lucy Show* and was thrilled that she was able to get him to co-star in her 1975 special *Lucy Gets Lucky*.

Lucy and Vivian with John Wayne during production of the *I Love Lucy* episode "Lucy and John Wayne."

Bob Weiskopf, who joined the writing staff alongside Jess Oppenheimer, Madelyn Pugh, and Bob Carroll Jr. In the first installment, "Lucy Visits Grauman's," Lucy and Ethel steal Wayne's footprints from the forecourt of Grauman's Chinese Theatre. In the second part, "Lucy and John Wayne," Wayne is brought in to replace the original footprints, after the cement slab is broken. Lucy later recalled that Wayne agreed to do the show after much persistence, but then backed out due to his limited experience in the new medium. He was finally coaxed into doing it and to prove that he was fully committed to the assignment, Wayne was the first one there in the morning for the first reading.

Wayne wanted publicity for his upcoming film, *Blood Alley*, and only accepted union scale, which was $280. *Blood Alley*, which opened two days before the first installment in the continuing story aired, was mentioned frequently in the two episodes. One scene even features a large poster of the film depicting Wayne and co-star Lauren Bacall.

When Wayne was scheduled to appear on *The Lucy Show*, Lucy wanted a script in which the Lucy character ordered Wayne around, which writer Bob O'Brien gladly wrote. Lucy thought it was hilarious that her character would stand up to the gigantic John Wayne.

Helen Hayes

Lucy later said she was in complete awe when she worked with Helen Hayes. The theater legend and two-time Academy Award winner was cast in the *Here's Lucy* episode "Lucy and the Little Old Lady." Hayes played Kathleen Brady from Dubuque, Iowa, who comes to Carter's Unique Employment Agency to look for a temporary job. She had come to California to visit her nephew, but it turns out he is out of town and she does not have any money. Lucy cannot find her suitable employment, so she invites Mrs. Brady to stay with her. Lucy said in regards to Hayes, "She was so super. She came in and she was just already prepared and knew every line . . . wasn't at all perturbed about anything." Hayes did have one request, though. When Lucy initially read the script, she asked the writers, Fred S. Fox and Seaman Jacobs, to take out certain things she felt they had written to make Hayes lovable. Lucy said that the actress was lovable enough without them. During rehearsals, Hayes said in regard to the script, "There's no little *diddly* stuff." Hayes made some suggestions for her character, and they turned out to be exactly what the writers originally had in mind.

Hayes was thrilled to be working on *Here's Lucy*. Several months earlier, she had to be hospitalized while performing in a Washington DC production of *Long Day's Journey into Night*. Doctors discovered that the actress was allergic to the large amount of dust found in theaters and urged her to end her theater career. That proved to be Hayes's final stage appearance. *Here's Lucy* reinvigorated her television career.

19

"That's What They Say on Lineup"

Other Desilu Series and Pilots

W hen you think "Desilu," you think of Desi and Lucy first and fore-most, their first names being combined to make up the compa-ny name, after all. People familiar with the work of Lucille Ball and Desi Arnaz, even the casual admirers, inevitably know of the company that produced *I Love Lucy*, as it would show up on the program's end cred-its. But Desilu was much bigger and more active than simply producing series in which Lucille Ball starred. Over a sixteen-year period (1951–67), Desilu went from what appeared to be just another company formed by stars for the sake of creative control to a studio empire to be reckoned with, producing several well-known series and attempting on a regular basis to create many more.

Listed below are the Desilu-produced series that actually got on the air as well as a partial list of their pilots, many of which ended up being shown and those that did not.

Series Produced by Desilu

Willy (CBS, 1954–55; June Havoc). Originally called *Miss Bachelor in Law* and then *My Aunt Willy* and *The Artful Dodger*, this comedy starred June Havoc as a lawyer (reportedly the first woman lawyer in the medium) who sets up practice in a small New England town. When this premise failed to attract enough viewers, the character moved to New York to work for a vaudeville organization.

The Lineup (CBS, 1954–60). Inspired no doubt by the success of *Dragnet*, this police procedural series used a similar documentary-like approach as detective Ben Guthrie (Warner Anderson) and his team fought crime in San Francisco. Receiving cooperation from the city's police department,

Lucy and Desi at the entrance of the studio they were under contract to, met at, and, ultimately, owned, in 1958.

the show featured dramatizations of actual cases. For the first four seasons, Anderson was supported by Tom Tully and Marshall Reed. When CBS decided to revamp the format, they expanded the program to an hour, moved in from Friday to Wednesday, and brought in William Leslie, Tod Barton, Skip Ward, and Rachel Ames to replace Tully and Marshall. It was cancelled by mid-season.

In 1958, Columbia Pictures released a feature of the same name directed by Don Siegel and starring Eli Wallach as a psychotic criminal, with Anderson and Reed repeating their television roles. Leslie was seen in the cast as well, although he played a different character than the one he would eventually do on the show.

December Bride (CBS, 1954–60). Following two years on CBS radio (with frequent *Lucy* player Doris Singleton in the cast) as Jack Benny's summer replacement, this comedy about lovable widow Lily Ruskin was brought to television by Desilu, earning character actress Spring Byington two Emmy nominations. Verna Felton (who had appeared memorably in the *I Love Lucy* episodes "Sales Resistance" and "Lucy Hires a Maid") played her best friend, Hilda Crocker. Landing in the Nielsen Top Ten for its first four seasons, Desi would call it Desilu's "second most successful comedy series." Desi appeared in an episode as himself, "Sunken Den" (2/29/1956).

Those Whiting Girls (CBS, 1955, 1957). Singer Margaret Whiting and her sister, actress-singer Barbara Whiting, portrayed themselves in this sitcom that served as the summer replacement for *I Love Lucy* in 1955 and then filled in its slot after its final season, in 1957. Their mother was played by Mabel Albertson, who had acted in the Lucy-Desi film *Forever, Darling*, and would later appear in the "Lucy and the Missing Stamp" episode (12/21/64) on *The Lucy Show*. Jerry Paris, who later directed the *Here's Lucy* episodes "Lucy Meets the Burtons" and "Lucy and Buddy Rich," was a regular during the second season.

Sheriff of Cochise/U.S. Marshal (syndicated; 1956–60). For its first two seasons, this modern-day western had John Bromfield portraying the sheriff of Cochise County, Arizona. When it returned for season three, he had been promoted to a federal marshal working for the state, hence the title change.

The Walter Winchell File (ABC, 1957–58). Columnist Walter Winchell hosted and narrated this anthology series based on stories he himself had covered in the papers. He later narrated *The Untouchables* for Desilu and performed the same task for *The Lucy Show*'s *Untouchables* takeoff "Lucy, the Gun Moll."

Official Detective (syndicated; 1957–58). This anthology crime series (based on the magazine of the same name) first played on radio from 1947 to 1957. Everett Sloane hosted the television version. The pilot had gone under the name *Official Detective Story*.

Whirlybirds (syndicated, 1957–60). Kenneth Tobey and Craig Hill were helicopter pilots engaging in all kinds of adventures in this syndicated half-hour series.

This Is Alice (syndicated; 1958–59). The Alice of the title was a nine-year-old girl, played by Patty Ann Gerrity, who later appeared in *The Lucy Show* episode "Lucy Is a Chaperone" (4/8/63). Tom Farrell (who later played several roles on *The Lucy Show* and *Here's Lucy*) and Phyllis Coates (of *Adventures of Superman*) were her parents.

The Texan (CBS, 1958–60). This half-hour western starred Rory Calhoun (who was also one of its producers) as a gunman fighting bad guys in the post-Civil War years.

Westinghouse Desilu Playhouse (CBS, 1958–60). Desi Arnaz hosted this anthology series and appeared in two episodes during the second season, "So Tender, So Profane" (10/30/59) and "Thunder in the Night" (2/19/60). Lucy was seen in the November 17, 1958 episode, "K.O. Kitty," written by Madelyn Martin and Bob Carroll, Jr., playing a woman who inherits a down-and-out boxer. This marked the first time she took on a television role in which she did not officially play the "Lucy" character.

Eight of the *Lucille Ball-Desi Arnaz* shows were first presented here as well: "Lucy Goes to Mexico" (10/6/58), "Lucy Makes Room for Danny" (12/1/58), "Lucy Goes to Alaska" (2/9/59), "Lucy Wants a Career" (4/13/59), "Lucy's Summer Vacation" (6/8/59), "Milton Berle Hides Out at the Ricardos" (9/25/59), "The Ricardos Go to Japan" (11/27/59), and the very last Lucille Ball-Desi Arnaz pairing, "Lucy Meets the Moustache" (4/1/60). Lucy's Desilu Workshop special, showing off the young talent from her stock company, was also shown as part of the series, under the name "The Desilu Revue." It aired on Christmas Day, 1959.

The Ann Sothern Show (CBS, 1958–61). In what is probably the first example of a character crossing over from one series to another, Ann Sothern reprised her *Private Secretary* role of Susie McNamara in the first of the Lucy-Desi specials, "Lucy Takes a Cruise to Havana," in November 1957. The following year she starred for Desilu in *The Ann Sothern Show*, portraying Katy O'Connor, the assistant manager of a New York hotel, the Bartley. Two of her *Secretary* co-stars, Don Porter and Ann Tyrrell, joined her on the new series.

Sothern received an Emmy nomination and won the Golden Globe for her performance. *The Ann Sothern Show* marked the only time Lucille played the character of Lucy Ricardo without Desi being present as Ricky. In the October 5, 1959 episode, entitled "The Lucy Story," Lucy Ricardo checked into the Bartley Hotel after getting fed up with Ricky.

Lucy had been friends with Sothern for years and had shared three film credits with her, *Broadway Thru a Keyhole*, *Kid Millions*, and *Thousands Cheer* (appearing in the same sketch). Sothern later appeared on *The Lucy Show* multiple times playing the Countess Framboise.

The Grand Jury (syndicated, 1959–60). This drama about two grand jury investigators starred the man who nearly played opposite Lucy in *The Greatest Show on Earth*, Lyle Bettger, and Harold J. Stone as a character named John Kennedy.

The Untouchables (ABC, 1959–63). Controversial in its day for its extreme violence, *The Untouchables* created stories around real-life law enforcement agent Eliot Ness, as played by Robert Stack, in an Emmy-winning performance. Earning two Emmy nominations for Outstanding Program Achievement in the Field of Drama, the series reached the Number 8 spot in the Nielsen ratings during its second season. The property was first launched as a two-part episode of *Westinghouse Desilu Playhouse* (airing April 20 and 27, 1959), which was later expanded into a theatrical feature, released as *The Scarface Mob*. Stack and cast members Bruce Gordon and Steve London, along with the show's narrator, Walter Winchell, spoofed their roles in "Lucy the Gun Moll," an episode (3/14/66) of *The Lucy Show*.

Guestward Ho! (ABC, 1960–61). This was originally conceived as a possible series for Vivian Vance (the pilot was produced in 1958, with Leif Erickson as her co-star), but network executives requested different casting before they would agreed to do the show, hence Joanne Dru replacing her in the series. She and Mark Miller played a New York couple who buy a dude ranch in New Mexico.

Harrigan and Son (ABC, 1960–61). Pat O'Brien and Roger Perry were the father and son lawyers in this situation comedy. Perry was a member of Lucy's Desilu Workshop stock company and had already appeared on several Desilu shows including *Whirlybirds* and *U.S. Marshal*.

Kraft Mystery Theater (NBC, 1962). When this summer replacement series for *Perry Como's Kraft Music Hall* returned for the second year, Desilu came aboard as producers. Some of the shows aired had already been seen on *Westinghouse Desilu Playhouse*, including Desi in "Thunder in the Night."

Fair Exchange (CBS, 1962–63). An attempt to do comedy in a full-hour slot, *Fair Exchange* was cancelled after three months, only to return later that same season in a safer, half-hour format. The story of two families, one in New York City, the other London-based, who swap teenage daughters for a year, it featured Eddie Foy Jr. (who had been in two early Lucy films, *Broadway Thru a Keyhole* and *Moulin Rouge*) and Audrey Christie, who had created the role in the Broadway version of *Without Love* that Lucy would later play on film. Another member of the stage cast of *Without Love* was Donald Briggs, who had played Lucy's boyfriend in 1939's *Panama Lady*. Briggs and Christie married, and at the time Christie was doing *Fair Exchange*, her husband was making frequent appearances as Eddie Collins, Vivian's boyfriend on *The Lucy Show*. Christie appeared with Lucy in her final film, *Mame*, as Mrs. Upson.

Glynis (CBS, 1963). At one point nearly titled *Be Careful, My Love*, this comedy, created and produced by Jess Oppenheimer, starred Glynis Johns as a ditsy amateur sleuth and Lucy's *Wildcat* co-star Keith Andes as her attorney husband. It was cancelled after only 13 episodes. The pilot for the series, which aired under the name *Hide and Seek*, had been shown on *Vacation Playhouse* on August 5, 1963. Reruns of *Glynis* would replace *The Lucy Show* in the summer of 1965 instead of the traditional *Vacation Playhouse*.

Vacation Playhouse (CBS, 1963, 1964, 1965, 1966, 1967). This anthology series ran comedies (including intended pilots) while serving four times as the summer replacement for *The Lucy Show*. In 1965, it filled in for *Gomer Pyle, USMC*, and presented dramas and adventures. During *The Lucy Show* period, episodes began with the voiceover, "While Lucy's on vacation . . . it's *Vacation Playhouse*."

The Greatest Show on Earth (ABC, 1963–64) Although it bore the same name as the 1952 Oscar-winning Cecil B. De Mille epic that Lucy *didn't* get to do because of her pregnancy, this series was not an extension or spinoff of that film. Jack Palance starred as circus boss Johnny Slate along with some actual Ringling Brothers, Barnum & Bailey performers. In order to help the show in the ratings, Lucy agreed to make her dramatic television debut on the December 10, 1963 episode, "Lady in Limbo," opposite Billy Mumy, who had appeared in the Desilu pilot *The Two of Us*.

You Don't Say (NBC, daytime: 1963–69; nighttime: 1964). This game show (produced in association with Ralph Edwards-Bill Yagemann Productions) had a pair of panelists (one a celebrity) trying to help the other identify the name of a famous person or place. Tom Kennedy was the host. Running on the daytime schedule from 1963 to 1969, it was also seen briefly at night, for part of 1964. Considering the premise seemed like a variation on *Password*, it is ironic that Lucy chose to be a frequent guest on *that* series and not the one produced by her own company.

Star Trek (NBC, 1966–69). This sci-fi series about the adventures of the crew of the starship *U.S.S. Enterprise* starred William Shatner as Captain Kirk and Leonard Nimoy as his Vulcan first officer, Mr. Spock. Running a respectable three years and earning back-to-back Emmy nominations for Outstanding Dramatic Series, the show's popularity grew during its years in syndication to unprecedented proportions, spinning off a franchise of movies and additional series. Arguably the most enduring non-*Lucy* show to come from Desilu, it became a Paramount production once that studio purchased Lucille's company.

Mission: Impossible (CBS, 1966–73). In its first season, this espionage series, about a team of specialized government agents, starred Steven Hill as the group's leader, Daniel Briggs. For season two, Peter Graves came aboard as James Phelps, and it was this character that made the more indelible impression on television fans. In its first two years on the air, the show won the Emmy for Best Dramatic Series. After the Desilu buyout, it became a production of Paramount Television.

Mannix (CBS, 1967–75) The last new Desilu series to debut turned out to be a success, reaching the Nielsen Top Ten in its fifth season on the air. By that time it had become a Paramount production, following that studio's purchase of Desilu. Mike Connors played the titular detective, a role he repeated on the October 4, 1971 *Here's Lucy* episode "Lucy and Mannix Are Held Hostage." Connors had previously starred in an unaired pilot for Desilu called *Personal Report. Mannix* was twice nominated for the Emmy for Best Dramatic Series, while Connors's co-star, Gail Fisher, won the trophy in 1970.

A Collection of Desilu Pilots, Both Aired and Unaired

1954:

Country Doctor. Charles Coburn, who appeared with Lucy in *Lured*, was the star of this proposed medical show, based on the 1935 novella by A. J. Cronin. Desi wrote in his autobiography that the powers-that-be asked, "Who wants to see a show about doctors?" *Country Doctor* did finally make it to television, in England, when Andrew Cruickshank played Dr. Angus Cameron in the BBC series adaptation, *Dr. Finlay's Casebook*, from 1962 to 1971.

1955–56:

Just Off Broadway. Desilu tried to create another musical sitcom similar to their summer replacement show, *Those Whiting Girls*. In this pilot, two sisters, one a singer (Rose Marie) and the other a dancer (Peggy Ryan) move into an apartment that comes complete with a struggling songwriter (Ray McDonald, Ryan's real-life husband).

1956–57:

Adventures of a Model (filmed 1956; NBC, Aug. 19, 1958, on *Colgate Theatre*, repeated: CBS, Sept. 9, 1960). Joanne Dru starred as a fashion model. She later got a chance to appear in a Desilu series with *Guestward Ho!* Lucy and Desi appeared as themselves in a segment at the end of the pilot with Joanne Dru.

1957–58:

A Night in Havana starred Ricardo Montalban and was set in Desi's homeland of Cuba.

Sad Sack was an adaptation of Sgt. George Baker's famous military comic strips and comic books, produced around the same time Jerry Lewis appeared in a film version. Tom Ewell was the star of the pilot.

1958–59:

Claudette Colbert Show (NBC, Sept. 30, 1958, shown on *Colgate Theatre*, as "Francy Goes to Washington," then repeated on CBS, August 23, 1960 on *Comedy Spot* as "Welcome to Washington."). Colbert was a newly elected congresswoman who moves to the capital with her family. The original title while the pilot was in development had been *Mrs. Harper Goes to Congress*.

Mr. Tutt (filmed in 1954; NBC, Sept. 10, 1958, shown as an episode of *Colgate Theater*). Walter Brennan played a folksy but crafty small-town lawyer, with Olive Blakeney as his secretary and Harry Harvey Jr. as an investigator.

The Orson Welles Show (Sept. 16, 1958, shown on *Colgate Theater*). The pilot for this anthology series, which was to include everything from dramatic plays to interviews, had Welles directing an adaptation of the John Collier story "Fountain of Youth." Welles had guest starred as himself on the October 15, 1956 *I Love Lucy* episode "Lucy Meets Orson Welles." "The Fountain of Youth" won a Peabody Award.

The Caballero (CBS, Apr. 13, 1959, shown as an episode of *The Texan*). Cesar Romero, who appeared with Lucy and Desi in "Lucy Takes a Cruise to Havana," played Mexican border patrol Captain Joaquin Acosta.

Chez Rouge (CBS, Feb. 16, 1959, shown on *Westinghouse Desilu Playhouse*). Janis Paige starred as a Panama-based nightclub owner known as "The Redhead."

The Abbotts were husband-and-wife detectives.

Black Arrow. This western had a schoolteacher moonlighting as a masked avenger.

The Last Marshal. Jim Davis portrayed the last lawman of his sort appointed before the western territories became states.

Personal Report. Future *Mannix* star Mike Connors co-starred with Wayne Morris in one of Morris's last roles (he died in 1959), as private eyes. The series was created by Desilu vice president Martin Leeds.

Ricky of the Islands. Rick Vega, who was a regular during the final season of *Our Miss Brooks,* was a thirteen-year-old boy shipwrecked on a tropical island.

The Wildcatters. The adventures of two oil field mechanics starring Charles Bronson. Desi later wrote in his autobiography that the network turned down the pilot because they felt Bronson was not good looking enough to be a leading man.

Lucy appeared without credit in three early George Murphy films, *Kid Millions* (1934), *Jealousy* (1935), and *I'll Love You Always* (1935) before co-starring with him in 1941's *A Girl, A Guy, and A Gob.* Murphy would become a Desilu executive and star in a pilot for the studio, *You're Only Young Twice.*

1959–60:

Six Guns for Donegan (CBS, Oct. 16, 1959, shown on *Westinghouse Desilu Playhouse*). Sheriff Lloyd Nolan and his five sons enforced the law in the western town of Donegan. Nolan had appeared with Lucy in the films *Two Smart People* and *Easy Living.*

Ballad of the Bad Man (CBS, Dec. 22, 1959, shown on *Westinghouse Desilu Playhouse*). Steve Forrest was a bounty hunter out west, just as Steve McQueen was on a CBS series airing that season, *Wanted: Dead or Alive.*

Meeting in Appalachia (CBS, Jan. 22, 1960, shown on *Westinghouse Desilu Playhouse*). Frank Behrens portrayed Chicago police sergeant Ed Croswell.

You're Only Young Twice (CBS, Aug. 1, 1960, shown on *CBS New Comedy Showcase*). An insurance agent adjusts to family life after retiring. Lucy's leading man in *A Girl, a Guy and a Gob*, George Murphy, who at the time was a Desilu executive, starred alongside Martha Scott.

Chick Bowdrie was a character (played by Chuck Wassil) who had appeared on an episode of *The Texan.*

The Man of Many Faces was a detective who used disguises to trap the guilty.

The Privateer. After guest starring in the *Lucille Ball-Desi Arnaz Show* episode "Lucy Goes to Sun Valley," Fernando Lamas was given his own pilot, as a pirate helping the poor.

St. Louis Man. A detective series set in 1870s St. Louis.

Private Eyeful. Lucy's friend Edward Buzzell (the director of *Best Foot Forward* and *Easy to Wed*) produced and directed this pilot for a projected half-hour series about a female detective starring Marilyn Maxwell. It was based on a 1959 novel of the same name by Henry Kane.

1960–61:

Always April (CBS, Feb. 23, 1961, shown as an episode of *The Ann Sothern Show*). Susan Silo was a teen hoping to achieve stardom like her famous parents, played by Constance Bennett and John Emery. Bennett was the star of two early Lucy films, *Moulin Rouge* and *The Affairs of Cellini*, while Emery had appeared in *Forever, Darling* and two *I Love Lucy* episodes: "The Quiz Show" (11/12/51) and "Little Ricky Gets a Dog" (1/21/57).

Pandora (CBS, Mar. 20, 1961, shown as an episode of *The Ann Sothern Show*). Pat Carroll had the title role playing secretary to actor Anthony Bardot (singer Guy Mitchell).

The Man from Telegraph Hill. Dan Dailey was cast as real-life San Francisco columnist Herb Caen. Dailey later guest starred on the *Here's Lucy* episode "Won't You Calm Down, Dan Dailey?" (11/8/71).

My Wife's Brother. The comedy team of Dan Rowan and Dick Martin co-starred with Lucy protégé Carole Cook in a sitcom about a brother living with his married sister and her husband. Cook appeared several times on both *The Lucy Show* and *Here's Lucy*, playing various characters, while Dick Martin had a recurring role on the first two seasons of the former, as Lucy's neighbor and occasional boyfriend Harry Conners.

You Can't Win Them All was based on the baseball-themed book *The Last Season.*

1961–62:

Ernestine (shown on *Comedy Spot*, July 3, 1962). Charlie Ruggles and Marie Wilson were a father-daughter business team who run a loan company. This was also known as *The Soft Touch.*

1962–63:

The Seekers (CBS) presented two different pilots in an effort to sell Barbara Stanwyck as a detective in the Chicago missing person's bureau. Both of them aired as episodes of *The Untouchables*: "Elegy" (11/20/62) and "Search for a Dead Man" (1/1/63).

The World of Floyd Gibbons (CBS) was originally presented as an episode of *The Untouchables* under the name "The Floyd Gibbons Story" (12/11/62), with Scott Brady as a globetrotting newspaper reporter. It again aired under its new name during the 1964–65 season.

Mickey and the Contessa (shown on *Vacation Playhouse*, Aug. 12, 1963). Mickey Shaughnessy was a football coach who hires a Hungarian housekeeper and ends up with a contessa played by Eva Gabor.

Swingin' Together (shown on *Vacation Playhouse*, Aug. 26, 1963). Pop star Bobby Rydell portrayed a singer hoping to make it in show business. Stefanie Powers, Lloyd Corrigan, and Bing Crosby's sons Dennis, Lindsay, and Philip were also on hand.

All About Barbara (CBS, Sept. 2, 1963). Written by Madelyn Martin and Bob Carroll Jr., this comedy found Barbara Nichols playing an actress who marries a small-town college professor (William Bishop).

Maggie Brown (CBS, shown on *Vacation Playhouse*, Sept. 23, 1963) Among the pilots produced during Lucille's first year as president of Desilu was a sitcom starring her good friend Ethel Merman. Ball and Merman first met when they appeared together in the Eddie Cantor musical *Kid Millions* in 1934. Although Merman had more success in Broadway musicals than anyone, major stardom in either motion pictures or television eluded her. She longed to do a sitcom and was thrilled when the Desilu deal came about. The show, entitled *Maggie Brown*, had the Broadway diva playing the title character, a widowed saloon owner in a place called Lobster Island. The plot of the pilot involved Maggie trying to keep the authorities from finding out she is in possession of an illegal beer machine and attempting to get her teenage daughter accepted into an exclusive private school in Connecticut. The test show, written by Bill Manhoff and directed by Jerry Thorpe, was filmed on February 4, 1963. During rehearsals, Merman attended the filming of that week's *Lucy Show,* "Lucy Is a Soda Jerk," and in turn, Lucy and Gary Morton were present for the *Maggie Brown* production.

Maggie Brown was shot in color, which was something *The Lucy Show* had yet to do. Merman was given the opportunity to reprise two songs she had introduced on Broadway in the pilot: "Friendship" from *Du Barry Was a Lady* (which later was filmed with Merman's redheaded friend in her old role) and "Mutual Admiration Society" from *Happy Hunting,* which she sang with *Bye Bye Birdie's* Susan Watson, who played her daughter, Jeannie. Like all the Desilu comedy pilots of the time, *Maggie Brown* did not sell. CBS aired it as the season finale of their *Lucy Show* summer replacement series, *Vacation Playhouse,* on September 23, 1963. The show was rerun on July 18, 1966 and July 10, 1967, also under the *Vacation Playhouse* banner. Unfortunately, Merman never got to star in her own situation comedy like she always wanted. (A second attempt, 1977's *You're Gonna Love it Here,* also failed.)

After her pilot was rejected, Merman was signed to do a guest shot on *The Lucy Show.* Lucy, Vivian Vance (who had been Merman's understudy in *Anything Goes* and *Red, Hot, and Blue*), and Ethel enjoyed working together so much that the episode, "Lucy Teaches Ethel Merman to Sing," was expanded into a two-part installment. During the filming of Merman's "Everything's Coming up Roses" finale in the second episode, "Ethel Merman and the Boy Scout Show," Lucy stood behind her TV son, Jimmy Garrett, and told him, "Watch closely because you'll never see a better performer."

The Victor Borge Comedy Theatre. This umbrella title for a comedy anthology series featured an airline sketch with Lucille Ball and Gale Gordon that later was revamped for the *Lucy Show* episode "Lucy Goes to London" (10/17/66). This sketch was directed by Desi Arnaz. The pilots included in the package were:

Suzuki Beane. This comedy about a girl from a Bohemian family starred Katie Sweet, who appeared in the episode "Lucy Misplaces $2,000" (10/22/62) on *The Lucy Show,* and Jimmy Garrett, who played Lucy's son Jerry on the same series for its first four seasons.

The Sound and the Fidelity found Tom Ewell and Sarah Marshall battling with their neighbor over their hi-fi system.

Working Girls, about four young women finding careers in New York, had Tuesday Weld among its cast.

Blue Fox referred to the San Francisco restaurant where a blind detective (years before *Longstreet* picked up on this concept) made his headquarters.

1963–64:

Hey, Teacher (CBS, June 15, 1964; shown as the premiere installment of *Vacation Playhouse*). Dwayne Hickman, who had a small role in Lucy's 1947 film *Her Husband's Affairs,* played a new teacher at an elementary school.

Papa G.I. (CBS, June 29, 1964). In his second Desilu-produced pilot, Dan Dailey played an army entertainer who adopts two Korean orphans.

Hooray for Hollywood (CBS, June 22, 1964). Herschel Bernardi and John Litel were rival studio heads in this comedy set in the nineteen-thirties. Joan Blondell also appeared. Litel had appeared on *I Love Lucy* in the episode "Mr. and Mrs. TV Show" (4/11/55) and in Lucy's movie *The Fuller Brush Girl.* The following year Blondell played Lucy's neighbor Joan on back-to-back episodes of *The Lucy Show:* "Lucy and Joan" (10/11/65) and "Lucy the Stunt Man" (10/18/65).

I and Claudie (CBS, July 2, 1964). Jerry Lanning played Clint and Ross Martin played Claudie in this sitcom about a con man.

1965–66:

Where There's Smokey (filmed in 1959; ABC, Mar. 1, 1966). Gale Gordon had already found a comfortable job on *The Lucy Show* by the time this pilot finally aired. In it he played a fireman, and Soupy Sales was his incompetent brother-in-law.

The Two of Us (CBS, Aug. 29, 1966; shown on *Vacation Playhouse*). Pat Crowley was an illustrator of children's books, and Billy Mumy played her imaginative son in this sitcom that featured animated segments. This was filmed *before* Mumy appeared opposite Lucy in the "Lady in Limbo" episode of *The Greatest Show on Earth* (12/10/63). Mary Jane Croft (whose husband, Elliott Lewis, co-produced and directed the show with Claudio Guzman) appeared in the pilot as a meddlesome neighbor with *Lucy Show* guest Barry Livingston (best known for playing Ernie on *My Three Sons*) as her son.

1965–66:
Good Old Days (NBC, July 11, 1966). An attempt to do a live-action spin on *The Flintstones,* with Darryl Hickman as a young caveman and Kathleen Freeman and Ned Glass as his parents. That same year CBS premiered another Stone Age comedy, *It's About Time* (which Freeman also appeared in). Freeman had been in five episodes of *The Lucy Show:* "Lucy Plays Florence Nightingale" (1/6/64), "Lucy and Viv Open a Restaurant" (2/17/64), "Lucy Takes a Job at the Bank" (2/24/64), "Lucy Enters a Baking Contest," (4/27/64), and "Lucy Gets Her Maid" (11/30/64).

Frank Merriwell (ABC, July 25, 1966). Jeff Cooper starred in this turn-of-the-century comedy about a daredevil always in competition with his nemesis, played by Beau Bridges. Another cast member in the show was Tisha Sterling, daughter of Ann Sothern.

My Lucky Penny (CBS, Aug. 8, 1966). The Penny of the title was Brenda Vaccaro as Jenny Penny, a secretary for a man who speaks to her only on a tape recorder. Richard Benjamin played her husband Ted, a dental student. Future Oscar winner Joel Grey also appeared.

My Son, the Doctor (CBS, Aug. 22, 1966). Kay Medford was the overbearing mom and Jeff Davis her son, a doctor.

Vacation with Pay. Sounding uncomfortably similar to *Hogan's Heroes,* this comedy involved freewheeling inmates at a German prisoner of war camp.

1966–67:
The Hoofer (CBS, Aug. 15, 1966) had Donald O'Connor paired off with comedian Soupy Sales as vaudeville performers. A later O'Connor pilot that didn't sell was shown as part of the Lucille Ball special *Lucy Moves to NBC* (2/8/80). Sales had done a small role in Lucy's 1963 film *Critic's Choice.*

Alfred of the Amazon (CBS, July 31, 1967). Mousy Wally Cox was the son of a wealthy tycoon sent to the Amazon to run a rubber plantation. Cox, a favorite of Lucy's, appeared in the December 30, 1963 *Lucy Show* episode "Lucy Conducts the Symphony," and returned for no less than four separate *Here's Lucy* guest roles: "Lucy and the Ex-Con" (1/13/69), "Lucy and Wally Cox" (2/9/70), "Lucy the Diamond Cutter" (11/16/70), and "Lucy Sublets the Office" (1/31/72).

Police Story (NBC, Sept. 8, 1967). Steve Ihnat, Rafer Johnson, and Gary Clarke were three special assignment cops.

The Recruiters were Dick Curtis, Elliott Reid, and Dick Patterson, running a booth in Times Square. Reid played the Edward Murrow-like interviewer on the *I Love Lucy* episode "The Ricardos Are Interviewed" (11/14/55), showed up on *The Lucy Show* in "Lucy Visits the White House" and "Lucy the Stockholder," and later appeared on three *Here's Lucy* installments: "Lucy's Burglar Alarm," "Lucy and Sammy Davis, Jr.," and "Milton Berle is the Life of the Party." Patterson was in *The Lucy Show* episode "Lucy and the Beauty Doctor" and four *Here's Lucy* episodes: "Lucy the Matchmaker," "Lucy's Lucky Day," "Lucy and Joe Namath," and "Lucy Is Really in a Pickle." He and his wife, Gita, also played *Password* with Lucy and Gary in 1966.

The Long Hunt of April Savage. Robert Lansing sets out to avenge the death of his family in this western.

1967–68:

Assignment Earth (NBC, March 29, 1968). Aired as an episode of *Star Trek*, this show featured Robert Lansing and Teri Garr as aliens who arrive on earth with the mission to stop us from self-destruction.

20

"When Lucy Came to London Town"

Lucy on Location

T he majority of Lucille Ball's motion picture career was spent during the "studio era," when location shooting was considered something of a luxury, suitable for an occasional western or action picture, but not the norm. If it could be done on a set simulating a location, the powers that be were more than satisfied. Lucille did, however, have her handful of assignments that included sequences filmed outside the confines of Hollywood, although she was not always keen on such trips.

As for her television years, the situation comedy is customarily a very intimate and visually limited one, usually confined to the domicile of its main protagonists, the living room being the area most readily available for plot developments involving family and friendly neighbors. *I Love Lucy* had not one but two living room areas (the latter adding a much-needed window) that became as familiar to millions of viewers as real dwellings in their lives. Because so many sitcoms were filmed before a live audience, it was necessary to restrict even the action that was supposed to be taking place outside to indoor settings, which meant that traveling outside the studio soundstages was out of the question. It was, of course, also very expensive. TV viewers grew accustomed to seeing stock footage or establishing shots of locales before the scene cut to the more controllable environment of the studio.

There were, however, select occasions when Lucille Ball decided she needed not only a change of scenery but some fresh air. She therefore requested that certain episodes of her series and some of her specials put her outside and show her against authentic backdrops. Whether her style of comedy came off in the real world as well as it did on the soundstage is open for debate. If nothing else, it made for some refreshing variations on the familiar format and unique additions to the Lucy output.

Here are the Lucy television episodes and specials that found the actress in settings beyond the Hollywood back-lots and stages, and the few movies she did that used some real back-drops.

Television

The Lucille Ball-Desi Arnaz Show: "Lucy Hunts Uranium" (CBS, January 3, 1958)

"Lucy Hunts Uranium," the third installment of *The Lucille Ball-Desi Arnaz Show*, featured scenes filmed in and around Las Vegas. To establish that Ricky's band is performing at the Sands Hotel, an exterior shot is shown with Ricky's name prominently displayed on the marquee (Jerry Lewis's name is visible as the next performer scheduled to play the hotel). The sequence in which the Ricardos, the Mertzes, and guest star Fred MacMurray try to beat each other back to the Sands to declare their discovery of uranium was filmed on location. At the time it was shot, the Sands was a mere five years old, having opened to the public at Christmastime of 1952.

In another scene, set in the Mojave Desert, a double for MacMurray was supposed to drive his car (a Ford, the show's sponsor) into a freshly black-topped road, causing the vehicle to get stuck. The stunt was performed several times, but each time the car skidded off camera. Fed up, Desi decided to do the stunt himself and executed it perfectly. A pleased Desi turned furious, however, when he was told that nobody had bothered to film him performing the action. The entire cast and crew burst into laughter. The rest of the episode was filmed at Desilu in front of a live studio audience.

After many years as one of the most celebrated destinations on the Vegas Strip, the Sands was shuttered and demolished in 1986.

The Lucille Ball-Desi Arnaz Show: "Lucy Goes to Sun Valley" (CBS, April 14, 1958)

The fifth hour-long *Lucille Ball-Desi Arnaz Show* was partially filmed in Sun Valley, Idaho, a favorite retreat for the Arnazes. They had spent part of their first summer hiatus from *I Love Lucy* in 1952 at the resort with their first-born, year-old Lucie. In 1959, after Lucy separated from Desi, she and the children spent Christmas in Sun Valley with Lucy's good friend Ann Sothern at Ann's home.

For the "Sun Valley" episode, the entire cast and crew travelled from California to Idaho by train. The Arnazes stayed at the Sun Valley Lodge for the fourteen days they were scheduled to shoot. Lucie and Desi Jr. went

The *Lucille Ball – Desi Arnaz Show* cast with guest star Fred MacMurray during "Lucy Hunts Uranium," partly filmed on location in the Mojave Desert.

along with them and appeared on camera as extras, not only in the show but in the closing Ford Motors commercial. Lucy loved the snow, but guest star Fernando Lamas was not as thrilled, saying, "It's okay if you like white." The footage being shot in Sun Valley was sent back to the studio by train, only to have the crew in Idaho receive a frenzied telephone call from Desilu saying that they never received the film. As a result, everything that had already been filmed had to be shot again. The original was found in a Desilu station wagon months later. The rest of the show was filmed, as usual, in front of a live audience at Desilu.

The Lucy Show: "Lucy at Marineland" (CBS, September 13, 1965)

The fourth season of *The Lucy Show* began with a change in locale, as Lucy Carmichael now became a resident of Los Angeles. The opening show of the season was "Lucy at Marineland," the majority of which was filmed at Marineland of the Pacific, an oceanarium theme park located on the Palos Verdes Peninsula, about twenty miles south of Los Angeles. Apparently CBS was very keen on having their stars promote the Southern California attraction, as both the Beverly Hillbillies and the Munsters had already filmed programs there prior to Lucy's visit.

The episode was a milestone for the series, as it was the first to be telecast in color. Although the previous two seasons had actually been filmed in color, CBS had aired them in black and white.

In addition to series regulars Jimmy Garrett (in his penultimate appearance on the show) and Gale Gordon, the cast also featured Lucie and Desi Jr., as extras. (They can be spotted sitting behind Lucy while watching whale trainer Larry Clark.) Also on hand was Jimmy Piersall of the California Angels baseball team, appearing as himself. Piersall's battle with bipolar disorder had been the basis of the 1957 biopic *Fear Strikes Out*, in which he had been portrayed by Anthony Perkins. The center fielder was good-natured enough to make light of his problems on the episode, remarking "and they call me a kook," after meeting up with Lucy.

The Marineland scenes were filmed under uncharitably cold weather conditions in May 1965 with Lucy (wearing a wet suit under her clothes) required to plunge into the chilly water of the pools at the facility. The night "Lucy at Marineland" was first shown, Lucy also guest starred on the premiere episode of *The Steve Lawrence Show*, which aired at 10:00 on CBS's Monday night schedule. As part of her guest stint, Lucy brought along outtakes from the Marineland show. There were plenty. The porpoises refused to cooperate and swam hard into Lucy several times, ruining shots and turning the whole experience into something of an ordeal. "Lucy at Marineland," however, was a unique enough departure from the *Lucy Show* format to earn a cover story in the August 28, 1965 issue of *TV Guide*.

Marineland closed its doors in 1987 after 33 years of operation.

A Lucille Ball Special: Lucy in London (CBS, October 24, 1966)

After doing *The Lucy Show* for several seasons, Lucy decided she wanted a change of pace. Lucy and her cousin Cleo came up with the idea of doing a television special filmed in another country. Paris was the original choice, with Zero Mostel considered to co-star until he proved unavailable. Cleo, Desilu executive Bernie Weitzman, and some other producers travelled to Paris to see if the production would be feasible, only to realize that the language barrier would be too big an obstacle to overcome. London was selected instead. It was decided that Lucille would play Lucy Carmichael in the special and that it would be the continuation of the *Lucy Show* episode "Lucy Goes to London," which would air the preceding week. Cleo

Lucy with her tour guide Anthony Fitz-Faversham (Anthony Newley) on the edge of the Thames in 1966's *Lucy in London*.

hired Dave Winters to co-produce and choreograph and Steve Binder to direct, both men having worked on the pop music show *Hullabaloo*. (Winters would later direct Lucille in the 1969 special *Ann-Margret: From Hollywood with Love*.) Lucy loved to travel every year in May, her favorite month, so filming was scheduled for May 1966. Figuring they might as well start at the top, the producers approached Laurence Olivier to co-star, but he was otherwise engaged. In the end, British singer-songwriter-actor Anthony Newley and the rock band the Dave Clark Five were signed to appear. Phil Spector wrote the special's title song, which was done in a flashy, "music video" style and featured Lucy in various mod costumes from Kings Road, Chelsea. The plot of the special found Lucy Carmichael, after winning a dog food jingle, spending a vacation in London for just one day. Her tour guide, Anthony Fitz-Faversham (Newley), takes her on a wild ride in a motorcycle sidecar, showing her parts of the city rarely seen by tourists.

One sequence found Lucy and her tour guide punting the Thames River. Lucy was warned that the river was so heavily polluted she would need a series of shots in order to do the stunt of her and Newley sinking into the water. As if that did not sound ominous enough, she was also told she would have to have her stomach pumped if she swallowed any of the water. Despite being advised to film the segment in a different river standing in for the Thames, Lucy refused and ended up doing the stunt with no problem. Another scene found Lucy playing Kate in *The Taming of the Shrew*. The sequence was filmed on the property of Great Fosters, an estate in Egham, Surrey, England. Lucy had to be costumed in her Elizabethan-era outfit for the *Shrew* scene inside the house early in the morning with the understanding that she be gone before the elderly man who occupied the house woke up. The man found Lucy in costume walking the halls one day and momentarily thought he was seeing the ghost of Anne Boleyn, who reportedly haunted the premises.

London locations for the special included Madame Tussaud's wax museum on Baker Street and the Scala Theatre on Charlotte Street, where the finale featuring Anthony Newley singing a medley of songs from his musicals *Stop the World—I Want to Get Off* and *The Roar of the Greasepaint—The Smell of the Crowd*, and Lucy performing pantomime and singing another Newley composition, "One Day in London," was shot. (The Scala was demolished three years later after being damaged in a fire.)

The special received a big buildup before it was broadcast, including a *TV Guide* cover story with the October 22, 1966 issue. *Lucy in London* aired on Monday, October 24, 1966 in the time slot usually occupied by *The Lucy Show* and *The Andy Griffith Show*. It was ranked third in the Nielsen ratings closely after *Bonanza* (in the midst of its third consecutive season as the number one show) and the first-ever airing of the Peanuts special *It's the Great Pumpkin, Charlie Brown*. The reviews, however, were not what Lucy was hoping for, with many critics expressing disappointment that the humor of the special was completely different from a typical *Lucy* episode. Pat McCormick and Ron Friedman's script did, however, earn a Writers Guild of America Award nomination for Best Comedy, Non-Episodic. Perhaps due to its soft critical response, Lucy was discouraged from filming any more on-location specials for the time being. Despite the high ratings the special received during its initial telecast, CBS never re-aired it.

Here's Lucy: "Lucy and the Great Airport Chase" (CBS, February 3, 1969)

During the first season of *Here's Lucy*, Lucille Ball did something she had never done before, filming an entire episode of her series on location. The show was shot like a movie, eschewing the three-camera, live studio audience technique her earlier series had pioneered. Series producer Tommy Thompson had come up with an idea for a *Lucy* script while he was waiting to catch a flight at Los Angeles International Airport. While eating at the airport's glass tower restaurant, he noticed two window washers rise up on a mechanical platform. Thompson instantly thought of Lucy and Gale Gordon in this same position, and a *Lucy* episode was born. Tommy himself wrote the script, entitled "Lucy and the Great Airport Chase."

Much of the filming, done in July 1968, took place early in the morning when the airport was least active. The plot involved Lucy and the kids taking Harry to the airport where he is supposed to catch a plane to an important business meeting in San Francisco. Lucy, however, bumps into a man who gives her a little book containing a secret formula, and she and Harry end up being chased throughout the airport by two enemy agents interested in what is in Lucy's possession. This episode proved to be so successful that it was decided to film more *Here's Lucy* episodes outside the studio.

Here's Lucy

Lucy wanted to take her children around the United States and figured that a great way to do this would be to combine their family vacations with their television program. Eight of the twenty-four shows of the second season of *Here's Lucy* were planned to be filmed entirely on location. Ultimately, only five were done. Lucille had been so impressed with cousin Cleo's work as producer on location in *Lucy in London* that she decided to have Cleo become producer of her latest series, replacing Tommy Thompson. George Marshall, who directed Lucy in her two western-themed films, *Valley of the*

Sun (1942) and *Fancy Pants* (1950), was hired to helm the shows. Gene Thompson (no relation to Tommy), who had never previously written for Lucy, was chosen to write the four opening shows of the season. Gene Thompson never wrote for the series again.

The location shows began with a two-parter set at the United States Air Force Academy in Colorado Springs, Colorado. It was reported that *Here's Lucy* was the first television film to be shot at the Academy, which had been established in 1954. (Among the buildings on view was the architectural marvel, the Cadet Chapel.) The cast and a crew of sixty people arrived in Colorado Springs in early May 1969. One major problem during the filming was the weather. The sun alternated with rain, snow, hail, and sleet and since the show was filmed out of sequence like a movie, it was difficult to match the shots. To compensate for lost time, interior scenes were filmed during the periods of bad weather. Lucie Arnaz had a great time being surrounded by 3,500 male cadets her age and happily accepted an invitation to attend the academy's annual Recognition Ball. Lucy returned in September 1969 shortly before the shows aired (September 22 and 29) to attend a large screening party held at the Academy. She stated at the time, "This may not be one of our funniest programs, but it is one of our nicest."

These two segments were followed by "Lucy and the Indian Chief" (October 6, 1969), which was filmed on a Navajo reservation in Arizona. Director George Marshall appeared as a sheriff in the fourth installment, "Lucy Runs the Rapids" (October 13, 1969), which found the company shooting on the Colorado River in the Grand Canyon. The fifth location show of the season, "Lucy and Wayne Newton" (February 16, 1970), was filmed at Newton's ranch outside Las Vegas. The opening scene of the episode was a drive down the Las Vegas Strip featuring the marquees of some of the famous casinos, heralding such performers as Dean Martin, Totie Fields, Bill Cosby, Abbe Lane, and Dick Shawn.

At the time, Lucy mentioned the possibility of doing a show in Alaska and perhaps one in her hometown of Jamestown. Neither ever materialized. A three-part episode was written for the third season of *Here's Lucy,* with the idea of filming the first two episodes aboard the *SS Lurline,* with the cooperation of the Matson Cruise Line. The third part was to be filmed on location in Hawaii. However, the season opener, "Lucy Meets the Burtons," was such an expensive episode to produce that the plans for further location shooting were scrapped. The three-part saga became a two-partner ("Lucy Goes Hawaiian;" airing February 15 and 22, 1971 and featuring Vivian Vance) and ended up being filmed on soundstage sets recreating the *Lurline.*

The Lucille Ball-Dean Martin Special (Lucy Gets Lucky) (CBS, March 1, 1975)

Lucille loved working with Dean Martin, and her second CBS television special following the end of *Here's Lucy* teamed the two again, nine years after they had acted together on the *Lucy Show* episode "Lucy Dates Dean Martin." Lucy's first post-*Here's Lucy* special, *Happy Anniversary and Goodbye*, had included a short scene featuring Lucy, Nanette Fabray, Don Porter, and Rhodes Reason at Caesar's Palace in Las Vegas. The Dean Martin special would be filmed entirely in Vegas (with the exception of a single day done in Los Angeles). What's more, it would dispense with a laugh track. Lucille played a new "Lucy" character named Lucy Collins for the first and only time. The plot had Lucy Collins arriving in Las Vegas from Los Angeles to see her favorite singer, Dean Martin, perform at the MGM Grand. When her reservation for Dean's show falls through, Lucy takes a job at the MGM Grand so she can see Dean do a special "employees only" show.

The opening sequence finds Lucy arriving at the MGM Grand and shows her walking through a hall of movie star photographs. Among those adorning the walls is Lucille Ball, seen in publicity shots from *The Long, Long Trailer; Ziegfeld Follies'* and *Best Foot Forward*. The MGM Grand had opened to tremendous fanfare at Christmas of 1973, as not only the largest hotel in Vegas but, at the time, the largest hotel in the world.

Lucy Gets Lucky aired on March 1, 1975 in the Saturday night time slot usually occupied by *Mary Tyler Moore* and *The Bob Newhart Show*. The special's competition on NBC was the first half of the two-hour made-for-television movie *Who Is the Black Dahlia?*, starring Lucie Arnaz in the title role!

Although Las Vegas still includes an MGM Grand among its many posh hotels, it is not the same building seen in this *Lucy* special. The original MGM Grand was sold to Bally's in 1985 and now goes under that name. The hotel now bearing the MGM Grand name is an expansion of what was once known as the Marina.

Stone Pillow (CBS, November 5, 1985)

Filming took place entirely on location in New York in April 1985 in unseasonably hot weather. A good deal of the shooting was done on the Lower East Side of Manhattan. (For further information on *Stone Pillow* see the "Who Are You, Catherine Curtis?—Not Lucy" section.)

Films

The Three Musketeers (RKO, 1935)

Lucy was known in her pre-fame movie days as the girl who would do anything. During the production of her first film, *Roman Scandals,* she impressed star Eddie Cantor by agreeing to wear a mudpack and be as unglamorous as possible when the other gorgeous Goldwyn Girls were reluctant to tamper with their looks. Lucy was, however, always quick to recount one instance in her early RKO days when she did rebel.

In a 1974 American Film Institute seminar on her work, Lucille said, "Once I complained. I was playing in *The Three Musketeers*—one of the original ones with Walter Abel, God knows who else—and we were way out in Calabasas. It was very hot, and I was wearing four petticoats and a velvet thing and plumes and I fainted and there had been a lot of cows there. And when I picked myself up, dusted myself off, I said, 'Sir, get me a car, I'm going back to the studio and I'm quitting.' So they sent me back to the studio. I got out of the things, and I was called to the casting office, and Mr. Piazza [Ben Piazza, the head of casting at RKO, with whom Lucille had a friendly relationship] said, 'What's the matter' and I said, 'I'm not going on any more locations. I can't stand heat.' That was my only complaint—I couldn't stand the heat. It wasn't that I minded being a showgirl—I just couldn't stay out there in those petticoats any longer. There was one tree in 52 acres or something, so he said, 'OK, OK. Don't say you're going to quit.' From then on I got better parts."

Lucy's next film assignment was a speaking part in *I Dream Too Much.* She did, however, continue to be little more than an extra in several films made that year. She soon moved into bigger and better roles.

Having Wonderful Time (RKO, 1938)

Following the completion of *Stage Door,* cast members Ginger Rogers, Lucille Ball, Eve Arden, and Ann Miller (among others) were all brought together for another RKO production, *Having Wonderful Time.* The film was based on a Broadway hit by Arthur Kober that had opened in February 1937 (the original cast included two actors who would later appear on *I Love Lucy,* Sheldon Leonard and Cornel Wilde). The screenplay had many differences compared to the script from the play. The Broadway version revolved around a group of Jewish New Yorkers who vacation at an adult summer camp in the Catskills. The Hays Office demanded that any reference to ethnicity be deleted. Lucy played Brooklyn-accented Miriam

Ginger Rogers, Peggy Conklin, and Lucille Ball at Big Bear Mountain, standing in for Camp Kare-Free in the RKO comedy *Having Wonderful Time* (1938).

(Muriel Campbell had played Miriam in New York), otherwise known as "Screwball," one of the girls sharing a cabin with Teddy (Ginger Rogers), Fay (Peggy Conklin), and Henrietta (Eve Arden). The male cast members included leading man Douglas Fairbanks Jr., Lee Bowman (as Miriam's beau, Buzzy Ambruster), Jack Carson (another *Stage Door* alumnus), and, in his film debut, Red Skelton. One of the many campers in the movie who were seen but given no dialogue was Lucy's cousin, Cleo.

The cast filmed for three weeks at Big Bear Mountain in San Bernardino, California, about sixty miles east of Los Angeles, which was used to represent the Catskill resort "Camp Kare-Free." Although Lucille had her share of stunts in the picture, including several pratfalls, star Ginger Rogers had it worse. She spent two days in the forty-degree Bartless Lake. Regardless of whatever stunts they had to perform, the youthful cast had a wonderful time on location for *Having Wonderful Time*. During her courtship with Desi a few years later, Lucy wanted to show him California as he was new to the state. One of the places she took him to was Big Bear.

Valley of the Sun (RKO, 1942)

In 1941, Lucille Ball was cast in her first (and only) serious western picture. RKO initially planned to put Dorothy Comingore in the lead, following her role in *Citizen Kane*. Comingore, however, rejected the property and was placed on suspension by the studio. Lucy was cast as Christine Larson, a frontier woman who is kidnapped along with her crooked fiancée by a group of angry Native Americans. The leading lady spent twenty-seven days on location in New Mexico beginning in September 1941. Much like her ordeal while filming *The Three Musketeers*, Lucy spent long hours in the blistering heat in layers of period costumes.

Desi accompanied his bride of less than a year to the Taos filming location and spent his time on the set teaching the Conga to the authentic Native Americans hired to appear in the picture.

Lucy only made one more western, this one a comedy, *Fancy Pants*, which, like *Valley of the Sun*, was directed by George Marshall.

Forever, Darling (MGM, 1956)

Lucy and Desi's follow-up film to the massively successful *The Long, Long Trailer* was the comedy *Forever, Darling*. The script, written by Helen Deutsch, had been floating around MGM for over a decade when Lucy and Desi became involved with it. William Powell and Myrna Loy were initially pitched the screenplay, and it was later offered to Spencer Tracy and Katharine Hepburn. To make the film more like the Lucy and Desi adventures the public was used to seeing on television each week, the Arnazes brought in their series writers, Bob Carroll Jr. and Madelyn Pugh, to punch up the script. This resulted in an extended camping trip segment that climaxes the film.

In the movie, Lucy plays Susan Vega, whose husband Larry (Desi) is a chemist working on a new insecticide. The Vegas' five-year marriage is in trouble until Susan receives help from her guardian angel, who looks like James Mason and coincidentally is played by James Mason. Susan eventually goes on a field trip with Larry to help him with his new formula and to help save their marriage. The camping scenes were filmed at Yosemite National Park, a location already seen in *The Long, Long Trailer*. The rest of the movie was filmed at Desilu's Motion Picture Center.

Yours, Mine and Ours (United Artists, 1968)

In 1961, *Lucy* writer Bob Carroll Jr.'s wife showed him a newspaper story about Frank Beardsley, a widower with ten children who married Helen

North, a widow with eight offspring of her own. Desi purchased the movie rights to the story a month after the Beardsleys married. Desi's ex-wife was to play Helen in a feature film adaptation, and Fred MacMurray was initially sought to play Frank. After years of discussions and postponements, production finally began in 1967 with Henry Fonda as the father of eighteen children. In that time between the purchase of the screen rights and the actual filming, the real Beardsley family added two more children (one of whom is depicted in the film), and Helen wrote a book about the large family, *Who Gets the Drumstick?* (1965).

Although the real Beardsley family lived in Carmel, California (in a home expanded from Frank's original one, *not* a newly purchased house, as indicated in the script), the movie Beardsleys resided in San Francisco. The exterior sequences of Helen and Frank's first date were filmed in San Francisco, including the two getting on a trolley car where it is revealed how many children they have respectively. A montage of Frank and Helen in various San Francisco sites (notably the Fisherman's Wharf area) during their courtship was also included.

Frank is a naval warrant officer and Helen, during the period between her marriages, works part-time as a nurse at the naval base's dispensary. Location filming was done at the Alameda Naval Air Station, including two memorable scenes in the base's commissary. The first is Helen and Frank meeting cute by bumping into each other's shopping carts. Later, we see the married couple at the commissary purchasing $126.63 worth of groceries for a family of twenty. (In 1967–68 dollars, this was a *lot* to spend on food.) Additional shooting was done aboard the *USS Enterprise*, although these scenes involved Fonda, not Lucy.

After years of developing the project under various working titles, the picture was finally released as *Yours, Mine and Ours*. It proved to be Lucille's most successful movie ever, grossing in excess of $11 million and placing ninth on the annual box office list of the highest-grossing films. Although it was neither set nor filmed there, *Yours, Mine and Ours* had one of its premieres in Carmel, California with Lucy and the real-life Beardsley family in attendance.

Ironically, Helen Beardsley would die exactly eleven years to the day after Lucille Ball passed away, on April 26, 2000.

21

"Who Are You, Catherine Curtis?"

The Seven Instances When Lucille Ball Acted on Television *Not* Playing Her Lucy Character

W hen performers make an impact playing a character on a television series week after week, it becomes next-to-impossible for certain viewers to think of them outside of the persona they have created.

The real Lucille Ball was most definitely *not* "Lucy Ricardo," but she played the part so well that as far as television fans were concerned, this is how they expected her to be throughout most of her career on the small screen. And so Lucille Ball complied, playing variations on the scatterbrained Lucy Ricardo on each of her subsequent series, going so far as to make sure that they were all named "Lucy" and had the "ar" sound in their last names. Hence, the "Lucy" character. Despite subtle variations on each lady's professions and personal status, Lucy Carmichael, Lucy Carter, and Lucy Barker all showed characteristics of Lucy Ricardo in different stages of her life.

But Lucille Ball was an actress, first and foremost, and wanted to remind her fans on occasion that she could step outside of "Lucy" and play roles of an entirely different nature, in a few instances leaving the laughs behind altogether. Whether it was simply a case of not wanting to veer too far from what television audiences loved her best for, Lucille Ball, alas, did far too few "non-Lucy" roles in the final four decades of her life, but when she did venture into these uncharted waters, the results were often very rewarding and always worth a look.

Here are the seven instances of Lucille Ball acting on the small screen outside of the world of "Lucy."

The Westinghouse Desilu Playhouse: "K.O. Kitty"
(CBS, November 17, 1958) Lucille Ball as Kitty Williams

Desi's dream of Desilu producing an anthology series came true when CBS greenlit such a program to be sponsored by Westinghouse. The series would consist of comedies, dramas, and musicals, with the occasional Lucy-Desi program included. Desi was the on-camera host for each episode, but Lucy did not want to appear on the show every week. Westinghouse felt otherwise, so writers Bob Schiller and Bob Weiskopf came up with an idea of having Lucy appear at the end of each program talking to Desi on the telephone about the show that just aired.

Lucy and Desi were both supposed to appear solo in multiple installments of the series. Although Desi ended up starring in two productions, "So Tender, So Profane" (October 30, 1959) and "Thunder in the Night" (February 19, 1960), Lucy only starred in a single solo show, the comedy "K.O. Kitty." Lucy's longtime writing team of Madelyn Martin and Bob Carroll Jr. wrote the script with Madelyn's husband, Quinn Martin, who was a producer on *Desilu Playhouse.* Lucy played Kitty Williams, a dance instructor who has had a long standing engagement to David Pierce (William Lundigan) who assures her that they will finally marry once he becomes partner in his law firm. When Kitty's Uncle Charlie dies, Kitty inherits a gold pocket watch, a diamond stickpin, and a boxer. What Kitty assumed would be a dog turns out to be a prizefighter, Harold Tibbets (Aldo Ray). Kitty becomes Harold's manager in memory of her late uncle, much to the chagrin of David and rival manager Barney Snyder (Jesse White).

Lucy never again appeared on *The Westinghouse Desilu Playhouse* by herself. In addition to the remaining *Lucy-Desi* episodes being broadcast as part of the anthology show, Lucy, Desi, Viv, and Bill appeared as themselves in "The Desilu Revue," which presented scenes from the show put on by Lucy's Desilu Workshop students, on Christmas Day, 1959.

The Greatest Show on Earth: "The Lady in Limbo"
(ABC, December 10, 1963) Lucille Ball as Kate Reynolds

As Lucy entered her second year as president of Desilu, the company had only two other network prime-time shows on television outside of her own, the circus drama *The Greatest Show on Earth* and the sitcom *Glynis.* (They also had the game show *You Don't Say!* on NBC's daytime schedule at the time; *Glynis* was pulled from the nightly lineup only a week after Lucy made her appearance on *Greatest Show.*)

The Greatest Show on Earth was filmed with the cooperation of Ringling Bros. and Barnum & Bailey Circus and aired in color, unlike *The Lucy Show*, which at the time was shown in black and white despite being filmed in color. *Greatest Show* featured guest stars in each episode (one installment played host to Betty Hutton, who had starred in the 1952 film), and Lucille agreed to make her dramatic television debut on the show. Her participation on a program of this name is of special interest because twelve years earlier she had been obliged to drop out of Hutton's Oscar-winning film of the same title because of her pregnancy.

Lucy played Kate Reynolds, an unfriendly horse trainer who is determined to be the best at what she does. The circus is sending one of their acts to Moscow as part of an exchange program, and Kate is anxious to get the assignment. When one of the circus workers is mauled by a bear, Kate takes the man's son Jeff (Billy Mumy) away from the scene of the accident and puts him to bed in her room. When it is discovered that Jeff's father died from his injury, Kate talks circus manager Johnny Slate (series regular Jack Palance) into letting the boy stay with her until a relative can be located for him to reside with permanently. Kate explains that she herself was an orphan and therefore knows what it is like to get attached to someone and then be separated from them. She is adamant that Jeff will not get attached to her and interfere with her goals. As the story goes on, Kate stern façade begins to crack as she reveals more and more about herself. It turns out that she went from one unloving foster home to the next, married the first boy who asked, and became a pregnant war widow at seventeen. In one of her big dramatic moments, she reveals that her baby "was smart. He didn't get born." Kate, of course, does grow attached to Jeff, who has grown to love her as well. Kate Reynolds was certainly a departure from the Lucy Carmichael viewers were watching each week ("Lucy and the Military Academy" aired on CBS the night before this episode was shown).

Two months after the December 1963 airing of "Lady in Limbo," ABC announced the cancellation of *The Greatest Show on Earth* but allowed the show to finish out the season, ending its first-run episodes in April 1964. The cancellation was reported as a major factor in Lucy returning to *The Lucy Show* for a third season since Desilu would otherwise not have had a single prime-time show on the air.

A Lucille Ball Special: *Happy Anniversary and Goodbye* (CBS, November 10, 1974) Lucille Ball as Norma Michaels

Following the demise of *Here's Lucy*, Lucy agreed to do multiple specials for CBS. The first was entitled *Happy Anniversary and Goodbye*, which teamed

Lucy opposite Art Carney, who previously played her husband in their brief vignette in 1967's *A Guide for the Married Man*. That project was only one day's work for the twosome, and Lucy was excited to act with Carney more extensively. (At the time the special aired, movie audiences could see Carney in his first leading role in a motion picture in *Harry and Tonto*, for which he would go on to win the Academy Award for Best Actor.) Lucy was thrilled to get back to work since the preceding months were the first time in decades that she did not have any professional commitments. She had spent much of that free time cleaning both her house and Desi Jr.'s and learning to play backgammon, which would become one of her passions for the rest of her life.

In *Happy Anniversary and Goodbye*, Lucy played Norma Michaels, an overweight, middle-aged housewife married to a dentist, Malcolm (Carney). Returning home from their daughter's wedding, the couple quarrels and decides to separate one month shy of their twenty-fifth anniversary. Nanette Fabray and Peter Marshall (who previously played Lucy Carmichael's brother-in-law Hughie in *The Lucy Show* episode "Lucy's Sister Pays a Visit") co-starred. Norma's oft-divorced friend Fay (Fabray) helps Norma become more physically attractive and tries to help her reenter the dating scene, while Malcolm's dentist associate Greg Carter (Marshall) introduces him to a succession of young, buxom blondes. Two of Lucy's *Mame* co-stars, Doria Cook (who played Patrick Dennis's boorish fiancée Gloria Upson) and Don Porter (who was Gloria's bigoted father, Claude) both appeared as well. Porter played divorce lawyer Ed Murphy, better known as "Mad Dog," who dates Norma. (This was actually the third project Lucy and Don Porter worked on together in 1974; in addition to *Mame*, he also guest starred in the *Here's Lucy* episode "Meanwhile, Back at the Office" as Ken Richards, the new owner of the Unique Employment Agency.) Cook appeared as the Michaels' pregnant, newlywed daughter, Linda. Another member of the cast was a former "Mr. Universe"—Arnold Schwarzenegger, playing Rico, an Italian masseuse who gives an uptight Norma a massage. Lucy and Gary had spotted Schwarzenegger during an appearance on *The Merv Griffin Show* opposite guest host Shecky Greene. Arnold was brought in for an audition and, although at that stage of his career had no idea what went on at an audition, won the role that marked his television acting debut. (Ironically, Art Carney would make his last on-screen acting appearance in the 1993 film *Last Action Hero*, which starred Arnold Schwarzenegger.)

Lucy returned to Paramount Studios, once Desilu, to film the special. The first cut ran nearly two hours and had to be edited down to fit the designated hour-long time slot. *Happy Anniversary and Goodbye* aired on November 19, 1974, which was, coincidentally, Lucy and Gary's thirteenth anniversary. The special won fourth place in that week's Nielsen ratings. At the time, Lucy said, "I'm mad for Art Carney. I'd go anywhere to work with that man again." Happily she did, as the two would team up the following season for another special.

A Lucille Ball Special Starring Lucille Ball and Jackie Gleason: *Three for Two* (CBS, December 3, 1975) Lucille Ball as Sally Walburton, Rita "Pussycat" Fledgeman, and Pauline

For Lucy's second television special, she returned to her familiar "Lucy" roots with *Lucy Gets Lucky,* portraying a character (Lucy Collins) that comfortably fit into her expected television persona. For her follow-up, she attempted another non-Lucy project; this time with Jackie Gleason. Although Lucy and Jackie Gleason had long wanted to do a film version of *Diamond Jim Brady and Lillian Russell* together, when the two comedy legends finally did team up, they did something completely different. *Three for Two* was comprised of three stories, each about a different couple. The husband-and-wife team of Joseph Bologna and Renée Taylor originally wrote the material under the title *Comedies in Apple Blossom Time.* Lucy's old friend from MGM, Charles Walters, who previously directed two *Here's Lucy* episodes ("Lucy's House Guest, Harry" and "Lucy and Aladdin's Lamp"), directed the special, and would repeat the chores for her next one.

In the first playlet, "Herb and Sally," sixty-four-year-old Lucy plays forty-five-year-old Sally Walburton, a housewife from Cleveland, Ohio on vacation with her husband Herb in Rome. Sally wants romance, but Herb is not interested. In "Fred and Rita," the two performers play an adulterous couple, Fred "Teddy Bear" Schneider and Rita "Pussycat" Fledgeman, meeting up at a dimly lit hideaway, Cookie's Tip Toe Inn. The final chapter, "Mike and Pauline," deals with a long-married couple who want to celebrate New Year's Eve with their two children but feel they are too old to carry on the tradition. Daughter Maureen (Tammi Bula) wants to get married, and son Alfred (Paul Linke) wants to drop out of college to become a stand-up comic. *Three for Two* ranked eighth in the weekly Nielsen ratings.

A Lucille Ball Special: *What Now, Catherine Curtis?* (CBS, March 30, 1976) Lucille Ball as Catherine Curtis

Lucy's second television special of the 1975–76 season, *What Now, Catherine Curtis?,* once again featured Art Carney and was also presented in three acts, a la *Three for Two.* This time, however, Lucille played the same character in all three segments, Catherine Curtis, a woman in her mid-fifties who leaves her neglectful, philandering husband of twenty-three years to begin life anew in Manhattan.

Under the opening credits was a montage of photos from Lucille Ball's real life used to represent Catherine Curtis's, including Lucy in her wedding gown from *Forever, Darling* (representing Catherine's marriage to her husband Bennett), several images of Lucie and Desi Jr. as babies (in this instance Desi Jr. was being passed off as a girl, as Catherine was the mother of two daughters), and Lucie's 1971 wedding to Phil Vandervort.

The first act, "First Night," is a nearly twenty-minute dramatic monologue performed by Lucy in which Catherine attempts to unpack her belongings in her new apartment as she deals with the fact that for the first time in her life she is really alone. The second act, "First Affair," depicts Catherine attempting to start a romance with a widowed handyman, Mr. Slaney (Art Carney), who is building shelves for her apartment. The third segment, "First Love," shows Catherine in love with Peter (Joseph Bologna, who had co-written Lucy's previous special), who is fourteen years her junior. (In reality, Bologna was twenty-three years younger than Lucille.) Impulsive, Peter wants to get married, but Catherine is ashamed of the fact that she is so much older than him. *What Now, Catherine Curtis?* came in sixteenth place in the Nielsen ratings the week it aired.

The Practice: "The Dream" (NBC, October 13, 1976)
Lucille Ball as Matilda Morrison

In 1976, Danny Thomas returned to television in a new sitcom, *The Practice*, which premiered on NBC's midseason schedule in the 1975–76 season. Thomas played Doctor Jules Bedford, whose son, David (David Spielberg), was also a doctor. Also seen on the program were Dena Dietrich as Molly Gibbons, Jules's nurse; Didi Conn as Helen the receptionist (Conn and Lucie Arnaz would both later play the role of "Bella" during the original Broadway run of *Lost in Yonkers*); and Shelley Fabares as David's wife, Jenny.

Lucy had previously guest starred on Thomas's two earlier sitcoms, *The Danny Thomas Show* (as Lucy Ricardo in the January 5, 1959 "Lucy Upsets the Williams Household" episode, with Desi) and *Make Room for Granddaddy* (as Lucy Carter in "Lucy Carter, Houseguest," which aired on January 21, 1971), and was approached to guest star on the second-season premiere of Thomas's new series. This time, however, Lucy would not be playing her "Lucy" character, but an original one, Matilda Morrison, an underwear saleslady who believes she is psychic. Matilda comes to Dr. Bedford's office complaining of headaches and says that she has dreams of dying on

October 14, a few weeks away. She also claims that Dr. Bedford, whom she has never met before, was in the dreams. At first, Bedford thinks she's crazy, but when her other premonitions come true, starts to believe her and tries to help.

On August 13, 1976, Lucy arrived at MGM Studios where *The Practice* was filmed and where she was once under contract, and was greeted by a banner that said, "Welcome Home, Lucy." Besides an unbilled cameo in an episode of *The Phil Silvers Show* ("Bilko's Ape Man," aired on March 18, 1959), this was Lucy's first appearance on someone else's sitcom in which she was not playing her "Lucy" character. A month after the October 1976 airing of "The Dream," Danny Thomas was one of the stars who appeared in *CBS Salutes Lucy: The First 25 Years*. His segment was filmed on the set of his series. *The Practice* was cancelled by the network at the end of the 1976–77 season.

Stone Pillow (CBS, November 5, 1985)
Lucille Ball as Florabelle

In the nineteen-eighties, Lucy was approached with a project unlike anything she had ever done before; to play a bag lady struggling on the streets of New York in the dramatic television movie *Stone Pillow*. CBS sent Lucy the book *Shopping Bag Ladies* by Ann Marie Rousseau to learn more about the subject. Lucille was interested in the issue the film dealt with and thought it would raise awareness for the plight of the homeless. She was also interested in working with the director, George Schaefer, best known for helming many installments of *Hallmark Hall of Fame* and as the recipient of five Emmy Awards. Rose Leiman Goldemberg, who achieved great acclaim in 1984 for her script for the television film *The Burning Bed,* was the writer. Once she came aboard, Lucy had some suggestions of her own for the film. She requested that her character be named Florabelle, after her grandmother because of "her fortitude and guts," and wanted her to be independent and capable rather than a beggar or thief. She also came up with the idea that Florabelle should be a vegetarian, and requested an "up" ending because she thought it could be possible. Showing her further commitment to the project, she met with New York City Mayor Edward Koch to discuss the homelessness crisis in the city.

Filming was scheduled to be done in the early months of 1985 in New York. Tragedy intervened, however, when Goldemberg's daughter was killed in a car accident just before shooting was to begin. As a result, *Stone Pillow* was postponed until April 1985, only to have the weather turn unseasonably hot during filming. Lucy, wearing layers of clothing, a wool hat, and a wig, lost twenty-three pounds in the heat. During the filming of a scene set in a boiler room, temperatures reached 122 degrees. Upon her return to California, Lucy had to be hospitalized for dehydration. As a further discomfort, she also tore a tendon in her right arm. Those close to Lucy later said her health was never the same after the ordeal of *Stone Pillow*.

The movie was shot entirely on location in New York, mostly on the Lower East Side of Manhattan. Although Lucy allowed herself to look as unkempt as possible, she refused to cut her nails for the role and instead just painted them black. Due to her haggard and grungy appearance, she went unrecognized the entire time she was working on the streets of New York. Forgetting that she was in costume, Lucy was actually denied entrance at a restaurant and at a jewelry store when people mistook the legendary actress for an actual bag lady.

Stone Pillow met with mixed reviews. Many did not want to see their beloved Lucy playing such a sad, atypical character; others praised her for having the courage to take on such an unflattering role. Despite criticism, the movie ended up a very impressive ninth in the Nielsen ratings that week and received a Gold Angel Award from the Religion in Media organization as best television special.

22

"Roll 'Em. Lights, Camera, Action. Quiet!"

The Studios Where Lucy Worked

I n the fifty-three years she spent acting before the cameras, Lucille Ball found herself at pretty much every major studio in the Los Angeles area. (One of the few she never worked at was the Disney facility in Burbank, although the *Mame* scenes taking place at the Burnside family plantation in Peckerwood, Georgia were actually filmed at the Disney Golden Oak Ranch in Santa Clarita.) As a product of the studio contract

Lucille Ball in the climactic fashion show sequence in *Roberta*, her first film for RKO. She made $50 a week under her first RKO contract. Twenty-two years later, she owned the studio.

era, much of Lucy's career was unfolding at a time when few productions left Southern California to film, and she was therefore quite accustomed to the idea of going to work at the established lots that stretched from Culver City to Burbank, with Hollywood in between. Here, in approximate order of when she first worked at each, is a list of the studios in Lucy's life.

SAMUEL GOLDWYN

The former Schmuel Gelbfisz Americanized his name to Samuel Goldwyn and created Goldwyn Pictures Corporation in 1916. His company was acquired by Marcus Loew, forever leaving his name in the middle of the corporation thus created, Metro-Goldwyn-Mayer, despite no hands-on involvement with that studio whatsoever. Goldwyn quickly established a new company of his own, Samuel Goldwyn Inc. After working out of First National's United Studios for a period, in 1929 he moved his operations to the lot where Mary Pickford and Douglas Fairbanks had made their headquarters, at Santa Monica Boulevard and Formosa Avenue in West Hollywood, becoming the most powerful and prominent independent producer of the nineteen-thirties and forties. At the time he moved in, the facility was known as the United Artists Studio (Goldwyn owned stock in that company), but by the end of the thirties it was officially renamed the Samuel Goldwyn Studios.

It was with Goldwyn that Lucy signed her first film contract (for $125 a week), reporting to the studio in July 1933 to appear among the ensemble of decorative ladies in the Eddie Cantor comedy *Roman Scandals*. She only expected to work in California for six weeks, but six months had passed before *Scandals* was completed. By the time the picture was released on December 29th of that year, three of Lucy's interim assignments for Twentieth Century Pictures had already debuted in theaters. Because Goldwyn produced so few pictures each year (for example, *The Masquerader* with Ronald Colman was the studio's only other 1933 release), Lucy spent a good deal of her contract doing loan-outs elsewhere. Ultimately, there were only three Goldwyn credits for the actress. Lucy would later quip that in her earliest days in films, she was "classified with the scenery" and liked to refer to herself not as an extra, but as "atmospheric background."

After the end of *Here's Lucy*, Lucille Ball Productions moved its headquarters to Samuel Goldwyn Studios because they no longer needed the large space at Universal when they were not producing a show. (They eventually moved to 20th Century-Fox.) Ironically, she would end her acting career on the very same lot (by that point owned by Warner Bros.) filming *Life with Lucy* there in 1986.

- 1933: *Roman Scandals* as Townsperson/Slave Girl (Eddie Cantor, Gloria Stuart, Edward Arnold; d: Frank Tuttle);
- 1934: *Nana* as Chorus Girl (Anna Sten, Lionel Atwill; d: Dorothy Arzner, George Fitzmaurice); *Kid Millions* as Chorus Girl (Eddie Cantor, Ann Sothern, Ethel Merman; d: Roy Del Ruth)

TWENTIETH CENTURY PICTURES

An independent company formed by Warners' production chief Darryl F. Zanuck, in partnership with United Artists president Joseph Schenck and an associate producer at Fox, William Goetz (son-in-law of MGM head Louis B. Mayer), Twentieth Century Pictures was launched in 1933. United Artists handled the distribution of their first eighteen titles and also rented them space at the United Artists Studios where Samuel Goldwyn's company was also in residence. Over the next two years they would produce a total of twenty-two movies (20th Century-Fox took over the distribution of their last five pictures), six of which featured Lucille (loaned from Goldwyn) in bit parts. Three of these titles, *The Bowery, Broadway Thru a Keyhole,* and *Blood Money,* all beat Ball's first filmed assignment, *Roman Scandals,* to movie theatres, thereby making *The Bowery* (released October 7, 1933) the first chance audiences had of seeing her on the big screen.

- 1933 *The Bowery* as "atmospheric background" (Wallace Beery, George Raft, Jackie Cooper; d: Raoul Walsh); *Broadway Thru a Keyhole* as Chorus Girl/Girl on the Beach (Constance Cummings, Russ Columbo; d: Lowell Sherman); *Blood Money* as Drury Darling's Racetrack Date (George Bancroft, Judith Anderson; d: Rowland Brown);
- 1934 *Moulin Rouge* as Chorus Girl (Constance Bennett, Franchot Tone; d: Sidney Lanfield); *The Affairs of Cellini* as Lady-in-Waiting (Constance Bennett, Frank Morgan; d: Gregory La Cava); *Bulldog Drummond Strikes Back* as Bridesmaid (Ronald Colman, Loretta Young; d: Roy Del Ruth)

FOX FILM CORPORATION

Theatre chain entrepreneur William Fox created the Fox Film Corporation in 1915. Rather than pay the steep prices production companies wanted to exhibit their product, Fox figured he would produce his own films. Moving from Fort Lee, New Jersey, to California, Fox first operated out of a facility at Western Avenue and Sunset Boulevard (the former Dixon Studios). Fox soon established itself as a major force in Hollywood during the silent era, becoming lucrative enough to seek a second base of operations. In 1926 the company bought some 300 acres of land from their own contract player, cowboy star Tom Mix, in an underdeveloped section west of Beverly Hills, to create one of the most impressive studio complexes of its day. When hard times hit in the Depression era, the studio was placed in receivership. Rescue came with the merger of Fox and Twentieth Century Pictures in 1935. Lucy did two loan-out assignments from Goldwyn at Fox, continuing her run of unbilled bits.

• 1934 *Hold That Girl* as Girl (James Dunn, Claire Trevor, Alan Edwards; d: Hamilton MacFadden); *Bottoms Up* as Party Guest/Chorus Girl (Spencer Tracy, Pat Patterson, John Boles; d: David Butler)

COLUMBIA

Founded in 1919 as CBC by brothers Harry and Jack Cohn, in partnership with Joe Brandt, the company released its first feature in 1922, *More to Be Pitied Than Scorned,* made at the Paulis Studio in a section of Hollywood referred to as "Poverty Row" because the various independent production offices and facilities located on Gower Street worked on a tight budget.

Lucy in *Her Husband's Affairs* (1947), her first Columbia release since 1935. Pictured with her (left to right) are Edward Everett Horton, Jonathan Hale, Mikhail Rasumny, Franchot Tone, and Gene Lockhart.

The newly christened Columbia Pictures officially launched in January 1924 with Harry Cohn as Vice President in Charge of Production, while his brother and Brandt ran the business end from the East Coast. Initially, two soundstages and an office were purchased at 6070 Sunset Boulevard, which was later expanded with the purchase of the nearby Poverty Row facilities, the Columbia lot taking over the area between Sunset on the north, Fountain Avenue to the south, and bounded by Gower Street and Beachwood Drive. Because little room was allotted for exterior shooting on standing sets, an additional back-lot was built at Hollywood Way and West Oak Street in Burbank and became known as the Columbia Ranch.

Lucille joined Columbia in 1934 as a $75-a week stock player, figuring it was time to leave Goldwyn and settle in elsewhere because she wanted to try her hand at comedy. During her brief period of employment at Columbia, she logged in miniscule roles in eight feature films and three short subjects. Her most prestigious credit of this batch was *Broadway Bill*, as it was directed and produced by the studio's top filmmaker of the era, Frank Capra. Many of the others were "B" offerings or programmers, including the gangster melodrama *Men of the Night*, which ran all of fifty-eight minutes. Lucy's one milestone at Columbia was being given on-screen billing for the very first time, in the romantic comedy-drama *Carnival* (which was, in actuality, made at the Mack Sennett Studios), where she was listed simply as "Nurse." However, by the time Columbia released the picture, Lucille Ball was no longer at the studio. Following three months of employment at Columbia, Lucy and the entire stock company were laid off.

In 1947, Ball returned to Gower Street on loan-out from her newest MGM contract for one freelance credit, *Her Husband's Affairs*, and then signed a three-picture deal in 1949, giving her two more comedy show-cases, *Miss Grant Takes Richmond* and *The Fuller Brush Girl*, and concluding with perhaps her most "notorious" screen appearance, the kitschy Arabian nights opus *The Magic Carpet*, which Harry Cohn had guessed wrongly that she would refuse to do. It was released only three weeks before *I Love Lucy*'s October 15, 1951 debut.

• 1934 *Fugitive Lady* as Beauty Operator (Florence Rice, Neil Hamilton, Donald Cook; d: Albert S. Rogell); *Men of the Night* as Peggy (Bruce Cabot, Judith Allen, Ward Bond; d: Lambert Hillyer); *Jealousy* as "atmospheric background" (Nancy Carroll, George Murphy, Donald Cook; d: Roy William Neill); *Broadway Bill* as Telephone Operator (Warner Baxter, Myrna Loy, Walter Connolly; d: Frank Capra)
• 1935 *Carnival* as Nurse (Lee Tracy, Sally Eilers, Jimmy Durante; d: Walter Lang); *Behind the Evidence* as Secretary (Norman Foster, Donald Cook; d:

Lambert Hillyer); *The Whole Town's Talking* as Girl in Bank (Edward G. Robinson, Jean Arthur; d: John Ford); *I'll Love You Always* as Lucille (Nancy Carroll, George Murphy; d: Leo Bulgakov)

• 1947 *Her Husband's Affairs* as Margaret Weldon (Franchot Tone, Edward Everett Horton; d: S. Sylvan Simon)

• 1949: *Miss Grant Takes Richmond* as Ellen Grant, secretary (William Holden, James Gleason; d: Lloyd Bacon)

• 1950 *The Fuller Brush Girl* as Sally Elliott, switchboard operator/unofficial Fuller Brush girl (Eddie Albert, Carl Benton Reid; d: Lloyd Bacon); *A Woman of Distinction* as Herself (cameo) (Rosalind Russell, Ray Milland; d: Edward Buzzell)

• 1951 *The Magic Carpet* as Princess Narah (John Agar, Patricia Medina, Raymond Burr; d: Lew Landers)

Short subjects

• 1934 *Perfectly Mismatched* as Secretary (Leon Errol, Dorothy Granger; d: James W. Horne); *Three Little Pigskins* as Daisy Simms (Three Stooges, Gertie Green; d: Ray McCarey)

• 1935 *His Old Flame* (Charles Murray, Geneva Mitchell; d: James W. Horne)

PARAMOUNT

Because its origins can be traced to the creation of Adolph Zukor's Famous Players Film Company on May 8, 1912, Paramount has the distinction of being the longest-surviving American movie studio (Universal officially came into being exactly one month later). In 1914 Famous Players combined forces with producer Jesse L. Lasky's Feature Plays, and what began as Famous Players-Lasky was re-christened Paramount Pictures two years later. Originally headquartered in Hollywood at Sunset, Vine, and Selma, the company relocated in 1926 to a larger, twenty-six-acre facility (previously owned by United Studios) at Marathon Street, bounded on the north by the Hollywood Cemetery and Van Ness Avenue to the East, with Film Booking Offices of America (FBO) as their neighbor (this studio would be taken over by RKO in 1929 and then by Desilu in 1957).

While contracted to Goldwyn, Lucy did a single loan-out to Paramount, playing yet another of her many bit roles of the time, in *Murder at the Vanities*, which featured the hit song "Cocktails for Two." Lucy returned to Paramount in 1948 to film *Sorrowful Jones* as Bob Hope's co-star. The film was so successful upon its release the following year (it narrowly missed being in the top ten box office films of 1949, coming in at number eleven) that Paramount reteamed the twosome in *Fancy Pants*. The second teaming proved to be almost as financially successful as the first.

Paramount became the first Hollywood studio to be owned by a conglomerate when Gulf & Western purchased them in 1966. The following year they bought Desilu from Lucille, bringing down the wall that had divided the two companies and expanding the lot. *The Lucy Show* soundstages now found themselves part of the Paramount lot, and Lucy remained there for her follow-up series, *Here's Lucy*, until moving over to Universal in 1971. Lucy filmed her first post-*Here's Lucy* special, *Happy Anniversary and Goodbye*, at the studio she once owned.

• 1934 *Murder at the Vanities* as Earl Carroll Girl Playing Stenographer (Carl Brisson, Victor McLaglen, Jack Oakie; d: Mitchell Leisen)
• 1949 *Sorrowful Jones* as Gladys O'Neill, singer (Bob Hope, William Demarest, Bruce Cabot; d: Sidney Lanfield)
• 1950 *Fancy Pants* as Agatha Floud, heiress (Bob Hope, Bruce Cabot, Jack Kirkwood; d: George Marshall)

RKO

The most important studio in Lucy's career came into being when the Film Booking Offices of America (FBO) was purchased by Joseph P. Kennedy in 1926. RCA President David Sarnoff then acquired substantial interest in (and then complete control of) the company two years later, the same year he gained control of the Keith-Albee-Orpheum circuit of vaudeville houses. This merger brought forth the newly named Radio-Keith-Orpheum Corporation with Sarnoff as chairman, Hiram Brown as president, and Joseph I. Schnitzer as president of film production. Kennedy, father of the future 35th President of the United States, quickly resigned from the organization he had helped to create, having no actual involvement once motion picture production began. RKO, or Radio Pictures as it was known in the on-screen credits of its films, opened for business at the dawn of the talkies, in 1929. Their first sizeable hit was an adaptation of the stage musical *Rio Rita*, starring comedians Bert Wheeler and Robert Woolsey.

For studio headquarters, RKO took over the lot that FBO had once occupied, 13½ acres located at Gower Street and Melrose Avenue in Hollywood, directly next to the United Studios rental facility, which, in 1926, had become the site of Paramount Pictures. Because the facility had no room for substantial exterior shooting, an additional 500 acres were purchased in the San Fernando Valley near Encino. Dubbed the RKO Ranch, it allowed for larger standing sets and wide-open spaces for westerns. When RKO purchased Pathé Exchange Inc. in 1931, this allowed them to use Pathé's Culver City facility (opened as Thomas H. Ince Studios in

Lucille Ball as Annabel Allison in *The Affairs of Annabel* (1938), the first time she played the title role of a movie.

1919) at Washington Boulevard as well. (It was at this studio that independent producer David O. Selznick would lease space for several years, calling it Selznick International and using the Colonial-style building in front as his logo.)

The night Lucy was given the news that she was let go from Columbia, her date Dick Green informed her of a call for showgirls at RKO. Designer Bernard Newman selected Lucille as one of the models to participate in the fashion show at the climax of the Fred Astaire-Ginger Rogers musical *Roberta*. Lucy earned a contract with a starting salary of $50 a week. She would make films exclusively for the company for the next seven years, eventually moving from bit player to star.

Ginger Rogers's mother Lela took Lucille under her wing and became her mentor. Lela was the director of RKO's Little Theater for young actors, of which Lucy became a part. In addition to her bit roles in RKO films at the time, she was also appearing in showcase productions the Little Theatre put on such as the title role in *Breakfast with Vanora*. Under Lela's tutorage, Lucy changed her physical appearance and speaking voice to be more suitable for pictures. Lela's clout kept Lucy under RKO contract during her early days when it looked like she would be let go.

While there she could lay claim to appearing in two features that received Oscar nominations for Best Picture, *Top Hat* and *Stage Door*, the latter a significant credit because it gave her the opportunity to be part of a stellar ensemble that included Katharine Hepburn, Ginger Rogers, Eve Arden, and Ann Miller among others. *Joy of Living* let Lucy play a mother for the

Lucy in her largest film role up to that point, playing temperamental actress Lillian Temple, in 1936's *Chatterbox*, with Erik Rhodes.

first time in her career—a role she would not have again in a feature film until *The Facts of Life* in 1960. She received her first gig as a leading lady, portraying Joe Penner's wife in *Go Chase Yourself,* was the title character in *The Affairs of Annabel* and its sequel *Annabel Takes a Tour,* and supported the Marx Brothers in *Room Service.* Lucy received top billing for the first time in the short subject *So and Sew* (1936), co-starring with comedian Billy Gilbert, and then first reached the top of the cast list in feature films with *Next Time I Marry* (released December 1, 1938), a programmer made for double bills, as were many of Lucy's starring assignments for the studio. She did, however, get her chance to participate in some of the company's more important releases, including the musical *Too Many Girls,* which was a major milestone in her life because it put her into close contact with screen newcomer Desi Arnaz, who was repeating his role from the original Broadway stage production. They married the same year as the picture's release, 1940. Ball's penultimate assignment for RKO, *The Big Street,* was a high point on her resume, showing her at her dramatic best as a callous nightclub performer softened by a guileless Henry Fonda. It was Lucy's favorite of her film roles.

Although Lucy felt that RKO did not properly distribute *The Big Street,* her performance did not go unnoticed by the rival studios. Lucy's old friend and new RKO production head Charles Koerner informed her that RKO had no plans for her at present and that both MGM and Paramount had expressed interest in her. Lucy decided to move on to MGM because of their reputation making movie musicals. MGM bought half her RKO contract, and Lucy still owed RKO one more picture. Koerner told Lucy he would not use her in her one remaining assignment until they had something really important. Koerner died in 1946 with Lucy never having worked for him again. Lucy finally went before RKO cameras again in 1948 in *Easy Living* opposite Victor Mature, who had co-starred in her last RKO film, *Seven Days Leave.* The film Lucy started (then titled *Interference*) bore little resemblance to the finished product that was released a year later. Lucy was originally cast as the wicked wife of football player Mature and Lizabeth Scott was set to play the team's secretary. However, it was thought Scott fit the role of the icy wife better and the parts were switched. After Lucy finished work on the picture, the ending was reworked so that Mature ended up with Scott's character rather than Lucy's. Not surprisingly, Lucy was not pleased with the final result.

Once Howard Hughes bought control of RKO in 1948, its best days seemed to be over as the company began losing money on a steady basis. The RKO ranch was razed in 1954, and shortly afterwards Hughes sold the studio to General Teleradio. RKO ceased producing movies in 1957.

Lucy with Victor Mature (left) and Paul Stewart in her final RKO film 1949's *Easy Living*. Mature had previously starred with Lucy in her penultimate RKO film, *Seven Days Leave* in 1942.

In one of the great reversals of fortune in the history of entertainment, Lucy returned to RKO Studios most triumphantly when she and Desi purchased the company's Gower Street and Culver City lots to house their own Desilu Productions in December 1957. Now owner of the studio, Lucy decided to create her own Little Theater just as Lela Rogers had done two decades earlier. Lucy auditioned thousands of young performers, and twenty-two were selected, among them Carole Cook, Robert Osborne, Dick Kallman, and Majel Barrett. Lucy became president of the studio in 1962.

In 1968 she sold Desilu to next-door neighbor Paramount, who expanded their operations by removing the wall that separated the two companies, turning the former RKO location into part of their own lot. At the time *The Lucy Show* was being filmed there.

• 1935 *Roberta* as Model (Irene Dunne, Fred Astaire, Ginger Rogers; d: William A. Seiter); *Old Man Rhythm* as Coed (Charles "Buddy" Rogers, George Barbier, Barbara Kent; d: Edward Ludwig); *Top Hat* as Florist Shop Clerk (Fred Astaire, Ginger Rogers, Edward Everett Horton; d: Mark

Sandrich); *The Three Musketeers* as Court Subject (Walter Abel, Margot Grahame, Paul Lukas; d: Rowland V. Lee); *I Dream Too Much* as Gwendolyn Dilly, tourist (Lily Pons, Henry Fonda, Eric Blore; d: John Cromwell)

• 1936 *Chatterbox* as Lillian Temple, actress (Anne Shirley, Phillips Holmes, Edward Ellis; d: George Nichols Jr.); *Muss 'Em Up* as "atmospheric background" (Preston Foster, Margaret Callahan, Alan Mowbray; d: Charles Vidor); *Follow the Fleet* as Kitty Collins (Fred Astaire, Ginger Rogers, Randolph Scott; d: Mark Sandrich); *The Farmer in the Dell* as Gloria Wilson, script girl (Fred Stone, Jean Parker, Esther Dale; d: Ben Holmes); *Bunker Bean* as Rosie Kelly, secretary (Owen Davis Jr., Louise Latimer; d: William Hamilton, Edward Killy); *Winterset* as "atmospheric background"; (Burgess Meredith, Margo, Eduardo Ciannelli; d: Alfred Santell); *That Girl from Paris* as Claire Williams, dancer [The character's name is alternately spelled "Claire" and "Clair" on screen.] (Lily Pons, Jack Oakie, Gene Raymond; d: Leigh Jason)

• 1937 *Don't Tell the Wife* as Ann Howell, secretary (Guy Kibbee, Una Merkel, Lynne Overman; d: Christy Cabanne); *Stage Door* as Judith Canfield, actress (Katharine Hepburn, Ginger Rogers, Adolphe Menjou; d: Gregory La Cava)

• 1938 *Go Chase Yourself* as Carol Meely (Joe Penner, Richard Lane, June Travis; d: Edward F. Cline); *Joy of Living* as Salina Garrett Pine (Irene Dunne, Douglas Fairbanks Jr., Alice Brady; d: Tay Garnett); *Having Wonderful Time* as Miriam; (Ginger Rogers, Douglas Fairbanks Jr.; d: Alfred Santell); *The Affairs of Annabel* as Annabel Allison, actress (Jack Oakie, Ruth Donnelly, Bradley Page; d: Benjamin Stoloff); *Room Service* as Christine Marlowe, actress/secretary (Marx Brothers, Ann Miller, Frank Albertson; d: William A. Seiter); *Annabel Takes a Tour* as Annabel Allison, actress (Jack Oakie, Ruth Donnelly, Bradley Page; d: Lew Landers); *Next Time I Marry* as Nancy Crocker-Fleming Anthony, heiress (James Ellison, Lee Bowman, Granville Bates; d: Garson Kanin)

• 1939 *Beauty for the Asking* as Jean Russell, cosmetician (Patric Knowles, Donald Woods, Frieda Inescort; d: Glenn Tryon); *Twelve Crowded Hours* as Paula Sanders (Richard Dix, Allan Lane, Donald MacBride; d: Lew Landers); *Panama Lady* as Lucy, dancer (Allan Lane, Stefi Dunna, Evelyn Brent; d: Jack Hively); *Five Came Back* as Peggy Nolan, "goodtime girl" (Chester Morris, Wendy Barrie, John Carradine; d: John Farrow); *That's Right—You're Wrong* as Sandra Sand, actress (Kay Kyser & His Band, Adolphe Menjou; d: David Butler)

• 1940 *The Marines Fly High* as Joan Grant, cocoa plantation owner (Richard Dix; d: Benjamin Stoloff, George Nichols Jr.); *You Can't Fool Your Wife* as Clara Fields Hinklin, housewife and Mercedes Vasquez (James Ellison, Robert Coote; d: Ray McCarey); *Dance, Girl, Dance* as Bubbles/Tiger Lily White, dancer (Maureen O'Hara, Louis Hayward; d: Dorothy Arzner); *Too*

Many Girls as Consuelo Casey, heiress (Richard Carlson, Ann Miller, Desi Arnaz; d: George Abbott)
• 1941 *A Girl, a Guy, and a Gob* as Dot Duncan, stenographer (George Murphy, Edmond O'Brien; d: Richard Wallace); *Look Who's Laughing* as Julie Patterson, personal assistant (Edgar Bergen and Charlie McCarthy; d: Allan Dwan)

Lucille Ball moving up to the second feminine lead in *That Girl From Paris* (1936). She loses Gene Raymond to Lily Pons.

• 1942 *Valley of the Sun* as Christine Larson (James Craig, Cedric Hardwicke, Dean Jagger; d: George Marshall); *The Big Street* as Gloria Lyons, dancer (Henry Fonda, Barton MacLane, Agnes Moorehead; d: Irving Reis); *Seven Days Leave* as Terry Havalok-Allen, heiress (Victor Mature, Harold Peary, Mapy Cortés; d: Tim Whelan)
• 1949 *Easy Living* as Anne, secretary (Victor Mature, Lizabeth Scott, Sonny Tufts; d: Jacques Tourneur)

Short Subjects
• 1935 *A Night at the Biltmore Bowl* as herself (Betty Grable, Preston Foster; d: Alfred J. Goulding); *Foolish Hearts* as Hat Check Girl (Tony Martin, Phyllis Brooks, Jack Norton; d: Ben Holmes)
• 1936 *Dummy Ache* as Lois (Edgar Kennedy, Florence Lake, Jack Rice; d: Leslie Goodwins); *Swing It* as Mary, waitress (Louis Prima and His Band; d: Leslie Goodwins); *So and Sew* as Sally Curtis (Billy Gilbert, Lorin Baker; d: Jean Yarbrough, Charles E. Roberts); *One Live Ghost* as Maxine, maid (Leon Errol, Vivien Oakland, Robert Graves; d: Leslie Goodwins)

Lucy in character for her first MGM film, *Du Barry Was a Lady* (1943). Her newly dyed red hair was hidden under a wig for much of the picture.

METRO-GOLDWYN-MAYER

Theater exhibitor Marcus Loew entered the world of film production when his company, Loew's Incorporated, purchased Metro Pictures. After a period of struggle, Metro joined forces with the equally shaky Goldwyn Pictures, and then brought in independent producer Louis B. Mayer to oversee the newly merged operations. Metro-Goldwyn-Mayer (known more commonly as MGM or Metro) officially launched in April 1924 and soon became the top studio in the business. Taking over the former Goldwyn lot in Culver City (placing MGM farther away from central Hollywood proper than any of the other majors), Mayer rapidly expanded the facility until it encompassed 117 acres and twenty-three soundstages. Throughout the mid twenties until the years following World War II, MGM reigned supreme as the gold standard studio of Hollywood production.

Metro's main lot was wedged between Culver Boulevard and W. Washington Avenue at Overland Avenue, while Lot 2 was located across the street at Overland. Lot 3 and no less than three additional utility lots were available farther south of the main headquarters, down Overland near Jefferson Boulevard.

Lucy signed a contract with the studio on August 6, 1942, her thirty-first birthday, starting with a $1,500-a-week salary ($500 more than she was making at RKO) and eventually ending up earning $3,500 a week during the five years she was under contract there. The studio gave her the dressing room recently vacated by newly retired, former MGM queen Norma Shearer. Ball's first assignment, *Du Barry Was a Lady*, was significant since it marked the first time (discounting her appearance in the finale of *Kid Millions*) that she appeared on screen in color, allowing audiences to see the flaming red hair that the studio designated be her look. MGM only released five feature films in color in 1943, and Lucy appeared in three of them: *Du Barry Was a Lady* and *Best Foot Forward,* which she starred in; and *Thousands Cheer,* which she, like many on the MGM roster,

Lucille Ball, movie star, plays Lucille Ball, movie star, in *Best Foot Forward,* her second MGM assignment.

made a cameo in. (*Lassie Come Home* and *Salute to the Marines* were the other two MGM color films.) Husband Desi was signed by Metro shortly afterwards at a starting salary $500 less than his wife. Only one film, *Bataan*, in which his performance garnered critical acclaim, resulted from this contract.

Of her nine assignments during her Metro contract period, Lucille played herself no fewer than four times, which, if nothing else, meant that she was being treated as the star she was. When the studio gathered its top talent together for a famous photo that ran in *Life* magazine in 1943, she was positioned in the front row, between Margaret Sullavan and Hedy Lamarr, two seats to the left of her future neighbor James Stewart; two seats to the right of former and future co-star Katharine Hepburn; and directly in front of her *Du Barry* co-star, Red Skelton. Lucille left MGM in 1946 and freelanced at Universal with *Lover Come Back*. Ball would sign a second

Although Lucy was given a supporting role in *Without Love*, she and partner Keenan Wynn received the picture's best notices.

contract with Metro before *Lover Come Back* was completed, but spent the entire time doing loan-outs. She never felt the loyalty she had with RKO to MGM, but she liked the security.

Lucy finally ended her association with the studio in the fall of 1947 during her run in *Dream Girl*. She said at the time, "I was getting a big salary for doing nothing and though that sounds like a soft deal, it wasn't getting me anywhere. Besides, they were making lots of money by lending me out and I decided I might as well collect that myself. If they couldn't figure out what to do with me after *Easy to Wed*, I thought I might as well go elsewhere."

When Lucy returned to MGM in the nineteen-fifties, it was for the two co-starring pictures she did with Desi during the run of *I Love Lucy*. (The second of these, *Forever, Darling*, however, used the Desilu soundstages, not Metro's.)

• 1943 *Du Barry Was a Lady* as May Daly, nightclub performer/Madame Du Barry (Red Skelton, Gene Kelly, Virginia O'Brien; d: Roy Del Ruth); *Best Foot Forward* as Herself (William Gaxton, Virginia Weidler, Tommy Dix; d: Edward Buzzell); *Thousands Cheer* as Herself (Gene Kelly, Kathryn Grayson, Frank Morgan; d: George Sidney)
• 1944 *Meet the People* as Julie Hampton, actress (Dick Powell, Virginia O'Brien, Bert Lahr; d: Charles Reisner)
• 1945 *Without Love* as Kitty Trimble, real estate agent (Spencer Tracy, Katharine Hepburn, Keenan Wynn; d: Harold S. Bucquet); *Bud Abbott and Lou Costello in Hollywood* as Herself (unbilled cameo) (d: S. Sylvan Simon);
• 1946 *Ziegfeld Follies* as Ziegfeld Girl (Fred Astaire, Virginia O'Brien; d: Vincente Minnelli; [Note: Although Minnelli is the credited director, Ball's sequence was actually directed by George Sidney.]); *Easy to Wed* as Gladys Benton, actress (Van Johnson, Esther Williams, Keenan Wynn; d: Edward Buzzell); *Two Smart People* as Ricki Woodner, con artist (John Hodiak, Lloyd Nolan, Hugo Haas; d: Jules Dassin)
• 1954 *The Long, Long Trailer* as Tacy Bolton Collini (Desi Arnaz, Keenan Wynn, Marjorie Main; d: Vincente Minnelli)
• 1956 *Forever, Darling* as Susan Buell Vega (Desi Arnaz, James Mason, Louis Calhern; d: Alexander Hall)

UNIVERSAL

Starting as a film distributor in 1906, Carl Laemmle began producing his own motion pictures three years later. In June 1912, his company, Universal Pictures, was officially established and its permanent headquarters, which opened in March 1915 on the former 230-acre site of the Taylor Ranch, became the first studio to have its own city built exclusively to house it, Universal City, north of Hollywood across the Cahuenga Pass.

Lucy would make only one feature film for the company, her first free-lance assignment after leaving Metro, the romantic comedy *Lover Come Back*. (The same studio's more famous film of the same name, released in 1961 and starring Rock Hudson and Doris Day, was *not* a remake.) In fact, *Lover Come Back* was subsequently retitled *When Lovers Meet* to avoid confusion

Lucy in one of the Travis Banton creations designed for her only Universal film, *Lover Come Back*. She and the clothes received the best reviews.

with the later Universal property. When the film was re-released in 1952 to capitalize on Lucille Ball's renewed fame, it was called *Lucy Goes Wild*! *Here's Lucy* moved its base of operations from Paramount to Universal in 1971, and a museum celebrating the actress, called Lucille Ball: A Tribute, was part of the Universal Studios tour from 1990 to 2008. (A similar attraction became a part of the studio's East Coast theme park, in Orlando, Florida.)

• 1946 *Lover Come Back* as Kay Williams, fashion designer (George Brent, Vera Zorina, Charles Winninger; d: William A. Seiter)

20TH CENTURY-FOX

By the time Lucy returned to the Fox fold twelve years after her last job there, for the noir *The Dark Corner* (on loan from MGM), the company had long established itself as 20th Century-Fox (the hyphen would stay until

Lucy and Mark Stevens in *The Dark Corner*. Lucy was not happy that MGM loaned her out for this Fox assignment and director Henry Hathaway unnerved her. She later said she had a near-nervous breakdown doing this film.

1985) and was mightier than ever. The soundstages and back-lot were located between Santa Monica Boulevard on the north and Pico Boulevard on the south. Another twenty-one years went by before Ball returned to work there, during which time the lot had decreased considerably, most of it being sold off for real estate to compensate for crippling financial losses on the ultra-expensive *Cleopatra*. The area became known as Century City, the construction of one of its buildings captured on film as the site of Art Carney's job in Lucy's segment of *A Guide for the Married Man*. Lucy shot her 1976 special *What Now, Catherine Curtis?* (again with Art Carney) here as well.

After Gary Morton's close friend Marvin Davis purchased 20th Century-Fox in 1981, the couple moved Lucille Ball Productions headquarters to the studio. The company produced the 1983 film *All the Right Moves* starring Tom Cruise (on which Lucy refused on-screen credit because of the R-rated language and sexual content in the movie) and the 1984 Jaclyn Smith TV movie *Sentimental Journey* for the studio.

• 1946 *The Dark Corner* as Kathleen Stuart, secretary (Clifton Webb, William Bendix, Mark Stevens; d: Henry Hathaway)
• 1967 *A Guide for the Married Man* as Mrs. Joe X (Walter Matthau, Robert Morse, Art Carney; d: Gene Kelly)

UNITED ARTISTS

Founded in 1919 by four of the most powerful names in the business, director D. W. Griffith and actors Charlie Chaplin, Douglas Fairbanks, and Mary Pickford, United Artists was set up to allow the creative forces in Hollywood the independence to work outside the studio system. In this respect, UA had no set base of operations akin to the other major companies in Hollywood (although the former Pickford-Fairbanks Studio on Santa Monica Boulevard went under the name United Artists Studios for a period). Throughout its many years of existence, it distributed the product of individual production companies and would rent space on various lots.

All of Lucille's assignments for both Samuel Goldwyn and Twentieth Century Pictures were distributed through United Artists (see separate entries for those titles), while further down the line she appeared in three other movies released by the company.

Lured was produced under the supervision of Hunt Stromberg, a former producer at MGM who decided to go independent in 1943. It was shot at the General Service Studios, which later became the first home of *I Love Lucy*. *The Facts of Life* was shot at Desilu and was a joint venture of Desilu, Bob Hope's company, and that of its creators, Norman Panama and Melvin Frank. *Yours, Mine and Ours* was a Desilu production, marking the only time the studio's name appeared in the credits of a movie produced directly for cinemas. *Yours, Mine and Ours* proved to be the highest-grossing United Artists release of 1968.

Lucy in a pose as Sandra Carpenter, a serial killer's bait, in the independent thriller *Lured* (1947).

• 1947 *Lured* as Sandra Carpenter, dancer/detective (George Sanders, Charles Coburn, Boris Karloff; d: Douglas Sirk)
• 1960 *The Facts of Life* as Kitty Weaver (Bob Hope, Don DeFore, Ruth Hussey; d: Melvin Frank)
• 1968 *Yours, Mine and Ours* as Helen Brandmier North Beardsley, a housewife and nurse (Henry Fonda, Van Johnson, Tim Matthieson; d: Melville Shavelson)

GENERAL SERVICE STUDIOS

Founded by former Charlie Chaplin employee John Jasper, this studio was built in 1919 and initially went under the names Jasper Studios and

Hollywood Studios Inc. During the nineteen-twenties and early thirties, comedian Harold Lloyd made it his base of operations (it was known as Metropolitan Studios at the time), and Howard Hughes filmed part of his much-hyped 1930 aviation epic *Hell's Angels* here as well. As a rental lot to various independent productions, General Service Studios (as it was re-named in 1933) played host to such productions as Paramount's Hopalong Cassidy series, Alexander Korda's patriotic *That Hamilton Woman*, the Marx Brothers' *A Night in Casablanca*, the James Cagney pictures *Blood on the Sun* and *The Time of Your Life*, and one of Lucy's titles, *Lured*. Independent pro-ducer Benedict Bogeaus purchased the studio in 1942 and in the postwar years made the wise decision of making the lot available for television pro-duction as well. The Nasser Brothers joined the operations in 1948 and then bought the studio two years later.

When Lucy and Desi went looking for a studio that would allow them to film their new television series with three cameras before a live audi-ence, they settled on General Service at 1040 North Las Palmas Avenue, in the heart of Hollywood, located between Santa Monica Boulevard and Romaine Street, and bounded on the east by Seward Street. Soundstage Number 2 was refitted to accommodate their needs and *I Love Lucy* ended up being shot there for the first two years of its run. *Our Miss Brooks* was pro-duced there as well as *The George Burns and Gracie Allen Show* (George Burns maintained offices on the lot until his death in 1996 at the age of 100) and *The Adventures of Ozzie and Harriet*, among others.

MOTION PICTURE CENTER STUDIOS

The area between Willoughby Avenue (on the north), Waring Avenue (south), Lillian Way (east), and N. Cahuenga Boulevard originally served as one of Metro Pictures' back-lots when it opened in 1915. During the nineteen-twenties it was used to shoot scenes from such movies as Ramon Novarro's *Scaramouche* and Jackie Coogan's *Little Robinson Crusoe*. An all-new facility was built on this location in 1946, intending to go under the name Equity Studios but instead quickly becoming Motion Picture Center Studios. As a rental lot it was where scenes from such pictures as *Champion*, with Kirk Douglas; *The Men*, with Marlon Brando in his film debut; and Jose Ferrer's Oscar-winning *Cyrano de Bergerac* were filmed.

By 1953 the tremendous success of *I Love Lucy* enabled Lucy and Desi to expand their operations, so they moved off the General Service Studios lot and ended up several blocks southeast at the Motion Picture Center Studios. After negotiating a long-term lease with the owners, the studio was revamped considerably and became known as Desilu-Cahuenga. It changed

Lucy's longtime makeup man Hal King gets Lucy ready for her close up for the final scene of the last *I Love Lucy* episode "The Ricardos Dedicate a Statue," as Desi looks on.

its name several times over the years from Television Center Studios to Ren-Mar and then most recently to Red Studios.

The 1992 film *The Mambo Kings* was shot at the studio. In it, Desi Arnaz Jr., portrayed his famous father, and the movie contained a re-creation of the first season *I Love Lucy* episode "Cuban Pals." Coincidentally, the scene was filmed on the same soundstage where the original series was filmed beginning in the third season. "Cuban Pals" preceded Desilu's move to the Motion Picture Center.

WARNER BROS.

The Brothers Warner (Jack, Sam, Harry, and Albert) went from film exhibition to production starting in 1918. They eventually set up operations on Sunset Boulevard in Hollywood and then moved to the 110-acre First

A final gathering of Lucy and some of her most significant co-stars, Vivian Vance (left), Mary Jane Croft (3rd from right), and Mary Wickes (right), for the 1977 special *Lucy Calls the President.* The men on hand (left to right) are Ed McMahon, Gale Gordon, and James E. Brodhead.

National Studios lot in Burbank in 1929, following the success of the first talking picture, *The Jazz Singer.* Located at West Olive Avenue, the facility changed its name to the Burbank Studios in 1972 when Columbia arranged to share the lot with Warners. It was going under this name at the time Lucy filmed *Mame* there in 1973. The name has since reverted back to Warner Bros. Studios. Warners was the last of the majors that Lucy got around to working for. She would not do a feature film for them until 1963's *Critic's Choice* and ended her motion picture career there as well, starring in *Mame,* eleven year later.

Her 1977 television special *Lucy Calls on the President* was also taped there. This show featured Lucy's final on-screen teaming with Vivian Vance, Mary Jane Croft, and Mary Wickes. Lucille played Lucy Whittaker from Bundy, Indiana, who calls up President Jimmy Carter to let him know that a nearby camp for unprivileged children is planned to be torn down in favor of a housing project. The president tells her that he will be passing through Indiana and would like to meet her at her house to discuss the matter. Lucy's planned meeting with the Carters and her family, which initially consists of her husband Floyd (Ed McMahon) and his father Omar (Gale Gordon), spins out of control when her next-door neighbor Vivian, her Aunt Millie (Mary Wickes) and the town's mayor (James E. Brodhead) and his wife, Midge (Mary Jane Croft) all want to be invited. They, in turn, invite their own guests.

The special also featured Steve Allen as himself and Miss Lillian Carter, the president's mother, in a cameo. This was the first project Lucy worked on after the death of her mother, DeDe, and it was difficult for her to get through it knowing that her mother was not in the audience for the first time in her television career. The set used as the Whittaker home was also seen in the special *High Hopes: The Capra Years,* which also featured Lucy.

Lucy and Bob Hope in a shot publicizing *Critic's Choice.* It was their fourth and final film together and their least favorite of their joint movie ventures.

Carl Reiner interviewed the Oscar-winning director Frank Capra on the set, while Lucy took viewers on a tour of the Warner Bros. back-lot where some of Capra's films were made. Although produced the same year as *Lucy Calls the President*, the Capra special did not air on television until 1981.

• 1963 *Critic's Choice* as Angela Ballentine, housewife and playwright (Bob Hope, Marilyn Maxwell, Rip Torn; d: Don Weis)
• 1974 *Mame* as Mame Dennis Burnside (Robert Preston, Beatrice Arthur, Jane Connell; d: Gene Saks)

Lucy as Mame Dennis in her opening scene in *Mame*, her final feature film.

23

"Real Gone with the Wind"

Films, Plays, Radio and Television Programs Lucy Nearly Did, Might Have Done, Should Have Done, Wasn't Able to Do, Had Second Thoughts About Doing, Etc.

A s is the case with all great stars, as much as we got to enjoy Lucille Ball in her six decades of work, there was always the hope she would give us more. Like anyone in demand in show business, there were always those intriguing "might have been" projects that slipped through the cracks, conflicted with something else she had already signed up for; those she toyed with or considered before deciding to pass, or got cancelled for reasons that were not her fault. Some of them are properties that never came to fruition one way or the other, leaving us to speculate on them altogether, while others did indeed get produced with other ladies in the roles once thought of for Lucy. Some were certainly well suited for her; others might seem a bit curious when comparing her against the women who claimed the parts for their own. You be the judge.

Films

Gone with the Wind

In 1936, producer David O. Selznick purchased the screen rights to Margaret Mitchell's recently published novel *Gone with the Wind* for a record $50,000. Who Selznick would cast in the lead roles became a chief topic of discussion in Hollywood, with nearly every actress, major or minor, considered for the coveted starring part of Scarlett O'Hara. Speculation on just who would embody Mitchell's resilient Southern heroine on celluloid became so intense that Selznick made the most of all the attention, turning this into one of the great publicity stunts in cinema history, with such notables as Katharine Hepburn, Bette Davis, Jean Arthur, Joan Bennett, and Paulette Goddard among the prime contenders. The RKO studio brass arranged an audition for Lucy, who spent several weeks with a dialogue coach trying to master a Southern accent. While on her way to the Selznick studio in Culver City, Lucille got lost and found herself caught in a huge rainstorm, unable to get the top down on her secondhand Studebaker Phaeton. When the drenched actress at last arrived at Selznick's office, she was met by her friend, Selznick's assistant, Marcella Rabwin, who ordered Lucy to take off her wet clothes and gave her a long, brown sweater to wear. Marcella then handed her a large snifter of brandy and led her to a fireplace in Selznick's office. Lucy knelt down in front of the fire and Selznick entered. The sweater she was wearing was not long enough to sufficiently cover her, so Lucy remained on her knees, performing the three scenes she was supposed to do without once standing up. When it was all over, Lucy burst into tears, certain she had muffed her big chance. Selznick offered his thanks for auditioning.

Vivien Leigh, of course, ultimately won the role and an Oscar for her performance. A decade after *Gone with the Wind* was released, Lucy was asked what she considered to be the greatest performance in the history of motion pictures. She answered Vivien Leigh as Scarlett O'Hara, saying, "It's a difficult role and she did a great job." By that point in time she claimed to have seen the film eight times.

Lucy did get the opportunity to play Scarlett O'Hara in a takeoff of the classic film in the 1971 *Here's Lucy* episode, "Lucy and Flip Go Legit." Two decades after her disastrous trip to the Selznick studio, Lucy ended up owning it and later confessed she still got lost trying to get there.

Night of January 16th

In 1939, Lucille was cast in the lead role in RKO's adaptation of Ayn Rand's play *Night of January 16th*. The plot revolved around Karen Andre, who is on trial for the murder of her boss and lover. The unusual thing about the play was that the "jury" was comprised of members of the audience, with the verdict for each particular performance dependent on how they voted that night. MGM originally bought the film rights to the play in 1934 when it was titled *Woman on Trial*, before its successful Broadway run in 1935–36, but never did anything with the property. RKO then paid Rand (who once worked for the studio in the wardrobe department) $10,000 for the screen rights. The studio's original intention was to star Claudette Colbert in the film, but they replaced her with Lucy. Like MGM, RKO ended up not making the property either. Next it was Paramount who purchased the rights, once again intending to put Claudette Colbert in the lead. When the film was finally made in 1941, Ellen Drew got the role (the character was now named "Kit Lane"), playing opposite Robert Preston. The completed film bore little resemblance to Rand's play, and the playwright went on record as being none too pleased with the final result.

The Smiler with a Knife

In 1940, Orson Welles, RKO's newest director, planned to make a suspenseful comedic film about a man who plotted to become dictator of the United States, *The Smiler with a Knife*. Welles wrote the screenplay based on a novel by Nicholas Blake, which had been published the previous year. For the feminine lead, who dons a series of disguises to expose the aspiring autocrat, Welles wanted Lucille Ball. The fledgling filmmaker had first met Lucille when RKO had him escort her to the premiere of one of the studio's films. However, an unhappy Welles left the theatre immediately after the picture began, leaving Lucy all alone. The two reunited under more pleasant circumstances in April 1940 when they appeared together on Welles's *Campbell Playhouse* production of *Dinner at Eight,* with Lucy as Kitty Packard, the role played by Jean Harlow in the 1933 film.

Welles later described Lucille Ball as "the greatest actress in the world," and he was desperate to get her to star in *The Smiler with a Knife*. However, RKO, to whom they were both under contract, balked and urged Welles to find a bigger name. Welles's friend Carole Lombard was approached, but opted to make *Mr. and Mrs. Smith* for Alfred Hitchcock instead. Rosalind Russell also turned down the role. Disenchanted, Welles soon stopped work on the film and immediately went into production on *Citizen Kane*. He regretted for years that the film was never made because he knew how superb Ball would have been in it. Lucy did get to work with Welles several times in the years following, including on *I Love Lucy*. In 1978 the two appeared together in an installment of Dinah Shore's talk show, *Dinah!,* in which they reminisced about their disastrous date and their never-made project.

Ball of Fire

The role of burlesque queen Sugarpuss O'Shea in the 1941 Samuel Goldwyn comedy *Ball of Fire* was offered to and rejected by some of the top female stars in Hollywood, including Ginger Rogers, Carole Lombard, Jean Arthur (who could not get a release from her home studio of Columbia), and Barbara Stanwyck. Lucy, however, loved the script by Billy Wilder and

Charles Brackett and wanted to play the part, which bore many similarities to her role of Bubbles in the previous year's *Dance, Girl, Dance.* The *Ball of Fire* plot, which was a variation on "Snow White and the Seven Dwarfs," found Sugarpuss hiding out from the police with a group of timid professors who are writing an encyclopedia. The youngest of these scholarly gentlemen finds Sugarpuss a great study in American slang, a subject he is not well versed in, and ultimately falls in love with the extroverted showgirl. Gary Cooper was cast in the male lead, and although it seemed all but certain that Lucy would star in *Ball of Fire*, it was decided that a bigger name should be paired opposite him. Stanwyck, who had just completed work on *Meet John Doe* with Cooper, was again offered the part, and this time she accepted, eventually earning an Oscar nomination for her performance. Although Lucy did not get a chance to play Sugarpuss O'Shea on film, she did play the role several years later on radio. On November 5, 1944, Lucille starred in a half-hour adaptation of the movie on *The Old Gold Comedy Theater*, with Cooper reprising his film role.

Shore Leave

In 1941, RKO cast Lucy in the lead role in their new film version of the 1927 Broadway musical *Hit the Deck*. This had been based on the 1922 straight play *Shore Leave*, which resulted in a 1925 silent film of the same name. Three years after its New York opening, RKO produced a film version of *Hit the Deck* and later reworked elements of the plot into a vehicle for the studio's red-hot dance team, Fred Astaire and Ginger Rogers. That version, entitled *Follow the Fleet* (1936), featured Lucy among the cast.

For their latest take on the ever-adaptable property, RKO assigned David Butler to produce and direct, with future *I Love Lucy* director James V. Kern writing the screenplay. Ray Bolger, Bert Lahr, and Buddy Ebsen were cast in supporting roles, which meant that they nearly had the chance to compensate for their previous, aborted project together. The three performers had worked on *The Wizard of Oz* until Ebsen was forced to leave the film when the aluminum dust in his "Tin Man" makeup made him seriously ill, relinquishing his part to Jack Haley.

Eddie Albert had just signed a three-picture deal with RKO, which handed him the male lead in what was initially called *Hit the Deck*, as his first assignment (another project considered for Albert was the role of "Little Pinks" in what would become *The Big Street*). However, Albert was soon replaced by George Murphy, who had recently starred with Lucy in *A Girl, a Guy, and a Gob.* (Albert would finally get to appear in a film with Lucy when they did *The Fuller Brush Girl* at Columbia in 1950.) Production was set to begin in late fall 1941 on the musical, which now reverted back to its original title, *Shore Leave*. Instead, RKO withdrew Lucy from the project, preferring that she do *Passage to Bordeaux*. The studio attempted to borrow Betty Grable from 20th Century-Fox to replace Lucy, but nothing ever came of it. Neither film ended up being made. As it turned out, RKO could not get the rights to the Vincent Youmans music from *Hit the Deck* and decided to abandon the project. MGM finally produced a new version of *Hit the Deck* in 1955 with a cast that included Jane Powell, Debbie Reynolds, Ann Miller, Tony Martin, Walter Pidgeon, Vic Damone, and Russ Tamblyn.

Passage to Bordeaux

RKO planned to have Lucille Ball enter the ranks of major stardom when they announced she would star in one of their biggest films of 1941–42, *Passage to Bordeaux*. Described as "a romantic adventure," the story centered on a group of Americans stranded in France when the Germans invade. Lucy would have played the role of a Texan showgirl. It was reported that RKO bought the script, written by Budd Schulberg (author of *What Makes Sammy Run?*), specifically for Lucille. Joseph Cotten and Ruth Warrick, who co-starred in the yet-to-be released *Citizen Kane*, were set to join her in the cast; Erich Pommer, who produced Ball's *Dance, Girl, Dance* a year earlier, was slated to perform the same duty for *Bordeaux*; and Robert Stevenson was named as director. The picture that RKO had built up for Lucille never materialized.

Footlight Serenade

In 1942, Lucille was put on suspension from RKO for the only time during her career for refusing to make a picture. The studio had planned to loan her out to 20th Century-Fox to play the second female lead in the Betty Grable film *Strictly Dynamite*, which was later retitled *Footlight Serenade*. Although she and Betty were good friends, having both appeared in the films *Old Man Rhythm* and *Follow the Fleet*, and Grable was looking forward to working with her again, Lucy refused the assignment, afraid the filming would interfere with the production of RKO's *The Big Street*, which she had already been signed for and was anxious to star in. Warner Bros. contract player Jane Wyman was instead cast in *Footlight Serenade* as Flo La Verne, the role intended for Lucy. Lucille was put on suspension from the studio for several weeks, and it was reported that, as a result, she was being replaced in *The Big Street* by Dorothy Comingore, best known for her role as the second Mrs. Kane in *Citizen Kane*. Happily for Lucy, she did get to stay in *The Big Street*, which she later cited as her favorite film role.

Seattle

In June 1944, Lucille was announced to star in MGM's *Seattle* alongside Clark Gable and Myrna Loy. This was to be the first film to star Clark Gable, the widower of Lucy's late friend Carole Lombard, after he returned home following his military service. The picture was described as a "comedy drama with music," to be produced by John Considine Jr. and directed by Norman Taurog. Gable, however, was not happy with the story and turned the project down. He ended up not returning to films for nearly a year after resuming civilian life, with 1945's *Adventure* co-starring Greer Garson (who was first considered to star opposite him in *Seattle*). *Seattle* was never produced. The cancellation of the film was one in a series of professional disappointments for Lucille at the time.

Yolanda and the Thief

By late 1944, Lucille was not pleased with MGM. Outside of filming her cameo in *Ziegfeld Follies* (which would not be released until early 1946), she had not been before the movie cameras in nearly a year. Lucy had initially been excited by her assignment in *Ziegfeld Follies* because she was promised she would dance with Fred Astaire. Although they appeared in the same segment of the film, they did *not* dance together, which was a tremendous disappointment for Lucille. However, it soon looked like Lucy would get a second chance to partner Astaire when she was cast alongside him in *Yolanda and the Thief.* Playing Fred's romantic interest, however, was another redheaded Lucille B, who *did* get to dance with Fred in *Ziegfeld Follies*—Lucille Bremer. In *Yolanda,* Astaire played a con artist who tries to fleece an heiress (Bremer) out of her fortune by posing as her guardian angel. Although it was reported in later years that Lucy was scheduled to play Astaire's partner in crime (a role that went to Frank Morgan), Lucy was actually cast as Amarilla, the heiress's flighty aunt (even though Ball was only five-and-a-half years older than Bremer). When production was postponed, MGM instead put Lucy to work in the supporting role of Kitty Trimble in *Without Love,* starring Katharine Hepburn and Spencer Tracy. Once production finally commenced on *Yolanda and the Thief,* Mildred Natwick (who was somewhat more believable playing Bremer's aunt, being *twelve* years her senior) assumed the part originally earmarked for Lucy.

Born Yesterday

In the late nineteen-forties, Lucille found a role that she thought she would be perfect for; however, she was not the only actress who felt that way. The role was Billie Dawn and the movie was *Born Yesterday*, based on a

Lucy and Fred Astaire during the filming of *Ziegfeld Follies* (apparently ignoring the "No Smoking" sign). Lucy wanted to dance with Astaire on film, but it never happened.

hit Broadway comedy written by Garson Kanin (who had directed Lucille in 1938's *Next Time I Marry*) for his friend Jean Arthur. The plot involved a scrap metal tycoon who hires a journalist to educate his uncultured girl-friend, Billie Dawn. When Arthur left the play during its out-of-town try-outs, the little known Judy Holliday was brought in to replace the movie star. *Born Yesterday* opened on Broadway on February 4, 1946 to rave reviews, particularly for Holliday. Columbia head Harry Cohn paid a then-record sum of $1 million to Kanin for the motion picture rights. Those in the industry were buzzing about who would play the much-coveted role of Billie Dawn in the film version. One person Cohn was dead set against was Judy Holliday. The most talked about name was Columbia's reigning star Rita Hayworth, who was Cohn's pick, even though most argued she was wrong for the role. Shortly afterwards, Hayworth walked out on her Columbia contract to marry Prince Aly Khan, putting an end to that possibility. The other name most frequently mentioned was Lucille Ball.

It was reported in December 1946 that Lucy, William Holden, and William Bendix would star in a Los Angeles production of the play, but nothing ever came of this. In April 1948, Lucy was offered the opportunity to play Billie Dawn onstage for a month, but she turned down the offer due to her picture commitments. In reference to the planned movie version, she said, "I'm not going to campaign for it: Columbia ought to realize I'm right for the role." Three months earlier, Lucy had signed a contract with Columbia for her to do one picture a year for the studio, and she hoped *Born Yesterday* would be one of them. Among the others under consideration for the role of Billie Dawn were Jan Sterling (who replaced Holliday on Broadway and did the show on tour), Celeste Holm, Gloria Grahame, and Lana Turner.

In May 1949, Judy Holliday left the cast of the Broadway play to do a supporting part in the Spencer Tracy-Katharine Hepburn film *Adam's Rib*, which was scripted by Garson Kanin and his wife, Ruth Gordon. In order to increase Holliday's chances of repeating on film the role she played onstage for over three years, Katharine Hepburn conspired to show Holliday off to her best possible advantage and planted items in the gossip columns that Holliday was stealing the picture from the two famous leads. As a result, Cohn relented and filmed a series of screen tests with Holliday, which finally landed her the part. Lucille's old flame Broderick Crawford and her *Miss Grant Takes Richmond* co-star William Holden were cast as the male leads. Judy Holliday won the Academy Award for Best Actress for her performance in *Born Yesterday*.

The Greatest Show on Earth

In October 1950, Lucy was offered a substantial role in Paramount's *The Greatest Show on Earth*, to be directed and produced by Cecil B. DeMille. Lucy was eager to work with the famed director, but an obstacle was standing in her way. She had only completed two films (*Miss Grant Takes Richmond* and *The Fuller Brush Girl*) as part of her three-picture deal with Columbia. When Lucy asked studio head Harry Cohn about the possibility of dissolving her contract with Columbia in order to make the Paramount picture, he refused. Defiantly, Lucy accepted DeMille's offer anyway. Several weeks later, Cohn sent Lucille a script for a low-budget Arabian Nights adventure entitled *The Magic Carpet*. Lucy was well aware that Cohn had deliberately sent her the inferior script knowing that any actress of her standing would reject it. If Lucy turned down the film, he could fire her and not have to pay her $85,000 salary for her third picture. Lucy called Cohn's bluff and told him she would love to make the picture. However, by the time filming began, Lucy discovered she was pregnant and managed to conceal her condition from Cohn to prevent him from finding another reason to fire her. Lucy completed *The Magic Carpet* in only five days and received her $85,000 payment.

Because of her condition, Lucy knew that she would be unable to appear in *The Greatest Show on Earth* after all. She tearfully told DeMille how much she would have liked to have done the picture, but she had waited ten years to have a child. DeMille turned to Desi, who had accompanied Lucy to DeMille's office, and said, "Congratulations, Desi, you are the only person in the world to screw Harry Cohn, Columbia Pictures, Paramount, Cecil B. DeMille, and your wife, all at the same time." Gloria Grahame replaced Lucy in the circus epic, playing Angel the elephant girl, whose act involves her dangerously placing her head under the foot of the trained pachyderms. *The Greatest Show on Earth* became a gigantic blockbuster and won the Academy Award for the Best Picture of 1952. Eleven years later Lucille could finally put the title *The Greatest Show on Earth* on her resume, when she appeared in an episode of the Desilu series of the same name.

The Star

In the late nineteen-forties, producer Jerry Wald approached the husband-and-wife writing team of Dale Eunson and Katherine Albert with an idea he had for a film. It would begin with a movie star who, having fallen on hard times, attends her own auction sale of her goods. Wald had produced *Mildred Pierce*, which starred the Eunsons' closest friend, Joan Crawford, so the writers modeled their fictitious aging star on Crawford. Rather than actually approach Crawford herself to play the part, the Eunsons wanted their friend Lucille Ball to play the lead. Lucy even announced in June 1950 that the Eunsons' *The Star,* would be one of the first projects done by the newly formed Desilu Productions.

Dale Eunson later recalled, "Once we had the script written, we tried to get the film made with Lucille Ball. But her movie career had never taken off, and we couldn't raise any money on her." The film was ultimately made in 1952 by another independent company, Bert E. Friedlob Productions, and distributed by 20th Century-Fox. Bette Davis was cast in the leading role of Margaret Elliot and earned her ninth Oscar nomination. Her character in the film was an Academy Award winner too and, in one scene, she memorably grabs her trophy and says, "Come on Oscar . . . let's you and me get drunk!" Apparently Crawford was all too aware of just who inspired the character of Margaret Elliot, and the Eunsons' friendship with the actress was irreparably harmed as a result of *The Star.* (One of Davis's competitors for the Oscar that year, ironically, was Crawford, for her performance in *Sudden Fear.* Neither lady won.)

By the time production began on *The Star* in July 1952, Lucy was pregnant with her second child and the star of television's most popular situation comedy.

The Manchurian Candidate

Two years after its publication, producer Frank Sinatra, director John Frankenheimer, and screenwriter George Axelrod were preparing a film adaptation of Richard Condon's 1959 novel *The Manchurian Candidate.* To play the role of Eleanor Iselin, one of the most villainous mother characters of all time, who trains her son to be an assassin and has an implied incestuous relationship with him, Sinatra wanted Lucille Ball. Frankenheimer's choice, however, was Angela Lansbury, whom he had just directed in the film *All Fall Down*, in which she played mother to Warren Beatty. Frankenheimer arranged a screening of *All Fall Down* for Sinatra and Frank was persuaded to cast Lansbury in the role.

Years later, during a press junket for *Mame*, Lucy stated that she was sent the script for *The Manchurian Candidate* while she was in New York doing *Wildcat* on Broadway. She recalled she was numb after reading it and thought that the film had no values. (Lucy made no reference to the fact that Lansbury, who originated the role of Mame onstage, ended up playing the part she had been offered.) It seems unlikely that fifty-year-old Lucy would have agreed to play the mother of thirty-three year-old Laurence Harvey no matter what the film's subject matter. Oddly enough, Lansbury was only thirty-six when she did the film—making her only three years older than her on-screen son. For her performance, Lansbury was nominated for an Academy Award and named Best Supporting Actress by the Golden Globes and the National Board of Review (the latter for her work in both *The Manchurian Candidate* and *All Fall Down*).

Sweet Bird of Youth

Tennessee Williams's *Sweet Bird of Youth* opened on Broadway in March 1959; eight months after MGM had already purchased the motion picture rights to the play. Richard Brooks was selected to direct and adapt the script to the screen. Paul Newman starred in the original production as Chance Wayne, an aspiring actor returning to his hometown with an aging movie star he hopes can help him get his break in Hollywood. While in town Chance tries to win back his one-time love, the daughter of a villainous political magnate.

Lucy, as well as several other major Hollywood actresses, was offered the leading lady role but turned it down, saying that, although the story was "beautifully written," she would be "embarrassed in that." Lucille felt she was all wrong to play the hard-drinking, hashish-smoking Alexandra Del Lago, otherwise known as Princess Kosmonopolis. While Lucy knew the movie would be Academy Award-worthy, she explained her reluctance, "I just don't feel that part at all."

With box office draw Paul Newman signed to recreate his Broadway role, it was decided that a major star was not necessary to play opposite him, so Geraldine Page, who originated the role of Alexandra onstage, ended up being cast in the film. Lucy later described Page's performance as "marvelous," and Page ended up with an Academy Award nomination for her efforts. In the nineteen-eighties, a television adaptation of the Williams play was planned. Reportedly, Lucy was again offered the role of Alexandra Del Lago and once more turned it down. Eventually Elizabeth Taylor agreed to play the part in the remake, which aired on October 1, 1989, several months after Lucy's passing.

The Great Sebastians

During the early nineteen-sixties, Lucille Ball was frequently mentioned in the press as the possible star of a film version of the play *The Great Sebastians*. The comedy/drama, written by Russel Crouse and Howard Lindsay, was about the efforts of a married couple, who have a phony mind-reading act, to get out of Communist Czechoslovakia. The husband-and-wife duo of Alfred Lunt and Lynn Fontanne had starred onstage in 1956 and then the following year in a television adaption as part of *Producers' Showcase*. Columbia purchased the film rights before the play even hit Broadway, initially thinking it might be turned into a vehicle for Judy Holliday and Ernie Kovacs.

By 1962, Columbia producer Arthur Hoffe decided to bring it to the screen with some major changes. Instead of nineteen-forties Czechoslovakia being the setting and the Communists being the enemies, Hoffe envisioned the film taking place in the Roaring Twenties Chicago with the Sebastians being the last people to see Judge Crater alive. (Hoffe's timeline was a bit off, as the headline-making disappearance of New York State Supreme Court Associate Justice Joseph Crater did not occur until August 1930.) Hoffe wanted Lucy and Bing Crosby to play Essie and Rudi Sebastian, while Danny Kaye was reportedly interested in co-starring with Lucy as well; the two having done a television special together at that time. Lucy and Bob Hope also chatted about doing the film as a follow-up to their fourth screen credit together, *Critic's Choice*. Around the same time, Ball was also in discussions to do *The Great Sebastians* opposite "The Great One," Jackie Gleason. None of these plans came to fruition. In the early seventies, Columbia attempted to star Sonny and Cher in a Mike Frankovich-helmed film version, which meant that the concept could not have veered any further away from the original casting of the Lunts. In any event, the film was cancelled and a movie adaptation of *The Great Sebastians* was never produced.

Cactus Flower

Lucy was sought after to co-star with Walter Matthau in 1969's *Cactus Flower*, based on a popular Broadway play by Abe Burrows that had starred Lauren Bacall and Barry Nelson. The plot involved an unmarried dentist, Julian Winston, telling his young girlfriend, Toni, he has a wife and children so he does not become too involved with her. When Toni attempts suicide, Julian decides he wants to marry the girl and asks his nurse to pose as his soon-to-be ex-wife. Lucy was offered the role of the nurse, Stephanie Dickinson, who is secretly in love with her boss. The character of Stephanie, who blossoms a great deal in the course of the film, is actually the "cactus flower" referred to in the title.

Although Lucy wanted to work with Walter Matthau, who was cast at the dentist, she had seen the play and decided that whoever they got to play the young lady would "take that picture and, if she didn't, there would be no picture." When Lucy told Mike Frankovich her reason for not doing the movie, the enraged producer instead hired Ingrid Bergman, who had not made a film in Hollywood in two decades, to play the role. At the time Lucy was approached to play Stephanie, Alexandra Hay was up for the role of Toni. Instead, *Laugh-In*'s Goldie Hawn won the part, and Lucy felt her initial hesitation was justified, as "she really walked away with it." In her later years, Lucy always put Goldie Hawn toward the top of the list of her favorite performers. Hawn won the Academy Award for Best Supporting Actress for her work in *Cactus Flower*.

Hello, Dolly!

In January 1964, the musical *Hello, Dolly!* opened on Broadway and became the biggest hit the Great White Way had ever seen. During the mid-sixties, Lucille Ball's name was constantly mentioned to play the role of widowed matchmaker Dolly Gallagher Levi on Broadway or on film. Lucy was reportedly one of the many actresses approached to star in the show after Ethel Merman, for whom composer Jerry Herman had specifically written the show, turned it down. Lucy did likewise. Instead, Carol Channing took the role and played it off and on over 5,000 times for more than thirty years. Lucy's protégé Carole Cook got to put her stamp on the role when she was chosen to headline the 1965 Australian touring production. Back on Broadway, Channing was succeeded by Ginger Rogers, Martha Raye, Betty Grable, Pearl Bailey, Phyllis Diller, and finally (and ironically), Ethel Merman. When the show closed in December 1970, it was the longest running musical in Broadway history.

Despite her initial rejection, producer David Merrick repeatedly offered Lucy the part of Dolly on Broadway and on tour, but with no success. Along with such actresses as Doris Day and Julie Andrews, Lucy was considered to be one of the front-runners for the film version, reportedly being Merrick's first choice although he would actually have no final say in the matter. However, in May 1967, it was announced that Barbra Streisand, then age twenty-five and in preproduction for her film debut in *Funny Girl*, had signed to star in *Hello, Dolly!* Carol Channing said, if she could not play the part, she was happier that Streisand, who was a completely different type than her, won the role rather than Lucy. Lucy did impersonate Carol Channing in her *Hello, Dolly!* guise in *The Lucy Show* episode "Lucy, the Undercover Agent" in 1966.

Plaza Suite

Neil Simon's *Plaza Suite* opened on Broadway in February 1968, the comedy consisting of three acts that confined the action to a suite in New York's fabled Plaza Hotel. The first act dealt with a long-married couple unhappily celebrating their wedding anniversary in the hotel where they spent their honeymoon; the second involved a Hollywood producer trying to seduce an old flame; and the third was about a couple trying to coax their daughter out of the bathroom after she locks herself in there minutes before her wedding. The "gimmick" was that the main couple in each of the three "playlets" was played by the same actors, with George C. Scott and Maureen Stapleton originating the roles. Paramount planned to make a film version and announced that the two original leads would reprise their roles in the first act, with Peter Sellers and Barbra Streisand appearing in the second, and Walter Matthau and Lucille Ball starring in the third. Instead, Matthau was cast as the man in all three segments, and Stapleton and Barbara Harris were signed to play opposite him in the first and second chapters, respectively. Lucy was still the first choice for the role of mother-of-the-bride Norma Hubley in the third section.

It was reported that Lucy wanted to play all three female roles, and when that was deemed impossible, she turned down the offer. Lucy, however, said, "I've been offered the script three different times and I keep turning it down. I think the play is awful." Lucy's refusal led to Lee Grant (who previously starred in a Los Angeles production of the play) being cast in sequence number three. Interestingly enough, another actress who reportedly actively pursued being in the film was Vivian Vance, who wanted the Maureen Stapleton role in the first act. This was yet another project that would have teamed Lucy with Walter Matthau that failed to materialize. Another film that was planned around the same time to star the two was a comedy entitled *The Contractor*. By the time they were ready to do the film, they felt that the script, although funny, was outdated. Lucy's brief cameo in *A Guide for the Married Man* marked the only motion picture collaboration between Ball and Matthau, although they shared no scenes together.

Diamond Jim Brady and Lillian Russell

One film project Lucy had her eye for a long time was a movie based on a three-year period during the forty-year relationship between extravagant millionaire "Diamond" Jim Brady and operatic singer and Broadway star Lillian Russell. Brady was known for his jewelry collection and voracious appetite for good food and high living, and he provided Russell with lavish gifts during their lengthy liaison in the late nineteenth and early twentieth century. During her time with Brady, Russell married four other men.

Jackie Gleason was the perfect choice to play Diamond Jim, and he was extremely interested in the property. *Lucy Show* writer Bob O'Brien was selected to write the screenplay, and filming was scheduled to commence in the first few months of 1969. Gleason, however, loathed traveling, and wanted to shoot the movie in Florida, where he did his television show. This was impossible since Lucy was doing her own series in Hollywood at the same time. When *The Jackie Gleason Show* was cancelled in 1970, it looked as if Gleason would no longer be tied to his Florida base and the movie could finally be filmed. However, as time passed it remained unproduced.

Giving a reason for the delay, Lucy stated that Gleason had lost a significant amount of weight and no longer looked "jolly" enough for the role.

In 1975, Lucy and Jackie did finally co-star together; not in their long-planned project, but in the television special *Three for Two*. At the time, the two were still discussing the possibility of the Brady-Russell film. Lucy was horrified by the explicit and adult nature of the films she saw during the early seventies and was determined to counterbalance this with family pictures. She felt that *Diamond Jim Brady and Lillian Russell*, like *Mame*, fit the bill. When describing the project, Lucy said, "it's opulent, it's nostalgic, it's a series of beautiful costumes and tunes and entrances—it's just a little puff of fun and nostalgia." According to Lucille Ball Productions vice president Howard Rayfiel, Bob O'Brien's script was nothing more than Lucy and Jackie making elaborate entrances in sumptuous clothing. There was no real depth to the characters. These shortcomings would never be dealt with regardless, because after a decade of talking about the movie, it never occurred.

Theater

Big Blonde

With her marriage to Desi beyond repair by 1959, Lucy began to seek out properties to make her Broadway debut once the hour-long Lucy-Desi shows had ceased production. Lucy met with producer/director Morton DaCosta (*The Music Man*) several times to discuss the possibility of her starring in a Broadway version of the Dorothy Parker short story "Big Blonde." DaCosta planned to direct the show as well as co-produce it with Kermit Bloomgarden, while the husband-and-wife team of Frances Goodrich and Albert Hackett, who had penned the screenplay for Lucy and Desi's 1954 comedy *The Long, Long Trailer*, were hired to adapt the story for the stage. The main character in the Parker tale deals with an unhappy marriage, alcoholism, relationships with many men, and a suicide attempt. Lucy decided that the subject matter was too depressing for her during that difficult period in her life and sought a more upbeat project. She found it with *Wildcat*. During the early performances of *Wildcat*, Lucy still considered the possibility of doing *Big Blonde* at a later date, but, having soured on Broadway following her difficulties with her maiden venture there, never pursued it further.

The Unsinkable Molly Brown

Another project Lucy was offered as a vehicle in which to make her Broadway debut was the musical *The Unsinkable Molly Brown*, composer Meredith Willson's first show after the tremendous success of *The Music Man*. Lucy was pleased with the first act of the script but not the second, and for that reason turned down the show. Molly Brown was a backwoods girl turned wealthy woman who tries to make her mark on society and ends up surviving the sinking of the *Titanic*. The character of Molly Brown in the musical's early scenes bore many similarities to the musical Lucy eventually did do, *Wildcat*. Both characters were tomboys. Both want to strike it rich; however, they have different reasons. Molly does it all for herself, hoping to become a member of high society. Wildy, on the other hand, wants nothing more than to help her physically lame sister, which Lucy found to be more sympathetic. Tammy Grimes took the part of Molly Brown and won a Tony Award, while Debbie Reynolds received an Oscar nomination for the 1964 film version. Lucy later sang one of the most famous songs from the show's score, "Belly Up to the Bar, Boys," on *The Carol Burnett Show* in 1967.

Pocketful of Miracles

After her run in *Wildcat*, Lucy always stated she had no interest in returning to the Broadway stage, but would instead consider doing short engagements in summer stock theaters throughout the country. However, in 1982, Lucy's close friend Lee Tannen suggested that Lucy play the role of Apple Annie in a proposed Broadway musical version of the 1961 film *Pocketful of Miracles*. Annie was an apple-selling beggar who turns to a gangster to help transform herself into a lady to impress her visiting daughter. The character originated in a 1929 Damon Runyon short story entitled "Madame La Gimp," which was adapted into the 1933 film *Lady for a Day*, directed by Frank Capra with May Robson receiving an Academy Award nomination for her portrayal of Apple Annie. Capra remade the film in 1961 under the title *Pocketful of Miracles* with Bette Davis as Annie. Lucy was no stranger to the Damon Runyon world, having starred in *The Big Street* based on the Runyon story "Little Pinks" and *Sorrowful Jones*, which had derived from his story "Little Miss Marker." The *Here's Lucy* episode "Dirty Gertie" was a spoof of the Apple Annie story, with Lucy posing as a drunken apple peddler who is associated with the underworld.

Tannen approached the two gentlemen who held the theatrical option on the property, Max Allentuck and Steve Martin, with the idea to star Lucy in the show. Lucy considered the offer, and composer Wally Harper and lyricist David Zippel were hired to write several songs with Lucy in mind.

Lucy liked the songs, but for a variety of reasons, the show never came to fruition. Gary Morton did not want to move to New York for an extended period of time and was not thrilled with the small amount of money his wife, who could still command a sizable salary on television, would make. Theatrical impresario James Nederlander, who also held the option on *Pocketful of Miracles*, remembered Lucy's ill health two decades earlier during *Wildcat* and was concerned that she would not be able to sustain the eight shows a week schedule. Furthermore, legal battles over who actually owned the property prevented the show from ever being mounted.

Radio

My Sister Eileen

In the nineteen-thirties, writer Ruth McKenney published a series of short stories in *The New Yorker* based on the colorful adventures she and her sister, Eileen, experienced as two Ohio girls settling in New York's Greenwich Village to pursue their dreams; Ruth to become a writer, Eileen an actress. The stories were republished as a popular book, *My Sister Eileen*, which was adapted by Joseph A. Fields and Jerome Chodorov into a 1940 Broadway play starring Shirley Booth as Ruth and Jo Ann Sayers as Eileen. Two years later, a film version, directed by Lucy's former flame Alexander Hall, with Fields and Chodorov adapting their work, starred Rosalind Russell as Ruth and Janet Blair in the title role. Both actresses later reprised their parts in an installment of radio's *Academy Award Theater*, on May 18, 1946. At the conclusion of the program, it was announced that Lucille Ball would star as Ruth in a *My Sister Eileen* radio series scripted by Arthur Kurlan. This show never materialized.

CBS instead created another radio show with a similar premise, *My Friend Irma*, with Marie Wilson in the lead. Kurlan sued CBS, claiming that rather than accept his idea for a potential *My Sister Eileen* radio program, the network had opted to produce something new they would not be obliged to pay him for. Kurlan further alleged the network had stolen his Lucy casting idea by attempting to engage the actress for their *Irma* series. CBS settled with Kurlan in 1953. *My Sister Eileen* later spawned a 1953 Broadway musical named *Wonderful Town*, with a Tony-winning Rosalind Russell recreating her screen role, and an unrelated movie musical of *My Sister Eileen* with Betty Garrett in 1955. Although a radio series was never produced, with or without Ball, a television sitcom starring Elaine Stritch ran on CBS from 1960 to 1961. Lucille Ball never got a chance to play Ruth Sherwood, but

Lucie Arnaz played the role in several Los Angeles productions of *Wonderful Town* in the nineteen-nineties.

Our Miss Brooks

Another radio project proposed to Lucille Ball was the situation comedy *Our Miss Brooks.* Shirley Booth was the original choice to play wisecracking schoolteacher Connie Brooks, and an audition show was produced. The producers decided they did not care for Booth's rather serious interpretation of the role, however, and so Lucy was approached, only to have her decline the offer. CBS then moved over to Eve Arden, who had many similarities to Lucille, who described the two of them as "drop gag girls," actresses whose part consisted of making a sarcastic comment and then exiting the scene. (The two previously appeared together on screen in *Stage Door* and *Having Wonderful Time.*) Arden initially passed on the role as well, but CBS head William S. Paley finally persuaded her to take the part.

Three ladies on the verge of stardom (left to right: Ann Miller, Eve Arden, and Lucy) share the screen with star Ginger Rogers (right) in one of the top RKO releases of the decade, *Stage Door* (1937).

Our Miss Brooks began as a summer replacement radio series on June 13, 1948; Lucy's own radio show, *My Favorite Husband*, premiered one month later on July 23. Gale Gordon, who was cast in *Our Miss Brooks* as Principal Osgood Conklin, soon found himself doing double duty when he took the role of bank president Rudolph Atterbury on *My Favorite Husband*. In 1952, *Our Miss Brooks* began its run on television, becoming the second show filmed by Desilu. Eve Arden won an Emmy for her performance in 1954, beating out Lucille Ball. Both the radio and television incarnations of *Our Miss Brooks* ceased production in 1956, the same year a theatrical film with Arden and the series regulars was released by Warner Bros.

Television

Lucy Goes to Broadway

Shortly after filing for divorce from Desi, Lucy moved to New York to start work on her Broadway debut. Lucy had been looking for a project to do on the New York stage for over a year and finally decided on a musical comedy, *Wildcat*. Desilu financed the entire production, and in return, the company was given 36 percent of the net profits, the rights to the cast recording, and the television rights. A television special was planned to feature Lucy preparing for her Broadway debut and would showcase some highlights from the musical. Madelyn Martin and Bob Carroll Jr. wrote a story outline for the project. Desi and Claudio Guzman were alternately announced to direct the special. Vivian Vance and Bob Hope would appear, as would William Frawley. Despite the disintegration of their marriage, Desi was also to have been featured in the special alongside his children with Lucy. One scene would have involved Lucy being given singing lessons by either Ethel Merman or Leonard Bernstein. Lucy reportedly wanted her real-life voice teacher, Kay Thompson, to be a part of the special as well.

Filming was originally scheduled for April 1961, but the starting date was repeatedly pushed back. It was announced in May that the special would air on December 3 of that year; that month would mark the one-year anniversary of when the show made its Broadway debut. Because of the toll it took on Lucy's health, *Wildcat* was forced to close on June 3, 1961. The television project, however, was not abandoned. Desilu, the sole investor in *Wildcat*, thought they could recoup some of their losses by going ahead with the planned special, although it could not be filmed right away because of Lucy's fragile state of health. In late 1961, the project was still a priority, but changes had to be made. Lucy had married Gary Morton, so Desi's on-camera participation had been dropped to avoid a confusing and awkward situation. William Frawley, who had been co-starring on *My Three Sons* since the Lucy-Desi shows ceased production, was also no longer part of the planning stage. However, according to Lucille, Vivian was still onboard, as was Bob Hope. *Lucy Goes to Broadway* was still considered a possibility as late as 1963, as Lucy's contract with CBS included a television special to be produced that season. Ultimately, Lucy did *The Lucille Ball Comedy Hour* with Bob Hope instead. *Lucy Goes to Broadway* was never produced, certainly one of the most frustrating of all the "what if" properties in Lucille Ball's career, as it would have afforded future generations some idea of what *Wildcat* had looked like onstage.

24

"It Took Years of Practice to Get My Voice Where It Is Today."

Lucy Sings . . . and Lucy "Sings"

A lthough she was by no means a trained singer, nor someone who entered show business with the belief that she would make her mark on the hit parade, Lucille Ball clearly loved performing in the musical genre and did so on many occasions. (Indeed, there were professional singers who probably didn't sing as frequently on television as Lucy did.)

When it came to actual singing, it was usually on a case-by-case basis whether Lucy would be allowed to do her own vocals or be dubbed by someone else. In films it was usually the latter, which could often be very disorienting, as the familiar Lucy voice would be heard speaking the dialogue leading up to the song, only to have a technically perfect sound come from her mouth that all too obviously belonged to someone else.

Once Lucille took television by storm and became "Lucy" to millions, it was harder to try to pull off the charade of professional singers passing themselves off as the star, although there were still occasions when this was done, even on her own series. More often than not Lucy's off-key vocalizing was used for some good-natured ribbing in the plotlines, especially on *I Love Lucy*, where the three other principals were, after all, a nightclub entertainer and two former vaudevillians. Nevertheless, by the time Lucy started her third show, *Here's Lucy*, she was more determined than ever to throw in a musical sequence or two, not just because she herself enjoyed doing them, but to showcase both her children's talents as well.

Here then is a list of the songs that Lucy (or Lucy's "ghost," as dubbers were often referred) was seen singing on screen, stage, and television, with as many of those who actually wrote the material credited as was possible to determine.

Lucy gets downright groovy with two members of a faux rock 'n' roll group called the DDT's in this off-camera shot from the episode "Lucy in the Music World" from season four of *The Lucy Show*.

Movies

Roman Scandals (Goldwyn, 1933)

Lucille's very first motion picture assignment, *Roman Scandals,* was a musical, although she was principally around to be "atmospheric background." However, in one of Eddie Cantor's numbers (which Cantor performed in blackface), "Keep Young and Beautiful," several of the Goldwyn Girls get to pipe in on a few lines, one of them being Lucy ("Keep young and beautiful, if you wanna be loved"), as she and another blonde-haired chorine are having their legs rubbed by attending bathhouse slaves. She later shows up in the number posed with another beauty to sing the lines "Shake well to slender thighs, roll your eyes around for exercise." Lucille is also visible in the film's first musical number, "Build a Little Home," which takes place during the present day, before the storyline jumps back to ancient Rome. Whether or not Lucille's real voice was used remains unclear.

• "Build a Little Home"; "Keep Young and Beautiful" (Music: Harry Warren; Lyrics: Al Dubin)

Kid Millions (Goldwyn, 1934)

In her second Goldwyn assignment starring Eddie Cantor, Lucy was once again a chorus girl. She is featured prominently in the "I Want to Be a Minstrel Man" production number led by thirteen-year-old Harold Nicholas. Ball and three other Goldwyn Girls receive a close-up on the line "and sings a song about his sugar candy." Lucille gives the camera a big wink while delivering this. The lyrics to the song were written by Harold Adamson, who two decades later would write the words to the theme song for *I Love Lucy*.

The Goldwyn Girls also serve as backup in "Mandy," which features Eddie Cantor, Ethel Merman, Ann Sothern, George Murphy, and the Nicholas Brothers. The girls pass around tambourines in synchronization. Lucy also appears in the three-strip Technicolor finale set in an ice cream factory. She is seen carrying a giant chocolate bar.

• "I Want to Be a Minstrel Man" (Music: Burton Lane; Lyrics: Harold Adamson); "Mandy" (Irving Berlin)

Old Man Rythm (RKO, 1935)

Lucille makes several brief appearances as a coed in the campus musical *Old Man Rhythm*. All of the college kids, including Lucy, sing "There's Nothing Like a College Education" on their way back to school via train. Lucy can later be seen sitting around a camp fire joining in the song "Boys Will Be Boys." These numbers also feature (more prominently) Lucy's pal Betty Grable. One of the movie's co-stars, Johnny Mercer, wrote the lyrics to the score.

• "There's Nothing Like a College Education" ; "Boys Will Be Boys" (Music: Lewis E. Gensler; Lyrics: Johnny Mercer)

Dance, Girl, Dance (RKO, 1940)

Playing a dancer who ends up bumping and grinding in burlesque in the drama/musical *Dance, Girl, Dance*, Lucy's character went under two unforgettable names, "Bubbles" and "Tiger Lily White." She was given three numbers (in "Beer Barrel Polka" she sang equally with the other girls in the chorus line) in which to strut her stuff and was actually allowed to use her own voice in this instance, since flawless vocalizing was not what her wisecracking, cynical character was all about.

• "Beer Barrel Polka" (Music: Jaromir Vejvoda; English Lyrics: Lew Brown); "Mother, What Do I Do Now?" (Chet Forrest and Bob Wright); "Jitterbug Bite" (Music: Edward Ward; Lyrics: Chet Forrest and Bob Wright)

Although it later developed a cult following as an early "feminist picture," *Dance, Girl, Dance* was poorly received upon its initial release. *New York Times* critic Bosley Crowther wrote, "… it is Miss Ball who brings an occasional zest into the film."

Too Many Girls (RKO, 1940)

The popular 1939 Richard Rodgers & Lorenz Hart stage musical *Too Many Girls* came to the screen within a year of its New York debut, with several cast members retained from the Broadway original including: Eddie Bracken, Hal LeRoy, chorus boy Van Johnson, and most significantly, where Lucille was concerned, Desi Arnaz. (Lucy's role of "Connie Casey" had been played in New York by Marcy Wescott.) Seven numbers were kept from the stage, including the biggest hit of the batch, "I Didn't Know What Time It Was," which became one of Lucy's songs, as dubbed by Trudy Erwin. A new tune Rodgers & Hart provided for the score, "You're Nearer," was also performed by Lucy (as the four male principals, including Desi looked on, swooning). She later reprised the song in a montage featuring Frances Langford, Ann Miller, Libby Bennett, and Desi. During the rousing fight song "Look Out!," Lucy can also be seen mouthing the lyrics with the company, spending most of the scene standing next to Van Johnson. Hugh Martin (who later wrote the music for *Best Foot Forward*) served as vocal arranger on the film, his first movie. He was the one who made the decision to dub Lucy's voice, a decision he said he later regretted.

• "You're Nearer"; "I Didn't Know What Time It Was"; "Look Out!"

A Guy, a Girl, and a Gob (RKO, 1941)

Lucy played stenographer Dot Duncan (the "girl") in *A Girl, a Guy, and a Gob*. Dot comes from an eccentric family and has a crazy navy boyfriend nicknamed "Coffee Cup" (the "gob," George Murphy). The family's unconventional behavior is evident when Dot's new boss, Stephen Herrick (the "guy," Edmond O'Brien), drops by the house and the family celebrates the birth of upstairs neighbor Mrs. Leibowitz's ninth baby. Dot leads the family in singing "Happy Birthday to You," which turns into a conga. It's fitting that Lucille is seen doing the then-enormously popular dance, since, at the time, she was dating the man who popularized it in the United States.

• "Happy Birthday to You"   (Mildred and Patty Hill)

The Big Street (RKO, 1942)

The Big Street, RKO's adaptation of the Damon Runyon story "Little Pinks" (produced by Runyon himself), required Lucille to portray a self-centered nightclub singer, so it only made sense that she be seen singing at least one song, even if Martha Mears had to do the actual, off-screen warbling.

Unlike most sequences featuring a different voice emanating from Ball's mouth, this one was made easier to accept because it began in extreme long shot and was occasionally interrupted by dialogue. Later, after she has been injured, Lucy is heard humming the tune (whether this was Mears's voice as well is uncertain) and then reprises it at a Miami club, backed up by Ozzie Nelson and His Orchestra. This moment is also interrupted by cutaway scenes and dialogue. Mears's most famous "ghost" credit was heard that same year (released, in fact, the same month as *The Big Street*, in August 1942), joining Bing Crosby on "White Christmas" in *Holiday Inn*.

• "Who Knows?" (Music: Harry Revel; Lyrics: Mort Greene)

Lucy, as ailing nightclub singer Gloria Lyons, is given one last dance by her ardent admirer, "Little Pinks" (Henry Fonda), in *The Big Street* (1942), Lucy's favorite of her movie roles.

Seven Days Leave (RKO, 1942)

In what would be her last RKO film for seven years, Lucy played heiress Terry Havalok-Allen in the comedy *Seven Days Leave*. One scene featured Terry and her escort, Private Johnny Grant (Victor Mature), attending the radio game show *Truth or Consequences*. Host Ralph Edwards selects Terry and Johnny as contestants, and Terry must quickly sing "Pop Goes the Weasel" while Johnny blows up a balloon.

• "Pop Goes the Weasel" (traditional)

Du Barry Was a Lady (MGM, 1943)

For her MGM debut in the studio's Technicolor production of the Cole Porter musical *Du Barry Was a Lady*, Lucy was handed a role that had been played in the 1939 Broadway original by her friend Ethel Merman. As was often the case in this era, most of the stage score was jettisoned to make way for new compositions so that the studio could profit from the royalties. Of the three Porter compositions retained, Lucy got to participate in one of them, certainly the most enduring of the score, "Friendship," sharing the moment with Red Skelton, Gene Kelly, and Virginia O'Brien. (Lucy would get to reprise the song on *I Love Lucy* in the memorable "Lucy and Ethel Buy the Same Dress" episode.) For this tune Ball was allowed to use her own voice, which made the contrast rather startling to audiences after earlier in the film hearing Lucy's *The Big Street* "ghost," Martha Mears, coming out of her mouth during the title song. Another new number, "Madam, I Like Your Crepe Suzettes," found Lucille cavorting and leaping on a trampoline-like bed with top-billed Red Skelton, but she did not sing any of the lyrics.

One of the few other aspects of the Broadway show that made it to Hollywood was cast member Charles Walters, called on here to stage the dances. By the end of the decade he had made the transition to full-fledged director (starting with *Good News* in 1947) and would end his career working four times with Lucy, helming two *Here's Lucy* episodes, "Lucy's House Guest, Harry" (1/25/71) and "Lucy and Aladdin's Lamp" (2/1/71), and directing the specials *Three for Two (A Lucille Ball Special Starring Lucille Ball and Jackie Gleason)* (1975) and *What Now, Catherine Curtis?* (1976).

• "Du Barry Was a Lady" (Music: Burton Lane; Lyrics: Ralph Freed); "Friendship" (Cole Porter)

Best Foot Forward (MGM, 1943)

The plotline of the 1941 Broadway musical *Best Foot Forward* involved a cadet inviting a movie star to be his date at the prom, so when it came time to transfer the show to film, MGM figured why not have a genuine star simply play herself? Whereas Rosemary Lane had portrayed the fictional "Gale Joy" onstage, for the movie Lucille was cast as "Lucille Ball," jumping in when Lana Turner's pregnancy made her unavailable to do the picture. Recruited from the original stage cast were Tommy Dix, June Allyson, Jack Jordan, and Kenny Bowers (all of them switching roles for the movie); Nancy Walker; and, in the ensemble, Gil Stratton (who had one of the leads on Broadway) and future film director Stanley Donen. Six songs were retained from Broadway, while Hugh Martin provided one new one, "Wish I May." Two others that had been intended for the stage but were dropped before opening night made their debuts here, "Alive and Kicking" (by Ralph Blane), and "You're Lucky" (Martin). The latter was given to Lucy to "sing," as she supposedly played the piano for Tommy Dix, with Gloria Grafton providing her vocal dubbing. Grafton had introduced Rodgers & Hart's "Little Girl Blue" in *Jumbo* on Broadway. She would "ghost" for Lucy a second time in *Meet the People*.

• "You're Lucky" (Hugh Martin)

Meet the People (MGM, 1944)

The third of Lucy's MGM assignments to come from a Broadway musical, *Meet the People* had actually begun life on the West Coast as a revue presented by the Los Angeles Assistance League Players. It was this particular production that earned one of its cast members, Virginia O'Brien, a contract with MGM. When the show moved to New York in December 1940, O'Brien was not on hand as she was already working at Metro. The Broadway cast included Jack Albertson, Nanette Fabray (billed then as Nanette Fabares), Jack Gilford, Peggy Ryan, and Doodles Weaver. The 1944 film version did bring back O'Brien, although her part was subordinate to Lucy's role as a theater star who decides to do her bit for the war effort by becoming a welder in a Delaware shipyard.

A sole tune from the show was retained for the film, the title number, which was performed several times in the picture, first by top-billed Dick Powell, then later reprised by Lucy during a Broadway rehearsal (backed up by chorus girls), using her same "ghost" from *Best Foot Forward*, Gloria Grafton, who also had an on-screen bit as a secretary. After Powell did his rendition of "In Times Like These," Lucille "dueted" with him on a follow-up reprise and then was joined by him, O'Brien, and the rest of the ensemble for the finale, "It's Smart to Be People," where Lucy (using her real voice) talked-sang the introductory verse.

Although Powell got Ball for the wrap-up, it was a supporting player, June Allyson, who captured his heart in real life, becoming his wife the following year. Coincidentally, "I Like to Recognize the Tune," the song Allyson performed in the picture, with Virginia O'Brien, Vaughn Monroe, and Viggie Talent, was a Richard Rodgers/Lorenz Hart number from *Too Many Girls* that did *not* make the transition from stage to screen when the 1940 movie (starring Lucy) was made. *Meet the People*'s producer (his only such credit) was lyricist E. Y. "Yip" Harburg, who was responsible for five of the songs.

• "Meet the People" (Music: Jay Gorney; Lyrics: Henry Myers); "In Times Like These" (Music: Sammy Fain; Lyrics: Ralph Freed); "It's Smart to Be People" (Music: Burton Lane; Lyrics: E. Y. Harburg)

Easy to Wed (MGM, 1946)

MGM's semi-musical remake of *Libeled Lady* found Lucy in the role previously played by the late Jean Harlow and brought her some of her best reviews to date. Lucy was given one song to sing as part of a stage show, backed up by chorus signers. She was dubbed yet again, this time by Virginia Rees, who had done similar chores for Lana Turner in *Ziegfeld Girl* and Angela Lansbury in *The Harvey Girls*.

• "Continental Polka" (Music: Johnny Green; Lyrics: Ralph Blane)

Sorrowful Jones (Paramount, 1949)

For her first of four films with Bob Hope, Lucy took on the role of nightclub singer Gladys O'Neill in this remake of *Little Miss Marker* (1934). The late Dorothy Dell had done the equivalent part in the earlier version (based on the 1932 Damon Runyon story), although the character had been named "Bangles Carson." Playing a singer, Lucy was naturally given a song, "Having a Wonderful Wish (Time You Were Here)," with Annette Warren providing the dubbing. (The sheet music for the song contradicts the movie's opening credits, calling it "*Havin'* a Wonderful Wish.") In the movie, Lucy runs through part of the song at a rehearsal in Bruce Cabot's nightclub, prompting Hope to insult her efforts, "You're off key, like always." She later gets to do a fuller version of it, with an audience present. Hope continues to criticize her singing throughout the picture, which one supposes can be taken more as a put-down of Annette Warren's vocal prowess than Lucille Ball's. Warren's most notable credit was singing for Ava Gardner in *Show Boat*, against the star's wishes.

• "Having a Wonderful Wish (Time You Were Here)" (Music: Jay Livingston; Lyrics: Ray Evans)

Fancy Pants (Paramount, 1950)

When Lucy (billed as *Miss* Lucille Ball) returned for her second Hope comedy the following year, she was now given two songs, the title number, and an ensemble piece, "Home Cookin,'" performed with her leading man, Jack Kirkwood, Joseph Vitale, and Joe Wong.

This very loose remake of *Ruggles of Red Gap* found her cast as wealthy "Agatha Floud," but since she ended up in love with the title protagonist, she was sharing aspects of *two* characters from the original story, pretentious "Effie Floud" and the widowed "Mrs. Judson." The 1915 Harry Leon Wilson novel had been filmed three times previously, so Lucy was taking over the "parts" originally done by Lillian Drew and Virginia Valli (1918), Louise Dresser and Fritzi Ridgeway (1923), and Mary Boland and ZaSu Pitts (1935). As with *Sorrowful Jones*, her vocals were again dubbed by Annette Warren.

This is one of the more curious examples of dubbing Lucy, as her own less-than-perfect vocal intonations were better suited to the rough hewn character of Agatha Floud than Ms. Warren's. Luckily, when she and Hope reteamed to do a shortened version of the script for *Lux Radio Theatre* (September 10, 1951), both songs were retained and Lucy did her own singing.

• "(Hey) Fancy Pants," "Home Cookin'" (Music: Jay Livingston; Lyrics: Ray Evans)

The Long, Long Trailer (MGM, 1954)

In their first motion picture outing since the tremendous success of *I Love Lucy*, Lucy and Desi chose, not surprisingly, to do a comedy, *The Long, Long Trailer*, but there was room for a musical number. For a scene showing the contented couple as they take to the road in the title vehicle, a standard from 1926, "Breezin' Along with the Breeze," was chosen for them to sing. Lucy's own voice was used.

Bob Hope and Lucy sing about the joys of "Home Cookin'" in this scene from their second film together, *Fancy Pants* (1950). Glimpsed in the background is Joe Wong as the Floud's family cook.

• "Breezin' Along with the Breeze" (Haven Gillespie, Seymour Simonds, and Richard Whiting)

Yours, Mine and Ours (UA, 1968)

In Lucy's most financially successful picture, she played a widow with eight children who married a widower with ten of his own. On Christmas morning, the family of twenty sings "Silent Night," moments after mother Helen (Lucille) gets a phone call informing her that there will be a new addition to the family.

• "Silent Night" (Music: Franz Xaver Gruber; Lyrics: Joseph Mohr; English translation: John Freeman Young)

Mame (Warner Bros., 1974)

For what would turn out to be her final theatrical feature, Lucy was chosen for the lead in Warner Bros.' motion picture adaptation of the hit Broadway musical *Mame*. The role had been created by Angela Lansbury, while in the original nonmusical version of Patrick Dennis's novel, *Auntie Mame* (1955), it had been played both on Broadway (1956) and on screen (1958) by Rosalind Russell. Joining Lucille for the 1974 movie were two original cast members from New York: Beatrice Arthur and Jane Connell (Audrey Christie, who played the role of Doris Upson in the film, had been one of Arthur's successors playing Vera Charles on Broadway).

Unlike so many of the earlier Broadway-to-Hollywood adaptations in which Lucille appeared, this one would retain almost the entire score, with only one number (which would have been sung by Lucy), "That's How Young I Feel," being dropped in the transition. (This makes *Mame*, by a wide margin, the most faithful adaptation to its stage source among Lucy's five musicals in the stage-to-screen category.) Lucy was joined by a backup chorus on "It's Today" and "Open a New Window;" by Connell, George Chiang, and Kirby Furlong in "We Need a Little Christmas;" Furlong in "My Best Girl;" and Arthur for "Bosom Buddies." All of the songs were composed by Jerry Herman.

• "It's Today"; "Open a New Window"; "My Best Girl"; "We Need a Little Christmas"; "Bosom Buddies"; "If He Walked into My Life"

Lucy in her first musical number, "It's Today!," in *Mame*. Lucy wanted her singing to be dubbed, but Warner Bros. wanted Lucy's own voice on the soundtrack. Rumors circulated before the film's release that Lucy's voice was dubbed by Lisa Kirk, but what movie audiences heard was all Lucy.

Stage

Wildcat (Alvin Theater; December 16, 1960–June 3, 1961)

When Lucy made it known that she wanted to star on Broadway, rather than take the safer route and do a comedy, she settled upon an original musical. This was not simply a case of an established star taking a backseat while the more experienced cast members did the real work, as the bulk of the thirteen numbers included Lucille's participation. The show's most enduring tune, "Hey, Look Me Over," performed by her with Paula Stewart, meant that Lucy could lay claim to having introduced a song that actually became a bona fide standard. It also became her "signature" number of sorts as she would reprise it on various variety shows and on her own series over the years. In addition to this showstopper, she also dueted with Don Tomkins on "What Takes My Fancy;" Keith Andes on "You're a Liar!" and "Give a Little Whistle" (joined by the company); and Edith King on "Tippy, Tippy Toes;" while Al Lanti, Swen Swenson, and the ensemble backed her up on "El Sombrero."

As with any new musical, many songs were written for the show, but cut before performances began. Among the those intended for Lucy's character, "Wildy Jackson," were "Thinkability," where she was to have been joined by the Countess and Janie; "Ain't It Bad?," which would have been sung by Wildy and Sookie; and "I Got My Man" and "Muy Simpatico," for Wildy and the chorus.

The eight performances-a-week demands of Broadway, however, took their toll on the star. The title song and "That's What I Want for Janie" were both cut from the score shortly after opening night in order to lighten the load. In February, Lucy became ill with a viral infection and was clearly suffering from exhaustion. Two weeks of performances were cancelled to allow her to recuperate in Miami. At the Saturday, April 22 evening performance, Lucy fainted onstage during the "Tippy, Tippy Toes" number. Edith King, who portrayed Countess Emily O'Brien and performed the number with her, tried to catch Lucy and, in the process, broke her own wrist. The star's understudy had already gone home for the night, so Shelah Hackett, the assistant choreographer, who had recently married co-star Keith Andes (she would later marry the show's choreographer Michael Kidd), was drafted into completing the performance as Wildy Jackson. One month later, Lucy collapsed onstage during the May 24 matinee. She had missed several performances the week before due to a throat infection. Her understudy, Betty Jane Watson, finished the show and went on for the evening performance, but Lucy never did return to Wildcat.

Performances ceased on June 3, but audiences were assured that the show would reopen on August 7 after Lucille had recuperated. Only a few days after this optimistic announcement, it was reported that because the local musicians' union demanded that the *Wildcat* musicians be paid during the hiatus, the producers would not be able to oblige and therefore were forced to close the show permanently. The musical ended up running 172 performances.

• "Hey, Look Me Over," "Wildcat," "That's What I Want for Janie," "What Takes My Fancy," "You're a Liar!," "Give a Little Whistle," "Tippy, Tippy Toes" (Music: Cy Coleman; Lyrics: Carolyn Leigh)

A publicity shot of Lucy, as "Wildy" Jackson, in her only Broadway credit, the Cy Coleman/Carolyn Leigh musical, *Wildcat* (1960).

Television: The Series

I Love Lucy

"The Diet" (10/29/51) The third aired episode is the first in the series in which Lucy sings, joining Desi onstage for the duet "Cuban Pete," playing "Sally Sweet," in a reprise of their nightclub routine. The song had already been done by Desi in his 1946 movie of the same name, although it had been written ten years earlier and recorded by several other performers in the interim.

• "Cuban Pete" (Jose Norman)

"The Quiz Show" (11/12/51) As a contestant on a radio show called *Females Are Fabulous*, Lucy sings "My Bonnie Lies over the Ocean," prompting a shot in the kisser from a seltzer bottle every time she says something "wet." The unctuous host, Freddie Filmore, is played by Frank Nelson in the first of eleven appearances on *I Love Lucy*.

• "My Bonnie Lies over the Ocean" (traditional Scottish folk song)

"Drafted" (12/24/1951) When "Drafted" was originally broadcast on CBS on Christmas Eve 1951, it included a Christmas-themed tag scene featuring the cast dressed as Santa Claus. The foursome sing "Jingle Bells" and soon notice that there is now a fifth Santa Claus among them. This tag would be repeated for the next two seasons at the end of whichever episode happened to air closest to Christmas ("Lucy's Show Biz Swan Song" and "Ricky's Old Girlfriend").

• "Jingle Bells" (James Lord Pierpont)

"The Benefit" (01/07/52) When Ricky, Ethel, and Fred sing "Shine on, Harvest Moon," Lucy joins in, but her off-key singing puts an end to the merriment. Ethel wants Ricky to star in a benefit for her club, but Lucy demands that she be a part of it too. Ricky selects "Auf Wiederseh'n, Sweetheart" for the two to sing, but Lucy only ends up with one line "Auf." When Lucy refuses to perform the song, Ricky must choose a new one.

In the finale, Lucy deliberately upstages Ricky's efforts to upstage *her* during their duet on "We'll Build a Bungalow," a sequence based on a bit they had done in their nightclub act, albeit with the song "Zing! Went the Strings of My Heart." Eighteen years later, Desi recreated the routine with daughter Lucie on the February 4, 1970 episode of *The Kraft Music Hall*.

• "Shine on, Harvest Moon" (Nora Bayes and Jack Norworth); "Auf Wiederseh'n, Sweetheart" (Eberhard Storch; English lyrics: John Turner and Geoffrey Parsons); "We'll Build a Bungalow" (Betty Bryant Mayhams and Norris the Troubadour)

"The Amateur Hour" (01/14/52) Lucy teams up with her rambunctious babysitting charges, played by Sammy Ogg and David Stollery, to perform in an amateur contest.

• "Ragtime Cowboy Joe" (Music: Lewis F. Muir and Maurice Abrahams; Lyrics: Grant Clarke)

"Breaking the Lease" (02/11/1952) The Ricardos and Mertzes stay up to all hours of the morning singing songs around the piano, including "I Want a Girl Just Like the Girl That Married Dear Old Dad." In one of the rare compliments about her singing voice to be sent in her direction, Ricky tells Lucy, "You even sounded good." At 2:00 a.m., they dedicate their next number, "Sweet Sue," to their wonderful friendship with the Mertzes. That friendship almost comes to an end a few minutes later, when Lucy and Ricky attempt to reprise "Sweet Sue" when the Mertzes are trying to sleep.

• "I Want a Girl Just Like the Girl That Married Dear Old Dad" (Music: Harry Von Tilzer; Lyrics: William Dillon); "Sweet Sue" (Music: Victor Young; Lyrics: Will J. Harris)

"The Operetta" (10/13/52) Eager to participate in a benefit for the Wednesday Afternoon Fine Arts League, Lucy believes she's going to be holding center stage, but, anticipating disaster, the other cast members make sure they drown her out whenever possible. (As Ricky tells Ethel, "Confidentially, when she sings, she hits a bad note once in a while," to which an incredulous Ethel replies, "*Once* in a while?!?!") The operetta numbers were written especially for this episode, with lyrics by Madelyn Pugh and Bob Carroll Jr., and music by Eliot Daniel.

• "I Am the Queen of the Gypsies," "We Are the Troops of the King"

"Ricky Loses His Voice" (12/01/52) Because Ricky is laid up in bed, Lucy stages the new show at the Tropicana. Naturally, she casts herself and the Mertzes. As part of a nineteen-twenties revue she dresses in a flapper outfit, strums the ukulele, and sings "Has Anybody Seen My Gal?"

• "Has Anybody Seen My Gal?" (Music: Ray Henderson; Lyrics: Sam M. Lewis and Joseph Widow Young)

"Inferiority Complex" (02/02/53) Her confidence having been built up by Ricky, Fred, and Ethel, Lucy now assumes they want her to sing and starts belting out a few lines of the Marilyn Miller hit "Who?" from the Broadway show *Sunny*.

• "Who?" (Music: Jerome Kern; Lyrics: Otto Harbach and Oscar Hammerstein II)

"Lucy's Show Biz Swan Song" (12/22/52) In one of the series' many episodes that bring attention to Lucy's lack of vocal skills, she and Ethel audition for the Tropicana's Gay Nineties revue with a tune she would return to over the years, "By the Light of the Silvery Moon." Lucy later attempts to get into Ricky's barbershop quartet by singing "Goodnight, Ladies," to which Ricky replies, "Goodnight!" After massacring the barbershop standard "Sweet Adeline" while rehearsing at home, she joins her cast mates for the same song when she sneaks her way into the show, despite Ricky's objections. They manage to temporarily silence her screechy vocals with their shaving brushes.

• "By the Light of the Silvery Moon" (Music: Gus Edwards; Lyrics: Edward Madden); "Goodnight, Ladies" (Edwin Pearce Christy); "(You're the Flower of My Heart) Sweet Adeline" (Music: Henry W. Armstrong; Lyrics: Richard H. Gerard)

"Lucy Hires an English Tutor" (12/29/52) When Lucy promises her English tutor (Hans Conried) a gig at the Tropicana, he tries to get the Ricardos and the Mertzes to participate in his ultra-cutesy ditty, "Tippy Tippy Toe." Lucy is given the refrains "Dilly Dilly Day" and "Hey Nonny Nonny." Despite the resemblance in titles, this had no connection to the song Lucille would later sing in *Wildcat*, "Tippy, Tippy Toes." Hans Conried had played the maitre d' at the nightclub where Lucille "sang" in *The Big Street*.

"No Children Allowed" (4/20/1953) Lucy attempts to get Little Ricky to sleep by singing "Rock-a-Bye Baby." Her off-key rendition is so painful that Ricky intercedes and tries to get the baby to sleep himself.

"The Indian Show" (05/04/53) Once again having schemed her way into the Tropicana show, Lucy joins Ricky on the duet "By the Waters of Minnetonka," with a few ad-libbed lyrics thrown in.

• "By the Waters of Minnetonka" (Thurlow Lieurance)

"Lucy's Last Birthday" (05/11/53) Thinking she's been forsaken, Lucy joins a lonely hearts group called "The Friends of the Friendless" and leads them in their self-named theme song as they march into the Tropicana.

"Lucy and Ethel Buy the Same Dress" (10/19/53) This time the Wednesday Afternoon Fine Arts League gets a chance to broadcast their revue on television. Lucy and Ethel end up destroying each other's matching outfits while singing a song Lucille had already performed on screen in *Du Barry Was a Lady*.

• "Friendship" (Cole Porter)

"The French Revue" (11/16/53) After Ricky says that he is going to do a French revue at the Tropicana, he, Lucy, Fred, Ethel, and a French waiter (Alberto Morin) all separately don straw hats and sing a line from "Louise," imitating Maurice Chevalier, who had first introduced the song in his talking picture debut, *Innocents of Paris*.

• "Louise" (Music: Richard A. Whiting; Lyrics: Leo Robin)

"Lucy Has Her Eyes Examined" (12/14/53) Hoping to impress a producer Ricky has brought to the house, Lucy, Ethel, and Fred give him their rendition of *Annie Get Your Gun*'s biggest hit, "There's No Business like Show Business."

• "There's No Business like Show Business" (Irving Berlin)

"Home Movies" (03/01/54) As part of a film they hope will serve as an audition for a television pilot, Lucy and Ethel sing in cowboy garb (including a moustache for Lucy!) a song Bing Crosby had introduced in his 1936 film *Rhythm on the Range*.

• "I'm an Old Cowhand from the Rio Grande" (Johnny Mercer)

"Ricky's Hawaiian Vacation" (03/22/54) Desperate to join Ricky on his band's trip to Hawaii, Lucy, Ethel, and Fred audition with some appropriate Hawaiian tunes, and a snatch from an inappropriate one as well.

• "King Kamehameha" (Johnny Noble and Ted Fio Rito); "Hawaiian War Chant (Kaua I Ka Huahua'i)" (Music: Prince Leleiohoku; Revised music and lyrics: Johnny Noble and Ralph Freed); La Cucaracha" (traditional Spanish folk corrido)

"Tennessee Ernie Hangs On" (05/10/54) In order to get houseguest Ernie Ford back to Bent Fork, Tennessee, the Ricardos and the Mertzes appear on *Millikan's Chicken Mash Hour* with him to raise the money for his trip. The gang sings "Y'all Come."

• "Y'all Come" (Arlie Duff)

"Mr. and Mrs. TV Show" (11/1/54) Having signed up for a husband-and-wife television show, Ricky, who previously rejected Lucy's suggestion that they do one, must now con his wife into doing the series. While doing house-work, Lucy sings "Sweet Sue" in her usual off-key way, and Ricky claims to be so impressed by her singing that he says he will demand that she co-star on the television show. Later, during the show, "Breakfast with Ricky and Lucy," the Ricardos and the Mertzes sing the "Phipps Department Store" jingle for their sponsor.

• "Sweet Sue" (Music: Victor Young; Lyrics: Will J. Harris)

(This episode was originally scheduled to be broadcast on November 1, 1954, but was preempted by a message from the Republican Party. The epi-sode was aired by some affiliates on that night, but rerun by CBS on April 11, 1955 for markets that did not get to see the initial airing.)

"Mertz and Kurtz" (10/11/54) Fred reunites with his old vaudeville partner Barney Kurtz (Charles Winninger). This gives the cast a chance to perform in a beach-set revue, with Lucy joined by Fred, Ethel, and Barney for "Peach on the Beach" (from the show *No, No, Nanette*) and "By the Beautiful Sea," while Ricky joins them for "On the Boardwalk" (from the movie *Three Little Girls in Blue*).

• "Peach on the Beach" (Music: Vincent Youmans; Lyrics: Otto Harbach); "By the Beautiful Sea" (Music: Harry Carroll; Lyrics: Harold R. Atteridge);

"On the Boardwalk (in Atlantic City)" (Music: Josef Myrow; Lyrics: Mack Gordon)

"Ricky's Contract" (12/6/54) Ricky is on edge waiting to receive a phone call about his recent screen test, so Lucy and the Mertzes attempt to get his mind off it by engaging in "a good old community sing." The trio tries to get Ricky to join in on "When You're Smiling." All three forget the lyric that follows, "But when you're cryin'." It is "you bring on the rain."

• "When You're Smiling" (Larry Shay, Mark Fisher, and Joe Goodwin)

"California, Here We Come" (01/10/55) In one of the most famous (and exhilarating) moments in *I Love Lucy* history, the cast sings the Sunshine State's unofficial theme song as they start off for Hollywood. The tune was first introduced by Al Jolson in the 1921 Broadway musical *Bombo*.

• "California, Here I Come" (Buddy DeSylva and Joseph Mayer)

"Tennessee Bound" (01/24/55) Lucy is locked up in a Tennessee jail for being sassy after Ricky gets pulled over for speeding. Ernie Ford has an idea to get Lucy out, supplying the gang with nail files so they can saw through the bars. In order to cover the filing noise, the group sings "Old MacDonald Had a Farm."

"Bull Fight Dance" (03/28/55) Wanting to be part of a benefit Ricky is doing for the Heart Fund, Lucy belts out a few lines of "Let Me Go, Lover!" while mimicking the woman who made the tune famous in 1954, Joan Weber. Later, while trying to duet with Ricky on a counterpart medley of "Old Folks at Home (Swanee River)" and "Humoresque," Lucy keeps segueing into the wrong song.

• "Let Me Go, Lover!"(Jenny Lou Carson and Al Hill); Old Folks at Home" (Stephen Foster); "Humoresque" (Music: Antonin Dvořák)

"The Dancing Star" (05/02/55) Set on convincing Caroline Appleby that she genuinely knows some movie stars, Lucy talks Van Johnson into letting her duet on "How About You?" in his nightclub act at the Beverly Palms Hotel. Lucy basically tosses in "ad libs" while Johnson does the actual singing of the song. In 1940, Johnson made his movie debut as a chorus boy in one of Lucille's films, *Too Many Girls*, and then, six years down the line, was billed *above* her in the comedy *Easy to Wed*. In 1968 he was a supporting player in her film *Yours, Mine and Ours* and guest starred on the episode "Guess Who Owes Lucy $23.50" on *Here's Lucy*.

• "How About You?" (Music: Burton Lane; Lyrics: Ralph Freed)

"Lucy and the Dummy" (10/17/55) This time Lucy is so set on performing at an MGM party that when Ricky chooses to go on a fishing trip instead, she substitutes a dummy with a model of his head, made by the studio for "trick shots." When demonstrating her dance for Fred and Ethel, she uses Ricky's record of "I Get Ideas" and then sings the song herself at the actual studio gathering.

• "(When We Are Dancing) I Get Ideas" (Music: Julio Caesar Sanders; Lyrics: Dorcas Cochran)

"Lucy Goes to the Rodeo" (11/28/55) Another "old crony" of Fred's (played by Dub Taylor) helps the Mertzes and Lucy rehearse some songs for a western show at Fred's lodge, with Lucy wailing through "Home on the Range." Told she'd do better keeping her mouth shut and jingling bells, she rehearses while singing some lines from "Down by the Old Mill Stream." During the actual presentation of the number (now done for Ricky's rodeo-themed show), only the bells are heard, as shaken by Lucy, Ricky, Fred, and Ethel.

• "Home on the Range" (Music: Daniel E. Kelley; Lyrics: Brewster M. Higley); "Down by the Old Mill Stream" (Tell Taylor)

"Second Honeymoon" (01/23/56) En route to Europe, Lucy sings the opening line of "Sailing, Sailing" (as in "over the bounding main") in her stateroom.

• "Sailing, Sailing" (Godfrey Marks)

"Lucy Goes to Scotland" (02/20/56) Definitely not your typical *I Love Lucy* episode, most of the half hour consists of Lucy's dream visit to the land of Kildoonan, set to new songs written by Larry Orenstein, who also played Mayor Ferguson in this episode. Lucy and the supporting company sing "A McGillicuddy Is Here," while Lucy and Ricky perform "I'm in Love with a Dragon's Dinner" and "The Dragon Waltz," the latter with the company. The two-headed dragon in question is played by Ethel and Fred.

• "A McGillicuddy Is Here," "I'm In Love with a Dragon's Dinner," "The Dragon Waltz"

"Lucy Meets Bob Hope" (10/01/56) Bob Hope agrees to perform at Ricky's nightclub, where he is joined by the Ricardos for a newly written song, "Nobody Loves the Ump," all of them dressed in the appropriate baseball attire.

• "Nobody Loves the Ump" (Music: Eliot Daniel. Lyrics: Larry Orenstein)

"Christmas Show" (12/24/1956) While Christmas decorating, Ricky begins to sing "Jingle Bells" in Spanish, and Ethel joins in in English. Lucy attempts to join the duet, but when her off-key voice is heard, all singing immediately ceases. Lucy says, "I don't know what's happened to my voice lately. I don't sing well anymore." Incredulous, Ricky replies, "Lately?!" and Ethel follows with, "Anymore?!" Ricky and Ethel recall the time Lucy loused up their barbershop quartet, which leads into a clip from "Lucy's Show Biz Swan Song."

• "Jingle Bells" (James Lord Pierpont)

The Ricardos (including Keith Thibodeaux, left, as 'Little Ricky') and the Mertzes perform "Man Smart, (Woman Smarter)" for the Westport Historical Society in the *I Love Lucy* episode "Ragtime Band."

"Ragtime Band" (03/18/57) At a benefit, Ricky sings the bulk of "Man Smart (Woman Smarter)," while Little Ricky plays bongos, and Lucy, Ethel, and Fred back him up on calypso instruments. Although Lucy gets to sing a verse, most of her participation (like Ethel and Fred) consists of the refrain "uhh! smarter!" Norman Span, who wrote the song, first recorded it in 1936 under the name King Radio, but it was Harry Belafonte's 1956 hit record that inspired this sequence.

• "Man Smart (Woman Smarter)" (Norman Span)

The Lucille Ball-Desi Arnaz Show

"Lucy Takes a Cruise to Havana" (11/06/57) "Your voice," Ricky remarks in horror, "it's terrible!," as Lucy joins him and Cesar Romero for a rendition of "Cielito Lindo" (the "ay, ay, ay, ay" song). Also, Ricky serenades her at a club with a song written for the episode, "That Means I Love You," which leads to a drumming "duel" between them. Later, the smitten Lucy, remembering the moment, sings a single line from the tune.

• "Cielito Lindo" (Quirino Mendoza y Cortés); "That Means I Love You" (Arthur Hamilton)

"Lucy Goes to Alaska" (02/09/59) Lucille joins her former *Du Barry Was a Lady* co-star Red Skelton for an appearance on his television show, with Red in costume as one of his most famous characters, Freddy the Freeloader. Lucy is dressed in similar hobo garb. The two sing a new song, "Poor Ev'rybody Else." (Coincidentally, Lucie Arnaz would later sing a song called "Poor Everybody Else" in the Cy Coleman-Dorothy Fields musical *Seesaw*.) Although Skelton spent nineteen seasons (1951–70) hosting his own variety show on CBS, Lucille never actually guest starred on his series.

• "Poor Ev'rybody Else" (Arthur Hamilton)

"Lucy's Summer Vacation" (06/08/59) Having drilled holes in Ricky's rowboat, Lucy must then join him in the leaky vehicle, along with Ida Lupino and Howard Duff. As they begin their journey the quartet breaks into a rendition of "Row, Row, Row Your Boat."

• "Row, Row, Row Your Boat" (traditional)

"Milton Berle Hides Out at The Ricardos" (09/25/59) As part of the Westport PTA's "Western Frolics," Lucy shows up dressed as an Indian to join guest star Milton Berle, as well as Ricky (in a horse costume), Ethel (as a schoolmarm), Fred (bartender), and Little Ricky (the sheriff) for the original song "Them There Days." Choreographer Jack Baker was actually in the horse costume, as Desi Arnaz was busy directing the episode.

"Them There Days" (Arthur Hamilton)

The Lucy Show

"Lucy Buys a Sheep" (10/29/62) With a bleating sheep named Clementine, it is only natural that Lucy would rock it to sleep by singing "My Darling Clementine," with some new lyrics thrown in for good measure, including "you're my lamb-y, I'm your mammy." Later, when she and Viv try to track down their lamb within a pen of other sheep, they reprise the tune.

• "My Darling Clementine" (Percy Montrose)

"Lucy Puts Up a TV Antenna" (11/26/62) After the TV set goes on the fritz, Lucy and Viv try to get the kids to join them in singing songs around the piano. Unfortunately, their out-of-date repertoire can't compare with "Papa-Oom-Mow-Mow." As a defeated Lucy says, "So much for *Sing along with Mom.*"

• "There's a Long, Long Trail" (Music: Zo Elliott; Lyrics: Stoddard King); "Wait 'Till the Sun Shines, Nellie" (Music: Harry Von Tilzer; Lyrics: Andrew B. Sterling); "Down by the Old Mill Stream" (Tell Taylor)

"Together for Christmas" (12/24/1962) Lucy and Viv, celebrating Christmas together for the first time, clash over the differences in their holiday traditions. Lucy wants a green tree, while Viv prefers a white one. They end up with two Christmas trees in the house. While trimming their trees, Lucy and Viv sing "Jingle Bells." Lucy ends up singing the song through tears after Viv steps on her beloved Santa decoration, which Viv then nicknames "Kris Krinkled."

• "Jingle Bells" (James Lord Pierpont)

"Lucy and Viv Become Tycoons" (02/11/63) When Lucy and Viv go into business to sell the latter's homemade caramel popcorn, they come up with their own "Crazy Crunch" jingle, to the tune of "Old McDonald Had a Farm" (i.e., "ee-i-ee-i-oh" becomes "c-r-a-z-y").

"Lucy's Barbershop Quartet" (02/04/63) This episode gives Lucy several opportunities to pipe in on some tunes. First, explaining to Chris who Wee Bonnie Baker was, she sings a few lines of that lady's hit, "Oh, Johnny, Oh, Johnny, Oh!" Later, hoping to be the replacement harmonist for Viv's barbershop quartet, The Four Alarms, she tries keeping up with the other three ladies (one of whom is Lucille's occasional dubber, Carole Cook) on "By the Light of the Silvery Moon," only to be told, not that she can't sing, as was the norm in the *I Love Lucy* days, but that she sings too soft. Lucy offers up another song to demonstrate her vocal abilities, "Be My Little Baby Bumblebee," only to have her fellow songbirds (or rather "bees") realize they've been shortchanged, given the unenviable task of mostly backing up Lucy with the repeated phrase "buzz around, buzz around." "Silvery Moon" returns for the big show at the finale, but not before Hans Conried is called upon to do a reprise of sorts of the role of the English tutor (here as a vocal coach) that he played on *I Love Lucy* more than a decade earlier in "Lucy Hires an English Tutor" (12/29/52).

• "Oh Johnny, Oh Johnny, Oh!" (Music: Abe Olman; Lyrics: Ed Rose); "Down by the Old Mill Stream" (Tell Taylor); "Be My Little Baby Bumblebee" (Music: Henry L. Marshall; Lyrics: Stanley Murphy); "By the Light of the Silvery Moon" (Music: Gus Edwards; Lyrics: Edward Madden)

"Lucy Is a Soda Jerk" (03/04/63) Filling in for Chris at her soda shop job at Wilbur's Ice Cream Shop (which includes Lucie Arnaz, in her acting debut, among its employees), Lucy and Viv demonstrate their knowledge of their inventory by composing a little jingle of the various flavors, to the tune of "The ABC" song.

"Lucy Is a Chaperone" (04/08/63) Serving as chaperones for Chris and her teenage friends at their beach house rental, Lucy (wearing a black wig) and Viv try awkwardly to fit in by singing the Four Seasons' recent number one hit "Big Girls Don't Cry." Among those appalled by their efforts are *A Hole in the Head* co-star Eddie Hodges; *My Three Sons*' Don Grady (who refers to Lucy as "that overgrown Gidget"); Patty Gerrity, who had starred in the syndicated Desilu series *This is Alice*; *The Children Hour*'s Karen Balkin; and eleven-and-a-half-year-old Lucie Arnaz.

• "Big Girls Don't Cry" (Bob Crewe and Bob Gaudio)

"Lucy Plays Cleopatra" (09/30/63) Hans Conried returns as the same voice teacher he played in "Lucy's Barbershop Quartet." This time he squirms as Lucy and Viv (joined by Mary Wickes, Mary Jane Croft, Hazel Pierce, and Renita Reachi, all in tights and top hats) rehearse their welcoming song, "Hello! Hello! Hello!" to the tune of "Ta-ra-ra Boom-de-ay."

• "Hello! Hello! Hello!" (Variation on "Ta-ra-ra Boom-de-ay," copyrighted by Henry J. Sayers; Music: unknown)

"Lucy and the Safecracker" (10/28/63) After Lucy accidently locks Mr. Mooney in the bank's vault, she persuades meek candy salesman Mr. Bundy (Jay Novello), a former safecracker, to attempt to get him out. Bundy will only do so if a jingle he wrote advertising his store is sung on television. Lucy and Viv sing the jingle for Grandma's Dandy Candy, to the tune of "I've Been Working on the Railroad," on the local Danfield news, much to the chagrin of the news reporter on the scene.

"Lucy Teaches Ethel Merman How to Sing" (02/03/64) Thinking Ethel Merman is a look-alike named Agnes Schmidlapp, Lucy figures she can pass her off as the real thing at her son's Boy Scout revue, but first decides to give her singing lessons. (It's only fitting that Hans Conried's character of Dr. Gitterman gets a mention, as Lucy and Merman perform nearly the same routine as the one done between Ball and Conried in "Lucy's Barbershop Quartet.") According to Lucy, in order to vocalize like The Merm, "all you have to do is sing loud and sound nasal," which she demonstrates by pinching her nose and singing a bit of the hit Ethel introduced in *Girl Crazy*, "I Got Rhythm." (Lucy later lip-synchs to a Merman recording on the song.)

• "I Got Rhythm" (Music: George Gershwin; Lyrics: Ira Gershwin)

"Ethel Merman and the Boy Scout Show" (02/10/64) In this follow-up episode, Lucy participates in the Boy Scout show, joining Viv, Mr. Mooney, and Ethel Merman in one of Ethel's signature tunes, "There's No Business Like Show Business." Playing a flapper, Lucy also duets with Mooney on a few lines of "I Love You!"

• "There's No Business Like Show Business" (Irving Berlin); "I Love You!" (Music: Harry Archer; Lyrics: Harlan Thompson); "Am I Blue?" (Harry Akst and Grant Clarke)

"Lucy Gets Her Maid" (11/30/64) Lucy and Viv attempt to become members of the prestigious Danfield Arts Society. Lucy is jealous that all the members have maids, so she takes a servant job in order to hire a maid for herself. When Lucy and Viv end up serving at a party for the members of the club, Lucy comes up with the idea for them to disguise themselves, donning a different costume based on the nationality of the course they serve. They also sing a bit of a song each time they serve. Lucy sings "Frère Jacques" while serving the French bread, "In a Little Spanish Town" while pouring the wine, and "Jingle Bells" when she enters with the Baked Alaska.

• "Frère Jacques" (traditional); "In a Little Spanish Town" (Music: Mabel Wayne; Lyrics: Sam M. Lewis and Joe Young); "Jingle Bells" (James Lord Pierpont)

"Lucy Meets Danny Kaye"(12/28/64) Several weeks after Lucille Ball appeared on *The Danny Kaye Show*, Lucy Carmichael showed up as an extra on Danny's variety series. Being Lucy, however, she isn't content with filling the background, so she is invited to partner her host on "All by Myself," joining him in some dance moves and then singing the final line.

• "All by Myself" (Irving Berlin)

"Lucy, the Disc Jockey" (04/12/65) In the last official *The Lucy Show* episode to feature Vivian Vance as co-star, Lucy wins a contest and becomes a DJ for a day. When the control board overheats, Lucy hoses the entire room down with foam, causing her to make her own on-air song request, singing the famous first line of "White Christmas." (This moment was featured—silently—in the montage that would open the show starting the following season.)

• "White Christmas" (Irving Berlin)

"Lucy and the Countess" (02/01/1965) Lucy's visiting friend, Rosie Harrigan (Ann Sothern), now the widowed Countess Framboise, is invited by Mooney to a wine tasting party given by the Danfield Wine Society. Rosie goes on the condition that Lucy is invited too. The Countess is actually flat broke, and she and Lucy expect to be fed. With no food in sight, the two drink more and more to quiet their hunger pangs. They end up drunkenly singing "Jeannie with the Light Brown Hair" and "I Love Paris" before sliding under the table.

• "Jeannie with the Light Brown Hair" (Stephen Foster); "I Love Paris" (Cole Porter)

"Lucy and Arthur Godfrey" (03/08/65) This time it's TV personality Arthur Godfrey, whom Lucy enlists to appear in a show. With an accent thicker than Spanish moss, Lucy plays Godfrey's daughter, a virtuous Southern belle. Rather than use traditional tunes, as was the norm in most episodes of this sort, for this occasion Max Showalter (music) and Bob Leeds and Peter Walker (lyrics) provide new songs. "Danfield" is performed by Lucy with Viv, Mooney, Godfrey, Showalter, and the rest of the cast.

• "Hanky Panky," "Dixie Lucy," "Danfield"

"Lucy in the Music World" (09/27/65) *The Lucy Show* goes groovy when Lucy gets a job working for the pop music show *Wing Ding*, at one point twisting and shouting to her rendition of the show's theme song. In order to help her neighbor Mel Tinker (Mel Tormé) get a gig on the show, the two of them pass themselves off as a pair of folk rockers called the Tearducts (Lucy is done up with a long red wig, boots and black stockings), and bring down the house with Mel's composition, "His Surfboard Came Back by Itself."

• "We're Gonna Have a Wing Ding" (Music and Lyrics: Mel Tormé; Additional Lyrics: Bob O'Brien); "His Surfboard Came Back by Itself" (Music: Mel Tormé; Additional lyrics by Bob O'Brien)

"Lucy and the Undercover Agent" (11/22/65) Pretending to be spies, Lucy and the Countess (Ann Sothern) decide to sneak into an army base by the most creative means possible. Finding out Carol Channing will be performing there, Lucy dons a costume reminiscent of the one Channing wore in the title number of "Hello, Dolly!" to imitate her, singing "Hello, Solly!" to the front gate security guard.

• "Hello, Dolly!" (Jerry Herman)

"Lucy, the Gun Moll" (03/14/66) Being mistaken for a gun moll named "Rusty Martin" gives Lucille a chance to play a dual role. Taken by a pair of lawmen (Robert Stack and Steve London spoofing their characters from *The Untouchables*) to the Domino Club so that she can successfully impersonate her twin, Lucy watches Rusty sing the song that had made another

Martin, Mary, famous, "My Heart Belongs to Daddy." Lucy Carmichael later reprises the song in the guise of Rusty.

• "My Heart Belongs to Daddy" (Cole Porter)

"Lucy and George Burns" (09/12/66) Lucy gets to play Gracie Allen, more or less, when she is invited by George Burns to partner him in his new act. Following some snappy George and Gracie-like banter, the two duet on "Some of These Days" ("you're gonna miss your red-haired mama"), with some soft shoe thrown in for good measure.

• "Some of These Days" (Shelton Brooks)

"Lucy and Carol in Palm Springs" (11/07/66) In a direct follow-up episode to the one that introduced Carol Burnett as Lucy's temporary roommate, Carol Bradford, the two ladies team up to do a dandy rendition of "Lazy River" while singing with the Vagabonds at a Palm Springs Resort.

• "Lazy River" (Hoagy Carmichael and Sidney Arodin)

"Lucy, the Babysitter" (01/16/67) An unsuspecting Lucy takes a job baby-sitting, only to discover that her charges are three rambunctious monkeys. She attempts to quiet them down with renditions of the traditional favorites "Ring Around the Rosie" and, of course, "Rock-a-Bye Baby." (Assessing her version of the latter, one critical chimp blows Lucy a raspberry.) Her co-stars were a legit act, the Marquis Chimps, famous for many variety show appearances, including several on *The Ed Sullivan Show*.

"Main Street U.S.A." (01/23/67) Lucy and Mooney visit the tiny town of Bancroft, where Lucy joins the crusade to stop a highway from ruining the tranquility of Main Street. A neighbor from Lucy's building in L.A., Mel Tinker (Mel Tormé, who had played this role in "Lucy in the Music World"), is there (as one of the town's native sons) to provide a song for the protestors (including Mel, John Bubbles, and even, eventually, Mooney) to sing, with Lucy leading the marchers as their baton-wielding majorette. The song is repeated in the second-part follow-up episode as well.

• "Main Street, U.S.A." (Mel Tormé)

"Lucy Puts Main Street on the Map" (1/30/67) Lucy and the residents of Bancroft reprise the song "Main Street U.SA." twice in this follow-up episode. Lucy also briefly joins in for Mel's new song "In Our Hometown."

• "Main Street, U.S.A.," "In Our Hometown" (Mel Tormé)

"Lucy and the French Movie Star" (9/25/67) When Lucy goes to work with French cinema idol Jacques DuPre (Jacques Bergerac), he serves her champagne, which quickly takes effect on Lucy. She tipsily sings "Darling, Je Vous Aime Beaucoup."

• "Darling, Je Vous Aime Beaucoup" (Anna Sosenko)

"Lucy, the Starmaker" (10/02/1967) Lucy tries to get bank president Mr. Cheever's talented nephew, Tommy (Frankie Avalon), discovered by movie producer Nelson Penrose (Lew Parker). Lucy gets Penrose to the bank on a pretext and then has Tommy impress him with his singing. Lucy and the other bank employees back Tommy up with "When the Feeling Hits You."

• "When the Feeling Hits You" (Bobby Doyle)

"Lucy Gets Her Diploma" (10/9/67) After the bank passes a new policy stating that all employees must have a high school diploma, Lucy reveals that she never graduated because she got the measles the week before finals her senior year (none of this follows the second-season episode "Lucy's College Reunion"). Now Lucy must go back to school to keep her job. In biology class, while giving an explanation of skeletal structures, Lucy breaks into a rendition of "Dry Bones." The entire class (which includes Lucie Arnaz, her future husband Phil Vandervort, and Robert Pine) joins in, along with the teacher (Olive Dunbar). At the graduation ceremony, Lucy gives a speech in which she compares her generation to the new generation of graduates. To show that her generation had strange-sounding music too, Lucy sings snatches of "The Hut-Sut Song," "Mairzy Doats," and "Three Little Fishies." (For the Lucy character, Lucille is once again shaving more than a few years off her real age, as these songs were all popular between 1939 and 1943, by which time she would have reached the age of thirty-two.)

• "Dry Bones" (James Weldon Johnson); "The Hut-Sut Song" (Leo V. Killion, Ted McMichael, and Jack Owens); "Mairzy Doats" (Milton Drake, Al Hoffman, and Jerry Livingston); "Three Little Fishies" (Josephine Judson Carringer; Adapted by Saxie Dowell)

"Lucy and Carol Burnett, Part 1" (12/11/67) As a break from the bank, Lucy is temporarily employed as an airline stewardess, along with Carol Tilford (Carol Burnett, who, the previous season, had shown up as an entirely different character). When the in-flight movie is ruined, Lucy and Carol decide to put on a show. Besides Carol singing variations on "That's Entertainment," the two redheads do several duets (the passengers join in for "When the Saints go Marching In").

• "Let Me Entertain You" (Music: Jule Styne; Lyrics: Stephen Sondheim); "Give Me That Old Soft Shoe (Soft Shoe Song)" (Roy Jordan and Sid Bass); "You Gotta Start Off Each Day with a Song" (Jimmy Durante); "When the Saints Go Marching In" (traditional)

"Lucy And Carol Burnett, Part 2" (12/18/67) In part two of Lucy's stopover in the world of Globe World Airlines, she and Carol participate in their stewardess graduation show. Handing out diplomas are Buddy Rogers and Richard Arlen, the stars of the first movie to win the Academy Award for Best Picture, *Wings* (which, according to the script, "opened the doors for the growth of aviation"). The two men join Lucy, Carol, and Mr. Mooney on "How 'Ya Gonna Keep 'Em Down on the Farm," while the entire cast wraps it up with Lucy's signature tune, "Hey, Look Me Over" (revised lyrics) and "The U.S. Air Force Song" ("off we go into the wild blue yonder"). Keeping up to date with the year in movies, Lucy and Carol don flapper outfits to dance with the chorus girls to an instrumental version of "Thoroughly Modern Millie."

• "Salute to Aviation" (Music: Marl Young; Lyrics: Bob O'Brien) including "Over There" (George M. Cohan); "How 'Ya Gonna Keep 'Em Down on the Farm (After They've Seen Paree?)" (Music: Walter Donaldson; Lyrics: Joe Young and Sam M. Lewis); "Chattanooga Choo-Choo" (Music: Harry Warren; New Lyrics: Bob O'Brien); "Hey, Look Me Over"(Music: Cy Coleman; New Lyrics: Bob O'Brien; Original lyrics: Carolyn Leigh); "The U.S. Air Force Song" (Robert MacArthur Crawford)

"Lucy and Phil Harris" (02/05/68) Making a nuisance of herself, Lucy enthusiastically tosses off some suggested tunes for lounge singer Phil Stanley (Phil Harris) to perform, drowning him out with her unmistakable vocals as he tries to sing "But Beautiful" and "Is It True What They Say About Dixie?" Later, as she encourages him to come up with some words for the melody he has written ("But I Love You"), she improvs some lyrics of her own. Needless to say, none of them show up in the final composition.

• "But Beautiful" (Music: Jimmy Van Heusen; Lyrics: Johnny Burke); "Night and Day" (Cole Porter); "In Other Words" (Bart Howard); "Is It True What They Say About Dixie" (Irving Caesar, Sammy Lerner, Gerald Marks); "But I Loved You" (Gordon Jenkins)

"Lucy Helps Ken Berry" (02/19/68) Trying to help out Ken Jones's (Kenny Berry) dancing school, Lucy gets him a gig on *Ralph Story's LA*, where the two of them, backed up by members of the Local Trucking Union, perform a rendition of "Lulu's Back in Town," appropriately renamed "Lucy's Back in Town." (This song had been introduced by Lucy's *Meet the People* co-star, Dick Powell, in the 1935 film *Broadway Gondolier*.) The finale finds Lucy, Ken, and the Truckers joined by Mr. Mooney and Ken's partner, Sid (Sidney Miller), for "Pick Yourself Up."

• "Lulu's Back in Town" (Music: Harry Warren; Original Lyrics: Al Dubin; Special Lyrics: Bob O'Brien); "Pick Yourself Up" (Music: Jerome Kern; Lyrics: Dorothy Fields)

"Lucy and the 'Boss of the Year' Award" (03/11/68) The very last episode of *The Lucy Show* finds Lucy trying to get Mr. Mooney a promotion so he'll be shipped elsewhere. Her efforts to come up with a letter of commendation in song produce variations on "Swanee" ("Mooney, how I love ya, how I love ya . . .") and "Moonlight and Roses" ("Mooney and Roses"). At the Boss of the Year Award Annual Dinner Dance (emceed and conducted by Gary Morton), Lucy sings her versions of "Seventy-Six Trombones," backed by a quartet, and Bob Hope's theme song, "Thanks for the Memory," both with all new lyrics.

• "Swanee" (Music: George Gershwin; Lyrics: Irving Caesar); "Moonlight and Roses" (Adantino in D-Flat) (Music: Edwin Lamare; Original Lyrics: Neil Moret); "Seventy-Six Trombones" (Meredith Willson); "Thanks for the Memory" (Music: Ralph Rainger; Original Lyrics: Leo Robin)

Here's Lucy

"Mod, Mod Lucy" (9/23/68) For the series premiere, Lucy makes it known that *Here's Lucy* is going to keep up with the mod, mod changes in pop culture by presenting a pretty "groovy" dance number (choreographed by Jack Baker) for Lucy and the ensemble. Pinch-hitting for Kim, who has lost her voice, as the singer for Craig's band, Lucy first does a funky update on the

1924 standard "All Alone" (with uncredited vocal assist), followed by some exuberant gyrating to an instrumental version of Petula Clark's hit "I Know a Place."

• "All Alone" (Irving Berlin)

"Lucy and Miss Shelley Winters" (10/14/68) Having some fun with Harry's tape recorder, Lucy sings a few bars of "The Man I Love," until her boss walks in on her, prompting him to dismiss her efforts with the topical jibe, "Thank you, Tiny Tim!"

• "The Man I Love" (Music: George Gershwin; Lyrics: Ira Gershwin)

"Lucy and the Ex-Con" (1/13/69) After Lucy secures a janitorial job for former safecracker Rocky Barnett (Wally Cox) by leaving out his prison record on his resume, he ends up being the prime suspect in a robbery at the company where Lucy managed to get him hired. Rocky believes he knows who actually committed the crime, so he and Lucy try to prove his innocence by dressing up as a pair of little old society ladies, "Abigail Throckmorton" (Lucy) and "Lydia Perkins . . . of the Pasadena Perkins" (Rocky), and investigating the owner of a dive bar. Lucy pretends to down a few Mai Tais and feigns drunkenness in order to gain access to a backroom. During the scene she sings an inebriated version of the 1937 Oscar winner "Sweet Leilani."

• "Sweet Leilani" (Harry Owens)

"Lucy and Carol Burnett" (1/27/69) Lucy and her family manage to talk Carol Burnett into appearing at a fund-raiser to build a gym for Kim and Craig's school, Angeles High. Lucy sits this one out vocally, as all of her singing is done by Carole Cook. (Presciently, this includes a song, "Lullaby of Broadway," that would be Cook's big number in the 1980 Broadway musical *42nd Street.*) The entire company participates in a parody of "Yes, We Have No Bananas" called "Yes, We Have No Gymnasium," although Lucy has little more than a quick line. Her duets on "Lullaby," "Saint Louis," and "Sheboygan" are with Burnett, with whom she once again performs with ease. The finale finds them and the company doing new lyrics to "Fit as a Fiddle." One nod to an old Lucy movie, *Best Foot Forward*, has the student band playing an instrumental of that show's biggest hit, "Buckle down Winsocki," but Lucy is not featured in the scene. When Burnett shows up again on *Here's Lucy*, she is no longer herself but playing a character, "Carol Krausmeyer."

Lucy and Carol Burnett sing "Mention My Name in Sheboygan" to raise money for a new school gym in the *Here's Lucy* episode "Lucy and Carol Burnett."

• "Yes, We Got No Gymnasium" (Frank Silver and Irving Cohn; with revised lyrics); "Lullaby of Broadway" (Music: Harry Warren; Lyrics: Al Dubin); "You Came a Long Way from Saint Louis" (John Benson Brooks and Bob Russell); "Mention My Name in Sheboygan" (Bob Hilliard, Dick Sanford, and Sammy Mysels)

"Lucy and Tennessee Ernie's Fun Farm" (3/10/69) As for their participation in Ernie Epperson's Fun Farm musical extravaganza, the Carter family dons hillbilly duds to join Ernie in "Heavenly Music" (Lucille is dubbed), previously performed with an equal degree of "sophistication" by Gene Kelly and Phil Silvers in *Summer Stock*. For the finale, the gang sings "Y'all Come," which Ernie and Lucy had already sung on *I Love Lucy*. This marked Ford's fifth and final guest appearance on one of Lucy's series.

• "Heavenly Music" (Saul Chaplin); "Y'all Come" (Arlie Duff)

Lucy and Lucie Arnaz give their impersonation of The Andrews Sisters, alongside the real deal, Patty Andrews (center), in the finale of the episode "Lucy and the Andrews Sisters," from the second season of *Here's Lucy*.

"Lucy and the Andrews Sisters" (10/27/69) With Patty Andrews as her guest, Lucy solos on a few lines of the Andrew Sisters' novelty hit "Three Little Fishies (Itty Bitty Poo)" by Josephine Judson Carringer. For the big finale (emceed by Gary Morton), Lucy, Kim, and Patty (done up in familiar Andrews Sisters' 40's outfits and hairstyles) reprise that song among a medley of further hits by the nineteen-forties trio: "Bei Mir Bist Du Schoen" (Music: Jacob Jacobs; English Lyrics: Sammy Cahn, Saul Chaplin); "South

America, Take it Away" (Harold Rome); "Don't Fence Me In" (Cole Porter, Robert Fletcher), with Craig joining them as Bing Crosby; "Pistol Packin' Mama" (Al Dexter), also with Craig; "Don't Sit Under the Apple Tree" (Lew Brown, Sam Stept, Charlie Tobias); "Boogie Woogie Bugle Boy of Company B" (Music: Hugh Prince; Lyrics: Don Raye); "Pennsylvania Polka" (Lester Lee, Zeke Manners); and "Beer Barrel Polka" (Music: Jaromir Vejvoda; English Lyrics: Lew Brown), joined by Craig and the audience.

"Lucy and Johnny Carson" (12/1/69) While attending a taping of *The Tonight Show Starring Johnny Carson*, Lucy manages to "stump the band" with a song she says was a novelty number her father sang to her as a child, "Snoops the Lawyer." (When Carson can't get her to stop singing, the defeated host rests on the arm of a chair occupied by Lucille's mother, DeDe.) The song did, in fact, make its debut when Lucille Ball was a child, in 1921, when it was written by Bert Kalmar and Harry Ruby.

"Lucy and the Generation Gap" (12/8/69) Appearing in a high school musical about the generation gap written by Kim and Craig, Lucy joins Harry and her offspring on "We're Just Bugged about Parents" (to the tune of Noble Sissle and Eubie Blake's "I'm Just Wild About Harry"), set in Roman times; "Parents/Children" (to the tune of Harry Dacre's "Daisy Bell") in the Gay Nineties (with a clearly dubbed Lucy); and a variation on Charles Strouse and Lee Adams's *Bye Bye Birdie* hit "Kids," as reinterpreted in the Space Age (with Lucy in something resembling a robot costume).

"Lucy and Liberace" (1/5/70) Sneaking into Liberace's house to replace a candelabra they think Craig has stolen, Lucy and Harry (Gale Gordon) end up auditioning for the pianist's TV special with a piece they "did together at the Kiwanis Capers," "By the Light of the Silvery Moon" (Edward Madden, Gus Edwards). They then join Liberace, Lucie, and Desi Jr. for Liberace's theme song, "I'll Be Seeing You" (Music: Sammy Fain; Lyrics: Irving Kahal).

"Lucy the Crusader" (10/12/70) Lucy and Kim sing "Happy Birthday" to Craig on his eighteenth birthday.

• "Happy Birthday to You" (Mildred and Patty Hill)

"Lucy Goes Hawaiian, Part Two" (2/22/71) The big shipboard finale finds the Carter family and Viv donning muumuus, leis, and grass skits for several Hawaiian numbers including "Ukulele Talk" performed by Lucy and Kim, strumming said instruments; "Mama's Muumuu" by Lucy and Viv (with

Harry showing up in said muumuu); and the whole company enthusiastically shimmying through "Hawaiian War Chant (Kaua I Ka Huahua'")."

• "Ukulele Talk" (Ervin Drake); "Mama's Muumuu" (Gene Burdette); "Hawaiian War Chant (Kaua I Ka Huahua'i)" (Music: Prince Leleiohoku; Revised music and lyrics: Johnny Noble, Ralph Freed)

"Lucy, the Co-Ed" (10/19/70) Needless to say, when Harry requires some performers for his college reunion, Lucy and her family fit the bill. As Ginger, the head cheerleader, Lucy joins some chorus boys for "Ain't She Sweet?;" Harry, Kim, Craig, and Robert Alda (portraying a dean) for "Collegiate," and, most nostalgically, a variation on "Buckle Down Winsocki" (here called "Bullwinkle" after Harry's alma mater), the rousing tune from a movie from Lucille's past, *Best Foot Forward.* The finale finds the entire cast chiming in on "Varsity Drag" from *Good News.*

• "Ain't She Sweet?" (Music: Milton Ager; Lyrics: Jack Yellen); "Buckle Down Bullwinkle" [Winsocki] (Ralph Blaine and Hugh Martin); "Collegiate" (Moe Jaffe and Nat Bonx); "Varsity Drag" (Music: Ray Henderson; Lyrics: Lew Brown and Buddy G. DeSylva)

"Lucy's Wedding Party" (11/2/70) When Lucy and Mary Jane's friend Cleo has no place to hold her wedding reception, Lucy volunteers Harry's house while he is away for a college reunion. When Harry unexpectedly comes home, Lucy tries to convince him that the people are there for a surprise birthday party for him and leads the guests in singing "Happy Birthday to You." After Harry discovers the truth, he wants credit for Lucy's gesture, so Lucy has the crowd serenade him with "For He's a Jolly Good Fellow."

• "Happy Birthday to You" (Mildred and Patty Hill); "For He's a Jolly Good Fellow" (traditional)

"Lucy and Aladdin's Lamp" (12/14/70) After finding an object that looks like Aladdin's Lamp among the things she plans to sell at a garage sale, Lucy decides to make a wish. After wishing for fifty dollars, so she can have her roof repaired, Lucy receives a telegram informing her that she won a jingle contest and the prize is fifty dollars. After Lucy sings her jingle for Murphy's Soup (to the tune of "Jingle Bells"), Craig says that it must be a magic lamp for *that* jingle to win a prize.

"Lucy and Rudy Vallee" (11/30/70) Getting nineteen-twenties crooner Rudy Vallee a gig at the Hungry Hippy (where no hippies, hungry or otherwise, appear to be in sight), Lucy and Kim join him onstage for a "groovy" version of one of his signature tunes, "The Whiffenpoof Song," where those "poor little lambs" have now become "hip little cats who have grooved our way." Dressed in tights and shaggy vest, Lucy does some gyrating to *Hair*'s anthem "Let the Sunshine In" and some whistling (dubbed) to "Winchester Cathedral."

• "The Whiffenpoof Song" (Todd Galloway and Meade Minnigerode)

"Lucy and Carol Burnett" (2/8/71) Quickly getting the storyline out of the way, Lucy and her friend Carol Krausmeyer (Carol Burnett) jump right into The Hollywood Unemployment Follies, or How to Starve in Show Biz Without Really Trying. The entire company sings "Hooray for Hollywood" with new lyrics that include mention of one of Lucy's co-stars, Henry Fonda. Kim and Carol join the star for a bit of "We're Off to See the Wizard," and then Lucie Arnaz does the dubbing chores for her mom as the latter cavorts onstage with Carol to "Chicago" and "Alexander's Ragtime Band." Then it's back to Lucy for her own throaty rendition of "Falling in Love Again," imitating Marlene Dietrich while Harry sits stoically wearing a German spiked helmet and monocle. For the finale, the whole cast chimes in on "Singin' in the Rain." Jack Benny's joke participation in this number is actually a connective one to its twenties origins, as he hosted the first movie in which it appeared, *The Hollywood Revue of 1929*. In another bit of trivia for insiders, a set replicating a Hollywood soundstage is papered with posters from many Paramount releases, including *The Greatest Show on Earth*, the film Lucy *nearly* did but had to drop out of in order to give birth to the girl sharing the scene with her, Lucie Arnaz.

• "Hooray for Hollywood" (Music: Richard A. Whiting; Lyrics: Johnny Mercer); "We're Off to See the Wizard" (Music: Harold Arlen; Lyrics: E. Y. Harburg); "Chicago" (Fred Fisher); "Alexander's Ragtime Band" (Irving Berlin); "Falling in Love Again (Can't Help It)" (Music: Friedrich Hollaender; Lyrics: Sammy Lerner); "Singin' in the Rain" (Lyrics: Arthur Freed; Music: Nacio Herb Brown)

"Lucy and the Astronauts" (10/11/71) Even astronauts get musical on *Here's Lucy*. When Lucy is forced to spend time in decontamination with three spacemen, she gets them (and, eventually, a doctor, played by Roy Roberts) to chime in with her on "Shine on, Harvest Moon," twice! Roberts's no-nonsense demeanor suited Lucy's comedy well, as he appeared five times on *Here's Lucy* after playing Mr. Mooney's boss, Mr. Cheever, on many episodes of *The Lucy Show.*

• "Shine on, Harvest Moon" (Nora Bayes and Jack Norworth)

"Ginger Rogers Comes to Tea" (11/22/71) Upon finding out that Lucy is going to a Ginger Rogers Film Festival, Harry announces that he will be joining her and, uncharacteristically, treating for the evening out because he worships the very ground that Ginger Rogers tap dances on. Harry and Lucy sing a bit of "Cheek to Cheek" (from the Astaire and Rogers picture *Top Hat,* which Lucille appeared in) and dance out of the office.

• "Cheek to Cheek" (Irving Berlin)

"Won't You Calm Down, Dan Dailey?" (11/22/71) Taking a break from driving Dan Dailey crazy, Lucy gushes over the actor's friendship with Betty Grable and the four movies they made together, reminding him of when he performed "I Want to Be Happy." He and Lucy then sing the song and do a little soft shoe, right there in his office. For the record, none of the four Grable-Dailey musicals included this song, which came from *No, No, Nanette* and was featured in the three different movie adaptations of the show.

• "I Want to Be Happy" (Music: Vincent Youmans; Lyrics: Irving Caesar)

"Lucy Helps David Frost Go Night-Night" (11/29/71) With Lucy seated next to him, does David Frost honestly expect his flight from L.A. to London to go peacefully? Especially when the redhead resorts to humming "Hey, Look Me Over" while clanking her silverware on a drinking glass?

• "Hey, Look Me Over" (Music: Cy Coleman. Lyrics: Carolyn Leigh)

"Lucy and Candid Camera" (12/13/71) Lucy, Kim, and Harry are fooled by an Allen Funt imposter who they think has hired them to perform *Candid Camera* stunts and unwittingly rob a bank. What makes this bank robbery so unusual is that it is done entirely in song. The three sing a medley of songs in which the lyrics are changed to reflect the bank robbery. Lucy, Harry, and Kim sing "Stealin' the Jack," a play on "Ballin' the Jack" (Music: Chris Smith; Lyrics: Jim Burris) and "Hello, Dollar!" (Jerry Herman's "Hello, Dolly!"). Lucy sings "Whatever Lucy Wants," her own version of "Whatever Lola Wants" (Richard Adler and Jerry Ross). The trio then performs "Give

Us Your Money," based on "We're in the Money" (Music: Harry Warren; Lyrics Al Dubin). Harry sings a bit of "The Impossible Dream" (Music: Mitch Leigh; Lyrics: Joe Darion) backed up by Lucy and Kim. The three end with "Please Don't Talk About Us When Go," their version of "Please Don't Talk About Me When I'm Gone" (Music: Sam H. Stept; Lyrics: Sidney Clare). As the three bank robbers take their bows, an instrumental version of "Hey, Look Me Over" plays.

"Lucy and Her All-Nun Band" (11/1/71) To help Harry's sister (who really is a Sister, played by Mary Wickes), Lucy forms the all-nun band of the title (called the Remnants), accompanying them on saxophone and singing "When the Saints Go Marching In."

The Remnants were a real all-nun band. Writer Madelyn Davis saw the group at a fund-raiser for St. John's Hospital where her husband, Dick Davis, was a doctor, and was inspired to include them in a *Lucy* episode. The benefit the Remnants and Lucy perform at in the episode is also for St. John's.

• "When the Saints Go Marching In" (traditional)

"Someone's on the Ski Lift with Dinah" (10/25/71) As Lucy and Harry reminisce about wintery pleasures like ice skating, they break into "The Loveliest Night of the Year," before Harry ad-libs some lyrics about firing his sister-in-law. (This song, based on Juventino P. Rosas's waltz, "Sobre las Olas," is most instantly equated with underscoring trapeze acts.) Later, Lucy manages to get stuck on a ski lift with Dinah Shore, whom she joins on two songs the latter had recorded.

• "The Loveliest Night of the Year" (Revised Music: Irving Aaronson; Lyrics: Paul Francis Webster); "Blues in the Night" (Music: Harold Arlen; Lyrics: Johnny Mercer); "Mississippi Mud" (Harry Barris and James Cavanaugh)

"Lucy's Lucky Day" (12/20/71) Hoping to win $1,000 on *The Milky Way to Riches* giveaway show, Lucy tries to teach a chimpanzee a trick. Instead, she Harry and Kim put on a musical Gay Nineties revue with the ape as Lucy's partner (with Lucy playing a man in straw hat, striped jacket and boater). One of the numbers, "Tell Me, Pretty Maiden," had already been done by Lucy and Henry Fonda in the 1962 special *The Good Years*.

• "The Fountain in the Park" (Ed Haley); "Tell Me, Pretty Maiden" (Music: Leslie Stewart; Lyrics: Edward Boyd-Jones and Paul Rubens); Daisy Bell" (Harry Dacre)

"Lucy and Petula Clark" (10/30/72) For once Lucy's vocalizing is appreciated, as Petula Clark's record producer thinks the weird sounds Lucy is making during rehearsals are just what they're looking for to enhance Clark's recording of "Goin' Out of My Head." Lucy therefore backs Petula up with some "wah-wah-wahs" and other noises. Clark had recorded this song on her 1965 album *I Know a Place* (the record's title tune was frequently heard on the early seasons of the series). Earlier in the episode, Lucy torments Harry by wailing a few lines of "Oh, Dem Golden Slippers" and then leaves the office triumphantly singing the title line from her signature tune, "Hey, Look Me Over."

• "Oh, Dem Golden Slippers" (James A. Bland); "Hey, Look Me Over" (Music: Cy Coleman; Lyrics: Carolyn Leigh); "Goin' Out of My Head" (Teddy Randazzo and Bobby Weinstein)

"Lucy Is Really in a Pickle" (01/01/73) Lucy gets a gig doing a commercial for Polly Parker's Perky Pickles, so she and Lucie end up dressed as pickles in order to sing the Perky jingle, set to the tune of "There's a Tavern in the Town."

"Lucy, the Peacemaker" (09/24/73) When Eydie Gorme arrives at the employment agency seeking a personal assistant, she walks in on Lucy singing one of Eydie's hits, "If He Walked into My Life," which, of course, Lucy had just sang for the movie of *Mame*, shot earlier that year and due for release in March 1974. Later in the story, when Steve Lawrence comes up with a plan to hire Lucy as his new stage partner, in a ploy to get the estranged Eydie back, he has Lucy join him in a duet of "Together (Wherever We Go)" as an audition. (Asked what key she sings in, Lucy timidly replies "I don't sing in the same key all the time.") Indeed, once Steve hears her vocalize, he promptly calls Eydie, begging her to come back to him. Steve and Lucy had already done a straightforward rendition of the same song in the former's 1965 series.

• "If He Walked into My Life" (Jerry Herman); "Together (Wherever We Go)" (Music: Jule Styne; Lyrics: Stephen Sondheim)

"Lucy Gives Eddie Albert the Old Song and Dance"(10/15/73) This time it's "The Girl Friday Follies," and the celebrity Lucy hopes to nab for the benefit is her *Fuller Brush Girl* co-star, Eddie Albert. Attempting to guilt him into doing the show, Lucy (whom Albert had earlier mistaken for a "ding-a-ling" stalker fan) reminds him that the underprivileged kids for whom they are hoping to raise money won't be able to sit around the camp-fire and sing "There's a Long, Long Trail." Albert joins her in finishing the song, which Lucy had already piped in on back in 1962 on *The Lucy Show* for the episode "Lucy Puts Up a TV Antenna." For the big finale of the follies, set aboard an ocean liner, Lucy and Eddie duet on "Makin' Whoopee," the signature song of the star of Lucille's very first movie, Eddie Cantor.

• "There's a Long, Long Trail" (Music: Zo Elliott; Lyrics: Stoddard King); "Makin' Whoopee" (Music: Walter Donaldson; Lyrics: Gus Kahn)

"Tipsy Through the Tulips" (11/12/73) Lucy's efforts to keep an alcoholic mystery writer (Foster Brooks) off the sauce are thwarted at every turn by the crafty and determined boozer. When he gets Lucy drunk on spiked punch, the two of them do a soused version of "Tiptoe Through the Tulips," first made famous in the nineteen-twenties by Nick Lucas, but better known at the time by Tiny Tim's immortal 1968 recording.

• "Tiptoe Through the Tulips" (Music: Joe Burke; Lyrics: Al Dubin)

"Lucy Carter Meets Lucille Ball" (3/4/74) Lucille, playing the *real* Lucille Ball, sings a commercial for "Mais Oui" perfume on television. Participants in the Lucille Ball look-alike contest later get their chance to sing a version of the jingle. The three finalists are Kim, Cynthia Duncan (Carole Cook), and, of course, Lucy, who is selected the winner for having, according to Ms. Ball, "a voice as unmusical as mine."

"Lucy and Phil Harris Strike Up the Band" (2/25/74) Lucy's efforts to pop-ulate Phil Harris's band with minorities looks like progress until feminists decry the absence of a woman. Not surprisingly, Lucy fills in, joining Harris for a song (along with his hired minorities), then a dance.

• "That's What I Like About the South" (Andy Razaf)

Life with Lucy

"Lucy and the Guard Goose" (Unaired) When Lucy wants to return the guard goose she rented, she only gets the owner's answering machine. The recording features Frankie Laine's popular song, "The Cry of the Wild Goose" (by Terry Gilkyson), which Lucy proceeds to sing a line of.

"Lucy and Curtis Are Up a Tree" (Unaired) When grandson Kevin over-hears Lucy and Curtis in his tree house talking about moving out because they are spoiling the children too much, he moves the ladder, trapping them up there until they make a decision. By the time the family finds them, it has started pouring rain. Lucy and Curtis both decide to stay, and the family is so happy that they sing "Singin' in the Rain."

• "Singin' in the Rain" (Lyrics: Arthur Freed; Music: Nacio Herb Brown)

"Breaking Up Is Hard to Do" (Unaired) Lucy is thrilled to go to work with-out having to deal with former business partner Curtis after she buys his share of the business. On her way to work, she sings and hums a bit of her old standby tune, "Hey, Look Me Over." Lucy later plays the song while act-ing as a one-man band to drum up business for the hardware store.

• "Hey, Look Me Over" (Music: Cy Coleman; Lyrics: Carolyn Leigh)

"World's Greatest Grandma" (Unaired) "Well, if ever there was anyone who *cannot* sing a note, it's you," Curtis tells Lucy in this last filmed (1986) epi-sode of *Life with Lucy,* making it the final episode of a Lucille Ball series to criticize her vocal abilities. To demonstrate to her granddaughter how she performed in high school as part of an act imitating the Andrews Sisters, she does a few lines of "Don't Sit Under the Apple Tree," but gets the tune wrong. (Of course when the Andrews Sisters made their first splash on the hit parade in 1938, Lucille Ball would have already been twenty-seven years old and starring in movies for RKO.) At the Grandma Talent Show, Lucy recites the lyrics to "Sunrise, Sunset," from *Fiddler on the Roof.*

• "Don't Sit Under the Apple Tree" (Lew Brown, Sam Stept, and Charlie Tobias); "Sunrise, Sunset" (Music: Jerry Bock; Lyrics: Sheldon Harnick)

Television: Specials and Guest Appearances

Inside U.S.A. with Chevrolet (CBS, Nov. 24, 1949)
Two years prior to *I Love Lucy,* Lucy guest starred on this early variety show, which was headlined by real-life married couple Peter Lind Hayes (who had performed at the Copacabana with Desi and was featured in Lucy's 1942 film *Seven Days Leave*) and Mary Healy. For her television singing debut, Lucy joins her hosts on "Louisiana Hayride," co-written by the series' pro-ducer, Arthur Schwartz. (This series was based on a 1948 Broadway revue he had written with Howard Dietz.)

- "Louisiana Hayride" (Music: Arthur Schwartz; Lyrics: Howard Dietz)

Show of the Year for Cerebral Palsy (NBC, June 10, 1950)
For their appearance on this live telethon, hosted in New York by Milton Berle, Lucy and Desi do the "Cuban Pete" duet that they would do again so memorably on the *I Love Lucy* episode "The Diet" (10/29/51). Although Desi starred in the 1946 film *Cuban Pete*, the song of the same name was written ten years earlier.

- "Cuban Pete" (Jose Norman)

Dinner with the President (CBS, Nov. 16, 1953)
At this live show in which President Dwight Eisenhower receives his Democratic Legacy Medal from the Anti-Defamation League of B'nai B'rith, Lucy and Desi reprise their "We'll Build a Bungalow" routine from "The Benefit" episode of *I Love Lucy*.

- "We'll Build a Bungalow" (Betty Bryant Mayhams and Norris the Troubadour)

Desilu Playhouse: K.O. Kitty (CBS, Nov. 17, 1958)
This hour-long episode (with laugh track) is significant as the first acting assignment Lucille had on television in which she was not playing "Lucy." As dance instructor Kitty Williams, who inherits a boxer (Aldo Ray) from her late uncle, she tries to teach her pugilist how to move correctly through some dance steps. As she does, she sing-speaks the opening phrase from "I Can't Give You Anything but Love, Baby." Later, she reprises the song as a way of encouraging Ray to be victorious in the ring. (She's joined at the climax by co-stars William Lundigan, Jesse White, Sid Melton, and the spectators at the match.)

- "I Can't Give You Anything but Love, Baby" (Music: Jimmy McHugh; Lyrics: Dorothy Fields)

The Ed Sullivan Show (CBS, Feb. 19, 1961)
While her show was running on Broadway, Lucy dropped by to sing the standout number from *Wildcat*, "Hey, Look Me Over," with co-star Paula Stewart. Included is the dialogue in the scene leading up to the song.

- "Hey, Look Me Over" (Music: Cy Coleman; Lyrics: Carolyn Leigh)

The Good Years (CBS, Jan. 12, 1962)

In this much-publicized special (treated as Lucy's "comeback" to television after relocating east to appear on Broadway) consisting of informational narration, sketches, stereopticon slides, and songs from the early years of the twentieth century, Lucy performed several numbers, including a duet, "Tell Me, Pretty Maiden" (from the 1899 stage hit *Floradora*) with her *Big Street* co-star, Henry Fonda. (Lucy reprised this song with Gale Gordon and Lucie Arnaz in the *Here's Lucy* episode "Lucy's Lucky Day.") Lucy's partner in the "Everybody's Doin' It" number is the show's choreographer, Matt Mattox.

• "Swing Me Higher, Obediah" (Music: Maurice Scott; Lyrics: Alf E. Rick); "Tell Me, Pretty Maiden" (Music: Leslie Stewart; Lyrics: Edward Boyd-Jones and Paul Rubens); "Everybody's Doin' It" (Irving Berlin); "Lowell Factory Girl" (traditional; writers unknown)

The Bob Hope Show (NBC, Oct. 24, 1962)
A Bob Hope Special (NBC, Sept. 28, 1966)

As it was the tradition to close most of his specials with his signature tune, the Oscar-winning "Thanks for the Memory" (from his feature debut *The Big Broadcast of 1938*), Hope was joined here on this occasion by guests Lucille Ball, Bing Crosby, and Juliet Prowse. Lucy was back to do the same on Hope's first special of the 1966–67 season.

• "Thanks for the Memory" (Music: Ralph Rainger; Lyrics: Leo Robin)

The Danny Kaye Show (NBC, Nov. 11, 1962)

In her first television appearance to be shown in color, Lucy joins Danny Kaye on this variety special, singing a medley of tunes in a spoof of variety shows (mimicking Judy Garland, Carol Channing, and Marlene Dietrich) and then joining Kaye for Irving Berlin's famous counterpart duet from *Call Me Madam*, "You're Just in Love," and a snatch of "Rock-a-Bye Your Baby with a Dixie Melody."

• "Swanee" (Music: George Gershwin; Lyrics: Irving Caesar); "Diamonds Are a Girl's Best Friend" (Music: Jule Styne; Lyrics: Leo Robin); "Falling in Love Again (Can't Help It)" (Friedrich Hollaender; English Lyrics: Sammy Lerner); "You're Just in Love" (Irving Berlin); "Rock-a-Bye Your Baby with a Dixie Melody" (Sam M. Lewis, Joe Young, and Jean Schwartz).

The Greatest Show on Earth: "Lady in Limbo" (Dec. 10, 1963)

After young Jeff (Billy Mumy) sees his father mauled by a bear, Kate

Reynolds (Lucy, in her dramatic television debut) takes the boy in. Kate sings "Buffalo Gals" to put him to sleep, saying "That's the only song I know besides 'Minnie the Moocher.'"

• "Buffalo Gals" (John Hodges)

The Steve Lawrence Show (CBS, Sept. 14, 1965)
In the memorable opening of the premiere of Steve Lawrence's variety series, he and Lucy make their entrance riding atop an elephant through Broadway's Shubert Alley, singing "Together (Wherever We Go)," from the musical *Gypsy*. Apparently this song became equated in Lucy's mind with Steve Lawrence, as she reprised it on the *Here's Lucy* episode in which he appeared, "Lucy the Peacemaker" (9/24/73). Lawrence later joined his guest on Lucy's *Wildcat* hit "Hey, Look Me Over."

• "Together (Wherever We Go)" (Music: Jule Styne; Lyrics: Stephen Sondheim); "Hey, Look Me Over" (Music: Cy Coleman; Lyrics: Carolyn Leigh)

The Danny Kaye Show (CBS, Nov. 4, 1964)
Guest starring on Kaye's weekly variety series, Lucy joins him for a bit of balloon popping in a specialty number written for the program, "Balloon" ("we believe in ba lowing balloons . . .") This number, choreographed by Tony Charmoli, was a last minute substitution. Danny did not feel the original musical number planned for Lucy was right for her and recommended that they save it for upcoming guest star Gwen Verdon. The following month, Kaye appeared on The Lucy Show for the episode "Lucy Meets Danny Kaye" (12/28/64).

• "Balloons" (Billy Barnes)

The Dean Martin Show (NBC, Feb. 10, 1966)
For the show's finale, Dean and guest Kate Smith do a medley of turn-of-the-century tunes while Lucy, as a perky chorus girl, chirps in at select moments. Bracketing the bit is George M. Cohan's "Give My Regards to Broadway," while the other songs are "In the Shade of the Old Apple Tree" (Harry Williams, Egbert Van Alstyne); "Wait 'till the Sun Shines, Nellie" (Music: Harry Von Tilzer; Lyrics: Andrew B. Sterling); "Asleep in the Deep" (Music: Henry W. Petrie; Lyrics: Arthur J. Lamb), where Lucy does a deep rendering of the word "beware" before being hoisted off the stage by the bell rope she is pulling; "A Bird in a Gilded Cage" (Music: Harry Von Tilzer; Lyrics: Arthur L. Lamb), where Lucy merely provides some "cheep-cheeps"; "I Don't Care" (Music: Harry O. Sutton; Lyrics: Jean Lenox); and "The Yankee Doodle Boy" (George M. Cohan).

Carol +2 (CBS, Mar. 22, 1966)

In one of the specials that led to her long-running variety show, Carol Burnett plays host to Lucy, who joins her in a sketch playing charwomen (a familiar characterization for Burnett) discussing big movie deals while cleaning up after hours at the William Morris Agency. This leads to a specialty song, "Chutzpah!," written for the show. Over the end credits Lucy, Carol, and Carol's other guest, Zero Mostel (one of Lucy's co-stars in *Du Barry Was a Lady*) bid farewell with another new number, "Bye Bye."

• "Chutzpah!," "Bye-Bye" (Ken Welch)

Lucy in London (CBS, Oct. 24, 1966)

Although she was playing her *Lucy Show* character of Lucy Carmichael and it aired in part of that show's time slot, this hour-long program was treated as "A Lucille Ball Special." On location in London, Lucy is shown the town by a tour guide named Tony (played by Anthony Newley). Minus any vocal participation, Lucy is the center of attention in the show's memorable "music video" sequence as the Dave Clark Five sing the title song ("Lucy's in London, Bridges are falling down . . ."). Lucy and Newley duet on his 1961 hit "Pop! Goes the Weasel," performed in counterpart with another traditional ditty, "London Bridge Is Falling Down," as done by the Dave Clark Five. The "teams" then switch numbers. For the finale, Lucy reprises a new song Newley sang earlier, "One Day in London."

• "Row, Row, Row Your Boat" (traditional); "Pop Goes the Weasel" (traditional); "London Bridge Is Falling Down" (traditional); "One Day in London" (Anthony Newley)

The Carol Burnett Show (CBS, October 2, 1967)

Dressed as Western bar room hostesses, Lucy and Carol do a rousing medley of "See What the Boys in the Backroom Will Have" (from the movie *Destry Rides Again*) and "Belly Up to the Bar, Boys!" (from the show *The Unsinkable Molly Brown*), then join the chorus in a dance.

• "See What the Boys in the Backroom Will Have" (Music: Frederick Hollander; Lyrics: Frank Loesser); "Belly Up to the Bar, Boys!" (Meredith Willson)

The Jack Benny Hour (Jack Benny's Carnival Nights) (NBC, Mar. 20, 1968)

Lucy (as Helen of Troy) sings the 1949 Dinah Shore hit "It's So Nice to

Have a Man around the House" while a quartet of musclemen strike poses. Her other song is prophetic, as she spoofs Cleopatra to the tune (with new lyrics) of "Mame."

• "It's So Nice to Have a Man Around the House" (Music: Harold Spina; Lyrics: John Elliot); "Mame" (Jerry Herman)

The Twentieth Annual Emmy Awards (NBC, May 19, 1968)
At the same ceremony where Lucille receives her fourth and final Emmy Award in competition, she and Carol Burnett do a version of *Gigi*'s "I Remember It Well" that references what has happened in television since the Emmys began twenty years earlier. They are introduced by ceremony co-host Frank Sinatra.

• "I Remember It Well" (Music: Frederick Loewe; Lyrics: Alan Jay Lerner)

The Carol Burnett Show (CBS, Nov. 4, 1968)
Playing Catherine the Great, Lucy joins Carol, Vicki Lawrence, and Nancy Wilson for a rendition of one of the songs made famous by Sophie Tucker (she's dubbed on the final notes).

• "A Good Man Is Hard to Find" (Eddie Green)

Jack Benny's Birthday Special (NBC, Feb. 17, 1969)
Paying tribute to her former next-door neighbor as he turned 75 (on February 14th, precisely), Lucy returned to her days of playing chorus girls in a flashback sequence that has her miming the lyrics to "Big Spender" from *Sweet Charity*, as Carole Cook does the actual singing.

• "Big Spender" (Music: Cy Coleman; Lyrics: Dorothy Fields)

Like Hep! (NBC, Apr. 13, 1969)
Host Dinah Shore and her guest Diana Ross explain to Lucy how "hip" is now "hep," as the three of them sing and dance to the title song. As the hillbilly White Bred Sisters, the three ladies sing "Hot Giddy Dang Do" and a Supremes-like rendition of "Dinah" for the end credits. In between, Lucy does some blackout gags with Dan Rowan and her one-time *Lucy Show* co-star Dick Martin. As a nightclub singer named "Joyce," Lucy lets go with a line from "Big Spender" and, as Mary Poppins, the title phrase from "A Spoonful of Sugar" (using Carole Cook's voice for both).

• "Like Hep!" (Billy Barnes and W. Earl Brown); "Big Spender" (Music: Cy Coleman; Lyrics: Dorothy Fields); "A Spoonful of Sugar" (Richard M. Sherman and Robert B. Sherman); "Hot Giddy Dang Do" (Billy Barnes and W. Earl Brown); "Dinah" (Music: Harry Akst; Lyrics: Sam M. Lewis and Joe Young)

The Carol Burnett Show (CBS, Nov. 24, 1969)
A sibling act from 1919 vaudeville, the Rock Sisters, accidently gets booked into a rock concert fifty years later. Lucy and Carol, as Polly and Dolly Rock, perform the catchy "A Happiness Cocktail," which is later reprised with some groovy backup moves by a band called the Frozen Nostrils.

• "A Happiness Cocktail" (Artie Malvin)

The Ann-Margret Show: From Hollywood with Love (CBS, Dec. 6, 1969)
Lucy plays both herself (leaving the studio where *Here's Lucy* is supposedly being filmed) and an autograph hound for a sketch/number with her host, Ann-Margret, called "Autograph Annie and Celebrity Lu." Two months later, Ann-Margret guest starred on *Here's Lucy*, in the episode titled "Lucy and Ann-Margret," although the main focus of that particular installment was on Desi Jr. (2/2/70).

The Carol Burnett Show (CBS, Oct. 19, 1970)
For her fourth and final appearance on Carol's show, Lucy joins the company in a salute to smog, singing "Put on a Happy Face." She later teams with her host for two original numbers, "Poof," and "Is This a Crime?," in a sketch in which they send up the 1959 comedy classic *Some Like It Hot.*

• "Put on a Happy Face" (Music: Charles Strouse; Lyrics: Lee Adams)

The Pearl Bailey Show (ABC, Jan. 30, 1970)
Guest starring on Pearl Bailey's short-lived variety show, Lucille sings a new song written for the occasion, "I'm the Girl Who Will Lead the Band," which includes snatches of other march numbers like "Yellow Rose of Texas" and "Stouthearted Men." She also duets with Pearl on "Everything's Coming Up Roses" (Music: Jule Styne; Lyrics: Stephen Sondheim).

The Flip Wilson Show (NBC, Sept. 16, 1971)
Working with a performer whose talents she greatly admired, Lucy makes her entrance in one sketch dressed as the front end of a horse. Flip is the

backside. As the two characters discuss their lowly status, Lucy sings a few lines of "There's No Business like Show Business."

• "There's No Business Like Show Business" (Irving Berlin)

Steve and Eydie . . . On Stage (NBC, Sept. 16, 1973)
Several months in anticipation of the release of *Mame,* Lucy shows up to sing one of its songs, "Bosom Buddies," with Eydie Gorme (joined at the end by Steve Lawrence), in a segment taped in Los Angeles for this otherwise Vegas-filmed special. The week after this aired, Steve and Eydie guest starred on the *Here's Lucy* episode "Lucy the Peacemaker" (9/24/73).

• "Bosom Buddies" (Jerry Herman)

Shirley MacLaine: Gypsy in My Soul (CBS, Jan. 10, 1976)
For her guest appearance on this Shirley MacLaine special paying tribute to chorus dancers (which MacLaine had started as), Lucy gets to sing (with Shirley) a song originally written for *Wildcat* but cut before the show opened, "Bouncing Back for More." She also sings along with the chorus boys and girls at the finale, "It's Not Where You Start, It's Where You Finish," from *Seesaw.*

• "Bouncing Back for More" (Music: Cy Coleman; Lyrics: Carolyn Leigh); "Bring Back Those Good Old Days" (Cy Coleman); "It's Not Where You Start, It's Where You Finish" (Music: Cy Coleman; Lyrics: Dorothy Fields)

Dinah! (Syndicated; Nov. 16, 1976)
Once again, Lucy performs the breakout song from *Wildcat,* but this time the performance has the added novelty of one of the dancers from the show's original company, Valerie Harper, joining in as well. Dinah Shore completes the trio.

• "Hey, Look Me Over" (Music: Cy Coleman; Lyrics: Carolyn Leigh)

Texaco Presents Bob Hope's All-Star Comedy Salute to Vaudeville (NBC, Mar. 25, 1977)
Lucy takes on the persona of brassy vaudevillian Sophie Tucker for her segment in this Bob Hope special, singing the lady's signature song, which she had previously done on an episode of *The Lucy Show* with George Burns.

• "Some of These Days" (Shelton Brooks)

Donny and Marie (ABC, Sept. 30, 1977)
Having appeared on the *Here's Lucy* episode "Lucy and Donny Osmond" (11/30/72), Donny invites Lucy to guest star on his and his sister Marie's series. In a unique number utilizing special effects, Lucille is able to dance with multiple images of herself as she performs the Emmy-nominated song "Leading Lady." Joining original *Wizard of Oz* cast member Ray Bolger, as well as Marie Osmond and Paul Williams, in a spoof of that movie, the quartet sings a variation on a number from *Damn Yankees*, "Three Lost Souls." The whole company does the Schwartz-Dietz tune "A Shine on Your Shoes."

• "Leading Lady" (Earl Brown); "There's No Business Like Business" (Irving Berlin); "Tin Lizzie" (Earl Brown); "Two Lost Souls" (Music: Richard Adler; Lyrics: Jerry Ross); "A Shine on Your Shoes" (Music: Arthur Schwartz; Lyrics: Howard Dietz)

Gene Kelly . . . An American in Pasadena (CBS, Mar. 13, 1978)
Looking back on his film career, Gene Kelly hosts several stars with whom he had shared the screen, including Lucille (planted in the audience), who joins him to reprise "Friendship" from *Du Barry Was a Lady*. For the finale, Gene's leading ladies Lucy, Cyd Charisse, Janet Leigh, Betty Garrett, Gloria DeHaven, and Kathryn Grayson help Gene with "Singin' in the Rain" and a line of "You are My Lucky Star."

• "Friendship" (Cole Porter); "Singin' in the Rain," "You Are My Lucky Star" (Music: Nacio Herb Brown; Lyrics: Arthur Freed)

CBS: On the Air (CBS, Mar. 26, 1978)
To celebrate the fiftieth anniversary of CBS, the network gathered together as many of its stars of past and present as possible. Co-host Mary Tyler Moore sings "Like a Member of the Family" about how people feel about the network. After all the stars have made their entrances, they sing the last line, "Have a happy birthday, CBS!" in unison. Lucy is very prominently positioned in front. Further back in the crowd is Vivian Vance, the last time she and Lucy appeared together on television. In the second night of the weeklong salute, Lucy and Beatrice Arthur perform a dance number to a tune entitled "What's So Funny About Monday?," but do not do any singing themselves.

• "Like a Member of the Family" (Jerry Herman)

Happy Birthday, Bob: A Salute to Bob Hope's 75th Birthday (NBC, May 29, 1978)
Happy Birthday, Bob: A Salute to Bob Hope's Eightieth Birthday (NBC, May 23, 1983)
Bob Hope birthday salutes were plentiful once he reached certain milestone ages, and his frequent co-star Lucy shows up to sing a version of "Hey, Look Me Over" (Cy Coleman/Carolyn Leigh) with new lyrics ("Hey, Look *Him* Over") on two separate occasions.

Lucy Comes to Nashville (CBS, Nov. 29, 1978)
Serving as the host of a variety special that puts more emphasis on country music acts than herself, Lucy joins Mel Tillis as he sings the bulk of "How Nashville Got Its Name." In a sketch, Lucy plays singing star "Lulajean Lupkin," the runner-up for the Best Female Country Singer Award, begrudgingly picking the trophy up for her competitor. She reminds the audience that she was in the running for a song Lulajean herself wrote (or as she boasts, "both the lyrics *and* the words"), memorably titled "I'd Rather Walk Barefooted Through a Cow Pasture Than Take a Chance with You."

• "How Nashville Got Its Name" (Floyd Huddleston and Nancy Adams Huddleston)

The Mary Tyler Moore Hour (CBS, Mar. 6, 1979)
This combination variety show/situation comedy found Lucy singing and dancing "The Girlfriend of the Whirling Dervish" (from the Warner Bros. musical *Garden of the Moon*) with her host, Mary Tyler Moore.

• "The Girlfriend of the Whirling Dervish" (Music: Harry Warren; Lyrics: Al Dubin and Johnny Mercer)

A Lucille Ball Special: Lucy Moves to NBC (NBC, Feb. 8, 1980)
In this special, Lucille Ball takes a job at NBC where she produces a sitcom pilot entitled *The Music Mart* starring Donald O'Connor and Gloria DeHaven. In the show, O'Connor and DeHaven, as Wally and Carol Coogan, perform at a political rally with Sister Hitchcock (Lucille Ball) playing the tambourine and joining in singing "When the Saints Go Marching In." This marks the second time Lucy performed this song as a nun, having done so on the *Here's Lucy* episode, "Lucy and Her All-Nun Band" (11/1/71).

An All-Star Party for Carol Burnett (CBS, Dec. 5, 1982)
In this Variety Clubs tribute to Carol Burnett, Lucy kicks off the salute to her friend by reading a letter from President Ronald Reagan. As the

show closes, Carol and all of the participants—including Lucy, Bette Davis, James Stewart, Glenda Jackson, Beverly Sills, Sammy Davis Jr., Tim Conway, Vicki Lawrence, Steve Lawrence, Jack Paar, and Jim Nabors—sing "Carol's Theme." Tim Conway's clowning around causes Lucy to laugh uproariously through much of it.

• "Carol's Theme" (Joe Hamilton)

Bob Hope's High-Flying Birthday Extravaganza (NBC, May 25, 1987)
On one of his many self-congratulatory birthday specials (this time celebrating his eighty-fourth), Hope duets with Lucy on "I Remember It Well" from *Gigi*.

• "I Remember It Well" (Music: Frederick Loewe; Lyrics: Alan Jay Lerner)

Happy Birthday, Bob (NBC, May 16, 1988)
In her last appearance not only on a Bob Hope special but in the genre of variety shows, Lucy, in tights and suit jacket, sings a song written especially for the event (Hope's eighty-fifth and his fiftieth anniversary working for NBC). She even does a few steps with the backup chorus. The number received an Emmy nomination.

• "Comedy Ain't No Joke" (Music: Cy Coleman; Lyrics: James Lipton)

Other

In August 1946, Desi had a recording session with his orchestra. Lucy went to watch her husband and, for fun, sang a bit of the "Peter Piper" tongue twister while Desi sang the song "Carnival in Rio." Lucy was shocked to discover several months later that her performance was released as part of the record with her name prominently credited. Lucy filed a lawsuit against Radio Corp. of America and their subsidiary, RCA Victor Records, who put out the record, claiming that the performance did not represent her true artistic ability. Lucy dropped her $100,000 lawsuit in March 1947 when a "satisfactory" out-of-court settlement was made and her name was removed from the records. Further editions are credited to "Desi Arnaz and 'Friend.'"

25

"Comedy Ain't No Joke"

Who Found Lucy Funny

L ucille Ball made millions of people laugh through the years, so it was only natural that a question frequently posed to her in interviews was, "Who makes *you* laugh?" Lucy always said she herself was not naturally funny. She did not make jokes in real life. She could, however, act out a story and make people howl with laughter. Lucy loved people who were naturally funny. At some point in the nineteen-eighties, Lucy wrote out a list of the people who made her laugh, saying, "Very few people can give me a real belly laugh." Here are those who could.

George Gobel

Although comedian George Gobel was the first name written in the list of people who made her laugh, Lucy never acted with him. The soft-spoken Gobel reached the peak of his popularity on television while *I Love Lucy* was dominating the medium, premiering his comedy variety series *The George Gobel Show* in 1954. It would run six years (first on NBC and then ABC), landing in the Nielsen Top Ten during its first season and giving "Lonesome George," as he was humorously known, a catchphrase with "Well, I'll be a dirty bird."

Two of Lucy's best friends, Vivian Vance and Paula Stewart, actually worked opposite Gobel at the same time, appearing with him in a 1969 segment of *Love, American Style* entitled "Love and the Medium." Vivian made her final acting appearance playing Gobel's wife in an episode of the short-lived show *Sam* in 1978.

Dean Martin

In 1980, Lucy named Dean Martin and Ann Sothern among her favorite comedy stars and said that they "make me laugh more in person than in pictures." Lucille stated, "Dean Martin has a curly mind." Lucy claimed that

The Lucy Show episode "Lucy Dates Dean Martin" was the favorite of all her television episodes. While Martin had started out as the straight man to Jerry Lewis and was often considered a singer first and an actor second, Lucy's opinion of his riotously funny on-set manner was one shared by many who worked with him. She would later team up with him on his variety series, *The Dean Martin Show* (Feb. 10, 1966), and her special *Lucy Gets Lucky* (March 1, 1975), in addition to being the target on one of his "roasts" (Feb. 7, 1975).

Vivian Vance

Another interview question Lucy was frequently asked in her later years was if she watched reruns of her old shows. She said she did, and when she did, she watched Viv. At her 1984 seminar at the Museum of Broadcasting, Lucy stated, "No one could take the place of Vivian Vance in my life. She was the greatest partner anyone could ever have." Lucy went on to say, "Nobody ever enjoyed their work more than we did . . . Vivian and I had an absolute ball." Lucy added, "We did everything together happily. We used to have so much fun on the set. Seriously, not just the two of us giggling. I'm not talking about that. By making things evolve, making things work out, making what the writers had written out." Lucy always praised Vivian as a brilliant "show doctor."

Mary Wickes

Character actress Mary Wickes was Lucy's closest friend for years, and the two worked together often. Whenever Wickes came on screen it was almost a guarantee that she would be playing a nurse, a nun, a maid, or someone's aunt. She did them all on Lucy's shows: nurse ("Lucy and Harry's Tonsils," "Lucy's Big Break," "Lucy and Eva Gabor Are Hospital Roomies), nun ("Lucy and Her All-Nun Band"), maid ("Lucy and the Diamond Cutter"), and aunt ("Lucy and the Sleeping Beauty," "Lucy's Mystery Guest"). With the exception of the 1964–65 season, Mary Wickes made at least one appearance on a Lucy show each season from 1962 to 1974.

The actresses first met when Lucy guest starred on CBS's weekly musical variety show *Inside U.S.A. with Chevrolet* in 1949, which starred Peter Lind Hayes and Mary Healy and featured Wickes among the regulars. Wickes would become a familiar and very welcome face on both the big (*The Man Who Came to Dinner, White Christmas,* etc.) and small screen, and could memorably cut someone down to size with a withering glance or an acerbic remark like few others. Outside all her Lucy projects, television saw her

Lucy as "Wucy," age five and Vivian, age four ("she's six if she's a day!") on the set of *The Lucy Show* episode "Lucy, the Stockholder"

playing publicist Liz O'Neal on *The Danny Thomas Show*, spinster neighbor Miss Cathcart on *Dennis the Menace*, and the rectory housekeeper Marie on *Father Dowling Mysteries*, among so many other roles.

Of all her *Lucy* appearances, Wickes's most memorable role was that of ballet teacher Madame LeMond in "The Ballet" episode of *I Love Lucy*. The last time the two friends worked together was in 1977 in *A Lucille Ball Special: Lucy Calls the President* (in which she played Lucy's aunt, when in reality she was only a year older than Lucy).

Gary Morton

Gary made Lucy laugh from the very first time she met him and this was certainly at a time when she needed a laugh, having just divorced Desi after nineteen years of marriage. "Besides liking his looks, I also liked his sense of humor," Lucy said. "Before I met Gary, I hadn't laughed in years. I'd made other people laugh, but I hadn't laughed. Mother noticed I would laugh whenever Gary was around. Pretty soon I started to notice the same thing."

When Lucy and Gary married, Paula Stewart said that she introduced the two "because Lucille hadn't been dating anybody and was very depressed. They started laughing and haven't stopped." They were still laughing twenty-seven years later. Betty White was with the couple on one of Lucy's final nights on the town in 1989, to see Gloria DeHaven perform at the Hollywood Roosevelt Cinegrill, and later said, "Gary could still make her laugh that big, gutbucket laugh. That's how I'll remember her, with the silliness we had that night."

Nancy Walker

Nancy Walker made her movie debut in one of Lucy's films, *Best Foot Forward*, repeating the role she had played on the Broadway stage. Lucy tried for years to convince the New York-based Walker to move back to California, but Nancy said she did not want to uproot her husband, David Craig. Craig was a musical theater teacher, and among his trainees was Lucie Arnaz. Following a career mostly in theater (*On the Town, Do Re Mi*, etc.), Walker eventually did come back to California in 1970, where she landed a guest role on *Mary Tyler Moore*. Playing the part of Rhoda's (Valerie Harper) overbearing mother would make her a television star. Lucy described Nancy Walker as "fabulous" and was convinced she could do *anything*.

Bob Newhart

Like Lucy, the deadpan Bob Newhart is famous for starring in CBS sitcoms with his name in the title. He came to fame in 1960 with the hit comedy album *The Button-Down Mind of Bob Newhart* and became a television favorite with *The Bob Newhart Show* and *Newhart*, to name but two of his series. However, he and Lucy never did act together.

Dick Martin

In 1962, Lucy wanted Dick Martin to play the role of Harry Conners, Lucy Carmichael's airline pilot next-door neighbor on *The Lucy Show*. Martin, however, was a member of the comedy team Rowan & Martin, and the comic duo already had several nightclub bookings filling up their schedule. Executive producer Desi Arnaz arranged it so they could schedule Martin's episodes around his nightclub commitments. However, when it came time to film Martin's first episode in the series, he and Rowan had a nightly booking in Nevada. Desi chartered a plane that could fly Martin between his two engagements for the four days the episode would be in production. Martin played Harry in eleven episodes during the first season. He would later star on *Rowan & Martin's Laugh-In*, scheduled opposite *The Lucy Show* and then *Here's Lucy*. It became number one in the ratings and turned Martin and his partner into two of the most famous performers in America.

Dick Martin was a guest on *The Mike Douglas Show* when Lucy served as the co-host for the week in 1978. Also on the show were Gary Morton and Bob Hope, two of Lucy's other favorite laugh makers. Martin joined Lucy for several weeklong stints on *Password Plus* in the early eighties and played on *Super Password* with her in 1988, which was her final game show appearance.

Lucie Arnaz

Lucy really admired the fact that her daughter was naturally funny. "I don't think funny," she said, "That's the difference between a wit and a comedian. My daughter Lucie thinks funny." In 1974, Lucy added "Lucie has a weird, woolly sense of humor. Desi's more the serious type, but when he plays comedy seriously, he's great." Lucy was consistently wowed by her daughter and, the following year said, "She is so talented. There isn't anything she can't do. She sings, she dances, she mimes, she acts—and I couldn't do all those things." Several years later, Lucy's praise for her daughter grew even more when she balanced all those things with raising her children.

Bea Lillie

Lucy never had the opportunity to act with Beatrice Lillie, but she was a big fan of the British comedian. Lucy did, however, have Lillie as a guest on her radio show, *Let's Talk to Lucy*. Miss Lillie's interview took place while she was starring in the 1964 Broadway musical *High Spirits*, which Lucy saw her in twice. Mostly a stage performer, Lillie was cherished for her giddily eccentric combination of comedy and song in such revues as *At Home Abroad* and *Inside U.S.A.* Like Lucille Ball, Beatrice Lillie inhabited the character of Mame Dennis, originating the role in the London production of *Auntie Mame* and being a replacement during its original Broadway run.

James Garner

Although Lucy never performed with him, Lucy liked James Garner a great deal and considered him to be a friend. Garner's busy career included two popular television series that displayed his low-key sense of humor, *Maverick* and *The Rockford Files*, as well as a long string of movie leads including *The Americanization of Emily*, *Victor Victoria*, and *Murphy's Romance*. The one chance fans had to see Lucy and James Garner together was when both guest starred on the May 16, 1977 episode of *Dinah!* Knowing that Garner loved chocolate chip cookies, Lucy presented him on the air with a whole batch in a bag that looked like a cookie.

Woody Allen

In a 1974 interview, Lucy said that she thought Woody Allen was "great." Lucy said, "I've never worked with him. I just love him. I don't know him, but I'd love to work around him." At the time of her comment, Allen had successfully made the transition from standup comedian to starring, directing, and writing his own movie comedies. In due time, he would be proclaimed one of the world's foremost filmmakers, earning three Academy Awards for his work. One of his early works was the play *Don't Drink the Water,* which Vivian Vance originally started in, only to leave the production before it reached Broadway. Lucy never got the chance to work with Allen.

Jack Albertson

Before winning an Oscar, an Emmy, and a Tony, Jack Albertson appeared on an episode of *I Love Lucy*, "Bon Voyage," and on *The Lucy Show* in "Lucy and Viv Open Up a Restaurant." In 1974, Albertson began starring in the sitcom *Chico and the Man*, of which Lucy was a great fan. Jack was not the only member of his family to work with Lucy. His sister, Mabel Albertson, had a small role in *Forever, Darling* and appeared in *The Lucy Show* episode "Lucy and the Missing Stamp."

Carol Burnett

Lucy said about Carol Burnett, "That's the lady I really laugh at. That girl can do anything. I don't think I've ever envied anyone in the business really, but I think I have a little envy for Carol Burnett. She absolutely can do anything . . . no way I can do what Carol does." Lucy first met Carol Burnett when she attended the second night performance of the (then)

Off-Broadway show *Once Upon a Mattress*, at New York's Phoenix Theatre on May 12, 1959. Following the performance, the two ladies engaged in a lengthy conversation, with Lucy telling Carol that if she ever needed her, to call. Lucy and Carol first got the opportunity to work together a year later when Lucy guest starred on the September 27, 1960 episode of *The Garry Moore Show*, on which Carol was a regular.

Carol Burnett had signed a ten-year contract with CBS and had a special to do. In need of a guest star, she remembered what Lucy had said to her in her dressing room in 1959 and called her. Lucy immediately said, "When do you want me?" The special was *Carol + Two*—the two being Lucy and Zero Mostel—which was broadcast on March 22, 1966. It ended up being the highest rated show on TV the week it aired. Carol paid Lucy back by guest starring in two episodes of *The Lucy Show* later that year, "Lucy Gets a Roommate" and "Lucy and Carol in Palm Springs." Carol played Carol Bradford, a shy librarian who answers Lucy's ad for a roommate and whom Lucy helps coax out of her shell.

When Carol began her variety series *The Carol Burnett Show* the following season, Lucy was a guest star on the show's fourth episode (October 2, 1967). Carol then returned to *The Lucy Show* in a two-part storyline, only this time playing Carol Tilford, who goes to flight attendant school with Lucy. Carol played herself for her first *Here's Lucy* appearance during the show's first season, but in her two subsequent guest stints played Carol Krausmeyer, a friend of Lucy's. Lucy would guest star on *The Carol Burnett Show* a total of four times.

Burnett called Lucy her idol and presented many awards and tributes to her through the years.

Wally Cox

Lucy said she adored Wally Cox, and "I worked with him every chance I got." First coming to prominence in 1952 playing a mousy science teacher in the NBC sitcom *Mr. Peepers*, Cox was actually something of a free-spirited nonconformist and nothing like the quiet characters he was famous for. He made his first appearance on *The Lucy Show* in "Lucy Conducts the Symphony." He would appear on four *Here's Lucy* episodes in four seasons playing four different characters—"Lucy and the Ex-Con," "Lucy and Wally Cox," "Lucy and the Diamond Cutter," and "Lucy Sublets the Office." Cox most certainly would have been invited back for more had he not died in 1973.

Lucy and Wally Cox go incognito in the first of Cox's four *Here's Lucy* appearances, "Lucy and the Ex-Con."

Paul Williams

On *The Tonight Show Starring Johnny Carson,* Lucy stated that if she was stranded on a desert island, the one person she would want to be with would be Paul Williams because she adored him. Lucy and the elfin actor/songwriter worked together on *Donny and Marie* in 1977, in which Williams played W. C. Fields to Lucy's Mae West. They also appeared in a *Wizard of Oz* parody together in the same show with Williams as the Cowardly Lion and Lucy as "Tin Lizzie."

Bob Hope

Lucy first got to know Bob Hope during World War II, working together on the radio show *G.I. Journal* in 1945. Lucy wrote in her memoirs about her first on-screen collaboration with Bob, *Sorrowful Jones,* "Going to Bob's set every day was like going to a party. I couldn't wait to get there. And I loved working with him." In regard to Hope himself, she stated, "Bob is predictable and never moody. He's fun, sweet, kind, good; a gentleman and

Bob Hope welcomes Lucy to the Peacock network in the 1980 special *Lucy Moves to NBC*.

a trooper. I can bounce vitriolic remarks off his big chest and they come out funny, not like acid. Because he's such a strong male figure, he makes me appear more feminine."

Ball and Hope would team up for three more feature films, *Fancy Pants* (1950); *The Facts of Life* (1960), which for both of them was one of their favorite movies, with or without each other; and *Critic's Choice* (1963), their least favorite of their collaborations. Lucy referred to their films as "three goodies and one baddie." Bob joked on *The Merv Griffin Show* in 1973 that after the first screening of *Critic's Choice,* "The manager of the theater came up to me and pressed something into my hand. It was a .38." (Bob and Lucy would also pair up for the radio adaptations of *Sorrowful Jones* and *Fancy Pants.*)

Hope appeared as himself in the sixth-season premiere of *I Love Lucy* and did a cameo in *The Lucy Show* episode "Lucy and the Plumber." He would go on to appear on Lucy's specials *The Lucille Ball Comedy Hour* in 1964; *CBS Salutes Lucy: The First 25 Years* in 1976; and *Lucy Moves to NBC* in 1980. Lucy would appear in dozens of Bob Hope programs through the years. The two also were featured on several talk shows together such as *The Mike Douglas Show, The Merv Griffin Show,* and *Dinah!* Lucy's final public appearance was on the *Academy Awards* on March 29, 1989 with Bob Hope. Bob made Lucy laugh throughout their entire segment.

Jack Benny

Lucy worked frequently with her longtime next-door neighbor Jack Benny. Wanting Lucy to loosen up while performing on radio, writer-producer-director Jess Oppenheimer had her go to Jack Benny's radio show to see how effortlessly Benny acted out a script, even though he was not being seen by an audience apart from the studio one. Lucy observed Benny and adopted the same technique for her *My Favorite Husband* program.

Their television collaborations began with the 1952 CBS special *Stars in the Eye,* which featured Benny messing up take after take of *I Love Lucy.* Jack appeared for the first time on *The Lucy Show* in the episode "Lucy and the Plumber," as a violin-playing plumber who happens to be a dead ringer for Jack Benny. Only four days after the airing of this episode, Lucy guest starred on *The Jack Benny Program* on October 2, 1964. Benny would subsequently play himself in a voice cameo in *The Lucy Show* episode "Lucy and George Burns" and would guest star in "Lucy Gets Jack Benny's Account." He later guest starred on two *Here's Lucy* episodes, "Lucy Visits Jack Benny" and "Lucy and Jack Benny's Biography," and made cameos in the third-season episodes "Lucy and Carol Burnett" and in "Lucy and the Celebrities."

Benny would make his final public appearance on Lucy's roast on *The Dean Martin Celebrity Roast,* which aired on February 7, 1975, several weeks after his death on December 26, 1974.

George Burns

Lucille Ball was the guest star in an episode of George Burns and Gracie Allen's radio show in 1944. Lucy and George Burns would work together several times through the years. He guest starred in the fifth-season premiere of *The Lucy Show*, "Lucy and George Burns," and would later do a cameo in the *Here's Lucy* episode "Lucy and Jack Benny's Biography." Ball and Burns appeared together in many specials and tributes to friends like Jack Benny and Bob Hope. They also co-hosted, with Beatrice Arthur and Arthur Godfrey, the salute to CBS's Monday night schedule in *CBS: On the Air* in 1978.

Betty White

One of Lucy's favorite television programs to watch or appear on was the game show *Password*. She guest starred several times on the various *Password* incarnations through the years and watched the daytime show every day when she was home. Allen Ludden, who was the original host of *Password*, married another frequent *Password* player, Betty White. Lucy played on the show with White several times, and Betty's ability to make Lucy laugh is evident in their appearances together.

Lucy and Betty were on *Password Plus* together in 1981 with Desi Arnaz Jr. and another one of Lucy's favorite laugh makers, Dick Martin. The two women competed against each on *Super Password* (which was taped on December 2, 1986, the day Desi died) with Lucy's *Life with Lucy* co-star Ann Dusenberry and Betty's *Golden Girls* cohort Estelle Getty. Lucy made her final game show appearance on *Super Password* in 1988 with Betty and Dick Martin again, this time joined by Carol Channing.

Lucy's mother DeDe and Betty's mother Tess were great friends. After DeDe died, Lucy sent flowers to Tess on Lucy's mother's birthday. Lucy was a big fan of White's series *The Golden Girls* and even attended the filming of an episode during the series' second season.

Charles Nelson Reilly

The jittery actor first gained notice in a pair of hit Broadway musicals, *How to Succeed in Business* and *Hello, Dolly!* The first time Charles Nelson Reilly and Lucy were on the same television show, their paths did not cross. Although Reilly was a regular on *The Steve Lawrence Show*, which welcomed Lucy as the guest on the premiere episode, the two did not appear on camera together.

They would finally perform together when Reilly portrayed department store exchange clerk Elroy P. Clunk in the *Here's Lucy* episode "Lucy, the Crusader." Although Lucy never appeared on *Match Game*, which gave Charles Nelson Reilly his greatest fame, the two did compete against each other on another game show, the charades-based *Body Language*, on a week's worth of episodes that aired in September 1984. Reilly told her on camera that he always remembered something from when they worked together. While reading a script, Lucy had said, "Great joke. Wrong place." This had taught Nelson that a line could be great, but it has to fit the situation.

Johnny Carson

Lucy watched *The Tonight Show Starring Johnny Carson* every night before going to bed. Despite having to wake up early in the morning, she would not go to sleep until one o'clock when his show ended. Regarding Carson, she said, "I love to watch him. I think he's very talented and I love him and the monologue, and I love to see himself get mired in and drag himself out. I think he's the best part of the show." There were also certain people Lucy loved to see on *The Tonight Show* opposite Johnny, including movie critic Rex Reed; Robert Blake, whose many roles as a child actor included a small part in Lucy's film *Meet the People*; impressionist Rich Little; author Gore Vidal; and Fernando Lamas. Lucy was asked to guest host *The Tonight Show*, but turned it down, thinking she was not cut out for the job. Carson guest starred on *Here's Lucy* and was featured in the specials *CBS Salutes Lucy: The First 25 Years* and *Lucy Moves to NBC*.

Ed McMahon

Lucy's love of *The Tonight Show Starring Johnny Carson* was not due entirely to the host. She also greatly enjoyed sidekick Ed McMahon. McMahon appeared twice on *Here's Lucy*. In the second-season episode, "Lucy and Johnny Carson," he portrayed himself. Ed later guest starred in the sixth-season episode "Lucy, the Wealthy Widow," playing banker Ed McAllister. McMahon had the distinction of being the only actor besides Desi Arnaz to play husband to the "Lucy" character, when he was cast as bowling alley proprietor Floyd Whittaker opposite Lucille's Lucy Whittaker in *A Lucille Ball Special: Lucy Calls the President* in 1977. When Lucy appeared on *The Tonight Show Starring Johnny Carson* in November 1977 to promote the special, she said that one of the people who made her laugh the most was Ed McMahon. Lucy told him he makes her laugh "when you are trying to help him [Johnny] out of those situations. I adore it."

Johnny Carson, before his stint hosting *The Tonight Show*, was master of ceremonies at Lucy's 1961 Friars' Club Roast in New York.

Paul Lynde

Lucy was a big fan of *The Hollywood Squares*, which featured Paul Lynde as the 'center square.' Although he considered himself an actor as opposed to an actual comedian, Lynde's acid-tongued put-downs and witty quips on the show made him one of the funniest performers in the business. Although Desi, Lucie, and Desi Jr. all served as squares during the show's long run, Lucy never made an appearance on the series. She and Lynde both appeared on *Donny and Marie* together in a *Wizard of Oz* sketch in which Lucy played "Tin Lizzie" and Lynde gave his interpretation of the Wicked Witch.

In the early seventies, when Lynde was at the height of his *Hollywood Squares* fame, he was deluged with offers for a series of his own. Lynde said at the time, "I had some other ideas in mind, but Lucy told me to stick with a family concept. 'You can't be a loner and survive,' she said. 'As a loner you might be smart and funny for a while, yet you won't last in the long haul. Do a family show, and the Beverly Hills cocktail set will ignore you, but you'll hit the people—the ones you fly over coming out from New York.'" Lynde ended up doing *The Paul Lynde Show,* which had a definite Lucy influence behind the scenes. William Asher, *I Love Lucy*'s most prolific director, was the producer/director of the series, and other longtime *Lucy* directors Jack Donohue and Coby Ruskin also helmed segments. One episode was even scripted by Bob Carroll Jr. and Madelyn Davis. Despite all the talent involved, the sitcom only lasted one season.

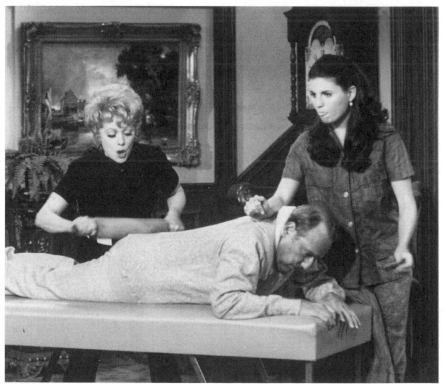

Lucy with two of the people who made her laugh the most, Gale Gordon and Lucie Arnaz, in an episode that made her laugh the most, "Lucy and Harry's Italian Bombshell."

Gale Gordon

It was no surprise, considering the number of times she called on him again and again to co-star with her on television, that Lucy adored working with Gale Gordon. Gale was nicknamed "Soggy Crotch" or "Old Wet Crotch" by the cast and crew because of how many of the series' best scenes involved him getting wet. Lucy said she loved seeing Gale and Lucie work together because they could break each other up so easily. Lucy once said Gale must "have a small hernia from laughing at my Lucie." Lucy especially enjoyed rehearsing with Gale because he gave a full-out performance from the first reading of the script on, something she loved.

Ad libs were a rarity on Lucy's series. Cameras moved on word cues, so added dialogue could result in confusion. However, Gale did think of a line to use while they were doing the *Here's Lucy* episode "Lucy and Harry's Italian Bombshell." When a door-to-door cosmetics saleslady (Vanda Barra) rings Harry's doorbell, he mistakes her for his long-lost love, Donna, whom he was expecting. When Harry hugs and kisses her, she beats him with her purse and storms out. Lucy says, "She swings a mean bag." To which Harry replies, "She *is* a mean bag." Gale followed this with a line he had thought he had mentioned to Lucy previously, but never did, "Good thing she wasn't selling doorknobs." This sent Lucy into a hysterical fit of laughter. In fact, Lucy laughed a lot during the filming of this episode. Kaye Ballard, who played Harry's now heavyset former love, struck Lucy as so funny that Lucy had to stop the filming because she was laughing so much. This was an incredibly rare thing for Lucy to do.

Betty Grable

The leggy blonde who became Fox's top musical star of the nineteen-forties and one of the great pinups of the war years, Betty Grable didn't exactly present herself on screen as a comical attraction, and yet Lucy described her off-screen as "one of the funniest women I ever met." Lucy said, "Ann Sothern and I used to laugh at Betty Grable." Lucy and Betty Grable shared two early film credits during their days as bit players—*Old Man Rhythm* (1935) and *Follow the Fleet* (1936), as well as the 1935 film short *A Night at the Biltmore Bowl.* Three years after her final movie, Betty Grable and her second husband, bandleader Harry James, guest starred on *The Lucille Ball-Desi Arnaz Show* episode "Lucy Wins a Racehorse."

While Desi Arnaz was starring on Broadway in *Too Many Girls,* he dated Grable who was concurrently in the cast of *Du Barry Was a Lady.*

Platinum blonde starlets Lucille Ball and Betty Grable appeared together in *Old Man Rhythm* (1935), *Follow the Fleet* (1936), and the short *A Night at the Biltmore Bowl* (1935). The two would later be reunited in *The Lucille Ball – Desi Arnaz Show* episode "Lucy Wins a Racehorse" (1958).

Jack Donohue

Jack Donohue's association with Lucy dated back to the forties when he was a choreographer and dance director at MGM while Lucy was under contract to the studio. In 1962, Donohue was hired to direct *The Lucy Show* and ended up helming more episodes of Lucille Ball's series than any other director.

Lucy had a habit of taking control on the set and telling the other actors what to do rather than allowing the director to do it. Donohue, when trying to get Lucy to stop doing *his* job, would typically fall back on his sense of humor, saying something like, "Lucy, please don't touch the actors. You don't know where they've been." Lucy could give it right back to Donohue. During the rehearsal for Lucy's production number, "The Continental Polka," in one of their movie collaborations, *Easy to Wed*, Donohue, then the dance director, was so angered by something that he reportedly punched a wall. The next day, Lucille reported to work in a wheelchair, bandaged, with blackened teeth, holding a sign that read, "I am not working for Donohue . . . Period."

Gary Coleman

Gary Coleman, then the star of NBC's popular *Diff'rent Strokes*, was one of the guests on Lucy's special *Lucy Moves to NBC*, which aired on February 8, 1980, Coleman's twelfth birthday. Lucy said, "I love Gary Coleman. He puts me away. He puts everybody away." While promoting *Lucy Moves to NBC*, Lucy also said about the young actor, "He's not only funny, he's bright." In fact, Lucy spent much of her promotional tour for the special praising Gary Coleman.

26

"What's That? Another Oscar?"

Lucy's Awards

1943: Golden Apple Award—Most Cooperative Actress of the Year (nominated)
At the 1943 Golden Apple Awards, Lucille Ball ended up a runner-up as Most Cooperative Actress of the Year, losing to Ann Sheridan. Carole Landis was also nominated for the honor. The Most Cooperative Actor of 1943 was Bob Hope.

1944: Golden Apple Award—Most Cooperative Actress of the Year (nominated)
For the second year in a row, Lucy narrowly missed out at being named Most Cooperative Actress of the Year. Betty Hutton was declared the winner. Maria Montez was the other nominee. Alan Ladd was the male recipient.

1946: Queen of Comedy
Lucille Ball was named The Queen of Comedy for 1946 by the Associated Drama Guilds of America in October 1946. Danny Kaye was her king.

1949: Jesters of America Award
In December 1949, comedy writers Leonard Stern and Martin Ragaway (who would later write five episodes of *Here's Lucy*) presented Lucy with a comedy achievement award from the Jesters of America. It is worth noting that Lucy was being commended for her skills at comedy *before* her television show premiered.

1951: Laurel Award—Best Comedienne
Lucy was presented the Laurel Award from *Motion Picture Exhibitor* in September 1951 as Best Comedienne of 1950. The winners were decided on a poll of film exhibitors. Lucy was awarded for her performance in *Fancy*

Gregory Peck presented Lucy with the prestigious Cecil B. De Mille Award at the Golden Globes in 1979.

Pants. Sharing in the female comedy honors was Judy Holliday for the role Lucy coveted in *Born Yesterday*.

1951: *Motion Picture Daily* Award—Most Promising Female Star
Although she was an eighteen-year veteran of films, Lucille Ball won the *Motion Picture Daily* Award for Most Promising Female Star for her new career in the medium of television. The polling for the award was conducted among the television critics of the United States.

1952: Emmy Award—Best Comedian or Comedienne (nominated)

Lucille Ball was nominated for her first Emmy at the Fourth Annual Emmy Awards. Lucy and Desi were the hosts of the ceremony, which was held on February 18, 1952, a little over four months after *I Love Lucy* first premiered. Lucy was nominated in the category Best Comedian or Comedienne alongside Sid Caesar, Imogene Coca, Jimmy Durante, Dean Martin & Jerry Lewis, Herb Shriner, and Red Skelton. Lucy's former co-star, Skelton, ended up winning. When Skelton accepted the award, he said, "Ladies and gentlemen, you've given this to the wrong redhead. I don't deserve this. It should go to Lucille Ball." Lucy would make her final appearance at the Emmys in 1986, when she presented Red Skelton with the prestigious Governor's Award. *I Love Lucy* was also nominated for Best Comedy Show, but lost to Skelton's series.

1952: *Motion Picture Daily* Award—Best Comedienne

Lucy won her second *Motion Picture Daily* Award, this time in the category of Best Comedienne. This was the third year the award was given out; Imogene Coca had won the first two years. *I Love Lucy* was also honored as Best Comedy Show.

1952: *TV Guide* Gold Medal Award

In the December 19, 1952 issue of *TV Guide* (before its April 3, 1953 national debut), Lucy was named Best Comedienne by the magazine's readers. She was also among those pictured on the cover that week. *TV Guide* presented their Gold Medal Award to Lucille on March 20, 1953 after the filming of her first *I Love Lucy* episode since her maternity leave, "No Children Allowed."

1953: Emmy Award—Most Outstanding Personality (nominee) and Best Comedienne

Lucy made her first public appearance after giving birth to Desi Jr. at the Fifth Annual Emmy Awards on February 5, 1953. Lucy was nominated for two awards: Most Outstanding Personality and Best Comedienne. Bishop Fulton J. Sheen ended up winning the award for Outstanding Personality over Lucy, Jimmy Durante, Arthur Godfrey, Edward R. Murrow, Donald O'Connor, and Adlai Stevenson. Lucy, however, emerged victorious in the category of Best Comedienne. She beat out Eve Arden, Imogene Coca, Joan Davis, and Martha Raye for the statuette. *I Love Lucy* also won the award for Best Situation Comedy.

1953: B'nai B'rith Woman of the Year
Lucille Ball became the first actress to be named Woman of the Year by
the B'nai B'rith. She accepted the award on November 21, 1953. Two days
later, she, Desi, Vivian Vance, and Bill Frawley performed for President
Eisenhower, which made it clear that no harm had come to Lucy following
the Red Scare.

1953: *Motion Picture Daily* Award—Best Comedienne
Lucy won her second consecutive *Motion Picture Daily* Award as Best
Comedienne.

1953: *Women's Home Companion* TV Award—Favorite Female Star
Lucille Ball topped Loretta Young and Eve Arden to receive *Women's Home
Companion*'s first annual TV Award for Favorite Female Star.

1954: Emmy Award—Best Female Star of Regular Series (nominated)
At the Sixth Annual Emmy Award ceremony held on February 11, 1954,
I Love Lucy was nominated for four awards. Lucy was nominated as Best
Female Star of a Regular Series, as was Eve Arden for *Our Miss Brooks*,
Imogene Coca for *Your Show of Shows*, Dinah Shore for *The Dinah Shore Show*,
and Loretta Young for *The Loretta Young Show*. Lucy's friend Eve Arden, starring in Desilu's *Our Miss Brooks*, was declared the winner. William Frawley
was nominated for Best Series Supporting Actor, but lost to *The Jackie Gleason
Show*'s Art Carney. Vivian Vance, on the other hand, was named the winner
of the Supporting Actress award and accepted it from Lucy's *My Favorite
Husband* co-star Richard Denning. Lucy and Desi gleefully ran up onstage
when *I Love Lucy* was named Best Situation Comedy for the second consecutive year. In their speech, Lucy and Desi told the Academy not to overlook
the writers. A writing category was established the following year.

1954: National Television Film Council Award
Lucy and Desi received an award from the National Television Film Council
for "their major contribution to films for television." Ed Sullivan presented
the trophy to the Arnazes at New York's Hotel Commodore on February
26, 1954. They were in New York for the opening of *The Long, Long Trailer*.

1954: *Motion Picture Daily* Awards—Best Comedienne and Best Comedy
Team
For the third consecutive year, Lucy was voted Best Comedienne in *Motion
Picture Daily*'s annual poll of television critics and editors. Lucy and Desi
were named as Best Comedy Team as well.

1955: Emmy Award—Best Actress Starring in a Regular Series (nominated)
I Love Lucy received five Emmy nominations in 1955 but no awards at the March 7, 1955 ceremony. Lucy was nominated in the category Best Actress Starring in a Regular Series along with Gracie Allen (*The George Burns and Gracie Allen Show*), Eve Arden (*Our Miss Brooks*), Ann Sothern (*Private Secretary*), and Loretta Young (*The Loretta Young Show*). Arden won the trophy. Vivian lost the award for Best Supporting Actress in a Regular Series to Audrey Meadows for *The Jackie Gleason Show,* while Bill Frawley (and *Our Miss Brooks's* Gale Gordon, among others) lost to Art Carney.

1955: *Motion Picture Daily* Awards—Best Comedienne and Best Comedy Team
Lucy was voted Best Comedienne in *Motion Picture Daily*'s annual poll of television critics and editors. Lucy and Desi were named as Best Comedy Team as well.

1955: *Motion Picture Daily* Award—Best Comedienne
Lucy won her fourth consecutive *Motion Picture Daily* Award as Best Comedienne.

1956: Golden Globe Award
Lucy and Desi were awarded for Television Achievement at the 13th Golden Globe Awards, held on February 23, 1956. This was the first year the Golden Globes recognized television.

1956: Emmy Award—Best Comedienne (nominee) and Best Actress—Continuing Performance
Lucy received two nominations for the calendar year of 1955 at the Eighth Annual Emmy Awards. She was nominated against Gracie Allen, Eve Arden, and Nanette Fabray for Best Comedienne with Fabray winning. Lucy was also nominated against Allen, Arden, Ann Sothern, and *Make Room for Daddy*'s Jean Hagen in the category of Best Actress—Continuing Performance. Lucy won the award, but was not present to accept it at the March 17, 1956 ceremony. Madelyn Pugh accepted it on Lucy's behalf. Madelyn, Bob Carroll Jr., and Jess Oppenheimer were nominated for their script for "LA at Last!," but lost to the writing team of *You'll Never Get Rich* (later known as *The Phil Silvers Show*). Bill Frawley lost the Best Actor in a Supporting Role trophy to *The Honeymooners*' Art Carney.

1956: *Motion Picture Daily* Awards—Best Comedienne and Best Comedy Team
For the fifth year in a row, Lucille Ball was voted Best Comedienne in *Motion Picture Daily*'s annual poll of television critics and editors. Ball and Desi Arnaz were honored for the second time as Best Comedy Team.

1957: Emmy Award—Best Continuing Performance by a Comedienne in a Series (nominated)
Desi was the host at the Ninth Annual Emmy Awards held on March 16, 1957. Lucy was nominated for Best Continuing Performance by a Comedienne in a Series, but lost to Nanette Fabray for *Caesar's Hour*. Other nominees in the category were Edie Adams for *The Ernie Kovacs Show*, Gracie Allen for *The George Burns and Gracie Allen Show*, and Ann Sothern for *Private Secretary*. Vivian and Bill Frawley were both nominated in the supporting categories, but lost to Pat Carroll and Carl Reiner, both of *Caesar's Hour*.

1957: *Motion Picture Daily* Award—Best Comedienne
Lucy was again named Best Comedienne in *Motion Picture Daily*'s annual poll.

1958: Genii Award
Lucy was the recipient of the Genii Award from the Radio and Television Women of Southern California in March 1958. In 1964, she presented the award to Vivian Vance.

1958: Emmy Award—Best Continuing Performance (Female) in a Series by a Comedienne, Singer, Hostess, Dancer, M.C., Announcer, Narrator, Panelist, or any Person Who Essentially Plays Herself (nominated)
Lucy received her final Emmy nomination for playing Lucy Ricardo in the bizarrely named category of Best Continuing Performance (Female) in a Series by a Comedienne, Singer, Hostess, Dancer, M.C., Announcer, Narrator, Panelist, or Any Person Who Essentially Plays Herself at the Tenth Annual Emmy Awards. Lucy did not attend the award show held on April 15, 1958, citing that the telecast was sponsored by Plymouth, rival to the *Lucy-Desi* sponsor Ford. Lucy, Gracie Allen, Dody Goodman (*Tonight Starring Jack Paar*), and Loretta Young (*The Loretta Young Show*) all lost out to Dinah Shore (*The Dinah Shore Show*). Vivian lost in the supporting actress race to Ann B. Davis for *The Bob Cummings Show*, while Bill Frawley was again defeated by Carl Reiner of *Caesar's Hour*.

1958: *Los Angeles Times* Women of the Year Award
In 1958, Lucille Ball was one of the ten recipients of the *Los Angeles Times* Women of the Year Award. This award was established in 1950 to honor outstanding Southern Californian women.

1958: *Motion Picture Daily* Award—Best Comedienne
Despite the fact that she was no longer on television every week, Lucy won the *Motion Picture Daily* Award as "Best Comedienne" for the seventh year in a row.

1959: *Motion Picture Daily* Award—Best Comedienne
Lucille Ball's eight-year streak as *Motion Picture Daily*'s Best Comedienne ends with this award. She will be absent from TV for the 1960–61 and 1961–62 television seasons.

1961: Aegis Theatre Club Award
Lucille did not go back to California empty-handed after making her Broadway debut, having won the Aegis Theatre Club Award for her performance in *Wildcat*. Gig Young was also recognized for his work in *Under the Yum-Yum Tree*. The awards were presented at the Manhattan Hotel on April 18, 1961.

1961: Golden Globe Award for Best Performance by an Actress in a Leading Role—Musical or Comedy (nominated)
Lucy was nominated for her performance as Kitty Weaver in *The Facts of Life*. She lost to Shirley MacLaine for *The Apartment*. Lucy's other competitors were Judy Holliday for *Bells Are Ringing*, Sophia Loren for *It Started in Naples*, and Capucine for *Song Without End*. *The Facts of Life* received two other nominations: one for Best Picture—Comedy and one for Bob Hope. The movie lost to *The Apartment*, and Hope lost to its lead, Jack Lemmon.

1961: National Laugh Foundation Award: Funniest Woman of the Year in Motion Pictures.
In March 1961, Lucille Ball won the National Laugh Foundation's award for Funniest Woman of the Year in Motion Pictures. Lucy's film *The Facts of Life* had just been released a few months prior.

1961: Laurel Award—Top Female Comedy Performance (nominated)
Lucy's performance in *The Facts of Life* placed her among the nominees for Top Female Comedy Performance for *Motion Picture Exhibitor*'s Laurel Awards. Lucy was, however, outranked by Janet Leigh for *Pepe*. Sophia Loren

(*It Started in Naples*), Paula Prentiss (*Where the Boys Are*), and Jean Simmons (*The Grass Is Greener*) were also listed.

1962: New York Film Critics Circle Award— Best Actress (nominated)
Lucille Ball's name was on the ballot for the prestigious New York Film Critics Circle Award for Best Actress for her performance in *The Facts of Life*. Although the film premiered at the end of 1960 in Los Angeles and qualified for the 1960 awards there, it did not actually open in New York until February 10, 1961. As a result, Lucy's name was placed on the ballot of the New York Film Critics Circle Award for the year of 1961, and the winner was announced in January 1962. Other names listed were Natalie Wood (*Splendor in the Grass*), Piper Laurie (*The Hustler*), Rachel Roberts (*Saturday Night and Sunday Morning*), and the eventual winner, Sophia Loren (*Two Women*).

1962: Fig Leaf Award
Lucy received the Fig Leaf Award from the Motion Picture Costumers. The award was given to performers who "most consistently distinguished themselves with effective use of costumes." Vincent Price presented the award to Lucy at the September 22, 1962 ceremony. Bob Hope was the male winner, and his daughter Linda accepted the award on his behalf.

1962: *Motion Picture Daily* Award—Best Comedienne
Back on television after a two-year hiatus, Lucille Ball was again named by *Motion Picture Daily* as Best Comedienne. *The Garry Moore Show*'s Carol Burnett received the honor the two years between Lucy's wins.

1963: Golden Apple Award—Most Cooperative Actress of the Year (nominated)
Lucy was nominated once again as Most Cooperative Actress of the Year in 1963; however. Bette Davis was named the most cooperative instead. Sandra Dee, Janet Leigh, and Connie Stevens were also in contention.

1963: Hollywood Advertising Club—Red Carpet Award
The Hollywood Advertising Club and the Los Angeles Advertising Women saluted Lucy at the Hollywood Roosevelt Hotel on February 4, 1963. The Hollywood Advertising Club presented Lucy with their Red Carpet Award, of which Lucy was the third ever recipient.

1963: Emmy Award—Outstanding Continued Performance by an Actress in a Series (Lead) (nominated)

Lucy received an Emmy nomination for her work in the first season of *The Lucy Show*. All of the contenders in the category of Outstanding Continued Performance by an Actress in a Series (Lead) besides Lucy were newcomers to the Emmy race. Shirley Booth of *Hazel*, Shirl Conway of *The Nurses*, Mary Tyler Moore of *The Dick Van Dyke Show*, and Irene Ryan of *The Beverly Hillbillies* all received their first Emmy nominations, and Shirley Booth won the statuette at the May 26, 1963 ceremony. *The Danny Kaye Show with Lucille Ball*, which aired on November 5, 1962, was nominated in the categories of Outstanding Program Achievement in the Field of Humor (where it lost to *The Dick Van Dyke Show*) and "Program of the Year" (the winner was *The Tunnel*). Lucy, however, failed to receive a nomination for her contribution to the special.

1963: *Motion Picture Daily* Award—Best Comedienne
Motion Picture Daily named Lucille Ball Best Comedienne for the second consecutive year.

1964: Women of Achievement Award
Lucille was the recipient of the Women of Achievement Award given by the women's journalism group, Theta Sigma Phi. She was honored for her acting and her role as president of Desilu. Magazine executive Margaret Hickey was the other recipient at the November 15, 1964 breakfast.

1964: *Motion Picture Daily* Award—Best Comedienne
For the third year in a row, Ball won the *Motion Picture Daily* Award for Best Comedienne.

1965: *Motion Picture Daily* Award—Best Comedienne
The television critics of the United States once again gave Lucille Ball the *Motion Picture Daily* Award for Best Comedienne.

1966: Emmy Award—Outstanding Continued Performance by an Actress in a Leading Role in a Comedy Series (nominated)
Lucy was nominated for the fourth season of *The Lucy Show* at the 1966 awards ceremony. Her competition was Mary Tyler Moore for *The Dick Van Dyke Show* and Elizabeth Montgomery for *Bewitched*. Moore won her second Emmy for the program. Lucy did not attend the ceremony, which was held on May 22, 1966, because she was in England working on *Lucy in London*.

1966: *TV Radio Mirror* Magazine Award—Best Female Star
Lucy was named Best Female Star on Television by *TV Radio Mirror* in 1966.

Dick Van Dyke was named Best Male Star, and his sitcom was also cited as the best series.

1966: *Motion Picture Daily* Award—Best Comedienne
Lucille Ball won her fifth consecutive and twelfth overall *Motion Picture Daily* Award for Best Comedienne. This will be her final win. The following year, Carol Burnett will begin an unstoppable streak, topping Lucy each year.

1967: Emmy Award—Outstanding Continued Performance by an Actress in a Leading Role in a Comedy Series
A shocked Lucille Ball was declared the winner of the Emmy for Outstanding Continued Performance by an Actress in a Leading Role in a Comedy Series in 1967. Lucy beat out Elizabeth Montgomery and Agnes Moorehead, both of *Bewitched*, and *That Girl*'s Marlo Thomas. Barbara Eden and Carl Reiner presented Lucy her award. During her acceptance speech, Lucy said, "The last time I got it, I thought they gave it to me because I had a baby." She obviously forgot her 1956 win that she was not present for. Lucy's win was called the highlight of the night. Gale Gordon was also nominated for his work on *The Lucy Show*, but lost to Don Knotts, who won his fifth Emmy Award for *The Andy Griffith Show.* Maury Thompson became the first and only *Lucy* director ever to be Emmy nominated, but he lost to James Frawley, director of *The Monkees*.

1968: Emmy Award—Outstanding Continued Performance by an Actress in a Leading Role in a Comedy Series
Lucille Ball won her second consecutive Emmy Award and her fourth overall at the 20th Annual Emmy Awards. One of the evening's hosts, Frank Sinatra, presented the award. Lucy emerged victorious over Barbara Feldon for *Get Smart*, Elizabeth Montgomery for *Bewitched*, Paula Prentiss for *He & She*, and Marlo Thomas for *That Girl.*

The Lucy Show received its greatest attention from the Emmys this year. Gale Gordon was nominated, but lost to Werner Klemperer from *Hogan's Heroes*. Milt Josefsberg and Ray Singer were nominated for scripting "Lucy Gets Jack Benny's Account," but *He & She* writers Allen Burns and Chris Hayward won for their script "The Coming Out Party." *The Lucy Show* received its only nomination for Outstanding Comedy Series, but lost to *Get Smart*.

This Emmy ceremony was criticized since the winners of the lead acting awards from the previous year all repeated: Lucy, Don Adams (*Get Smart*), Bill Cosby (*I Spy*), and Barbara Bain (*Mission: Impossible*). The TV Academy discussed the possibility of restricting nominations to programs only in their first season. This did not happen. This was Lucy's final Emmy nomination, but she would receive several more honors from the television Academy in later years. In 1969, they held a gala dinner for Ball and officially proclaimed her "The First Lady of Television." In 1973 on *The Merv Griffin Show,* Lucy was presented with a plaque celebrating all her Emmy nominations. James Stewart presented Lucy with this same plaque in 1976 on the special *CBS Salutes Lucy: The First 25 Years.* On the Emmy telecast in 1981, the Academy presented Lucy with a special certificate celebrating her thirtieth anniversary on television.

1968: Golden Globe Award for Best Actress in a Television Series (nominated)
Lucy was nominated for *The Lucy Show* at the 25th Annual Golden Globe Awards, but lost to her friend Carol Burnett for *The Carol Burnett Show.* The other nominees were Barbara Bain for Desilu's *Mission: Impossible,* Nancy Sinatra for the special *Movin' with Nancy,* and Barbara Stanwyck for *The Big Valley.*

1968: Laurel Award—Female Comedy Performance
Lucy received the Laurel Award for playing Helen North Beardsley in *Yours, Mine and Ours.* Lucy topped Jane Fonda for *Barefoot in the Park,* Debbie Reynolds for *Divorce American Style,* Inger Stevens for *A Guide for the Married Man* (in which Lucy had a cameo), and Doris Day for *Where Were You When the Lights Went Out? Yours, Mine and Ours* was cited for General Entertainment, and Henry Fonda was nominated for his performance, but *The Odd Couple*'s Walter Matthau received the top slot.

1969: Golden Globe Award for Best Performance by an Actress in a Leading Role—Musical or Comedy (nominated)
Lucy received a Golden Globe nod for her performance as Helen North Beardsley in *Yours, Mine and Ours.* Barbra Streisand ended up being named winner for her performance as Fanny Brice in *Funny Girl* (two months later she would win the Oscar in a historic tie with Katharine Hepburn). In addition to Lucy, Streisand beat out Julie Andrews for *Star!,* Petula Clark for *Finian's Rainbow,* and Gina Lollobrigida for *Buona Sera, Mrs. Campbell. Yours, Mine and Ours* would also be nominated for Best Motion Picture—Musical/Comedy, but would lose to *Oliver!,* which would also take the Best Picture award at that year's Oscar ceremony.

1969: Golden Apple Award—Star of the Year (nominated)
In 1969, the Hollywood Women's Press Club voted Mae West Star of the Year over Lucille Ball and Katharine Hepburn.

1970: Golden Globe Award for Best Actress in a Television Series—Musical or Comedy (nominated)
Lucy was nominated for the calendar year of 1969 at the 27th annual ceremony for *Here's Lucy*. Lucy lost in a tie between Carol Burnett and *The Governor & J.J.*'s Julie Sommars. Debbie Reynolds of *The Debbie Reynolds Show*, Barbara Eden of *I Dream of Jeannie*, and Diahann Carroll of *Julia* were also nominated.

1971: Golden Globe Award for Best Performance by an Actress in a Television Series—Musical or Comedy (nominated)
Lucy was again unsuccessful in winning a Golden Globe when she lost to Mary Tyler Moore for her self-titled series in 1971. Moore also beat out *The Partridge Family*'s Shirley Jones, *The Nanny and the Professor*'s Juliet Mills, and *Bewitched*'s Elizabeth Montgomery.

1971. International Radio and Television Society Gold Medal Award
To commemorate Lucy's twentieth anniversary on television, the International Radio and Television Society hosted a gala dinner for her on March 11, 1971 at New York's Waldorf-Astoria Hotel and presented her with their Gold Medal Award. Lucy was the first woman to receive the honor, which was established in 1960. Glen Campbell was the evening's headliner. Carol Burnett so wanted to be a part of the evening that she moved her Los Angeles-based variety show to New York for a week so she could participate. Lucy, Carol, and Lucie appeared on *The Dick Cavett Show*, done in New York, that week as well.

1971: Comedienne of the Century
On May 23, 1971, Lucy was proclaimed "Comedienne of the Century" at a "To Lucy, With Love," gala by the Diabetes Association of Southern California held at the Dorothy Chandler Pavilion. Bob Hope, Jack Benny, George Burns, Phyllis Diller, and Andy Williams were among the participants.

1972: Golden Globe Award for Best Actress—Musical or Comedy Series or Television Movie (nominated)
Lucy lost her third consecutive bid in this inconsistently named category. Carol Burnett once again received the award, triumphing over Shirley Jones for *The Partridge Family*, Mary Tyler Moore, and Jean Stapleton for

All in the Family. That same night, Desi Arnaz Jr. was named Most Promising Newcomer based on his performance in the film *Red Sky at Morning.*

1973: Golden Apple Award—Star of the Year
Lucy was named Star of the Year by the Hollywood Women's Press Club on December 16, 1973. Barbra Streisand and Liv Ullmann were nominated against Lucy. Robert Redford was named male Star of the Year. Lucy was the only one of the six nominees for Star of the Year to actually attend the ceremony.

1974: Ruby Award
Lucy received the Ruby Award as Entertainer of the Year from *After Dark* magazine in 1974. In a brunette *Mame* wig, she accepted the award at the February 28, 1974 ceremony from *Mame* composer Jerry Herman. The award was established in 1971 and named after Ruby Keeler. Lucy, in a pose from *Mame*, graced the cover of the March 1974 issue of *After Dark*.

1974: Sunair Home for Asthmatic Children Humanitarian Award
Lucy was named Humanitarian of the Year for 1973 by the Sunair Foundation, a California-based company specializing in the research and development of social sciences. Bob Hope hosted the foundation gala at the Beverly Hilton Hotel on May 15, 1974 where Lucy was presented her award.

1974: Mrs. Wonderful
Lucy was named the first ever Mrs. Wonderful by the Thalians organization, run by her friends Debbie Reynolds (who was unable to attend because she was starring on Broadway in *Irene*) and Ruta Lee. The organization was created in 1955 by a group of celebrities interested in helping children with mental health issues. In 1966, the Mr. Wonderful award was created to honor those involved in entertainment and philanthropy. In 1974, Lucy became the first woman honored. Among the stars paying tribute to Lucy were Liza Minnelli, Doris Day, Eve Arden, Raquel Welch, and Steve Allen and Jayne Meadows. One highlight was an *I Love Lucy* sketch with Lucie and Desi Jr. playing Lucy and Ricky Ricardo, supported by Ruta Lee and Shecky Greene as Ethel and Fred. Lucie also performed a musical tribute to her mother. Lucy was presented the Mrs. Wonderful award (designed by Walt Disney) by the previous year's honoree, Sammy Davis Jr. Lucy appeared many times at the Thalians' gala, most notably recreating the title number from *Mame* when co-star Robert Preston was honored in 1984.

1975: Golden Globe Award for Best Performance by an Actress in a Leading Role—Musical or Comedy (Nominated)

Lucille Ball received her final Golden Globe nomination, for *Mame* in 1975. Raquel Welch was named the winner for her performance in *The Three Musketeers*. The other nominees in the race were Diahann Carroll for *Claudine*, Helen Hayes for *Herbie Rides Again*, and Cloris Leachman for *Young Frankenstein*. Lucy's *Mame* co-star Beatrice Arthur was nominated for Best Performance by an Actress in a Supporting Role in a Motion Picture, but lost to *The Great Gatsby*'s Karen Black.

1975: Golden Award

Lucille Ball received the Golden Award for American Guild of American Guild of Variety Artists. The awards were held at Las Vegas' Caesar's Palace on December 22, 1975 with Jackie Gleason, whose TV special with Lucy aired a few weeks earlier, serving as host.

1977: Women in Film Crystal Award

In 1977, the Women in Film organization created the Crystal Award to "honor outstanding individuals who, through their perseverance and the excellence of their work in film, have helped to expand the role of women within the entertainment industry." In the first year, Lucy, Nancy Malone, Eleanor Perry, and Norma Zarky were the recipients. In 1994, Women in Film created a new award, the Lucy Award, which was given to "talented individuals who exemplify the extraordinary accomplishments embodied in the life and work of Lucille Ball."

1977: Friars Club Life Achievement Award

Lucy was honored with the Friars Club Life Achievement Award on November 4, 1977. Milton Berle was the host of the star-studded event that included Lucie, Desi Jr., Carol Burnett, Beverly Sills, Sammy Davis Jr., Frank Sinatra, Henry Fonda, Mary Tyler Moore, Danny Thomas, Ann-Margret, and Steve Lawrence and Eydie Gorme.

Lucy and Desi received a Friars' Club roast in 1958, which went on to become perhaps the most infamous in the club's long history. Held at the Beverly Hilton Hotel, the evening was emceed by Art Linkletter and included entertainment by Milton Berle, Dean Martin, Sammy Davis Jr., Danny Thomas, George Murphy, and Tony Martin, among others. Comedian Harry Parke (known as "Parkyakarkus") roasted the couple and then went to his seat, where he had a heart attack and died.

Lucy received a solo testimonial in 1961. Women were not actually allowed to become members until 1988. Lucy was among the first group of females to be made honorary members, alongside such notables as Carol Burnett, Barbra Streisand, Phyllis Diller, Elizabeth Taylor, and Dinah Shore.

1979: Golden Globe Awards—Cecil B. DeMille Award
Lucy received the prestigious Cecil B. DeMille Award at the 36th Annual Golden Globe Awards. Gregory Peck, who received the award in 1969, presented it to Lucy.

1980: The Gift of Laughter Award
Lucille Ball was honored by the Children's Diabetes Foundation at their third annual Carousel Ball in Denver, Colorado on June 14, 1980. The event was organized by Lucy and Gary Morton's close friends Marvin and Barbara Davis. The Mortons attended the event, which attracted the biggest stars in Hollywood, each year.

1982: Iris Award of the Year
Lucy received the Iris Award of the Year from the National Association of Television Programming Executives in March 1982. The previous year, Lucy had presented the award to Phil Donahue.

1982: *TV Guide* Life Achievement Award
During *The Fourth Annual TV Guide Special: 1982—The Year in Review,* Carol Burnett presented a Life Achievement Award to the *TV Guide* cover queen. The special was eventually telecast on January 24, 1983.

1983: Jack Benny Memorial Award
The March of Dimes presented Lucy with their Jack Benny Memorial Award on June 2, 1983. The organization said Lucy was being cited for her "outstanding accomplishments as a great entertainer" and for "her many charitable contributions to our community." Carol Burnett, who was the 1981 honoree, presented Lucy with the award named after Lucy's late neighbor and co-star. Benny's best friend George Burns was the award's first recipient in 1977.

1984: Television Academy Hall of Fame
In 1984, the Academy of Television Arts and Sciences established the Television Academy Hall of Fame. Of the seven people inducted in the first year, Lucille Ball was the only woman. Milton Berle, Norman Lear, and William S. Paley were also inducted, and Paddy Chayefsky, Edward R. Murrow, and General David Sarnoff all were inducted posthumously. At

the ceremony, held on January 21, 1984, Lucy was first saluted by her son Desi, who introduced a taped tribute by his sister Lucie. Lucie was unable to attend because she was on the East Coast starring opposite her husband Laurence Luckinbill in a production of *The Guardsman* at the Paper Mill Playhouse in New Jersey. Lucie sang a song entitled "My Mother, the Star," which caused the entire audience to burst into tears. Carol Burnett then formally inducted Lucy into the Hall of Fame. In Lucy's tearful speech, she said, "This night has got to top them all." Later on, Lucy said that the show was the most emotional she had ever done.

Lucy returned to the Hall of Fame ceremony in 1987 when she inducted Bob Hope. In 1991, Desi Arnaz was posthumously inducted, with Lucie and Desi Jr. accepting the honor on their father's behalf. At that same ceremony, *I Love Lucy* became the first television show ever to be inducted into the Hall of Fame with many of the surviving cast and crew members, including Madelyn Davis, Bob Carroll Jr., Bob Schiller, Bob Weiskopf, Mary Jane Croft, Doris Singleton, Jerry Hausner, and William Asher, attending the ceremony.

1984: Variety Clubs Children's Charities Award

In 1984, Lucille Ball was the ninth celebrity honored by the Variety Clubs International with "An All-Star Party." Lucy followed in the footsteps of John Wayne, Elizabeth Taylor, James Stewart, Ingrid Bergman, Jack Lemmon, Burt Reynolds, Carol Burnett, and Frank Sinatra. One of the features of the tribute was a hospital wing being named after the honoree. The Barbara Davis Juvenile Diabetes Hospital in Denver, Colorado unveiled the Lucille Ball Research Library. Barbara Davis was the wife of the Mortons' friend Marvin Davis.

Saluting Lucy at her tribute were Monty Hall, Joan Collins, Frank Sinatra, Cary Grant (who read a letter from President Ronald Reagan), Sid Caesar and Carl Reiner, John Ritter, Vicki McClure, Shelley Long, Dean Martin, James Stewart, Sammy Davis Jr., and Burt Reynolds. The event was held on November 18, 1984, the eve of Lucy and Gary's twenty-third wedding anniversary. Gary presented Lucy with an Olympic medal with an inscription that read, "You are truly a gold medal wife." Lucie, seven months pregnant, and Desi Jr. sang to their mother the *I Love Lucy* theme with a new arrangement by Nelson Riddle and lyrics by Sammy Cahn. The song left Lucy in tears. *An All-Star Party for Lucille Ball* aired on CBS on December 29, 1984 and was a ratings winner. Two years earlier, Lucy was a speaker at Carol Burnett's All-Star Party, in which she read a letter from Ronald Reagan. In 1986, Lucy participated in Clint Eastwood's tribute.

1985: Will Rogers Memorial Award
The Beverly Hills Chamber of Commerce and Civic Association named Lucy the winner of their annual Will Rogers Memorial Award in 1985. Lucy received the honor on March 1, 1985 at a dinner celebrating the organization's twenty-fifth anniversary.

1986: Kennedy Center Honor
On December 5, 1986, the day after Desi Arnaz's memorial service, Lucy travelled to Washington DC to receive the prestigious Kennedy Center Honor. The other recipients in 1986, the ninth year the honors were given out, were Ray Charles, Hume Cronyn and Jessica Tandy, Yehudi Menuhin, and Antony Tudor. Lucy and the other honorees each received their Kennedy Center Medal Honor at the White House on December 6. The following night was the Kennedy Center Honors ceremony. Walter Matthau and Robert Stack were on hand to participate in Lucy's tribute. Stack read a statement written by Desi in which he credited the success of *I Love Lucy* to Lucille. Current sitcom stars Beatrice Arthur (*The Golden Girls*), Valerie Harper (*Valerie*), and Pam Dawber (*My Sister Sam*) performed a musical tribute for Lucy that featured a medley of "I Love Lucy," "Mame," and "Hey, Look Me Over" with special lyrics. Bea Arthur and Valerie Harper had special connections to two of the songs since Arthur co-starred in *Mame* and Harper was a dancer in *Wildcat*. Lucy would return to the Kennedy Center the following year when she presented her friend Sammy Davis Jr. his honor.

1986: Working Women Hall of Fame
In celebration of their tenth anniversary, *Working Woman* magazine created the Working Women Hall of Fame in 1986. Lucy was among the first six inductees, cited for being the first female head of a TV studio.

1987: American Comedy Award—Lifetime Achievement
The American Comedy Awards were established in 1987. At the first ceremony, which was televised on May 19, 1987, five women were awarded with lifetime achievement awards: Lucy, Carol Burnett, Mary Tyler Moore, Bette Midler, and Lily Tomlin. Midler and Tomlin were the only winners present. Lucy taped an acceptance speech for the evening. When Midler and Tomlin jointly accepted their awards, Lily spent her time onstage saying that she wanted to meet Lucy. Lucy soon went out to dinner with the two ladies.

1988: Hasty Pudding Woman of the Year
Hasty Pudding Theatricals, Harvard University's all-male revue, named Lucille Ball their Woman of the Year in 1988. Lucy had been offered the honor, which was established in 1951, many times over the years, but was forced to turn it down due to other commitments. Lucy gladly travelled to Massachusetts to accept the honor at the February 16, 1988 ceremony. The festivities began with a parade through Cambridge. Later in the day, she received the Woman of the Year Hasty Pudding Pot prize at a ceremony that included an *I Love Lucy* trivia quiz for her and a sample of real hasty pudding for Lucy to try. The day concluded with a black tie dinner in Lucy's honor.

1988: National Association of Broadcasting Hall of Fame
On April 10, 1988, Lucy and Milton Berle became the first two people inducted into the National Association of Broadcasting Hall of Fame specifically for television. The Hall of Fame was established in 1977, but all previous inductees had been for radio.

1989: Eastman Second Century Award
In March 1989, it was announced that Lucy would receive the Eastman Second Century Award given by the Directors Guild of America. The award was to recognize Lucy's "continuing contribution to the development of young talent in the entertainment industry." Lucy was to receive the award at a banquet on April 24. This became impossible when she was hospitalized on April 18. Lucie and Gary attended the ceremony, and Carol Burnett presented the award to Lucie on behalf of her mother. This would be the last honor bestowed on Lucille Ball in her lifetime.

Bibliography

"Actor Gale Gordon Was Born in Trade." *Montreal Gazette* 19 July 1962.

Andrews, Bart, and Thomas Watson. *Loving Lucy: An Illustrated Tribute to Lucille Ball.* New York: St. Martin's, 1980.

Andrews, Bart. *The "I Love Lucy" Book.* Garden City, NY: Doubleday, 1985.

Arnaz, Desi. *A Book.* New York: William Morrow, 1976.

Ball, Desiree. "My Favorite Actress." *The Illustrated Press* 291 (2001).

Ball, Lucille, and Betty Hannah Hoffman. *Love, Lucy.* New York: Putnam, 1996.

Ball, Lucille. *Lucille Ball: An American Film Institute Seminar on Her Work.* Beverly Hills, CA, 1977.

————. *The Museum of Broadcasting Seminar Series: Lucille Ball Seminar at the Citibank Auditorium.* 10 Apr. 1984.

Ballard, Kaye, and Jim Hesselman. *How I Lost 10 Pounds in 53 Years: A Memoir.* New York: Back Stage, 2006.

Beck, Marilyn. "Hollywood Closeup." *Milwaukee Journal* 16 Feb. 1971.

————. "Lucy's Cousin Her Producer." *Calgary Herald* 21 May 1971.

————. "New Movie on Tap for Ball, Gleason." *Hartford Courant* 5 June 1969.

Bergman, Ronald. *The United Artists Story.* New York: Crown, 1986.

Berle, Milton, and Haskel Frankel. *Milton Berle: An Autobiography.* New York: Delacorte, 1974.

Bergquist, Laura. "Lucille Ball, the Star That Never Sets." *Look* 7 Sept. 1971.

"Bob and Lucy Practice Togetherness." *Pittsburgh Press* 29 Jan. 1963.

Brady, Kathleen. *Lucille: The Life of Lucille Ball.* New York: Hyperion, 1994.

"Brilliance, Purpose, and Achievement Distinguish 1958 Times Women of Year." *Los Angeles Times* 21 Dec. 1958.

Brockway, Laurie Sue. "Those Who Loved Lucy Flock to Jamestown to Remember Her." *The Pittsburgh Press* 15 Oct. 1989.

Browning, Norma Lee. "Lucy's Special May Spur Series." *Chicago Tribune* 15 Nov. 1974.

Castelluccio, Frank, and Alvin Walker. *The Other Side of Ethel Mertz: The Life Story of Vivian Vance.* Manchester, CT: Knowledge, Ideas & Trends, 1998.

Churchill, Douglas W. "Fox Seeks Betty Grable and Barbara Stanwyck for Two Pictures." *New York Times* 30 Oct. 1941.

————. "Screen News Here and In Hollywood." *New York Times* 21 Oct. 1941.

————. "Screen News Here and In Hollywood." *New York Times* 27 Apr. 1939.

————. "Screen News Here and In Hollywood." *New York Times* 8 Sept. 1941.

Considine, Shaun. *Bette & Joan: The Divine Feud.* New York: E. P. Dutton, 1989.

Cuthbertson, Ken. "Gale Gordon Talks about Comic Style." *The Leader-Post* [Regina, Saskatchewan] 17 Feb. 1978.

Davis, Madelyn Pugh, and Bob Carroll. *Laughing with Lucy: My Life with America's Leading Lady of Comedy.* Cincinnati, OH: Emmis, 2005.

De La Hoz, Cindy. *Lucy at the Movies.* Philadelphia: Running, 2007.

"Desi Arnaz Jr.—A Child of Hollywood." *Palm Beach Post* 16 Oct. 1971.

"Desi Arnaz Jr. Dances to a New Tune, Marries Ballerina." *Deseret News* 29 Oct. 1987.

"Desi Arnaz Jr. Ties Knot." *Lawrence Journal-World* 14 Jan. 1980.

"Desilu's 'Whiting Girls' May Chart Trade Course to Musical Comedy." *Billboard* 7 May 1955.

"Desi's Back, with a New Name." *Milwaukee Journal* 21 Sept. 1982.

"Dorothy Comingore Is Offered Leading Feminine Role in 'The Little Pinks' at RKO." *New York Times* 27 Dec. 1941.

"Dream Girl." *Billboard* 30 Aug. 1947.

Eames, John Douglas. *The MGM Story.* New York: Crown, 1979.

———. *The Paramount Story.* New York: Crown, 1985.

Edelman, Rob, and Audrey E. Kupferberg. *Meet the Mertzes: The Life Stories of I Love Lucy's Other Couple.* Los Angeles: Renaissance, 1999.

Edwards, Elisabeth. *Lucy & Desi: A Real Life Scrapbook of America's Favorite TV Couple.* Philadelphia: Running, 2004.

"Eliott Lewis; Actor, Producer, Mystery Writer." *Los Angeles Times* 26 May 1990.

Fantle, David, and Tom Johnson. *Reel to Real: 25 Years of Celebrity Interviews from Vaudeville to Movies to TV.* Oregon, WI: Badger, 2004.

Fidelman, Geoffrey Mark. *The Lucy Book: A Complete Guide to Her Five Decades on Television.* Los Angeles: Renaissance, 1999.

Fleeman, Michael. "Comedy Star Lucille Ball Dies." *Daily Union* [Kansas] 26 Apr. 1989.

Fonda, Henry, and Howard Teichmann. *Fonda: My Life.* New York: New American Library, 1981.

"For Lucy." *Sarasota Journal* 5 Feb. 1963.

"Frank Gorey." Interview by Stu Shostak. *Stu's Show.* Shokus Internet Radio. 12 Dec. 2007.

"Frank Sinatra Will Tape Another One-Hour Special." *Los Angeles Times* 10 May 1966.

"Gale Gordon." *Sherbrooke Telegram* 27 May 1948.

Gertner, Richard. *International Television Almanac.* New York: Quigley, 1971.

"Gleason Suggests Lucy Act." *Evening Independent* 9 Aug. 1963.

Graham, Sheilah. "Flashes From Film." *Milwaukee Journal* 12 Nov. 1944.

"Grateful Desi Pledges Hospital for Mexicans." *Hartford Courant* 28 July 1967.

Gregory, James. *The Lucille Ball Story*. New York: New American Library, 1974.

Harrison, Paul. "Lucille Ball, Worn Thin and Jittery by 'Vacation' . . ." *Pittsburgh Press* 19 Oct. 1941.

"Hippodrome." *Reading Eagle* 21 May 1921.

Hirschhorn, Clive. *The Columbia Story*. New York: Crown, 1989.

———. *The Hollywood Musical*. New York: Crown, 1983.

———. *The Universal Story*. New York: Crown, 1983.

———. *The Warner Bros. Story*. New York: Crown, 1979.

Hopper, Hedda. "Ann Sothern, Lucille Ball May Do Series." *Los Angeles Times* 12 Feb. 1962.

———. "Ball on Broadway." *Los Angeles Times* 15 Apr. 1959.

———. "'Born Yesterday' Scheduled For Screening in Hollywood." *Youngstown Vindicator* 5 Dec. 1946.

———. "Columnist in a Nostalgic Mood." *Los Angeles Times* 30 May 1958.

———. "Drama and Film." *Los Angeles Times* 27 Sept. 1947.

———. "Lucille Ball Retains Charm of Girlhood." *Los Angeles Times* 25 May 1947.

———. "Lucille Has Ball on Manhattan Trip." *Los Angeles Times* 26 Nov. 1962.

Jacobs, Jody. "Ball, Wolper in C of C Awards Spotlight." *Los Angeles Times* 21 Feb. 1985.

Jewell, Richard B., and Vernon Harbin. *The RKO Story*. New York: Arlington House, 1982.

"Jill, David Frost Birds of a Feather." *Los Angeles Times* 18 May 1970.

Kulzer, Dina-Marie. *Television Series Regulars of the Fifties and Sixties in Interview*. Jefferson, NC: McFarland, 1992.

Lester, Peter. "Ask Her Anything About Desi Sr., Divorce, Drugs, Gay Rights—Lucy Ball Hasn't Become Bashful at 68." *People* 11 Feb. 1980. Web.

Lewis, Dan. "Ingrid Bergman Eyed as Lucy's Show Guest." *Waycross Journal-Herald* 3 Apr. 1971.

Los Angeles Times 21 Dec. 1958.

Lowry, Cynthia. "Lucy Radiant as a Newlywed; Gary's Career Faces Big Test." *Hartford Courant* 10 Dec. 1961.

———. "New Lucy TV Series This Fall Poses Big Comeback Question." *Montreal Gazette* 21 Aug. 1962.

———. "Vivian Vance Likes Role Better Than Ex-Lucy Part." *Tri City Herald* 9 Dec. 1962.

———. "Novelist-Divorcee Sees Goofs Explode on Lucy Show." *Evening Independent* [St. Petersburg] 7 June 1963.

"Lucie Arnaz." Interview by Arthur Unger. 1971. The New York Public Library for the Performing Arts.

"Lucie Arnaz Weds Actor." *Wilmington Morning Star* 24 Jan. 1980.

"Lucille Ball, Bob Hope Get Fig Leaf Awards." *Ocala Star-Banner* 24 Sept. 1962.

"Lucille Ball Faints." *New York Times* 23 Apr. 1961.

"Lucille Ball Feted By Two Ad Clubs." *Los Angeles Times* 5 Feb. 1963.

"Lucille Ball, Gig Young Cited." *New York Times* 29 Mar. 1961.

"Lucille Ball." Interviews by Arthur Unger. 1974, 1975, 1984, 1985. The New York Public Library for the Performing Arts.

———. Interviews by Dinah Shore. *Dinah!* 1 Dec. 1975, 16 Nov. 1976.

———. Interview by Johnny Carson. *The Tonight Show Starring Johnny Carson.* NBC. 18 Nov. 1977.

———. Interview by Mike Douglas. *The Mike Douglas Show.* 1 Nov. 1978.

"Lucille Ball Signs Contract for $1,000 Weekly Increase." *Reading Eagle* 28 Mar. 1946.

"Lucille Ball Tasting Fame, Finds It Fun." *Reading Eagle* 10 Oct. 1948.

"Lucille Ball's Cousin Acts as Her Producer." *Sarasota Journal* 6 Aug. 1969.

"Lucy—After Two Decades." *Victoria Advocate* 28 Feb. 1971.

Lucy and Desi: The Scrapbooks. New York: Education Through Entertainment, 1996.

"Lucy's Change of Mind Upsetting Vivian Vance." *Hartford Courant* 20 Apr. 1964.

"Lucy's Sidekick Bounces Back on Comeback Trail." *Victoria Advocate* 1 Mar. 1959.

"Lucy's Sidekick Has Long Trip to Get to the Studio." *Washington Reporter* 19 Dec. 1963.

"Lucy's Wedding A Crowd Pleaser." *Miami News* 20 Nov. 1961.

Lyon, Herb. "Tower Ticker." *Chicago Tribune* 21 Dec. 1960.

"Mannequin Wins Film Contract." *Los Angeles Times* 24 Sept. 1934.

"Master of the Slow Burn." *TV Guide* 4 Aug. 1961. Web.

McClay, Michael, and Deanna Gaffner-McClay. *I Love Lucy: The Complete Picture History of the Most Popular TV Show Ever.* New York: Warner, 1995.

McLellan, Dennis. "Cecil Smith Dies at 92; Times TV Critic Advocated Literate, High-quality Shows." *Los Angeles Times* 14 July 2009.

Musel, Richard. "Lucy Goes Mod in London." *TV Guide* 22 Oct. 1966.

"News of the Stage." *New York Times* 26 Sept. 1940.

Oller, John. *Jean Arthur: The Actress Nobody Knew.* New York: Limelight Editions, 1999.

O'Neil, Thomas. *The Emmys: Star Wars, Showdowns, and the Supreme Test of TV's Best.* New York: Penguin, 1992.

Oppenheimer, Jess, and Gregg Oppenheimer. *Laughs, Luck . . . and Lucy: How I Came to Create the Most Popular Sitcom of All Time.* New York: Syracuse UP, 1996.

Oviatt, Ray. "No 'Method' Acting for Gale Gordon." *Toledo Blade* 12 July 1966.

Parsons, Louella. "Hollywood." *Calgary Herald* 28 Oct. 1957.

Peck, Harvey. "Vivian Vance Recalls Early Days." *Toledo Blade* 5 Feb. 1970.

Pierce, Arthur, and Douglas Swarthout. *Jean Arthur: A Bio-bibliography.* New York: Greenwood, 1990.

"Pleasing Program at the Orpheum." *Desert Evening News* [Salt Lake City] 23 Jan. 1920.

Polier, Rex. "Bill Frawley Is Topping Success at 67." *Palm Beach Post* 25 June 1961.

"Producer Charges Plagiarism in 'Sister Eileen' Broadcast." *Los Angeles Times* 18 June 1947.

Purdum, Todd S. "The Street Where They Lived." *Vanity Fair* Apr. 1999. Web.

Quigg, Jack. "Artful Gale Gordon Paid Well to Keep Mouth Shut." *Reading Eagle* 11 July 1951.

Quint, Ruth. "Role of Stamford Housewife Is Preferred by Television Star." *New Haven Register* 4 Oct. 1965.

Rabwin, Marcella. *"Yes, Mr. Selznick": Recollections of Hollywood's Golden Era.* Pittsburgh: Dorrance, 1999.

"Radio-TV Notes." *New York Times* 24 Jan. 1951.

Rayfiel, Howard. *Where the Hell Is Desilu? How to Fail in Hollywood Without Really Trying: A Memoir.* New Canaan, CT: Paribus, 2007.

"Red Alert! 'Life with Lucy' Goes on." *Rock Hill Herald* 5 Oct. 1986.

Rogers, Ginger. *Ginger: My Story.* New York: HarperCollins, 1991.

Rosenfield, Paul. "Compulsively Lucy." *Los Angeles Times* 12 Oct. 1986.

Sanders, Coyne Steven, and Tom Gilbert. *Desilu: The Story of Lucille Ball and Desi Arnaz.* New York: Morrow, 1993.

Schallert, Edwin. "Newlyweds Ball, Arnaz Will Costar for R.K.O." *Los Angeles Times* 12 Mar. 1941.

Scheuer, Philip. "'Great Sebastians' Up for Lucy, Bing." *Los Angeles Times* 11 May 1962.

Scott, Vernon. "Desi Arnaz Jr. Serious About Earning Living." *Youngstown Vindicator* 20 Mar. 1973.

———. "Gale Gordon as Funny as a Crutch When He's Not Screaming at Lucy." *Schenectady Gazette* 11 Aug. 1973.

———. "Legendary Lucy Basks in Praise with My Memories, No Regrets." *Anchorage Daily News* 8 Dec. 1984.

————. "Lucy Back on MGM Lot." *Reading Eagle* 14 Sept. 1976.

————. "TV Hall of Fame Is Created." *Hollywood Reporter* 27 Feb. 1983.

"Screen News Here and in Hollywood." *New York Times* 11 May 1944.

Sharbutt, Eve. "Lucille Ball Hasn't Quit TV, She's Just Adding Movies." *Sarasota Herald-Tribune* 24 May 1974.

Shearer, Lloyd. "Dino, Desi & Billy—Hottest Young Trio in the Business." *Reading Eagle* 6 Feb. 1966.

Shepard, Elaine. "Lucy Sees Nothing Funny in Today's Films." *Pittsburgh Press* 11 Jan. 1973.

Shnay, Jerry. "Lucy Drops a Nice Bomb." *Chicago Tribune* 23 Sept. 1969.

————. "Lucy Knows Value of Timing and It Holds Her Popularity." *Chicago Tribune* 22 Sept. 1969.

Skirbunt, Peter D., and Kevin L. Robinson. *The Illustrated History of American Military Commissaries.* Fort Lee, VA: Defense Commissary Agency, Office of Corporate Communications, 2008.

Smith, Cecil. "A Walking History of TV." *Los Angeles Times* 21 Nov. 1977.

————. "An Hour Play and How It Grew." *Los Angeles Times* 30 Sept. 1974.

————. "Having a Ball with Lucy, Ingrid, Bette and Ginger." *Los Angeles Times* 12 Apr. 1981.

————. "Lucie: Truly a Child of the Tube." *Los Angeles Times* 3 Jan. 1980.

————. "Lucy: They Can't Help Loving That Gal." *Los Angeles Times* 11 June 1961.

————. "Lucy's Career to Take Off Again." *Los Angeles Times* 3 Feb. 1969.

————. "Summit Meeting with Lucille Ball." *Los Angeles Times* 1 Mar. 1971.

"Son Born to Lucie Arnaz." *Associated Press* 9 Dec. 1980.

Swallow, Elizabeth. "Miss Ball Gives Housewarming." *Los Angeles Times* 21 Nov. 1937.

Tannen, Lee. *I Loved Lucy: My Friendship with Lucille Ball.* New York: St. Martin's, 2001.

"Television Highlights." *Desert News and Telegram* 17 Feb. 1964.

Thomas, Bob. "Hollywood News." *Florence Times* 27 Apr. 1948.

————. "Lucille Ball Explains Why She Called Off Contract with MGM." *Meriden Daily Journal* 15 Oct. 1947.

————. "Lucy, Vivian Together Again." *Daytona Beach Morning Journal* 31 Aug. 1962.

————. "Movie Stars List Greatest Roles in Film History." *Evening Independent* [St. Petersburg] 1 June 1949.

————. "New Man in Lucille Ball's Life; He's Gary Morton." *Evening News* 14 Aug. 1961.

————. "Vivian Vance Finds New Life in 'I Love Lucy' Role." *Reading Eagle* 24 Dec. 1952.

Thomas, Tony and Aubrey Solomon. *The Films of 20th Century-Fox*. Secaucus, NJ: Citadel Press, 1985.

"TV Star Desi Arnaz Opens Multi-Million Dollar Hotel." *Saskatoon Star-Phoenix* 1 Apr. 1957.

Tweedell, Bob. "Lucy Show Acquires New Look." *Los Angeles Times* 12 May 1969.

"Vivian Vance Gives Up 'Lucy,' Tries Game Shows." *Herald-Journal* 12 June 1965.

"Vivian Vance's Return to Television Revived." *Rock Hill Herald* 19 July 1976.

Weiler, A. H. "Team of Ball and Arnaz Will Make Own Movies." *New York Times* 18 June 1950.

Welles, Orson, Peter Bogdanovich, and Jonathan Rosenbaum. *This Is Orson Welles*. New York: Da Capo, 1998.

Whitney, Dwight. "Lucy Remembers." *TV Guide* 31 Mar. 1973.

Wilson, Earl. "It Happened Last Night." *Lakeland Ledger* 20 Nov. 1961.

Winchell, Walter. "Desi Grateful to 800 Mexicans." *Herald-Journal* 9 Aug. 1967.

Wolters, Larry. "Name Winners in Many Fields by Video Poll." *Chicago Tribune* 9 Jan. 1955.

Yablonsky, Lewis. *George Raft*. New York: McGraw-Hill, 1974.

Zolotow, Sam. "Lucille Ball Ill; 'Wildcat' Halted." *New York Times* 7 Feb. 1961.

———. "Musical Cancels Aug. 7 Reopening." *New York Times* 8 June 1961.

Zylstra, Freida. "Home Ec Lessons Set the Stage." *Chicago Tribune* 27 Jan. 1967.

Index